Theological Anthropology at the
Beginning of the Third Millennium

Theology at the Beginning of the Third Millennium
Series Preface

Theology at the Beginning of the Third Millennium is a new series of theological monographs which seek to examine the *status quaestionis* of various sub-disciplines within the field of theology in this third decade of the third millennium and some half a century after the conclusion of the Second Vatican Council. While the impetus for the series has come from scholars at the University of Notre Dame (Australia), the Catholic Institute of Sydney, and Campion College (Sydney), contributors to the volumes come from a diverse array of theological academies. A feature of the series is the fact that although the majority of the contributors are situated within the Catholic intellectual tradition, scholars from other traditions are also welcome.

The various sub-disciplines which form the subject of each volume are examined from the perspective of scripture scholarship, fundamental, systematic and dogmatic theology, spirituality, historical theology, ecumenical and pastoral theology and the theology of culture. This is consistent with the Balthasarian metaphor that "Truth is Symphonic" and thus created by a harmonious integration of different disciplines or "sections" of the theological orchestra. Consistent with the charism of St. James the contributors share a high degree of respect for the deposit of the faith, a Johannine interest in integrating spirituality and mystical theology with dogmatic and fundamental theology, a Pauline sensitivity to the influence of the Holy Spirit, a Petrine interest in official magisterial teaching and, above all, a Marian disposition of receptivity to the Divine *Logos*.

Theological Anthropology at the Beginning of the Third Millennium

EDITED BY
Kevin Wagner, Peter John McGregor,
AND M. Isabell Naumann

FOREWORD BY *Renée Köhler-Ryan*

☛PICKWICK *Publications* · Eugene, Oregon

THEOLOGICAL ANTHROPOLOGY AT THE BEGINNING OF THE THIRD MILLENNIUM

Theology at the Beginning of the Third Millennium

Copyright © 2022 Wipf and Stock Publishers. All rights reserved. Except for brief quotations in critical publications or reviews, no part of this book may be reproduced in any manner without prior written permission from the publisher. Write: Permissions, Wipf and Stock Publishers, 199 W. 8th Ave., Suite 3, Eugene, OR 97401.

Pickwick Publications
An Imprint of Wipf and Stock Publishers
199 W. 8th Ave., Suite 3
Eugene, OR 97401

www.wipfandstock.com

PAPERBACK ISBN: 978-1-6667-0925-4
HARDCOVER ISBN: 978-1-6667-0926-1
EBOOK ISBN: 978-1-6667-0927-8

Cataloguing-in-Publication data:

Names: Wagner, Kevin [editor] | McGregor, Peter John [editor] | Naumann, M. Isabell [editor]

Title: Theological anthropology at the beginning of the third millennium / edited by Kevin Wagner, Peter John McGregor, and M. Isabell Naumann.

Description: Eugene, OR: Pickwick Publications, 2022 | Series: Theology at the Beginning of the Third Millennium | Includes bibliographical references.

Identifiers: ISBN 978-1-6667-0925-4 (paperback) | ISBN 978-1-6667-0926-1 (hardcover) | ISBN 978-1-6667-0927-8 (ebook)

Subjects: LCSH: Theological anthropology | Theological anthropology—Christianity | Catholic Church—Doctrines | Theology, Doctrinal

Classification: BT701.3 W34 2022 (print) | BT701.3 (ebook)

Contents

Contributors vii

Foreword xi
—*Renée Köhler-Ryan*

Preface xvii
—*Kevin Wagner*

1. Theological Anthropology at the Beginning of the Third Millennium 1
   —*Tracey Rowland*

2. Finding One's Self in Foucault, Aquinas, and Girard 23
   —*Sr. Mary Julian Ekman, RSM.*

3. Christ and the Interweaving of Spirit and Matter:
   The Contribution of Eric Mascall to Theological Anthropology 37
   —*Nigel Zimmermann*

4. Beyond Boethius: The Clarity and Capacity of Relational Personhood 55
   —*Simon R. Wayte, MGL*

5. Rethinking the *Imago Dei*: Rationality and Relationality 76
   —*Thomas V. Gourlay*

6. *Dasein* and Love: A Philosophical and Theological Reflection on Being and Anxiety 94
   —*Lawrence Qummou*

7. Anthropology of the Image: The Human Person as Mirror 116
   —*Helenka Mannering*

8   Becoming a Social Human Being: Communal Life as a Path
    to Deification in the Ascetical Works of Basil of Caesarea   151
    —*Kevin Wagner*

9   A "New Creation in Christ" (2 Cor 5:17)—
    Mary, the Immaculata, as Anthropological Model   171
    —*M. Isabell Naumann, ISSM*

10 Theological Anthropology and Evolutionary Science
    at the Beginning of the Third Millennium: An Overview   185
    —*Colin Patterson*

11 More Than a Mind: 4E Cognition and Eastern Christian
    Liturgical Experience   207
    —*Antonios Kaldas*

12 Resources for a Theological Anthropology of the Heart   228
    —*Peter John McGregor*

13 *Homo orans*: The Human Person as Defined by Prayer   254
    —*Rev. Dr. Paschal M. Corby, OFM Conv.*

14 Wisdom or Eloquence? Insights from Josef Pieper's
    Anthropology for Secondary Religious Education   271
    —*Paul G. Chigwidden*

Contributors

Paul G. Chigwidden is a secondary school teacher from rural NSW. He teaches religion, English and history. He lives on a small farm with his wife and four children.

Fr. Paschal M. Corby is a priest of the Order of Friars Minor Conventual. He is a lecturer in Moral Theology at the University of Notre Dame, Australia (Sydney) and the University of Divinity/Catholic Theological College (Melbourne). With a background in Medicine, he has a particular interest in Bioethics. He is the author of *The Hope and Despair of Human Bioenhancement* (Pickwick, 2019).

Sister Mary Julian Ekman is a Religious Sister of Mercy of Alma, Michigan and a Lecturer in Philosophy at the University of Notre Dame Australia, teaching in the areas of Moral Philosophy, Natural Law, and Personalism. Sister Mary Julian worked and studied in Rome, Washington, DC, and the United Kingdom before returning to Sydney and her convent in Camperdown.

Thomas V. Gourlay is the National Director of Chaplaincy and Faith Formation, and Lecturer in the School of Philosophy and Theology at The University of Notre Dame Australia. In addition to being the editor of the volume *1968: Culture and Counterculture—A Catholic Critique* (Wipf & Stock), he has contributed papers to a number of scholarly books and journals, including New Blackfriars, the Heythrop Journal, and the eJournal of Catholic Education in Australasia. Tom is the president and co-founder of the Christopher Dawson Society for Philosophy and Culture (Inc.) and the managing editor of *Macrina Magazine*.

Antonios Kaldas lectures in philosophy at St. Cyril's Coptic Theological College under the Sydney College of Divinity. His research interests include Philosophy of Mind and Cognitive Science, Liturgical Theology, and Natural Theology. He serves as parish priest at Archangel Michael and St. Bishoy Coptic Orthodox Church.

Renée Köhler-Ryan is Head of School of Philosophy and Theology at the University of Notre Dame Australia. William Desmond supervised her doctoral dissertation on an Augustinian understanding of Sacred Space at the Katholieke Universiteit of Leuven (Belgium). Her book *Companions in the Between – Augustine, Desmond, and their Communities of Love* was published by Cascade Books in 2020. Her research interests include the work of St. Augustine and of William Desmond, Aesthetics, the thought of Edith Stein, and the Catholic Intellectual Tradition.

Helenka Mannering is a doctoral candidate at the Catholic Institute of Sydney and a sessional academic at the University of Notre Dame, Australia. Her areas of interest are moral theology, and theology and culture.

Peter John McGregor is a lecturer in Theology and Spirituality at the Catholic Institute of Sydney. His research has been published in theological journals such as the *Irish Theological Quarterly, New Blackfriars, Pro Ecclesia*, and *Radical Orthodoxy*, and he is the author of *Heart to Heart: The Spiritual Christology of Joseph Ratzinger*. His research interests include the theology of Joseph Ratzinger, the nature of theology, the relationship between theology and spirituality, missiology, and the theological anthropology of the heart.

M. Isabell Naumann, ISSM, is the President of the Catholic Institute of Sydney (Ecclesiastical Faculty of Theology) and a Professor of Systematic Theology. She is a Member of the Secular Institute of the Schoenstatt Sisters of Mary (ISSM). For over ten years, she served as the Academic Dean of Studies at the Seminary of the Good Shepherd, Sydney and taught Systematic Theology at the Catholic Institute of Sydney. She is also an Adjunct Professor in Systematic Theology at the University of Notre Dame, Sydney. She has served on various national and international academic boards and councils, including two terms at the Pontifical Council for Culture, Rome. She is a member of the International Theological Commission.

Colin Patterson is an independent scholar who was on the faculty of the John Paul II Institute for Marriage and Family, Melbourne, until its closure in 2019. Prior to this work, he was employed as a psychologist, a minister of the Uniting Church in Australia and a secondary teacher. He was received into the Catholic Church in 2004.

Lawrence Qummou is a doctoral candidate at the University of Notre Dame Australia and a sessional lecturer of Theology at Campion College. His research focuses on theological epistemology and the relationship between Catholicism and Russian Orthodoxy. He has completed postgraduate studies in Theology and Education at the University of Notre Dame Australia and Western Sydney University. Lawrence currently works as a researcher in the Archdiocese of Sydney.

Tracey Rowland holds the St. John Paul II Chair of Theology at the University of Notre Dame (Australia). In 2014 she was appointed to the IXth International Theological Commission and in 2020 she was the winner of the Ratzinger Prize for Theology. Her most recent work is: *Beyond Kant and Nietzsche: The Munich Defence of Christian Humanism* (Bloomsbury, 2021).

Kevin Wagner is the principal convener of the *Theology at the Beginning of the Third Millennium* conference series and co-editor of the eponymous book series. He is a lecturer in Theology at the University of Notre Dame, Australia—Sydney, specializing in Early Church History and Scripture. Kevin was previously the Director of the Emmanuel School of Mission in Rome, a role he shared with his wife, Helen.

Simon R. Wayte, MGL, is a priest of the Missionaries of God's Love and dean of studies at the MGL house of formation in Melbourne. He completed a doctorate in Theology at Catholic Theological College of the University of Divinity where he now lectures in Ecclesiology and Mariology. His DTh, supervised by Prof Gerald O'Collins, SJ, focused on developing a Christology organized around the concept of presence. Using a holographic analogy, he highlighted the importance of pneumatology in Christology and emphasized the indivisible nature of the continuing presence of the risen Christ in the Church and her liturgy. He has a background in science having previously completed a PhD in astrophysics at Mount Stromlo Observatory, ANU. His current research interests include the areas of Christology, Ecclesiology, Mariology and the dialogue between faith and science.

Nigel Zimmermann is Adjunct Senior Lecturer with the Institute for Ethics and Society at the University of Notre Dame Australia and Senior fellow with the PM Glynn Institute at Australian Catholic University. He is author of *Levinas and Theology* (2013), *Facing the Other: John Paul II, Levinas, and the Body* (2015) and editor of *The Great Grace: Receiving Vatican II Today* (2015) and co-editor (with Sandra Lynch) of *Faith and Reason: Vistas and Horizons* (2021).

Foreword

—Renée Köhler-Ryan

One of the finest philosophical and theological protagonists for the importance of anthropology of the twentieth century is most certainly Pope St. John Paul II. Whenever I teach in courses on the Human Person at the University of Notre Dame Australia, I am reminded of the challenge that preoccupied him when he took up the task of thinking through what is significant about human personhood. During the days of the Second Vatican Council, the then Karol Wojtyla wrote a letter to his friend Henri de Lubac, remarking:

> I devote my every rare free moments to a work that is close to my heart and devoted to the metaphysical sense and mystery of the PERSON. . . . The evil of our times consists in the first place in a kind of degradation, indeed in a pulverization, of the fundamental uniqueness of each human person. . . . To this disintegration planned at times by atheistic ideologies, we must oppose, rather than sterile polemics, a kind of 'recapitulation' of the inviolable mystery of the person.[1]

The work that Wojtyla was doing, in his spare moments, was writing *Person and Act*, which most of us know in English translation as *The Acting Person*. What strikes me when reading about the circumstances of writing such a work—squeezed between the small moments of a momentous Council—is that Wojtyla's task is now ours. The Second Vatican Council strove to situate the church in what in *Gaudium et Spes* calls a "new stage of history," characterized by "profound and rapid changes . . . spreading

---

1. Letter to Henri de Lubac; see de Lubac, *At the Service of the Church*, 171–72.

by degrees around the whole world."[2] The fast pace of the sixties is outstripped today, particularly through the medium of technology.

But time is still our own: a gift from God. If, as Wojtyla so well knew, humans are made in God's image, then our Christian task is to recognize this mystery, and to articulate it for our age of immediacy. When the world demands quick fixes that toss away human lives, it is up to us to pause to contemplate our kinship in and through Christ. Moreover, we can think through what the mystery of personhood means for the world, and how, in this third millennium, we can live up to the task of being salt and light to our age.

John Paul II is, of course, one in a long line of Catholic figures who remind us how important it is to consider anthropology—as a way to know ourselves and at the same time to become closer to God. Taking a giant leap back in time, I would like to consider Saint Augustine, whose whole task was—as he claimed in the *Soliloquies*—to know "God and the soul" and nothing more.[3] Augustine thought that to know something of God was to appreciate more of the soul, and also that understanding the soul led to greater understanding of God. But lest we find this all a bit too individualistic and self-centered, it is important to recall that Augustine thought that we can only really know God and the self through community—particularly with other Christians—and through creation. Augustine stressed a deep kinship in creation, and particularly between human persons. The Christian faith, in fact, revealed the depth of that realization. Always drawn toward friendship, Augustine is delighted, as he converts and matures as a Christian, to find that knowing persons by no means entails excluding God. In fact, the exact opposite is the case. Loving others with Christ-like *caritas*—being, as it were, outwardly-directed—brings a depth of self-knowledge beyond comparison.

This deep mystery is, as John Paul II would put it, metaphysical. One can hear it throughout Augustine's letters to friends. One set of letters is worth noting in this regard, to a friend named Martianus. Augustine and Martianus were friends from way back—enjoying the same activities and interests. This was a pretty good start, but it was going to get better. First, Augustine becomes Christian, and realizes that the grace of God makes him, *per se*, better able to love, and so to be a better friend. Then, years later, Martianus converts to Christianity, and Augustine tells him

---

2. Second Vatican Council, *Gaudium et spes*, no. 4.
3. Augustine, *Soliloquies* 1.7.

that now they can really enjoy a full friendship together. Augustine opens what is now known as "Letter 258" with the words: "I have snatched or rather torn and in a sense stolen myself from the many tasks that occupy me so that I might write to you, my friend of long standing, whom I did not have as long as I did not possess you in Christ."[4] Like Wojtyla, Augustine has to wrest time from daily commitments, to write about what is most important. Whether Augustine or John Paul II, administrators trained in philosophy and theology still struggle to find pockets of time to think about and communicate with persons. This struggle is, I would argue, still one of the most important tasks of our time. Augustine goes on to meditate, in the letter, on the course of his friendship with Martianus. Their love now is capable of new depths, because: "it turns out that between friends who do not agree on things divine there cannot be a full and true agreement on things human either."[5] Now, Augustine declares them companions "in things divine."[6] After all, he argues, "things divine" are the greatest objects of mutual knowledge and desire.

Augustine's letter to Martianus serves to remind us that among theologians who believe in the triune God, much can be accomplished. Augustine refers to the friendship between believers not only as *caritas*, or *charity*, but also as *concordia*. That is, the hearts of Christian friends correspond with each other. They beat, as it were, in unison. One should not let the sappiness of commercialized love fool us here. The balloon hearts and cupid bows of Valentine's Day are not quite what Augustine has in mind. The martyr Valentine knew this, of course! Augustine thinks that the hearts of Christian friends can beat in accord, because they are in harmony with the love between the Persons of the Trinity.

This trinitarian love is at the basis of all—for Augustine and all the church Fathers, and for Christian thought throughout the ages. Such love can be very difficult to articulate, and a book like this meets a noble challenge: to find, for and in our own time, the words to think through the implications of trinitarian, theological anthropology. And, we can avoid any temptation toward pulverization. When John Paul II—or, at least, John Paul II in translation—used the term "pulverization", it was mainly in the context of the political discourse that contributed to the atrocities of national socialism and of the communist state. Such destruction

---

4. Augustine, *Letter* 258.1.
5. Augustine, *Letter* 258.2.
6. Augustine, *Letter* 258.2.

still happens in political regimes. But we should not forget that it is also present in public conversation, in societies that pride themselves as being more enlightened. Scoring the point in a verbal slinging match can often appear more important than working toward truth and the common good. And sometimes even those who might seem to be on the same side can be guilty of harming each other verbally.

Augustine experienced the threat of verbal pulverization from none other than a fellow future saint. Astonishingly, St. Jerome once threatened Augustine in a letter, saying that if the young upstart didn't watch out, Jerome would beat him to a pulp—like an ancient warrior in Virgil's *Aeneid* had defeated a younger, seemingly stronger, opponent.[7] Jerome's threats were not actually physical, but Augustine found the sentiment behind them quite shocking at the time. Yearning for harmony, because of shared love of God, Augustine found instead derision and distrust. Scholarship has shown that Jerome had very recently been burned in friendship, and his wounds were too raw for him to trust a stranger—albeit a fellow Christian scholar—from a distant land. Later, Augustine and Jerome came to a kind of gentleman's agreement—but one which fell far short of Augustine's deepest desire for the enjoyment of Christian love. Tellingly, Jerome is willing in the end only to play in what he calls the field of Scripture. Augustine proves to have somewhat more intense demands on charity: Christian scholars should help each other, as they gasp in the rarefied air of the Scriptures.

My great hope is that those who read the contributions to this book will not miss the opportunities to climb such mountains together. After all, if delight in shared ideas about God is possible in an age such as ours—so fractured that it is often even difficult to find out what it is that we so adamantly disagree about—then the work of its editors and contributors will be noble indeed.

Knowing God and the soul, and nothing more, was the life's ambition of one of the greatest minds in History. But such ambition would, by his own reasoning, have yielded nothing, if it had not first submitted to the love of God. All the chapters here, taken as a whole, epitomize Christian concord, delving into the "sense and mystery" of being human persons—all the while refusing to submit to the forces of pulverization.

---

7. Jerome, *Letter 68.2*, in Augustine, *The Works of Saint Augustine—Letters 1–99*, 262.

Bibliography

Augustine. *Soliloquies*. In *Nicene and Post-Nicene Fathers, Series 1, Vol. VII*, edited by Philip Schaff. Grand Rapids: Eerdmans, 1888. https://ccel.org/ccel/schaff/npnf107/npnf107.i.html.

———. *The Works of Saint Augustine—Letters 1–99*. Edited by John E. Rotelle. Translated by Roland Teske. Hyde Park, NY: New City, 2001.

———. *The Works of Saint Augustine—Letters 211–270*. Edited by Boniface Ramsay. Translated by Roland Teske. Hyde Park, NY: New City, 2005.

Lubac, Henri de. *At the Service of the Church: Henri de Lubac Reflects on the Circumstances That Occasioned His Writings*. San Francisco: Ignatius, 1989.

Second Vatican Council. *Gaudium et spes*. https://www.vatican.va/archive/hist_councils/ii_vatican_council/documents/vat-ii_const_19651207_gaudium-et-spes_en.html.

Preface

KEVIN WAGNER

One of the great benefits of the study of history is its ability to teach us something about the limits of human capabilities. The great world wars, for instance, reveal to us both the seemingly limitless capacity we have for perpetrating evil and depraved acts, and our propensity to spend ourselves for others, for greater goods. Our own time is no less a lesson in humanity for those who choose to open their eyes to the world.

For the Christian, one moment in human history stands out among all others. It was the occasion of an event that occurred in the backwaters of the Roman Empire some two-thousand years ago. And the event was a person. And this event reveals to us not only something about ourselves, but in a unique and particular way it unveils to us the Face of God himself. History and historical beings up to this singular moment of revelation and beyond, are now to be viewed in a new way in the light of Jesus of Nazareth, God-made-man. This book is principally concerned with the way the Christ-event reveals God to us through our humanity and with the insights this event gives us into our own selves.

Chapter One begins with a magisterial account of the history of Catholic theological anthropology from the time of Newman up to the present age. Here Rowland paints a picture of a dynamic discipline that has responded to the signs of the times. For instance, we discover that Newman's accounts of the imagination, conscience, and the heart offered an antidote to secular forces such as Nietzsche's anti-Christian humanism. Similarly, Rowland introduces us to the theological anthropology of Matthias Scheeben, the Second Vatican Council's *Gaudium et spes*, Dietrich von Hildebrand, John Paul II and Benedict XVI, and the contributions from the International Theological Commission. In an age where sexual difference is widely contested—and, one could argue, poorly understood—these figures stand as sure lights to guide us in confusing times. Rowland's contribution, which covers far more than we can articulate here, is a valuable first port of call for anyone seeking to orient her or himself with the field of Catholic theological anthropology.

Chapters 2 to 4 could be broadly classified as engagements with Thomistic theological anthropology. Sr Ekman, in chapter 2, presents the self-nullifying accounts of human selfhood offered by Foucault, Girard, and Oughourlian, and contrasts these with Aquinas's theory of the self. *Contra* these modern thinkers, Aquinas offers a hope-filled vision of the individual self that: preserves the unity of body and soul, recognizes the primacy of reason for self-knowledge and self-determination, and extols charity as the ultimate source of self.

Chapter 3 introduces the overlooked theological anthropology of Dr Eric Lionel Mascall OGS (1905–1993), an Anglican Thomist, who engaged critically with the secularizing trends in theology of the mid to late twentieth century. Zimmermann presents us with an intriguing insight into the eccentric character of Mascall and his innovative theology, which brought Thomism and twentieth century Orthodoxy into dialogue. Of particular interest in this wide-reaching contribution is the strong influence of Chalcedonian incarnational theology on Mascall's ecclesiology, anthropology, eschatology, and spirituality.

Chapter 4, by Fr Wayte, begins with a useful historical overview of personhood from Ancient Greece, through to Tertullian, the Cappadocians, and Boethius. Next, Wayte presents the views of Aquinas, Henry of Ghent, and Richard of St. Victor, in order to develop a general definition of person based on relation. Wayte argues that this definition highlights the triadic structure of being and enables the distinction between individual, subject and self to be clarified. This chapter finishes with an examination of the perfect man Jesus Christ—in whom the divine and human natures interpenetrate without confusion or change—and role of the incarnate Son (and the Spirit) in the divinization of human persons.

The next two chapters proffer solutions to the problems of individualism and isolation. Chapter 5 goes back to the beginning to explore more deeply the notion of the person as *imago Dei*. Here Gourlay sets out to show that it is not only in the rational faculty, but also in the communion of persons, that the *imago Dei* is found. Walking us through the writings of Ratzinger, Schindler, and others, Gourlay persuasively argues for a relational ontology that may be "best exemplified" by the act and wonder of Mary's *fiat*; an act that opened the whole of creation to reality Itself.

Chapter 6 is a fascinating exposition of the approaches of Heidegger and Balthasar to the problem of being and anxiety. Here, Qummou demonstrates convincingly that the christological meta-anthropology of Balthasar offers a far more hopeful view of existence than the phenomenological ontology of Heidegger. For Balthasar, the "kenotic nature of God's love" expressed in the person of Christ and his death on the cross, bridges the ontological gap between God and his people, grounding the relationship between Creator and creature. Ultimately, Qummou argues that "the concrete human experience of anxiety solidifies the foundation of Being as love."

Chapter 7 addresses the problem of consumer culture and conformity to the *imago Dei*. After a short reflection on the nature of image, Mannering proceeds to analyze three categories of images—idols, aniconic images, and icons—in order to discover "the way different types of images elicit different desires." Her work provides for the reader an insight into the dangers of both the idolatrous and the aniconic gaze, both of which are promoted by our modern consumeristic culture. As a corrective to these ways of looking at the world, Mannering presents the iconic gaze, which, when directed towards persons, has the potential to enable full and adequate vision of beauty, both human and divine, and to facilitate conformity to the likeness of Christ, "the image with the perfect likeness."

My contribution in chapter 8 seeks to show how Basil of Caesarea's rules for monastic life help to shape the monk into what we may call a "social human being." What we discover in Basil's works is that his desire to embrace monasticism is directed towards becoming like God, that is, to deification. But this work of becoming like God was not, for Basil, merely an exercise that was carried out in the chapel. Rather, Basil leaves a legacy of practical guidelines for guiding the Christian to become a person for others and an *alter Christus*.

Naumann, in chapter 9, presents Mary, the immaculate and sinless one, as a model for Christian identity and personality. In particular, through her "unique role in the drama of salvation," Mary demonstrates perfect receptivity to God's will and the "total free response" demanded by God's creatures. Indeed, Naumann contends, it is "the integral beauty of her personality and her femininity in the distinctiveness of her being" that make her "the exemplary model" for every human person.

Chapters 10 and 11 are explicit attempts to bring science into dialogue with theology. The first of these chapters deals with the relationship between theological anthropology and evolutionary science at the beginning of the third millennium. Here Patterson provides an overview of modern responses to three questions of particular importance for our time: the difference between humans and other species; theories of evolution and the Christian faith; and non–rational evolutionary explanations for human religious impulses.

Chapter 11 takes a different angle as it seeks to draw on the findings of 4E cognition to present a new way of looking at liturgical experience in Eastern Christianity. Beginning with a useful explanation of 4E Cognition, Fr Kaldas goes on to argue for the "natural harmony" of 4E cognition with Eastern Christian anthropology. Not content to stop at the level of theory, Kaldas provides first a compelling case for the expression of 4E cognition principles in Eastern Christian liturgical practice, and then a strong argument for 4E cognition practitioners to look to Eastern Christian liturgical experience as a fertile field for deepening their own research into the cognitive sciences.

Chapters 12 and 13 bring theological anthropology into dialogue with prayer and the spiritual life. In chapter 12, McGregor focuses on the human heart as a place of encounter with God. Here he begins the admirable task of rescuing the term "heart" from misuse and miscomprehension (a situation perhaps attributable to a forgetting of its scriptural roots), such that it may serve to bear fruit for theological anthropology and, thus, deepen our understanding of human mystery and friendship with God. Drawing on both Eastern and Western traditions, McGregor demonstrates that a renewed theology of the heart offers an antidote to the "disassociation of the intellectual faculty from the sensual–emotional–volitional faculties." In short, McGregor argues for a re-focusing on the heart—the seat of both human affectivity and knowledge—as a means for negotiating successfully this current "Age of Emotion" or "Affectivity."

The contribution of Fr Corby in chapter 13 makes the claim that the human person is best defined as the one who has the capacity "to think about God and pray to him." Noting first that this capacity is rooted in the human person's creation in the image of God, Corby walks the reader through the scriptures in order to demonstrate first, that human persons are made for worship, and second, that this worship is both fulfilling and liberating. This disposition to pray and to seek union with God, Corby claims, is rooted in our real likeness to God and our relationship to the incarnate Word, who is "the onto-logical foundation for prayer."

Our final chapter brings insights from Josef Pieper's theological anthropology into the secondary religious education (RE) classroom. From the outset, Chigwidden states his claim that wisdom must take precedence over eloquence in the teaching of RE in order that Catholic secondary schools may be reinvigorated. His study begins with a definition of secularism based on the work of Charles Taylor and an examination of its effects on religiosity and practice drawing on survey data from the USA and Australia. Chigwidden then presents key elements of Pieper's anthropology—concerning our receptivity, our need for contemplation, and our *telos*—that can serve as foundations for an educational program designed to prepare students for life (rather than other more utilitarian ends).

This book is offered as a gift to a world that often seems to have forgotten what it means to be human. Its contents serve as a reminder to its readers that there is something strong and dignified in the human person that is waiting to be revealed to a world that sorely needs hope. The source of this strength and dignity is the Christian God, and it is to him that we look for our hope!

1

Theological Anthropology at the Beginning of the Third Millennium

—Tracey Rowland

The human person, the central subject of theological anthropology, is a creature made in God's image to grow into the likeness of Christ. In order to explain how this is possible a large number of theological "building blocks" are gathered. They form a multi-dimensional mosaic of the human person. New "blocks" or "tiles" are added as new questions arise and other "tiles" get cleaned and polished. In patristic and medieval times scholars sought to understand how different faculties of the human soul interact with each other. These contributions today provide many of the old "tiles" that are studied and clarified. New issues have however arisen in the last two and a half centuries. While eighteenth century scholarship focused on the powers and limitations of the human intellect, the nineteenth century was the time of the Romantic movements with their interest in the affective side of the human person, and thus concepts like the human heart, memory and imagination. When studied within a theological context these interests fostered a re-examination of topics in fundamental theology. This included a re-appraisal of the late scholastic understandings of the relationship between nature and grace, and faith and reason. In the twentieth century, in the wake of Hegel and Heidegger, the history and ontology relationship found itself added to the list of "hot button" issues foundational for theological anthropology. Finally, the sexual revolution of the 1960s forced theologians to address questions about the meaning and purpose of human sexuality and the theological significance of sexual difference. A theology of the body developed to complement the theology of the soul so that Catholic scholars could address the pastoral crises of late modern and post-modern cultures. The theology of the body was thus a new "tile" added to the mosaic.

The Influence of St. John Henry Newman

An examination of the mosaic in the third decade of the twenty-first century begins with a visit to Victorian Oxford. St. John Henry Newman (1801–90)—the most illustrious church "Doctor" of the nineteenth century—made significant contributions to the field of theological anthropology. Newman's motto was *"cor ad cor loquitur"* (heart speaks to heart). He was interested in the affective side of the human person and the relationship between love and reason as expressed in his famous "Sermon 12." He also addressed the faith and reason relationship in his *Essay on the Grammar of Assent* known for its treatment of what Newman called the "illative sense," described as the intellectual counterpart of Aristotle's *phronesis*.

Newman was also interested in the role of the human imagination in spiritual development. The imagination had been a neglected faculty of the human soul. Over the centuries the faculties of intellect and will tended to attract the lion's share of academic analysis, but Newman understood the power of the imagination and what is today called *mythopoesis*. There could be no C. S. Lewis or J. R. R. Tolkien without a highly developed Christian imagination. The late Michael Paul Gallagher, a professor of fundamental theology at the Gregorian University, explained that Newman offered an "epistemology of the imagination" as a "key mediator between theology and spirituality," and that "his pedagogy of faith does not begin with arguments but with paying attention to preconceived spiritual attitudes."[1] Gallagher argued that "Newman always proposed the integration of rationality, heart and imagination, seeing the whole self as an instrument of truth."[2] Gottlieb Söhngen also drew attention to the importance of affectivity and the imagination in Newman's anthropology. He noted that on the title page of *The Grammar of Assent* Newman

---

1. Gallagher, "Realisation of Wisdom," 127–28.
2. Gallagher, "Realisation of Wisdom," 127.

had copied the saying of St. Ambrose: *Non in dialectica complacuit Deo salvum facere populum suum*—God did not accomplish the salvation of his people through dialectics.[3] In other words, Newman was attentive to the fact that the human person not only has an intellect, but also has an imagination, a memory, and above all, a heart.

Newman's theological anthropology can also be read as the intellectual antidote to Friedrich Nietzsche's radically anti-Christian humanism. As Gottlieb Söhngen remarked, Newman recognized the problem of an "ethical atheism," that is, an atheism that sees itself as morally superior to Christian theism. He understood that "contemporary atheism had become a dogma, that is, a lived reality of which one is convinced and for which one is willing to die."[4] Newman understood that one cannot defeat this new kind of atheism with logic. The new atheism is an alternative humanism. For this reason it requires a counter-narrative, a counter-theological anthropology, a counter-Christian humanism that addresses the kinds of issues raised by the new atheists, above all, their assertion that Christianity fetters human freedom, undermines human dignity, and is at war with *Eros*.

By far the most influential of Newman's contributions to the field of theological anthropology was, however, his account of the human conscience. This has had significant flow-on effects in the field of moral theology, including the moral theology of Joseph Ratzinger. It was Newman's treatment of conscience that inspired the White Rose resistance movement in Nazi Germany. While in Anglophone circles for much of the twentieth century, Newman was best known for his conversion from Anglicanism, in German circles it was his theological anthropology as presented in the *Essay on the Grammar of Assent* and his fundamental theology as presented in his *Essay on the Development of Christian Doctrine*, that most attracted attention, along with his treatment of conscience as it was mediated to a German audience through the work of Romano Guardini and Theodor Haecker. Guardini was both a scholar and the leader of the German Catholic youth movement "Quickborn" while Haecker was a translator and mentor to the students in the White Rose resistance group. In a lecture delivered in 1933 Guardini stated that the conscience is not a mirror or a camera, not a magnetic needle or any other kind of mechanical instrument, nor is it a "law that hangs

---

3. Söhngen, *Kardinal Newman*, 38.
4. Söhngen, *Kardinal Newman*, 46–47.

somewhere," "not a simple idea," "not a concept in the air," but rather the conscience is "the living voice of God's holiness in us."[5] By the third decade of the twenty-first century, Newman's idea of conscience has become an important "tile" in the mosaic.

Matthias Scheeben and the Nuptial Mystery

Another contender for the status of most significant church "Doctor" of the nineteenth century is the Rhinelander Matthias Joseph Scheeben (1835–88). His two most famous works were *Handbuch der katholischen Dogmatik* (1873–87) and *Mysterien des Christentums* (1865–97)—the latter published in English as *The Mysteries of Christianity*. For those who lack the time to read the several thousand pages of material that remains untranslated, Aidan Nichols has provided a summary in his *Romance and System: The Theological Synthesis of Matthias Joseph Scheeben* (2010). According to Nichols, the great virtue of Scheeben's theological anthropology is that it combines both "romance" and "system":

> Owing to its emphasis on the mysteric, it must perforce press into service a range of imagery in order to express what lies beyond reason. That is a feature which links it to Romanticism in philosophy and the arts: hence my term "romance." At the same time, its concern to do full justice to the epistemic status of theology as a science ... also obliged Scheeben to make a serious effort towards "system." That is the feature which links his work to classicism in philosophy and the arts—both pre-romantic and, in the shape, not least, of neo-Thomist metaphysics and theology, post-Romantic too. In Scheeben's case both romance and system are in the service of recreating what in the High Middle Ages was a self-evident thesis. To wit, the human being, with his knowing and experiencing, is encompassed within a greater, more comprehensive, supernatural whole.[6]

In the same year that Nichols produced *Romance and System*, John Milbank contributed an essay to *Modern Theology* entitled "The New Divide: Classical versus Romantic Orthodoxy." His thesis was that contemporary Catholic theologians are divided between those who seek to the defend the rationality of the faith with reference to philosophical propositions and doctrinal pronouncements and those interested in an engagement with

---

5. Guardini, *La coscienza*, 32–33.
6. Nichols, *Romance and System*, 4–5.

Romantic-movement issues. Milbank explained the division in the following terms with reference to key concepts in theological anthropology:

> The "romantics" think that the collapse of a reason linked to the higher *eros* led to the debasement of scholasticism and then to secular modernity. Resistance to the latter had therefore to oppose rationalism and even to insist more upon the role of the "erotic"—the passions, the imagination, art, *ethos* etc., than had been the case up to and including Aquinas. The exponents of "classicism" on the other hand (largely located in the United States) trace secularity simply to a poor use of reason and regard the scholastic legacy, mainly in its "Thomistic" form, as sustaining a true use of reason to this very day.... The conflict between these two parties is therefore one between opposed metanarratives.[7]

Nichols presents Scheeben as an exemplar of a via-media between what he identifies as the two main schools of Catholic theology in nineteenth century Germany: the Catholic Tübingen School and neo-Scholasticism. These two schools are the forerunners to what Milbank called the opposing metanarratives. The former (Tübingen) was engaged with Romantic issues, the latter (the neo-Scholastics) defined themselves by their opposition to all entanglements with Romantic interests like history and culture.

In a romantic key Scheeben argued that "a truth that is easily discovered and quickly grasped can neither enchant nor hold. To enchant and hold us it must surprise us by its novelty, it must overpower us with its magnificence, its wealth and profundity must exhibit ever new splendours, ever deeper abysses to the exploring eye."[8] Here Scheeben anticipated what Balthasar and following Balthasar, St. John Paul II, called "the splendor of the truth."

From the eighteenth through to the twenty-first centuries there were also German Catholic theologians who sought to defend the faith before the tribunal of German Idealism. Karl Rahner was the prize twentieth century example of someone who shared this interest. Scheeben was not however one of these. On the contrary, his concept of faith has been categorized as a kind of *Autoritätsglaube*: "authority-faith." Nichols describes this as "a firm holding as true or a decided judgement of the mind, that does not rest on its own insight or direct acquaintance (*Kenntnisnahme*)

---

7. Milbank, "The New Divide," 26.
8. Scheeben, *Mysteries of Christianity*, 5.

with the object of that judgment, but on the insight or knowledge made over to us by another intelligent being."[9] Nichols concludes that Scheeben regarded reason's authority as a participation in the authoritative rationality of God.[10]

Consistent with this anti-Kantian orientation, Scheeben was of the view that philosophy *can be* Christian. Like the humanity and divinity of Christ, faith and reason may be distinguished (faith is faith and reason is reason) but they should not be quarantined from one another in different autonomous university faculties prevented from meeting and integrating. The master of the quarantine policy was Immanuel Kant. In contrast, Nichols observes that Scheeben begins with exceedingly clear distinctions (an intellectual virtue of the scholastic system builders) but he then seeks to "marry" them to each other and uses a variety of nuptial metaphors to describe their union (a typically romantic academic habit).[11]

This approach to the faith and reason relationship makes Scheeben a precursor to Etienne Gilson (1884–1978) who was a leading figure in the 1930s French debates over the issue of whether there can be such an animal as "Christian philosophy."[12] It also makes him a precursor to the theological anthropology of Balthasar and Ratzinger. In his *Theology of Karl Barth*, Balthasar drew attention to the following paragraph from Josef Pieper's *Über das Ende der Zeit* that is highly critical of the tendency of the German Idealists to sharply separate theology and philosophy:

> All real philosophizing necessarily oversteps the boundary of "pure philosophy" to make statements the import of which are not the result of the human effort to know but come to us as something to be accepted. And indeed the basic impulse to pursue philosophy that gets to the roots of things goes beyond the border that divides philosophy from theology, faith and revelation. Thus a philosophy that would insist on remaining a "pure philosophy" would be untrue to itself and would cease being philosophy.[13]

Scheeben's nuptial mysticism was taken up by scholars in the late twentieth century, foremost among them Angelo Scola, author of *The*

---

9. Nichols, *Romance and System*, 22.

10. Nichols, *Romance and System*, 23.

11. Nichols, *Romance and System*, 65.

12. The best Anglophone account of these debates is Sadler, *Reason Fulfilled by Revelation*.

13. Balthasar, *The Theology of Karl Barth*, 347.

Nuptial Mystery (2005). In every case the interest is in the "marriage" of fundamental theology's "critical couplets" such as faith and reason, nature and grace, scripture and tradition, history and ontology, the divinity and humanity of Christ, and last but not least, trinitarian theology and the *imago Dei*. Nichols concludes that "everywhere the Trinity is central to [Scheeben's] construction," and that within the Trinity Christ constitutes, "the 'heart' or 'knot' of that *nexus mysterium* in his own person."[14]

The Anthropology of *Gaudium et spes*

The relationship between Christology and the human person, and indeed, more broadly, the relationship between all three Persons of the Trinity and the human person, was the *leitmotiv* of the pontificate of St. John Paul II. As an auxiliary bishop of the Archdiocese of Kraków, the young John Paul II contributed to the drafting of the Conciliar document *Gaudium et spes*. The reception of this document differed widely depending upon what readers took to be its central idea and depending on their attitude to the culture of modernity. Some scholars, foremost among them Edward Schillebeeckx, treated the document as a mandate to correlate the church's teachings to trends in contemporary social theory.[15] Walter Kasper noted that some sections of the document were explicitly trinitarian while others sections spoke of God without any differentiations between the Persons within the Trinity.[16] David L. Schindler used the expression "merely theistically hued" to refer to the sections that refer to God in general.[17] Other aspects of the document that generated difficulty in interpretation are that it alternates between statements addressed to all people of good will and statements that are only for the faithful, and between sections that are theological and sections that are sociological. The sociological generalizations were applicable to some parts of the world and not others. Liberation theologians criticized the document for being a manifesto written by and for middle class Europeans while some

---

14. Nichols, *Romance and System*, 490.

15. See, for example, Schillebeeckx, *The Real Achievement of Vatican II* and Schillebeeckx, *World and Church*, and for a recent study of this subject see Minch, "Eschatology and Theology of Hope."

16. Kasper, "The Theological Anthropology of *Gaudium et spes*," 129–40.

17. Schindler, "Christology and the *Imago Dei*" 156–84.

such Europeans argued that its unreserved embrace of "modernity" was naïve.

Notwithstanding all these issues St. John Paul II thought that the document could receive a positive reception if paragraph 22 was construed as its hermeneutical lens. This is the most Christocentric paragraph of the document and it becomes the linchpin for the relationship of Christology to theological anthropology. According to paragraph 22,

> The truth is that only in the mystery of the incarnate Word does the mystery of man take on light. For Adam, the first man, was a figure of Him Who was to come, namely Christ the Lord. Christ, the final Adam, by the revelation of the mystery of the Father and His love, fully reveals man to man himself and makes his supreme calling clear. It is not surprising, then, that in Him all the aforementioned truths find their root and attain their crown.[18]

Paul McPartlan argues that this paragraph was inspired by Henri de Lubac's 1938 book *Catholicisme*.[19] It became a recurring theme in John Paul II's speeches and homilies and it was central to his first encyclical *Redemptor hominis* (1979).

A young Professor Joseph Ratzinger also endorsed the trinitarian Christocentric reading of *Gaudium et spes*. In a long essay on "The Dignity of the Human Person" published in Herbert Vorgrimler's *Commentaries on the Documents of Vatican II*, Ratzinger lamented the sloppy drafting of the document but stated that notwithstanding the drafting issues, the document did, in a positive way, offer a "daring" new theological anthropology that was Christocentric and trinitarian. This commentary is Ratzinger's most extensive engagement with the territory of theological anthropology outside of his book *Principles of Catholic Theology: Building Stones for a Fundamental Theology*. In this essay he engages with issues such as the relationship between nature and grace, and faith and reason, the understanding of natural law and human freedom, the place of experience in spiritual development and the complex nature of atheism. He follows the trajectory of Henri de Lubac in criticizing extrinsicist constructions of the relationships between faith and reason, and nature and

---

18. Second Vatican Council, *Gaudium et spes*, no. 22.
19. McPartlan, "Henri de Lubac," 343–46.

grace. He declares his preference for an Augustinian understanding of these relationships and is expressly critical of the idea of "pure reason."[20]

The Papacies of John Paul II and Benedict XVI

The combined magisterial works of the papacies of John Paul II and Benedict XVI read as an exercise in unpacking and re-presenting what the young Ratzinger identified as a theological anthropology explicitly trinitarian and Christocentric. Central to this anthropology is an understanding of the missions of the Persons of the Trinity in the life of the world and the spiritual development of the human person. Common themes are the work of the theological virtues—faith, hope, and love—on the faculties of human soul, and the soul's receptivity to truth, goodness, and beauty. The trinitarian encyclicals of John Paul II (*Redemptor hominis*; *Dives in misericordia*; and *Dominum et vivificantem*) and the theological virtues trilogy of the papacy of Benedict XVI (*Deus caritas est*; *Spe salvi*; and *Lumen fidei*) outline the major principles of this trinitarian Christocentric anthropology.[21] To obtain a comprehensive account of this anthropology it is necessary to combine the content of all six encyclicals.[22] The trilogy on the Trinity gives an account of how the human person relates to God the Father, God the Son, and God the Holy Spirit, while the trilogy of encyclicals on the theological virtues of faith, hope, and love, narrows the focus to the work of each of these virtues in the human person.

In addition to his trinitarian encyclicals, two other encyclicals of St. John Paul II are directly relevant to theological anthropology. *Veritatis splendor* (1993) reset moral theology on a firm christological foundation thus linking moral theology to dogmatic, especially trinitarian theology, and linking conceptions of the moral life to the transcendental properties of the true, the beautiful, and the good. *Veritatis splendor* cuts through the layers of casuistic analysis typical of Jesuit-style scholasticism by presenting the moral life as a sharing in the virtues of Christ himself.[23] *Fides et ratio* (1998) offered the most significant magisterial engagement with the topic of the faith and reason relationship over the last century. Although

---

20. Ratzinger, "The Dignity of the Human Person," 115–63.
21. *Lumen fidei* was drafted by Benedict XVI but settled and promulgated by Francis.
22. Scola, "On the Trinitarian Encyclicals of John Paul II."
23. Melina, *Sharing in Christ's Virtues*.

this encyclical did not directly address the debates of the 1930s internal to the Thomist tradition, the weight of scholarly opinion comes down on the side of reading this document as, at least, implicitly Gilsonian.

The most academically original contribution to the field of theological anthropology of these two pontificates was however St. John Paul II's catechesis on human love, delivered in a series of Wednesday audience addresses in the early years of his pontificate and marketed to the world as his "theology of the body." These lectures set the relationship between men and women and their sexual intimacy into the context of trinitarian theology with exegetical assistance from the accounts of creation in the book of Genesis. From this exegesis St. John Paul II dredged a whole raft of concepts that are now a standard part of any lexicon of theological anthropology. They include: original solitude, original shame, original nakedness, original innocence, original unity, the law of the gift, and the nuptial or spousal meaning of the body. These lectures are a case study in the integration of biblical exegesis with phenomenology.[24]

The Contribution of Dietrich von Hildebrand

Many of the themes in St. John Paul II's theology of body were anticipated by Dietrich von Hildebrand (1889–1977) who shared John Paul II's interest in phenomenology and personalist philosophy. This is especially so of the more phenomenological dimensions of the theology including the notion of the spousal meaning of the body and the law of the gift. St. Pius XII described Hildebrand as a twentieth century doctor of the church, while St. John Paul II described him as one of the greatest ethicists of the twentieth century, and Benedict XVI said that his life and work had left an indelible mark on the history of the church in the twentieth century.[25] So strong was Hildebrand's opposition to the Nazi regime that the National Socialists passed a death sentence against him *in absentia*. He had to flee Europe for the United States where his research focused upon themes in moral, sacramental, and theological anthropology and the nexus of all

---

24. For the best English translation of the lectures, see Waldstein, *Male and Female He Created Them*. For an introduction to the theology of the body see Anderson and Granados, *Called to Love*.

25. Hildebrand, *The Soul of a Lion*.

three. Like Newman and Ratzinger he was interested in the integration of cognition and affectivity.[26]

Hildebrand famously supported Paul VI's encyclical *Humanae Vitae* (1968) because he believed that "the sinfulness of artificial birth control is rooted in the arrogation of the right to separate the actualised love-union in marriage from a possible conception, to sever the wonderful, deeply mysterious connection instituted by God."[27] For Hildebrand contraception belonged to the same league of sins as suicide and euthanasia. In each case human persons act as if they, and not God, were the giver of life. Two of the passages illustrating the influence of personalist philosophy upon his defense of *Humanae vitae* are the following:

> If sex were really nothing more than a biological instinct, such as thirst or hunger, it would be incomprehensible why the satisfaction of an instinct implanted in man's nature by God should be something immoral outside of marriage, especially if it led to procreation.[28]

> Instead of saying that the sinful satisfaction of sexual desire becomes legitimate through marriage, we should say that the sexual act, because it is destined to be the consummation of this sublime union and the fulfillment of spousal love, becomes sinful when desecrated by isolation.[29]

In line with Newman, Ratzinger, and Guardini and against the so-called "New Morality" of the 1970s, Hildebrand insisted that the human conscience does not instruct the person about whether something is morally good or evil; rather, he argued that this question needs to be answered *before* conscience can speak. He described the conscience as the *advocatus Dei*, that is, God's advocate, in the soul of man. This is essentially the same account of conscience as Guardini's "living voice of God's holiness in us" and as that offered by Ratzinger in his book simply titled *On Conscience* (2006).

---

26. Hildebrand, *The Heart*. For a comparison of Ratzinger and Hildebrand's understanding of the heart, see McGregor, *Heart to Heart*, 303–7. McGregor argues that whereas Ratzinger broadens the notion of heart, Hildebrand narrows it to a particular kind of affectivity.

27. Hildebrand, *Love*, 45.

28. Hildebrand, *Love*, 18.

29. Hildebrand, *Love*, 22.

The Contribution of the International Theological Commission

Running alongside the magisterial work of the pontificates of St. John Paul II and Benedict XVI and into the era of Francis there have been a number of documents produced by the International Theological Commission (ITC) relating to theological anthropology. The three most directly relevant are: *Theology, Christology, Anthropology* (1981), *Propositions on the Dignity and Rights of the Human Person* (1983), and *Communion and Stewardship: Human Persons Created in the Image of God* (2004).

In an address to celebrate the Commission's 50th anniversary, Philippe Vallin remarked that the documents of the Commission (1969–2019) have contributed to the development of a theological anthropology based on a metaphysical vision of the human person made in the image of God that finds its dynamics in a sacramentality of active imitation of Jesus Christ and in a moral theology of eschatological responsibility.[30] Vallin further spoke of the Commission's desire to bridge the "huge gap that had arisen between an ontological discourse that dealt with intra-Trinitarian correlations and a soteriological discourse that was considered 'functional' and that dealt more with biblical narratives and the concrete economy of salvation."[31] A significant element in the bridge created is the notion that "the fundamentally relational character of the *imago Dei* itself constitutes its ontological structure and the foundation for the exercise of freedom and responsibility."[32] This insight has given rise to numerous scholarly examinations of the roles of relationality and receptivity within the *imago Dei*. Some of the leading names in this area are: William Norris Clarke (1915–2008), Kenneth L. Schmitz (1922–2017) and David L. Schindler. Balthasar's trinitarian anthropology is also hugely influential in this context.

Once one ventures into the territory of receptivity and relationality it is difficult to avoid the issue of the theological significance of sexual difference. The key principle identified by the ITC is found in the document *Communion and Stewardship: Human Persons Created in the Image of God* (2004):

---

30. Vallin, "Un filo rosso antropologico," 1.
31. Vallin, "Un filo rosso antropologico," 1.
32. Vallin, "Un filo rosso antropologico," 4.

Far from being an accidental or secondary aspect of personality, sexual difference is constitutive of personal identity. Each of us possesses a way of being in the world, to see, to think, to feel, to engage in mutual exchange with other persons who are also defined by their sexual identity. According to the *Catechism of the Catholic Church*: "Sexuality affects all aspects of the human person in the unity of his body and soul. It especially concerns affectivity, the capacity to love and to procreate, and in a more general way the aptitude for forming bonds of communion with others." The roles attributed to one or the other sex may vary across time and space, but the sexual identity of the person is not a cultural or social construction. It belongs to the specific manner in which the *imago Dei* exists.[33]

St. John Paul II's Apostolic Letter *Mulieris dignitatem* (1988) on the Dignity and Vocation of Women also addressed the issue of the theological significance of sexual difference. Like his theology of the body lectures this document drew upon the accounts of creation in the book of Genesis. In paragraph 6 he wrote,

Let us enter into the setting of the biblical "beginning." In it the revealed truth concerning man as "the image and likeness" of God constitutes the immutable *basis of all Christian anthropology*. "God created man in his own image, in the image of God he created him; male and female he created them" (Gen 1:27). This concise passage contains the fundamental anthropological truths: man is the highpoint of the whole order of creation in the visible world; the human race, which takes its origin from the calling into existence of man and woman, crowns the whole work of creation; *both man and woman are human beings to an equal degree*, both are created *in God's image*.[34]

John Paul II further asserted that "the biblical text provides sufficient bases for recognising the essential equality of men and woman from the point of view of their humanity.... The woman is another I in a common humanity."[35] Henceforth they are called not only to exist "side by side" but to "exist mutually one for the other."[36] Léonie Caldecott and others have argued that John Paul II's interpretation of Genesis 2:18-20, the passage

---

33. International Theological Commission, *Communion and Stewardship*, no. 33.
34. John Paul II, *Mulieris dignitatem*, no. 6.
35. John Paul II, *Mulieris dignitatem*, no. 6
36. John Paul II, *Mulieris dignitatem*, no. 7.

referring to the creation of Eve as Adam's helpmate, is making a point about the ontological complementarity of men and women. It is not a statement inferring an ontological inferiority of women to men.[37]

The approach to theological anthropology that begins from the position of trinitarian theology and works downwards to humanity has the merit of offering a foundation for the principle of an equality of the sexes while respecting their differences. The three Persons of the Trinity exist in precisely such a relationship of equality with difference. It is for this reason that Cardinal Angelo Scola has argued that a culture that does not accept the revelation of the trinitarian God ultimately renders itself incapable of understanding sexual difference in a positive sense.[38] Scholars who are working on developing the notion of an equality within difference include: Deborah Savage, Margaret Harper McCarthy, Michele M. Schumacher, and Mary Frances McKenna.[39] In her publications McKenna develops Ratzinger's notion of the person in conjunction with his scriptural exegesis where he identifies a "female line" in the Bible, typologically linking the taking of Eve from Adam's side to the piercing of Christ's side and the creation of the church. McKenna suggests that while the "male line" in the Bible (from Adam to Christ) represents "humanity," that is, every human being both male and female, the "female line" (from Eve to Mary) represents the communal aspect of humanity.[40]

More generally, in the third decade of the twenty-first century, Catholic scholarship exploring the theological significance of sexual difference often begins, positively or negatively, with an engagement with the theology of Balthasar and Adrienne von Speyr (1902–67) where the nuptial mystery theme is strong and issues such as sexual difference, generativity and fruitfulness are explored within a trinitarian framework.

Re-uniting Eros and Agape

A sub-theme of the issue of sexual difference is the relationship between *Eros* and *Agape*. This theme has risen in prominence since the sexual

---

37. Caldecott, "Sincere Gift," 64–81.
38. Scola, "The Dignity and Mission of Women," 52.
39. Savage, "The Nature of Woman in Relation to Man"; Schumacher, *Woman in Christ*; McCarthy, "The Feminine Genius and Women's Contributions in Society and in the Church"; McKenna, "The Female Line in the Bible."
40. McKenna, "The Female Line in the Bible."

revolution of the 1960s but it had appeared much earlier in Friedrich Nietzsche's indictment of Christianity on the grounds that it had waged war against *Eros*. Sigmund Freud's *Three Essays on the Theory of Human Sexuality* (1905) also made the issue of the nature of sexual desire one of the most debated subjects in the twentieth century.

In the first decade of the twentieth century Pierre Rousselot (1878–1915), a French Jesuit whose life was tragically cut short in the battle of Éparges, published *Pour l'histoire du problem de l'amour au Moyen Age* (1908), later translated into English as *The Problem of Love in the Middle Ages: A Historical Contribution*. The work explores the relationship between *amor concupiscentiae* and *amor amicitiae* in medieval thought with a special emphasis on the Thomistic synthesis. Rousselot's pioneering work was followed by the publication of two reflections on the relationship between *Eros* and *Agape* by Söhngen in 1946[41] and Martin D'Arcy's *The Mind and Heart of Love: Lion and Unicorn, a Study in Eros and Agape* in 1954. Between these Catholic publications Anders Nygren, a Danish Lutheran, published *Eros and Agape* in two volumes in 1930 and 1936. Typically the two Jesuits (one French and one English) and the German-speaking Söhngen, sought to effect a reconciliation of *Eros* and *Agape*, while the Lutheran took the Protestant either/or approach and championed *Agape* over the allegedly selfish *Eros*.

The issue of the relationship between the two reappears in *Deus caritas est* (2006), the first encyclical of the pontificate of Benedict XVI, where Benedict gave his papal seal of approval to the union of the two in his account of the unity of love in creation and salvation history. As Beáta Tóth explains,

> Remarkably, the concept of love in the encyclical avoids an overly voluntaristic/rational interpretation by emphasising also the feeling aspect of love which is seen as engaging the whole of what we are: the intellect, the will, and the sentiments in an all-embracing act. The sentiments accompanying love are taken seriously and human feelings are not undervalued or scorned as superfluous elements that disturb the intellectual act of the will. There is no suggestion of an obligation to love one's neighbour through indifference to subjective emotions.[42]

---

41. Söhngen, *Von Gottes Herrlichkeit*; Söhngen, *Humanität und Christentum*.
42. Tóth, *The Heart Has Its Reasons*, 164.

Here perhaps the influence of Newman and Söhngen on Ratzinger were factors steering him away from either overly voluntarist or overly rationalist approaches to the meaning of human love and its relationship to the divine. A symphonic understanding of the faculties of the soul and their relationship to the body is the theological foundation stone allowing for the integration.

In the twenty-first century the recognition of the heart as a locus of anthropological integration has emerged alongside a renewal of interest in the spirituality of the Sacred Heart, especially in French Catholicism, and in the Divine Mercy spirituality fostered by St. John Paul II and St. Faustina of Poland. Beáta Tóth's *The Heart Has its Reasons: Towards a Theological Anthropology of the Heart* (2016) along with Hildebrand's earlier *The Heart: An Analysis of Human and Divine Affectivity* (1977) affirm Benedict's reconciliation of *Eros* and *Agape* and thus his defence of Christianity against Nietzsche's charges.

Trinitarian Theological Anthropology and Sacramental Theology

The magisterial emphasis on a Christocentric trinitarian anthropology has had flow on effects in the field of sacramental theology. The sacraments inaugurate what Vallin calls a "configuration to Christ." They are not mere social milestone markers for people open to "Gospel values." As Vallin notes in the context of the sacrament of Orders, "the Christian called to the priestly ministry does not receive only an external function with ordination, but a radical participation in the priesthood of Christ."[43] A priest acts *"in persona Christi capitis."* There are also pneumatological and paterological dimensions to sacramental theology. Building and strengthening the bridges between theological anthropology and sacramental theology is one of the tasks of the twenty-first century.

In the context of the sacrament of marriage some of the scaffolding work has been completed in the works *The Nuptial Mystery* (2005) by Cardinal Angelo Scola, and *Divine Likeness: Toward a Trinitarian Anthropology of the Family* (2006) and *Mystery and Sacrament of Love: A Theology of Marriage and the Family for the New Evangelisation* (2015) by Cardinal Marc Ouellet. In *Divine Likeness*, Ouellet argued that the gifts of creation, of life, and of *fides* within the sacrament of marriage signify

---

43. Vallin, "Un filo rosso antropologico," 4.

the uncreated love between the divine persons, while the "Holy Spirit prolongs in marriage what he does in the relationship of Christ and the Church, he makes of it the nuptial incarnation of the "Nuptial Mystery" par excellence."[44]

In the context of the sacrament of penance St. John Paul II addressed many of the foundational issues in his Apostolic Exhortation *Reconciliatio et paenitentia* (1984). In the following statements in paragraph 18 he linked the loss of a sense of sin to a flawed anthropology fostered by the social sciences, and to a flawed moral theology:

> [A] reason for the disappearance of the sense of sin in contemporary society is to be found in the errors made in evaluating certain findings of the human sciences. Thus on the basis of certain affirmations of psychology, concern to avoid creating feelings of guilt or to place limits on freedom leads to a refusal ever to admit any shortcoming. Through an undue extrapolation of the criteria of the science of sociology, it finally happens ... that all failings are blamed upon society, and the individual is declared innocent of them. Again, a certain cultural anthropology so emphasizes the undeniable environmental and historical conditioning and influences which act upon man, that it reduces his responsibility to the point of not acknowledging his ability to perform truly human acts and therefore his ability to sin.
>
> The sense of sin also easily declines as a result of a system of ethics deriving from a certain historical relativism. This may take the form of an ethical system which relativizes the moral norm, denying its absolute and unconditional value, and as a consequence denying that there can be intrinsically illicit acts independent of the circumstances in which they are performed by the subject. Herein lies a real "overthrowing and downfall of moral values," and "the problem is not so much one of ignorance of Christian ethics," but ignorance "rather of the meaning, foundations and criteria of the moral attitude."[45]

The severance of dogmatic theology from moral and pastoral theology has flow on effects in the understanding of theological anthropology and conversely a flawed theological anthropology will have flow on effects in the realm of moral theology. Dogmatic theology protects the two from falling into error.

---

44. Ouellet, *Divine Likeness*, 234.
45. John Paul II, *Reconciliatio et paenitentia*, no. 18.

Mediating History in the Realm of Ontology: Rahner or Balthasar

While the relationships between the critical couplets of nature and grace, and faith and reason generated a large amount of debate over the course of last century, by far the most serious theological crisis zone has been that of explaining the relationship between history and ontology. The key question is: how does the fact that a human person is immersed within history and a particular culture or cultures influence his or her identity and moral formation? There is general agreement that the two theologians who have had the courage to stare the problem in the face and respond to it are Rahner and Balthasar. In *Principles of Catholic Theology* Ratzinger identified the crisis but did not attend to the task of providing his own definitive account of the mediation of history in the realm of ontology. He did however argue that Karl Rahner's attempt to deal with the issue in *Hearers of the Word* (1941) made the mistake of making man's being itself historical in character. The epistemological side of Rahner's project has been described as an attempt to "baptize" German Idealism while his account of the relationship between nature and grace, employing his concept of the supernatural existential, has been noted for its tendency to naturalize the supernatural and even, by some interpreters, to affirm the secularization of formerly Christian cultures. Against these orientations Ratzinger rhetorically asked,

> Is the Christian really just man as he is? Does not the whole dynamism of history stem from the pressure to rise above man as he is? Is not the main point of the faith of both Testaments that man is what he ought to be only by conversion, that is, when he ceases to be what he is? Does not such a concept which turns being into history but also history into being, result in a vast stagnation despite the talk of self-transcendence as the content of man's being?[46]

Peter McGregor, affirming Ratzinger's reservations, put the issue this way:

> The problem with Rahner's beginning with anthropology and then proceeding to Christology is that anthropology is the noun and theology is the adjective. Nor would its opposite, an anthropological theology which begins with God and then moves to man, resolve this dilemma. The danger of the first is an over-emphasis on the humanity of Christ, and of the second,

---

46. Ratzinger, *Principles of Catholic Theology*, 166.

an over-emphasis on his divinity. Ratzinger chooses neither. Rather, he sees the reconciliation of the two in Christology, more specifically, in the Christological dogmas of the Creed. The being of God and human action, as well as the action of God and being human, are reconciled in Christ.[47]

In *Principles of Catholic Theology*, Ratzinger further argued, contrary to the whole trajectory of German Idealism, that the whole is always communicated to man in the particular and that this explains "the fragmentary character of all his efforts to comprehend the unity of history and being."[48] This notion of the communication of the whole in the particular was a dominant theme in Balthasar's 1963 work *Das Ganze im Fragment* published in English as *A Theological Anthropology* (1967). In his Foreword Balthasar took a swipe at the pretensions of German Idealism. He wrote,

> For the philosopher and the theologian alike history is only a fragment; but if one does not know whether a part of a symphony is a fifth or a twentieth of the whole, then he cannot reconstruct the whole. Not even Hegel, who knew everything else, could construct the future. We, who know less than he, must abandon the attempt to establish, by means of the fragments of the world, the totality of the absolute world-transcending Spirit.[49]

Later in the same work Balthasar addressed the theme of the fragmentary nature of the human perception of the world with reference to the theological virtues. He argued that "faith, hope and charity move through a fragmentary existence towards an unforeseeable perfection. . . . As a blind man feels with knowing hands the sharp edges of broken pottery, so they learn from the fragments of existence in what direction toward wholeness God points them."[50]

Theological anthropology is always partnered by philosophical presuppositions and when seeking to understand the mediation of history in the realm of ontology, the options for partners are numerous, a fact that Rahner recognized when he coined the concept "gnoseological concupiscence." It is something of an academic cliché to say that Catholic theological anthropology in the twenty-first century is divided into

---

47. McGregor, *Heart to Heart*, 30.
48. Ratzinger, *Principles of Catholic Theology*, 171.
49. Balthasar, *A Theological Anthropology*, ix.
50. Balthasar, *A Theological Anthropology*, 95–96.

Rahnerian and Balthasarian camps, with the "open-to-history" existential Thomists finding themselves welcome within the Balthasarian camp, but nonetheless this *is* how the territory looks at the beginning of the twenty-first century. The root cause of the division would appear to be Rahner's openness to Kant and the general legacy of German Idealism and the contrary belief, shared by Newman, Scheeben, Gilson, Balthasar, and Ratzinger, that reason is never theologically neutral.

Conclusion

This chapter began by comparing theological anthropology to a mosaic since it is only possible to approach it by integrating elements from fundamental and dogmatic theology, including trinitarian theology and Christology, personalist philosophy and phenomenology. These elements include an understanding of the role of each of the Persons of the Trinity in the economy of salvation, the symphonic interaction of the faculties of the soul, the soul's attraction to the transcendental properties of being, the work of the theological virtues, the role of the heart understood in the biblical sense, and the nature of conscience. There are also the "critical couplets" of fundamental theology, including nature and grace, faith and reason, history and ontology, male and female, and *Eros* and *Agape*, to name only the most important of these relationships. It is the last three of these couplets that are attracting the lion's share of the research interest at the beginning of the twenty-first century.

Bibliography

Anderson, Carl, and José Granados. *Called to Love: Approaching John Paul II's Theology of the Body*. New York: Doubleday, 2014.
Balthasar, Hans Urs von. *A Theological Anthropology*. New York: Sheed & Ward, 1967.
———. *The Theology of Karl Barth*. San Francisco: Ignatius, 1992.
Benedict XVI, Pope. *Deus caritas est*. Rome: Editrice Vaticane, 2006.
———. *Spe salvi*. Rome: Editrice Vaticane, 2007.
Caldecott, Léonie. "Sincere Gift: The Pope's New Feminism." *Communio* 23.1 (1996) 64–81.
Gallagher, M. P. "Realisation of Wisdom: Fruits of Formation in the Light of Newman." In *Entering into the Mind of Christ: The True Nature of Theology*, edited by Deacon James Keating, 121–39. Omaha, NE: The Institute of Priestly Formation, 2014.
Francis, Pope. *Lumen fidei*. Rome: Editrice Vaticane, 2013.
Guardini, Romano. *La coscienza*. Brescia: Morcelliana, 2009.

Hildebrand, Alice von. *The Soul of a Lion: The Life of Dietrich von Hildebrand.* San Francisco: Ignatius, 2000.
Hildebrand, Dietrich von. *The Heart: An Analysis of Human and Divine Affectivity.* Denver: St. Augustine's Press, 2007.
———. *Love, Marriage, and the Catholic Conscience: Understanding the Church's Teaching on Birth Control.* Manchester, NH: Sophia Institute Press, 1998.
International Theological Commission. *Communion and Stewardship: Human Persons Created in the Image of God.* Rome: Editrice Vaticane, 2004.
John Paul II, Pope. *Dives in misericordiae.* Rome: Editrice Vaticane, 1980.
———. *Dominum et vivificantem.* Rome: Editrice Vaticane, 1986.
———. *Fides et ratio.* Rome: Editrice Vaticane, 1998.
———. *Mulieris dignitatem.* Rome: Editrice Vaticane, 1988.
———. *Reconciliatio et poenitentia.* Rome: Editrice Vaticane, 1984.
———. *Redemptor hominis.* Rome: Editrice Vaticane, 1979.
———. *Veritatis splendor.* Rome: Editrice Vaticane, 1993.
Kasper, Walter. "The Theological Anthropology of *Gaudium et spes*." *Communio* 23 (1996) 129–40.
McCarthy, Margaret Harper. "The Feminine Genius and Women's Contributions in Society and in the Church." In *Promise and Challenge: Catholic Women Reflect on Feminism, Complementarity, and the Church,* edited by Mary Rice Hasson, 105–27. Huntington, IN: Our Sunday Visitor, 2015.
McGregor, Peter J. *Heart to Heart: The Spiritual Christology of Joseph Ratzinger.* Eugene, OR: Pickwick, 2016.
McKenna, Frances Mary. "The Female Line in the Bible: Ratzinger's Deepening of the Church's Understanding of Tradition and Mary." *Religions* 11.6 (2020) 1–18.
McPartlan, Paul. "Henri de Lubac - Evangeliser." *Priest and People* 6 (1992) 343–46.
Melina, Livio. *Sharing in Christ's Virtues: For the Renewal of Moral Theology in the Light of Veritatis Splendor.* Washington, DC: Catholic University of America Press, 2001.
Milbank, John. "The New Divide: Classical versus Romantic Orthodoxy." *Modern Theology* 26.1 (2010) 26–38.
Minch, Daniel. "Eschatology and Theology of Hope: The Impact of *Gaudium et spes* on the Thought of Edward Schillebeeckx." *Heythrop Journal* 59 (2018) 273–85.
Ouellet, Marc. *Divine Likeness toward a Trinitarian Anthropology of the Family.* Grand Rapids: Eerdmans, 2006.
———. *Mystery and Sacrament of Love: A Theology of Marriage and the Family for the New Evangelisation.* Grand Rapids: Eerdmans, 2015.
Nichols, Aidan. *Romance and System: The Theological Synthesis of Matthias Joseph Scheeben.* Denver: Augustine Institute Press, 2010.
Ratzinger, Joseph. "The Dignity of the Human Person." In vol. 5 of *Commentary on the Documents of Vatican II,* edited by Herbert Vorgrimler, 115–64. New York: Herder & Herder, 1969.
———. *Principles of Catholic Theology: Building Stones for a Fundamental Theology.* San Francisco: Ignatius, 1987.
Rousselot, Pierre. *The Problem of Love in the Middle Ages: A Historical Contribution.* Milwaukee: Marquette University Press, 2002.
Sadler, Gregory B., ed. *Reason Fulfilled by Revelation: The 1930s Christian Philosophy Debates in France.* Washington, DC: Catholic University of America Press, 2011.
Savage, Deborah. "The Nature of Woman in Relation to Man." *Logos* 18.1 (2015) 71–93.

Scheeben, Matthias Joseph. *Mysteries of Christianity*. New York: Crossroad, 2008.
Scola, Angelo. "The Dignity and Mission of Women." *Communio* 25 (1998) 42–56.
———. "On the Trinitarian Encyclicals of John Paul II." *Communio* 18.3 (1991) 322–29.
Schillebeeckx, Edward. *The Real Achievement of Vatican II*. New York: Sheed and Ward, 1967.
———. *World and Church*. New York: Sheed and Ward, 1971.
Schindler, David. L. "Christology and the *Imago Dei*: Interpreting *Gaudium et spes*." *Communio* 23 (1996) 156–84.
Schumacher, Michele M. *A Trinitarian Anthropology: Adrienne von Speyr and Hans Urs von Balthasar in Dialogue with Thomas Aquinas*. Washington, DC: Catholic University of America Press, 2014.
———. *Women in Christ: Toward a New Feminism*. Grand Rapids: Eerdmans, 2004.
Second Vatican Council. *Gaudium et spes*. https://www.vatican.va/archive/hist_councils/ii_vatican_council/documents/vat-ii_const_19651207_gaudium-et-spes_en.html.
Söhngen, Gottlieb. *Humanität und Christentum*. Essen: Wibbelt, 1946.
———. *Kardinal Newman: Sein Gottesgedanke und seine Denkergestalt*. Bonn: Götz Schwippert, 1946.
———. *Von Gottes Herrlichkeit in Seiner Schöpfung un din Seiner Liebe*. Köln: Luthe-Druck, 1946.
Tóth, Beata. *The Heart Has Its Reasons: Towards a Theological Anthropology of the Heart*. Eugene, OR: Cascade, 2016.
Vallin, Philippe. "Un filo rosso antropologico, sacramentario ed etico attraverso i documenti della Commissione Teologica Internazionale (1969–2019)." Address before the International Theological Commission, Pontifical Lateran University, November 20, 2019.
Waldstein, Michael. *Man and Women He Created Them: A Theology of the Body*. New York: Pauline, 2019.

2

Finding One's Self in Foucault, Aquinas, and Girard

Mary Julian Ekman, RSM

One of the most puzzling realities we want to understand is ourselves. With such privileged access, we nevertheless struggle to know our true desires, intentions and motivations that are manifested in varying degrees within our consciousness.

Questions surrounding human intentionality and selfhood have fascinated thinkers across various cultures, interests, and metaphysical backgrounds. Among them we find St. Thomas Aquinas, who was primarily interested in the theological significance of these notions.[1] Aquinas offers a sophisticated theory of human self-knowledge which addresses notions of subjectivity, intentionality, and selfhood within the dynamism proper to human beings. For Aquinas, having being made in the image and likeness of God, we have the capacity to create ourselves *in action*: we cause our actions, we can reflect upon them, and we are ultimately responsible for the way in which they actualize us.

In contrast to many modern thinkers, Aquinas assumed the existence of a human soul and the notion of selfhood. Michel Foucault, René

1. See Cory, *Aquinas on Human Self-Knowledge*, 46.

Girard, and Jean-Michel Oughourlian, whose ideas have considerable relevance to contemporary notions of personal identity, accentuate self as a 'construct' (of the society/group, desire and imitation) and raise important questions about human freedom and agency. In this chapter, I will suggest that Aquinas's account of selfhood and subjectivity, grounded within a hylomorphic anthropology,[2] provides us with a more intuitive explanation for how it is that the human person—the *subject-as-a-being*—is both the datum of self-knowledge and the agent of self-determination, where knowledge and love are co-principles of finding self.

Part One

Michel Foucault argues that the individual is formed by power and by power relations and that we acquire a sense of self through our experience within these relations. In an essay called "The Subject and Power," Foucault defines power as "a way in which certain actions modify others," that is, every relationship of power involves a strategy of struggle in which the adversaries constitute for one another "a point of possible reversal."[3] The struggle is resolved only through the stabilizing effect of certain mechanisms which can be used to control the behavior of others.[4] In light of all this, Foucault sees the self as a social and cultural construct shaped and modified by the structures and institutions of modern Western society. This means that the individual is inextricably linked to the production and functioning of social and political discourse.

For Foucault, subjectivity is the product of social institutions dominating some part of the individual's identity; to be a subject is to be the product of the discourses of power. An individual is *made* a subject through various structures of objectification including the "whole technology of power over the body."[5]

Foucault outlines three modes of objectification of the individual: the human sciences; the "dividing practices"; and sexuality. This last structure is of particular interest to Foucault as he sees sexuality as the

---

2. That is, the human person is a matter-form composite in which body and soul constitute a single body.
3. Foucault, "The Subject and Power," 788, 794.
4. Foucault, "The Subject and Power," 794.
5. See Foucault, *Discipline and Punish*, 30.

way in which a human being turns himself into a subject.[6] He argues that from birth our bodies are subjugated and formed by the strategies of power so that what we perceive to be an "inside" of our relationship to self is really the product of constantly changing external forces.[7] In fact, the idea that humans have an "inner depth" that *needs* to be discovered is, he would argue, simply another manifestation of control imposed upon the individual by external forces of domination. Therefore, trying to answer the question "Who am I?" involves, for Foucault, pushing against not a class, individual, or institution but against a technique, a form of power.[8]

In his essay, "Technologies of the Self," he sets out to scrutinize the structures of power within Western society, the "very specific 'truth games' related to specific techniques" which we use to form ourselves, to relate to self and to relate to others. He outlines four major technologies or techniques: technologies of production; technologies of sign systems; technologies of power; and technologies of the self. While he sees these technologies as interrelated, Foucault is primarily interested in technologies of the self as they allow individuals "to effect by their own means or with the help of others a certain number of operations on their own bodies and souls so as to transform themselves."[9]

In the same essay, Foucault presents two hermeneutics of the self: one from Greco-Roman philosophy, the other from Christian spirituality. He argues that in Greco-Roman culture, knowledge of oneself was the consequence of taking care of oneself, but modern Western society changed this.[10] The change came about for two reasons: the transformation of moral principles in Western Society, and the philosophy of Descartes and Husserl. The first, he argues, was largely due to Christianity, which refashioned the previously integrated notion of self-care into something negative and self-indulgent; the second shifted self-knowledge out of the domain of self-care into that of epistemology. When an individual has

---

6. Foucault, "The Subject and Power," 777–78.

7. Foucault, "The Ethics of the Concern of the Self as a Practice of Freedom," in Foucault, *Ethics*, 300.

8. Foucault, "The Subject and Power," 781.

9. Foucault, "Technologies of the Self," 224–25.

10. Foucault, "Technologies of the Self," 225–26. In this section he argues that the Delphic principle "know yourself" was "technical advice" and was an admonition to "not suppose yourself to be a god" or "Be aware of what you really ask when you come to consult an oracle." In the ancient world, self-knowledge implied self-care since one's first concern had to be with oneself before one could know oneself.

neglected work by self on the self—which is essential for developing the practice of freedom or the formation of the self through techniques of living—domination of others results.[11]

For Foucault, then, the task of self-discovery involves deconstructing and reconstructing self through freedom and power; that is, constituting or inventing "self" through various technologies of the self. He argues that we must continually work at not being bound to a fixed identity; each individual has his or her own way of changing and this changeability characterizes what one is. To self-create and care for oneself is to model our life as a work of art and create an aesthetic experience out of it. The self is a process of modern identity, a social product. Thus, we inherit from Foucault what we could call the "sociological" or "technological" self.

According to René Girard, self is constructed, but for a different reason to Foucault: it is constructed specifically by "the strategies of mimesis."[12] In his book, *Deceit, Desire and the Novel: Self and Other in Literary Structure*, Girard develops his theory of mimetic desire; that we are mimetic, imitational creatures and our desires and ideas are modelled on the desires and ideas of people we admire. Girard distinguishes between instinctual needs and desires: he argues that while the former can be satisfied by objects, desires can never really be satisfied.[13] In fact they can never be satisfied because ultimately they have no real object: desires (and by extension human relations) are fundamentally mimetic.

In fact, for Girard we are not technically individual beings but *interdividual* ones.[14]

This implies that the self is not "in you" and it is not "in the other" but is constituted by the *interplay* between the two. The self is literally "transferable."[15] Just like desire, the self has no objective reality. Insofar as desire is not ultimately object orientated, self is the product of mediation

---

11. Foucault, "The Ethics of the Concern for Self as a Practice of Freedom," in Foucault, *Ethics*, 288. The practices associated with self-governance were varied: meditation, letter writing to friends, examination of self and conscience (all Stoic techniques he argues) then also Christian asceticism.

12. Girard, *Things Hidden Since the Foundation of the World*, 286.

13. Girard, *Violence and the Sacred*, 146.

14. Girard, *Things Hidden Since the Foundation of the World*, 299–300.

15. René Girard writes in *Things Hidden Since the Foundation of the World* that "everything that constitutes us as human beings on the level that we call 'psychic,' must result from the infinitely slow, but ultimately monumental work achieved by the disorganisation and increasingly complex reorganisation of mimetic functions" (284).

by another human (model). Girard thus describes the structure of desire as "triangular": the subject desires because he or she knows, imagines or suspects the model desires that object (which is the third point of the triangle).[16] In fact, it is because we do not know what to desire that we look to others in order to make up our minds: "We desire what others desire because we imitate their desires."[17] That we believe these desires are really our own is, for Girard, "the dearest of all our illusions."[18]

If there is no essence to the Girardian self how does he account for its origin, however illusory? The self is a product of cathexis. It is generated by the mechanism of imitation, especially at the point when that imitation turns into rivalry, conflict and a "mimetic crisis." By transferring or "channeling" the social conflict caused by mimetic rivalry onto a single victim, who effectively functions as its "shock absorber,"[19] order is restored and human relations are stabilized. Thus, we have in the "scapegoat victim" the first "other" who by default also infers the first self.[20]

One of the most important books Girard produced was called *Things Hidden Since the Foundation of the World*. It was in the form of a dialogue with two psychiatrists, Jean-Michel Oughourlian and Guy Lefort. Oughourlian, a close collaborator of Girard's, went on to develop the implications of Girard's "interdividual psychology" in his own book called *The Puppet of Desire: The Psychology of Hysteria, Possession and Hypnosis*, which applies Girardian theory within a clinical context.[21] He follows Girard's argument that our desires are inauthentic (borrowed from others) making us into "puppets of desire," specifically in the context of humans being prone to suggestion and hypnosis which, he also argues, is mimetic in nature. Oughourlian's psychological concept of self like Girard's is "a function of all the relationships in which the

---

16. Girard, "Triangular Desire," 35.

17. René Girard quoted in Oughourlian, *The Puppet of Desire*, x.

18. Girard, "To Double Business Bound," ix.

19. It is interesting to note that *ammortizzare* (Ital.) means to "cushion" or "absorb" (= redeem or pay off).

20. Girard, "Mimesis and Violence," 9, 12. Girard argues that primitive man actually stumbled upon the solution to this threat: the scapegoat. Here we touch on Girard's highly controversial anthropological theory of consciousness, inspired by Freud's hypothesis of a primal collective murder in *Totem and Taboo*. According to his theory, the experience of this first great scapegoat event is the genesis of human consciousness: the differentiation between "us" and "it."

21. His most recent work, *The Mimetic Brain*, recapitulates and further develops many notions within *The Puppet of Desire*.

self is involved."[22] He views *self* as a mythic notion or an ever-changing, "ultimately evanescent structure"—like the *mimetic desire* that produces it.[23] Although he also concludes that the self is permanently becoming, always in a state of modification by its relation to the other, "by the pull of the other's desire,"[24] he hints at an unorthodox model of consciousness in line with his view that the study of hypnosis can be a "touchstone for the anthropological theory of mimesis" and a way for its experimental verification. In effect, Oughourlian demonstrates experimentally the age-old hierarchic or emanatory consciousness comprised of multiple layered or nested selves (higher and lower selves) which he discovered in clinical hypnosis sessions. But even in this *vertical* rather than horizontal mimetic model, he still notes that each individual "persona" is contingent on the one above. He once again verifies, experimentally, that consciousness is rooted in otherness.[25]

Thus far, we have seen how Foucault and his "sociological self" gives primacy to power structures which pervade human action, challenging the classical idea of an autonomous, essential self. We have also seen how the "psychological self" of Girard and Oughourlian presents the subject as intrinsically unstable and other-dependent. A notable problem with these concepts is that in abolishing the traditional "interior" of the individual they simultaneously abolish the traditional rationale for a defense of the subject, having lost its essential reality. In short, the individual seems to dissolve into the happenstance of an inexorable mechanism. There is no traditional "interior" let alone "desire" proper to an individual. There is arguably a problem of self-defeatism in the anti-essentialist philosophy of Foucault and Girard: namely, how can one essentially value something that does not essentially exist?

As we have seen, the problem of "self" is the problem of "desire." For Aquinas, working within a hylomorphic (body-soul) philosophy, human desire is never in vain. Unlike Girard, Aquinas does not categorically distinguish instinct and desire. He simply conceives desire in classical terms, that is, a response to what we perceive as good or "fitting" *for us*. In other words, human desire is bound up not with discourses of power or mimesis but with a rational soul and its powers of intellect and will (these

---

22. Oughourlian, *The Puppet of Desire*, 11.
23. Eugene Webb in Oughourlian, *The Puppet of Desire*, xviii.
24. Oughourlian, *The Puppet of Desire*, 198.
25. Oughourlian, *The Puppet of Desire*, 188.

denote ways by which the soul interacts with reality).[26] Our capacity to know all that is true and love all that is good characterizes us as free moral agents, responsible for what is traditionally termed "self-actualization." In this case, human desire has a *rational dynamic* because the object of desire is not the mimetic other but the good, which when acquired, is moreover completive and perfective of the human person.[27] Going deeper into Aquinas's concept of the individual subject we find a twofold notion of "subjecthood" and "selfhood" (although Aquinas himself does not use these terms) where the former is a wholistic account of the human person within which the latter, psychological, one is grounded.[28] While the latter (*"self-soul"*) can subsist in itself, for Aquinas it does not have the complete nature of being human.[29] Nevertheless, he argues that the soul is properly "the knower"[30] and for this reason grounds selfhood in the individual subject. That is, the intellect and will can reflect upon themselves and upon each other, sharing a unique relationship of reflexivity. Thus, we could formulate these notions in contemporary terms and say that for Aquinas, selfhood denotes the individual's experience of himself or herself within the world as "I." In perceiving my thinking and acting, I am perceiving my "self," and I come to know myself in a conscious manner as I engage with the world around me.[31]

In other words, the individual for Aquinas is primarily a rational not a mimetic animal: reason, not desire, is primal.[32] Unlike the Foucauldian and Girardian Selfs, one can meaningfully say "I" and in the order of action, one can genuinely claim that "I" am responsible for this action. Because the intellect and will are able to reflect upon themselves and upon each other, we are able to exercise conscious control over our

26. As an Aristotelian, Aquinas takes the role of mimesis as a given in the human learning experience.

27. Aquinas, *Summa Theologiae*, I-II.1.5.

28. Aquinas, *In I Sent.*, 25.1.1, in *Scriptum super libros Sententiarum*. Thomas goes beyond Boethius's definition of person as "an individual substance of a rational nature" in emphasizing the aspect of subsistence, existing in itself (in the mode of substance) with its own act of existence. See Norris Clarke, *Person and Being*, 29.

29. This is because the human person is a substantial union of soul and body. The soul is united to the body by its essence, even though the mode in which the human soul is united to the body is not one of total dependence. See Aquinas, *De veritate*, 13.4.

30. Aquinas, *Commentary on the Book of Causes*, prop. 15.

31. See Cory, *Aquinas on Human Self-Knowledge*, 69–75.

32. See Aquinas, *The Power of God*, 9.1.3.

judgments and also enjoy consciousness of our desires.[33] For Aquinas, nothing can be the object of the will unless it is known: I desire things because I perceive that they are good *for me*.[34] At length I experience an awareness that my decisions contribute to my becoming "someone" (who may be good or bad).

Part Two

Foucault famously stated that "man is an invention of recent date. And one perhaps nearing its end. . . . If those arrangements were to disappear as they appeared . . . then one can certainly wager that man would be erased, like a face drawn in sand at the edge of the sea."[35] Here our suspicion concerning the connection between Foucault's concept of self and the defense of that self is justified. Since there is no lasting self, we should probably not even be trying to "find" one. In the case of Girardian theory, the denial of the primacy of reason in human behavior perhaps also explains its strange neglect of the very real, clear, and present danger of rational—especially technological—forces and determinisms that define the modern world where most mesmerizing mimesis and models are not even human. Girard nevertheless intimates a uniqueness in the modern malaise. Here we refer to what Girard calls the "absurd mimetic project of self-divinization" in which the other becomes more fascinating the more inaccessible they are. The mimetic project ends up going "beyond the animal to the automatic and even the mechanical. The individual becomes increasingly bewildered and unbalanced by a desire that nothing can satisfy and finally seeks the divine essence in that which radically denies his own Existence: the inanimate."[36] Even so, Girardian thinking on modernity seems somewhat reminiscent of Foucault's. It is a question of defense of the self and a mode of thinking that undermines the idea of an innate self and self-ownership. We know Foucault cannot and does

---

33. Aquinas, *De veritate*, 22.12.
34. Wojtyla, *Person and Act*, 363.
35. Foucault, *The Order of Things*, 387.
36. See Girard, *Deceit*, 286. As Raymond Schwager notes in his essay entitled "Mimesis and Freedom," desire moves beyond human models "and beyond the world of the animal to the inanimate." However, Schwager himself does not seem to appreciate the degree to which the "inaccessible animate" can also paradoxically converge with the God model i.e., in the prophet, sage, and shaman who can be seen as "passionless, pitiless and perfect" (like a machine). See Schwager, "Mimesis and Freedom," 40.

not care to defend the self. Likewise, what could the interdividual theory of Girard possibly say to modern transhumanist philosophy of technologists, the philosophy of human erasure? Was there ever really a place for self-actualization in either theory? Is the self-nullification of Foucault and Girard yet another sophisticated modern ideology?

In any case, the burden of proof for an immutable, rational self or soul is on the one who asserts or presumes its reality.[37] At least traditionally, the *soul-self* did not have any particular importance or stability apart from its relation to the divine. There is no getting around the fact that any ontology of the self must have some divine or transcendent basis. Here, interestingly, Oughourlian looks to the traditional *imago Dei* in his exploration of the mimetic self: "in creating man in his own image, man inscribed in him the spatial dimension of mimesis . . . it is this feature that makes man radically different from all other animals and calls him to mastery over them."[38] His mimetic account of "the Fall" offers further elaboration of this idea. In this account the serpent represents the principle of mimetic desire being responsible for inciting the "mimesis of appropriation" and rivalry and thus difference.[39] The model, God, is presented by the serpent as "having given all but the tree; all but the difference which is also the obstacle and which constitutes the desirable."[40] Oughourlian calls this "ontological desire" (in this instance, the desire to be like God), and this is what sets us in motion. The goal of this ontological desire is ultimately desire for the model's being—"the secret that is difference [and] the essential factor in the mimetic."[41] Adam and Eve's consciousness of being naked thus becomes the symbol of their consciousness of selfhood, or individuation, the sin which draws us to talk in terms of "subject" and "object," notwithstanding with the advent of Christ the perfect Model the cycle of rivalry and pathological mimesis is resolved.

So, we now seem to have a convergence of Aquinas and mimetic theory in the *imitatio Christi*. We can also sympathize with Foucault's uncritical acceptance of the washing away of man's selfhood which might simply be thought of as a washing away of primal sin.

37. Oughourlian, *The Puppet of Desire*, 24.
38. Oughourlian, *The Puppet of Desire*, 22.
39. Oughourlian, *The Puppet of Desire*, 24.
40. Oughourlian, *The Puppet of Desire*, 24.
41. Oughourlian, *The Puppet of Desire*, 25.

We are left with the problem of interiority. For Aquinas, being made "to the image" infers a certain movement or tendency to perfection innate to the individual.[42] Aquinas did, however, also pose the question "whether the image of God is found in every man."[43] He concludes that we are the image of God by reason of our intellectual nature; in other words, how we participate in the image of God (a positive ontological desire), is actually developmental and presupposes a free *subject-as-agent*. That is to say, "a person is most perfectly like God according as that intellectual nature can most imitate God."[44] In what way does our intellectual nature imitate God? Aquinas gives three ways. First, in that we possess a natural *aptitude* for understanding and loving God, which is common to all human beings; this is image from *creation*. Second, the image of God is in man "inasmuch as we actually or habitually know and love God however imperfectly." This image is one of *re-creation* and consists in becoming more like God; that is, we strive, via reason, free choice and will to imitate God. Importantly, however, grace is required to actively know and love God as our ultimate end.[45] And third, Aquinas says human beings are in the image of God inasmuch as we know God actually and love him perfectly; this image consists in the *likeness of glory*.[46] In this state of being "Godlike" there is not even "room" for mimesis let alone rivalry and conflict.

From a Girardian perspective one can also reconcile with God through Christ the Perfect Model, albeit in such a way that our identity is still absorbed into the other (and necessarily so, since he is still a *Model*). And so, a question lingers: Am I still not a generated mimetic self with no essential freedom or personhood? For example, if I am not my own judge and not my own "self" am I still not just a mechanistic imitator, a *puppet of God*?[47] Some will reply in the affirmative, and even celebrate

42. Aquinas, *Summa Theologiae*, I.35.1.3.

43. Aquinas, *Summa Theologiae*, I.93.4.

44. Aquinas, *Summa Theologiae*, I.93.4.

45. Since "no created nature is a sufficient principle of an act deserving of eternal life" unless grace is added. See Aquinas, *Summa Theologiae*, I-II.114.2.

46. Aquinas, *Summa Theologiae*, I.93.5.

47. Raymund Schwager responds to critics of Girard who say that he holds two contradictory versions of freedom in his explanation of the origin of violence. Schwager suggests, however, that the actual problem is not the "quasi character of mimesis" but the enslavement of freedom. Schwager seems to use the classic "God of the Gaps" argumentation—but one does not get to do this in Girardian-mimetic theory because, as we will see, the real problem is not just the nature of the model but also the nature of imitation itself. See Schwager, "Mimesis and Freedom," 41–43.

FINDING ONE'S SELF IN FOUCAULT, AQUINAS, AND GIRARD 33

the fact. But others who believe in the individual subject, even one cooperating with grace, may nevertheless remain perturbed by the image of an innately mimetic creature, however healthy its mimesis and however perfect its Model. Perhaps they are haunted by Pascal's words that "man is neither angel nor beast, and the misfortune is that he who wants to play the angel plays the beast."[48]

The problem is the God model does not remove the problem of mimetic theory and the double bind of *imitate me-do not imitate me*. The blasphemous, the satanic, consists precisely in the *imitation* of God. We are now touching on the problem of imitation being an inherently pejorative concept. At length we are dealing with the concept of *anti* which means both "against" and also "like." The *evil* of the anti-Christ turns precisely on the fact that he *resembles* Christ. Mere internalization of God without any critical intent, or belief without understanding, is precisely what we call a parody of the thing.

The Girardian response to this criticism is naturally that the God model is self-rectifying because the model is also the ground of being in itself. But we still face the No True Scotsman fallacy. Who is the true model?

In Girardian theory we know that Christ as model is the one exception to the mimetic rule. And yet history shows us that this model was never unambiguous or universally agreed upon. Even in a communitarian context one only has to read the letters of St. Paul regarding the internal strife of the first communities and the problem of different Jesus' to wonder whether Christ as simply *Model* is sufficient for highly mimetic creatures.[49] Part of the problem lies in the fact that the very notion of a Model fosters a distance of a kind not especially conducive to fellowship or friendship. In fact, friendship is a key concept, or juxtaposition, in the problem of mimetic self, rivalry, and the role of the other. If it is true that knowledge and the self are constructed, and the subject can never be extricated from the object then there is no escape from the relation of co-creator and fellowship. The concept of friendship seems to be a way out of the impasse of mimesis and the mischief of models.

One of the greatest writers on friendship is Marcus Tullius Cicero. In *De amicitia*, he defines friendship as mutual goodwill and affection, a

---

48. Pascal, *Pensées*, 358: "L'homme n'est ni ange ni bête, et le malheur veut que qui veut faire l'ange fait la bête."

49. For example, see 1 Corinthians 1:10–15 on divisions within the early church.

gift unsurpassed by anything but wisdom itself.[50] Friendship, he says, is always unassailable. There is nothing mechanistic or pretended (*simulatum*) in friendship; it is genuine and spontaneous or not at all.[51] Moreover, writes Cicero, a true friend is "another self," for each human being naturally longs for another whose soul may "so blend (*misceat*) with his own as almost to make one out of two."[52] Friendship can only exist between good people.[53] Cicero would see no room for mimetic rivalry within true friendship. One might even *define* friendship as the transcendence or transgression of the mimetic power relationship, and that it is friendship with God which is arguably the most authentic relation precisely because it integrates and acknowledges all our human attributes. Above all, it does not pretend to be both a child of God (a harmonious will) and a slave of God (a subordinate will). That a model can be perfect does not mean it is good. A perfect model may even *destroy the good*.

The assertion that the concept of friendship with God is a conceit, if not a blasphemy, misses the point that it is not an option. Friendship is not a familiarization but a mystery. The chasm between God and man simply highlights the significance and role of grace as a quality of creation itself. As Aquinas reminds us, we cannot speak of charity which is universal in scope and depth without reference to "a certain friendship of man for God" for God's own sake.[54] In fact, charity is not dependent on any human virtue, but on the goodness of God himself.[55]

In short, we have seen three interrelational categories of self: the sociological, Foucauldian focused on subordination; the psychological, Girardian based on mimesis; and the "amicable," Ciceronian/Thomistic relation focused on harmony, friendship. The key issue for our purposes is that one does not *converse* with enemies, one converses with friends. One cannot converse with mimetic or inauthentic others. For Aquinas,

---

50. Cicero, *De amicitia*, v, 19. Furthermore "friendship excels relationship in this, that goodwill may be eliminated from relationship while from friendship it cannot; since, if you remove goodwill from friendship the very name of friendship is gone; if you remove it from relationship, the name of relationship still remains."

51. Cicero, *De amicitia*, viii, 27: "in amicitia autem nihil fictum, nihil simulatum est et, quidquid est, id est verum et voluntarium."

52. Cicero, *De amicitia*, xxi, 80; xxi, 81.

53. Cicero, *De amicitia*, xxvii, 21.

54. Aquinas, *Summa Theologiae*, II-II.23.1; II-II.23.5.1.

55. Aquinas, *Summa Theologiae*, II-II.23.3.1.

charity is the fellowship of the spiritual life; it is friendship with God *and the ultimate source of self*.[56]

Bibliography

Aquinas, Thomas. *The Disputed Questions on Truth (De veritate)*. Translated by Robert W. Mulligan et al. Chicago: Regnery, 1952.
———. *Commentary on the Book of Causes*. Translated by Vincent A. Guagliardo et al. Washington, DC: Catholic University of America Press, 1996.
———. *The Power of God*. Translated by Richard J. Regan. New York: Oxford University Press, 2012.
———. *Scriptum super libros Sententiarum*. Vol. 1. Edited by P. Mandonnet. Paris: Lethielleux, 1929.
———. *Summa Theologiae*. Translated by the Fathers of the English Dominican Province. New York: Benzinger Brothers, 1947.
Cicero, Marcus Tullius. *De Senectute, De amicitia, De divinatione*. Translated by William Armistead Falconer. Loeb Classical Library 154. Cambridge: Harvard University Press, 1923.
Clarke, W. Norris. *Person and Being*. Milwaukee: Marquette University Press, 1993.
Cory, Therese. *Aquinas on Human Self-Knowledge*. Cambridge: Cambridge University Press, 2014.
Foucault, Michel. *Aesthetics, Method, and Epistemology: Essential Works of Foucault, 1954–1984*. Vol. 2. Edited by James D. Faubion. London: Penguin, 1994.
———. *Discipline and Punish: The Birth of the Prison*. Translated by Alan Sheridan. New York: Random House, 1979.
———. *Ethics: Essential Works of Foucault, 1954–1984*. Vol. 1. Edited by Paul Rabinow. London: Penguin, 1994.
———. *The Order of Things: An Archaeology of the Human Sciences*. London: Routledge, 1989.
———. "The Subject and Power." *Critical Inquiry* 8.4 (1982) 777–95.
———. "Technologies of the Self." In *Technologies of the Self*, edited by Luther H. Martin et al., 16–49. Amherst: University of Massachusetts Press, 1988.
Girard, René. *Deceit, Desire, and the Novel: Self and Other in Literary Structure*. Translated by Yvonne Freccero. Baltimore: Johns Hopkins University Press, 1977.
———. "Mimesis and Violence: Perspectives in Cultural Criticism." In *The Girard Reader*, edited by James G. Williams, 9–19. New York: Crossroad, 1996.
———. *Things Hidden Since the Foundation of the World*. Translated by Stephen Bann and Michael Metteer. Stanford: Stanford University Press, 1978.
———. *"To Double Business Bound": Essays on Literature, Mimesis and Anthropology*. Baltimore: John Hopkins University Press, 1978.
———. "Triangular Desire." In *The Girard Reader*, edited by James G. Williams, 33–44. New York: Crossroad, 1996.
———. *Violence and the Sacred*. Translated by Patrick Gregory. Baltimore: Johns Hopkins University Press, 1977.

---

56. Aquinas, *Summa Theologiae*, II-II.25.2.2.

Oughourlian, Jean-Michel. *The Mimetic Brain*. Edited by William A. Johnsen. Translated by Trevor Cribben Merrill. East Lansing: Michigan State University Press, 2016.

———. *The Puppet of Desire: The Psychology of Hysteria, Possession and Hypnosis*. Translated by Eugene Webb. Stanford: Stanford University Press, 1991.

Pascal, Blaise. *Pensées*. London: Dent & Sons, 1913.

Schwager, Raymond. "Mimesis and Freedom." *Contagion* 21 (2014) 29–45.

Wojtyla, Karol. *Person and Act and Related Essays*. Vol. 1. Translated by Grzegorz Ignatik. Washington DC: Catholic University of America Press, 2021.

3

Christ and the Interweaving of Spirit and Matter

The Contribution of Eric Mascall to Theological Anthropology

NIGEL ZIMMERMANN

Introduction

The Anglican Thomist Eric Mascall (1905–93) crafted an inimitably Christo-centric theological anthropology in critical engagement with the secularizing trends in mid twentieth century English-speaking theology. Two great mysteries beckoned Mascall's scholarship: that of the triune God, known through Christian revelation; and the human person, an embodied rational creature made in the divine image and likeness. Unfenced by strict denominational limitations, Mascall engaged in a lively fashion with the controversies of contemporary Christianity, offering a vision of the human person as an ecclesial mystery. That is to say, for Mascall, questions about the nature and destiny of the human person, and the contradictions of human existence, find their answers in a lived and sustained immersion in the mystery of Christ and his body the church.

As an Anglican Catholic, Mascall drank deeply from the wellsprings of Eastern Christian spiritual writings as well as those of Western Catholic sources, and ultimately argues that without the mystery of the church, the mystery of the human person is a problem without a resolution.[1]

Mascall in His Time, and the Interweaving of Spirit and Matter

In his Boyle Lectures of 1965, published as *The Christian Universe*, Eric Mascall wrote,

> God's ultimate purpose for the human race and for the whole material universe is that they should be taken up into Christ and transformed into a condition of unimaginable glory, and that it is for this that God took our human nature, in which spirit and matter are so mysteriously and intricately interwoven.[2]

The interweaving of spirit and matter is an intricate act that draws the human person into the challenges of material and spiritual life. In Christ, the taking up of human nature into the divine life is a double movement including both humanity's joining into God, and of "God's universal offer of himself to man."[3] For Mascall, the Incarnation of Christ Jesus is not so much the story of two static objects becoming enjoined in a mysterious manner, but of two mysteries becoming united in a way that carries its own logic and order. Those two mysteries are human nature and divine nature, the latter transforming the former in what Holy Scripture calls glory. It is impossible to understand the place of Mascall in the debates of twentieth century theological debate without grasping the orientation this fundamental belief grants to all his writings, and the way this simple point of Christian orthodoxy, defined by the Council of Chalcedon (451), serves as Mascall's departure point in the midst of contemporary discussion.

---

1. I am thankful to the Institute for Ethics and Society at the University of Notre Dame Australia and especially to Sandra Lynch and John Rees for their support, enabling me to pursue a research project on Eric Mascall which brought me to his archives in Pusey House in Oxford, and where I spent time with his final unpublished manuscript *The Overarching Question*.
2. Mascall, *The Christian Universe*, 109.
3. Mascall, *The Christian Universe*, 88.

Chalcedon might seem a peculiar place to start. The fathers of Chalcedon committed themselves and their successors to an understanding of the Incarnation, such that without dilution or magnification, the two natures—being human and divine—were perfectly united, and that same person, Jesus Christ, is of one substance with the Father as touches the Godhead. In other words, Christ is both fully human and fully divine, and likewise is the Second Person of the Trinity, "without confusion, without conversion, without division, never to be separated."[4] At the close of the Council, the Monophysite position became clearly viewed as heretical, while nonetheless remaining the popular Christian position in Egypt thereafter (although some outstanding questions have been resolved between Coptic Orthodoxy and Western Catholicism in more recent times). It was determined about two centuries later that the operation of two wills (according each to their nature) and two operations in Christ was in conformity with the previous five Councils, thus cementing the Chalcedonian position as lasting and effective.[5] More will be said on this topic later in the chapter; suffice it to note the fundamental contribution that Chalcedon made to Christian doctrine was in terms of Christology.

In his contemporary context, both theologically and personally, Mascall was a thoroughgoing eccentric. An Anglican Thomist, a celibate priest of the Church of England, a professor of theology, a member of the Oratory of the Good Shepherd, a committed parish clergyman, a poet and story-teller, a prolific writer and combative letter-writer, he could write like a rigorist unreconstructed theist driven by fierce logic as much as he could write with delightful whimsy and attractive self-deprecation. His two poetry collections, *Pi in the High* (1959) and *Compliments of the Season* (1985), are said to have been written in the bath. In them, he managed to laugh at himself, as well as the foolishness of current debates among scholars. See for example the first stanza of his 1965 poem "Swinburne Among the Theologians":

> O pale Heideggerian orphan, O pilgrim of *Sorge* and *Angst*.
> How vacuous, vile and *geworfen* is the hook of the hope where thou hang'st!
> Condemned to exist willy-nilly, contrive to rebel and depart

---

4. See especially Sellers, *Two Ancient Christologies*, 46; Prestige, *God in Patristic Thought*.
5. Jedin, *Ecumenical Councils of the Catholic Church*, 42.

> For the rose and raptures of Tillich and the lilies and languors of Barth.[6]

Other less literary tropes appear in his verse, bemusing on life as an English clergyman and the personalities of the Church of England. For a well-travelled scholar, Mascall's creativity can often be seen most clearly when he makes links between the past and the present, especially on matters of faith and history.

For his book of Augustinian reflections, *Grace and Glory*, Mascall received the following endorsement by Michael Ramsay, sometime Archbishop of York, and of Canterbury:

> Here is theology for Everyman, like all true theology profound in thought and simple in language. Here is wisdom, drawn from one of the timeless classics of Christian writing, and applied with sympathetic understanding to our own time. Here is one of the doctrines of our faith, often pushed way to the far horizons of our attention, brought vividly near to us.[7]

In a relatable manner, *Grace and Glory* offers a simple account of Christian hope inspired by the language of St. Augustine who spoke of how we shall "rest," "see," "love," and "praise" without ceasing. The grounding of a spiritual hope for human destiny explained analogously through the categories of bodily senses is one Mascall enjoyed putting forward as a positive Christian contribution. In it, one can see the strength that logic plays in Mascall's thought. In his autobiography, Mascall remarks on his lack of formal theological training, and the unlikely manner in which he, a Cambridge trained mathematician, ended up teaching theology at Oxford.[8] Without any sense of irony, he observes that the discipline of logic and reason in mathematics proved a solid foundation for theological research.

Equally however, Mascall could be merciless with his theological foes, perhaps no more so than in his tome *The Secularisation of Christianity*, in which he takes on two theological writers who had gained celebrity for their deconstructive accounts of Christianity, J. A. T. Robinson (then Bishop of Woolwich) and his book *Honest to God*, and Paul van Buren and his book, *The Secular Meaning of the Gospel*.[9] In that important work,

---

6. Mascall, *Compliments of the Season*, 16.

7. Michael Ramsey, "Preface," in Mascall, *Grace and Glory*, 8.

8. Mascall, *Saraband*, 378.

9. Mascall, *The Secularisation of Christianity*; Robinson, *Honest to God*; van Buren, *The Secular Meaning of the Gospel*.

Mascall entered what had become a very public and bitter conflict about the truthfulness and substance of Christianity. A primary focus of Mascall's critique is that both Robinson and van Buren misunderstand and misrepresent the classical Christian formularies regarding the person of Christ, in that they regard the church as disregarding the humanity of Christ. Mascall went to the church Fathers, especially St. Athanasius, and to the Council of Chalcedon, to stake his claim that orthodox Christian faith has maintained a steady commitment to the full operative humanity found in the person of Jesus of Nazareth, and that Christian orthodoxy is doctrinally resistant to all claims otherwise. Buren ultimately argued that what he called the "supranaturalistic" approach of Chalcedon was unsustainable, but that the Christian celebration of Christ's arrival—Christmas—contained a myth-like quality that had a place in the secular world. Mascall pointed out the inherent lack of logic in Buren and Robinson's approach, which seems to try and hold on to a loosely metaphorical conceptualization of Incarnation emptied of its human, divine, or metaphysical content. Mascall identifies the fundamental problem with such a "de-mythologizing" in which Christmas is celebrated despite its incoherence: "This does credit to the warmth of his human emotions, but on the plane of belief it would seem to involve him in sheer naturalism."[10] Elsewhere Mascall is concerned with writers like Piet Schoonenberg SJ, and also Norman Pittenger, who in many ways complement Robinson, not because they offer a wholesale rejection of Christian faith, but because they so over-emphasize one element of orthodox faith through a fundamental misreading of Christian dogma and history that they find themselves endorsing views contrary to the faith. In other words, such writers fall, not into mere apostasy, but very specific heretical categories:

> For, however mistaken we may judge their basic Christological assumption to be—and this would apply specially to such writers as Pittenger and Robinson, the latter of whom appears to have considerably influenced Schoonenberg—they were concerned with a quite fundamental Christian truth, that of the genuine humanity of Jesus, and this should be recognized although, in their fear of anything approaching to Docetism, they drifted into Nestorianism, adoptionism, or even some kind of sophisticated twentieth-century psilanthropism.[11]

---

10. Mascall, *The Secularisation of Christianity*, 145.
11. Mascall, *Theology & the Gospel of Christ*, 175.

Mascall's solution to these drifting positions in error was not so much to "go back" to Chalcedon, but to begin there and move forwards. His counter-intuitive approach to the constant dialogue at work between thinkers separated by much time and history makes Mascall a theologian able to think and write beyond the limitations of the present moment, viewing his work as a small part in a much larger conversation. Strikingly, the title page of *The Secularisation of Christianity* contains quotes from two writers not known for being linked in their intellectual commitments or contexts, St. Paul and Martin Heidegger.[12] At this point in his career, Mascall was Professor of Historical Theology in the University of London, having established himself as a formidable intellectual ready to make a coherent Christian case for belief in the halls of Oxford or Cambridge, as well as in the pages of the newspaper. By entering directly into the debates of the day, Mascall was stepping into a conflict with what, in other places, he would call the "New Approach."[13]

If his concern with writers of the "New Approach" was focused on their misunderstanding of the Christian doctrine of the two natures in Christ, Mascall was equally attentive to explaining from the mystery of Christ a vision of the human person, who is always a blend of good and bad amid the complexities of worldly existence. For Mascall, the Christian is the creature who is *re-created* in Baptism and is therefore conversant in some way with all that Christ has touched in history, both fallen and glorified.[14] Mascall's anthropology is not a flight from the world but a maturation to glory within it. Despite Mascall's affirmation of the joys of the world (he was no Calvinist), he has an acute sense of the underside of earthly joys, of the nearness of death and decay and the limitations upon us in time and space. Without denigrating the good things of the world, Mascall meditates upon them momentarily so that he can glean from them a flight towards that heavenly gift of a life in plenitude and of the eternal over-flowing cup. It is as if the fleeting beauty of nature, such as the rose or the smile of a friend, gives way to something more lasting and affective within the soul. He writes,

---

12. From St. Paul's Letter to the Romans: "I am debtor both to the Greeks and to the Barbarians, both to the wise and to the unwise" (Rom 1:14); and from Heidegger: "Conscience summons Dasein's Self from its lostness in the 'they'" (*Being and Time*, 274/319).

13. Mascall, *Theology & The Gospel of Christ*, 194.

14. Mascall, *Christ, the Christian, and the Church*, 106.

> One of the most haunting features of the world's literature—and especially of the literature of the ancient pagan world—is the recurrent sense of the transience and elusiveness, the fragility and fleetingness of even the best things that life can offer, the note of heartbreak at the very root of things. Swinburne's "Thou has conquered, O pale Galilean; the world has grown grey from thy breath" embodied a grotesque falsehood.[15]

Haunted as he finds this theme, Mascall is not fatigued by it. Like other Christian theologians committed to a sacramental account of grace, he finds in the pagan mind an openness to the divine and a nod towards what is ultimately gifted to us in the ragged body of Christ upon the Cross—a beauty of self-gift that surpasses every otherwise beautiful thing created and uncreated. The good things of the world are not cast aside but taken up into the Cosmic Christ, and at the heart of the transformation is the image and the likeness of God in the human person, glorified. The theological vision—the *Christian* vision—offered by Mascall is a fulsome one and an inspiring one, enabling those of faith to care for the dignity of the lost and the fallen and rescue the world from a depleted anthropology in which there is little hope and no promise.

In his own time, Mascall's engagement with contemporaries held in place a vision of the human person as well as an account as to why the salvific promise of Christ mattered. Moreover, in the scattered and demythologizing tendencies in the works he critiqued, he wished to give an account of the Gospel, which contains a re-unification of what has been lost and a re-integration of what was once unified:

> I suggest that we should see the primary effect of Adam's fall as consisting essentially in a breaking of unity: first of all the breaking of Adam's own unity with God, and then the weakening of the unity which would otherwise have bound him and his descendants together in an organic body and have bound that organic body in unity with God.[16]

The mystery of re-unification experiences its first steps—its foretaste—in the ecclesial mystery, that slow and sometimes unattractive community called the church, called to be a "sign" with a sacramental and liturgical life, as even Martin Luther maintained.[17] Mascall defended

---

15. Mascall, *Grace and Glory*, 81.
16. Mascall, *The Importance of Being Human*, 83.
17. Mascall, *The Recovery of Unity*, 103.

(critically) the long term role of Thomas Aquinas against and in critical engagement with the versions of Transcendental Thomism he found in figures such as Karl Rahner and Bernard Lonergan. In his Gifford Lectures, titled *The Openness to Being*, Mascall grounded himself in what he called "Existential Thomism," despite many contemporary critics.[18] His key interlocutor over time, and his close friend, was Austin Farrer. Among his students were the sometime Archbishop of Canterbury, Baron Rowan Williams of Oystermouth and the Catholic theologian Fr. Thomas Weinandy OFM Cap. The English theologian Aidan Nichols OP considered Mascall one of the faithful inheritors of the Oxford Movement, along with figures such as Darwell Stone, Kenneth Kirk, and Austin Farrer, as well as Henry Chadwick and John Macquarrie, and wrote "the orthodox Roman Catholic can recognise with but little effort 'separated doctors' of the Catholic Church."[19] In his remarkable study of Anglican theology, *The Panther and the Hind*, Nichols even devotes the whole book to "Eric Lionel Mascall, *magistro catholicae veritatis*."[20] Nichols sees in the proliferation of reports and paper from the church's bureaucracy a sad losing of its direction, manifest in what he calls the "*Ecclesia photocopians*," of new publications but not, perhaps, new fruits of the Gospel.[21] Mascall himself despaired of the committee-centric and bureaucratic establishment that had overcome the Church of England, and its resultant loss of the mission and purpose of the Gospel. He had written that the spate of Commission-written publications were soul-less, heart-breaking documents, concerned not with what to believe but how: "Not the *fides quae* but the *fides qua*."[22] For Mascall, some church leaders, as well as her teachers, had lost their way.

The place of Mascall is important, albeit overlooked, but it cannot be appreciated without understanding his constant return to the theme of Christ's two natures, and the way in which the Lord's Incarnation begins the work of more perfectly uniting the interweaving threads of spirit and matter.

18. Mascall, *The Openness of Being*.
19. Nichols, *The Panther and the Hind*, 128.
20. Nichols, *The Panther and the Hind*.
21. Nichols, *The Panther and the Hind*, 158.
22. Mascall, "Wither Anglican Theology?," 39.

Onwards from Chalcedon

Mascall's presentation of Christianity bequeaths a full Christian vision and Catholic imagination, intellectually integrated and confidently engaging with the liberal theologies of the twentieth century. His poetry and incorporation of reflections on great Western art and writing, such as the work of Dante Alighieri, illustrates a healthy good humor for the quibbles and personalities encountered in ecclesial life as well as the great debates about the place of Christianity in a rapidly changing contemporary world, and this is complemented by a liturgical prayer life that contextualized his perceived foolishness when it came to practical matters. In many ways this is a study of a perfect eccentric: he was a celibate in a church that did not require it; a Thomist in a communion that was becoming more Protestant; a Religious in a country where the Reformation triumphed over traditional Christian vocations such as his; and a theologian despite his first intellectual love of logic and mathematics. Since the 1990s Mascall has been overlooked and marginalized in theological literature, but increasingly his contribution is timely and relevant.

A recurring theme in Mascall's work is theological anthropology, especially in his book, *Whatever Happened to the Human Mind?*, a sequel to *Theology and the Gospel of Christ*.[23] In his treatment of the human person, Mascall is very much a traditional theist and a Thomist. For him, the confusions of contemporary anthropology, the meaning and purpose of what it is to be a human person, can be worked through and clarified by a Thomistic account of creation. To understand the human person, we do well to recognize him to be a rational creature immersed in a world whose origin lies in the creative will of another—that being to which the language of divinity belongs. In fact, it becomes fragile and dangerous ground to attempt to build an anthropology apart from a serious account of Creation. Mascall writes,

> A God who is merely a *primus inter pares* provides, as has been repeatedly urged, no ground for either his own existence or that of anything else; but it is not true that the only alternative view is that creation is internal to God. According to the doctrine of *analogia entis*, God as self-existent Being is altogether distinct from the world, while the world is entirely insufficient and dependent, although, at the same time and indeed for this very

---

23. Mascall, *Whatever Happened to the Human Mind?*; Mascall, *Theology & the Gospel of Christ*.

reason, it is most intimately interpenetrated by the creative act through which he is present to it at the heart of its being.[24]

Mascall follows Thomas in drawing an unambiguous distinction between God and the world, the Creator and Creation, but nevertheless holds the biblical notion of all things being *held* by God as a witness to God's ongoing, intimate involvement in that same Creation. Mascall brings Thomas into dialogue with twentieth century Orthodox thought, especially figures such as Fr. Paul Florensky and Vladimir Solovyev. He was in a rich dialogue and friendship with members of the Orthodox diaspora, and there is that constant reminder from the East that Christian anthropology cannot be separated from either Creation or an eschatology. Creation has no inherent finality in its own order, but carries a longing and a hope for an ultimate union of some sort with its Creator.

We ought to keep in mind the developed way in which St. Thomas dwelt on the role of the Beatific Vision to inform not just our future hope but the moral life here and now. Thomas wrote that "Grace is nothing else than a beginning of glory in us."[25] The work of grace carries a mysterious dimension because it refers to immaterial change; the kinds of change that do not give themselves to material discovery in a direct fashion. Nevertheless, Mascall argues that the logic of the Thomist also allows us to better understand the language used by the great mystics. That is to say, because human beings are material and spiritual creatures, our typical knowledge in and of the world is achieved through sensory awareness, which in turn is directed towards explanation and communication. For all the stillness and intimacy of what is obtained in mystical experience, there are countless words devoted to attempting to explain it, which requires the analogical language of sensory experience. Mascall is resistant to the assumption that the Thomist-Aristotelian tradition has been severely undermined by modern empiricism, while at the same time he is content in the observation that the world of intelligible knowledge is not comprehensive as the Angelic Doctor had always perceived it. Strangely perhaps, Mascall steps from this to the world of the mystics as an avenue by which we can reflect reasonably on human existentiality, although Mascall would not have used precisely that language.

This, I think, helps to explain Mascall's fascination with Catholic mystical writers like St. John of the Cross. Mascall had written a

24. Mascall, *He Who Is*, 140.
25. Aquinas, *Summa Theologiae*, II-II.24.3.2.

theological reflection on the Ascent of Mount Carmel and believed the Spanish Mystics offered a proper integration of orthodox theology and mystical experience without being sidetracked by personal extravagances.[26] That also explains something of the context in which Mascall drew from the wells of Thomas's thought and, in turn, engaged with theologians of the East.

According to Mascall, the great drama of our reflections on the mystery of the human person in Christian theology is lost if it ignores or tries to surpass the commitments of earlier generations of the faithful. Specifically, Mascall finds inspiration, as I described above, in the Council of Chalcedon. For him, it offers a vision, the implications of which we have only begun to consider with any sense of adequacy. Mascall sums up the elegance of the Chalcedonian formularies in contemporary terms by quoting Dorothy L. Sayers: "The Christian formula is not: 'Humanity manifests certain adumbrations of the divine', but: 'This man was very God.'"[27]

Mascall observes that in the twentieth century and going back to the Renaissance we have been in an era in which it was the divinity of Christ that seems to require the most explicit defense, but in fact it is Chalcedon's insistence upon the reality and completeness of Jesus' humanity that might surprise us.[28] Chalcedon excluded the Apollinarian view that in Jesus the person of the divine Word took the place of a rational soul and body. Later in the Council of 680 (that of Constantinople III), the church insisted that the rational soul included the human will. Nothing of his humanity needed to be discarded so that the fullness of the divine Word could dwell within this person, and not as a " . . . *part* of the human nature but its metaphysical *subject*; *person* and *nature* are not on the same level of being."[29]

Secondly, as complete and concrete as the human nature present in the person of Jesus of Nazareth was, its subject, its person, is "literally divine."[30] Mascall took on both the ancient Antiochenes as well as those doing "process theology," in committing to the Chalcedonian formulation that the impassability of God is not in any way threatened by the

---

26. See the meticulous study Mascall makes in *A Guide to Mount Carmel*.
27. Mascall, *Whatever Happened to the Human Mind?*, 28.
28. Mascall, *Whatever Happened to the Human Mind?*, 33.
29. Mascall, *Whatever Happened to the Human Mind?*, 33.
30. Mascall, *Whatever Happened to the Human Mind?*, 33.

presence of the eternal Word in the person of Jesus, who is also fully human. While Mascall regarded himself as a traditional theist and one who was also a Thomist in a fairly straightforward manner, he admits that Chalcedon was not attempting to do metaphysics, but simply formulating the truth of the Gospel. Nevertheless by implication it made a metaphysical distinction, that God who is the Creator is not totally bound by his own nature, and there is a capacity for openness in, and according to the divine nature, allowing for the possibility of a fully human existence cooperating perfectly with the divine.

This of course can be seen clearly in the Eastern distinction of the essence of God and the divine energies of God, as St. Gregory Palamas argues, and which today remains a point of contention between Western and Eastern Christianity.

In all of this, the fundamental point made by Mascall is that the reasonableness of the Chalcedonian position in its retention of the faith of the Gospel resists heresies both ancient and modern, and that attempts to belittle or ignore it will leave us a few steps away from the risen Lord to whom the first disciples gave their lives and witness. Mascall says,

> There is indeed mystery at the heart of the Chalcedonian doctrine, as there is at the heart of the Gospels, but mystery is not absurdity. And everything depends upon the fact which neither Christian thinking nor Christian devotion have found it easy to cling on to, that person, hypostasis, is not a *part* of nature, not even a tiny and indetectible part, but is its *subject*.[31]

Keep in mind that Christian orthodoxy would say that it is not merely God that has become man, but God the Son who has taken human nature, and so the humanity witnessed in the Sonship of Christ has its own particular relational aspect with regard to the other persons of the Trinity. Mascall makes reference to this distinction, but views in it a mystery that can only be explored speculatively.

In any case, Mascall holds that before we discuss Christian initiation, sacramental grace, the church as the Body of Christ or Christian discipleship, the very fact of the Incarnation means there is manifest a change in the human condition. The nature that we share in our humanity has been taken up, and not as some other thing, into the life of God. In this way all science, intellectual discovery, politics, and social reflection

---

31. Mascall, *Whatever Happened to the Human Mind?*, 35.

carries within it the air of possibility, a promise of becoming something more, the anticipation of what we might call deification.

Here it is important to understand that for Mascall Christian discipleship is always an ecclesial reality. It is the immersion into the waters of Baptism by which one dies to oneself and can rise from those waters marked as a new creature. The nature of the church, according to Mascall, is inherently eschatological, finding particular expression in the celebration of the Eucharist.[32] To understand this immersion in mystery, and the way that the ecclesial dimension reveals and aids the work of glorification in the human person, one must reflect on the teaching of Chalcedon in resistance to its detractors.

What might seem an eccentric focus on Chalcedon is also a logical one, and it lifts Mascall's work into a broader scope than simply the context of late twentieth century debate.

Theology and the Spiritual Battle

With the above in mind, let us consider briefly the spiritual dimension of Mascall's theology. While the topic of the angelic realm appears in many of his writings, two key texts concern us here: The chapter "Unseen Warfare" in *The Christian Universe* and the importance Mascall gave to his edited collection *The Angels of Light and the Powers of Darkness: A Symposium by Members of the Fellowship of S. Alban and S. Sergius*. Mascall drew deeply from St. Athanasius and the Eastern Orthodox tradition to insist on the reality of angelic warfare to any serious attempt to live a Christian life. Into that argument, Mascall included the thought of contemporary writers such as C. S. Lewis and G. K. Chesterton, indicating a dialogue between West and East, as well as the past and the present. For Mascall, to understand what it is to truly be human, one must engage in the spiritual battle. In *The Christian Universe* Mascall writes,

> You may perhaps feel that some apology is due for the fact that this lecture has been devoted almost entirely to the warfare in the unseen realm, about which most Christians today rarely think and which many would dismiss as at best picturesque myth and at worst pure fiction. It is for this very reason that it has seemed to me urgent to emphasise it. Scripture, tradition and Christian experience combine in assuring us that the struggle against evil

---

32. Mascall, *Christ, the Christian, and the Church*, 107.

> with which Christians on earth are concerned can be seen in its true proportions only against the background of a vaster and more mysterious conflict in the unseen world in which they too are caught up. When we are faced with the claim that Christians in a secular age ought to live as completely secularised men we can only reply that such a programme does no justice either to the true nature of this world or of existence as a whole, and that it totally misunderstands the nature of the forces with which we are opposed.[33]

Here Mascall is concerned with facing down the embarrassed feet-shuffling of his peers at the mention of the angels, and of re-discovering the Christian meaning of the "unseen realm." For him, the anthropological task is a deeply spiritual one; the need to articulate the meaning of human existence in its material and spiritual dimensions in light of the Christian Gospel, which is a path through the thorny thickets of a fallen world still aching with the violence of spiritual warfare, but looking hopefully towards a promised future. Mascall takes a long view in this, always drawing deeply from the past while raising the human condition up as something called to participate in what is splendid, beautiful, lovely, and hospitable to truth. In Mascall's anthropology, rooted as it is in the way the church baptizes and raises up a person towards glory, the human person is an ecclesial mystery, and an eschatological hope frames what might be said. However, Mascall is not blind to history. He quotes the words of Nikolai Berdyaev: "one of the greatest tragedies of Christians is that they are always too late."[34] The lateness of Christian wisdom in moments for which it is most needed, and the miseries of human fallen-ness under the banner of the Cross are not evaded by Mascall but confronted, and considered within a broader arc of both eschatology and history. The movement of the human person, as it were, through history and through the grace-filled moments of gradation in transformation in Christ is one in which an interaction with angels, fallen and unfallen, is necessary. Ignorance or embarrassed rejection of this idea might be commonplace, but such reactions fall outside the logic of Christian faith.

With regard to the spiritual battle into which the Christian person is called and baptized, Mascall's approach is much the same as in his moral approach to warfare as we might see in material history. For example,

---

33. Mascall, *The Christian Universe*, 129.

34. Berdyaev, "The Christian and the Social Order," 9, quoted in Mascall, *The Christian Universe*, 162.

CHRIST AND THE INTERWEAVING OF SPIRIT AND MATTER

in September of 1938, when Germany conducted undeclared war in Czechoslovakia, ultimately leading to the Munich Agreement of 30 September 1938, a young Mascall, as Sub-Warden of Lincoln Theological College, declared,

> The Christian has two main duties with regard to war. The first is to do all in his power, by both prayer and personal action, to remove its causes and prevent its occurrence. The second is to act rightly if and when it comes.[35]

The difference in spiritual battle is of course that the first duty is not really an option. One finds oneself already in the heat of battle, even if sin and death have already been robbed of their ultimate victory.

It is the second duty, of acting rightly, although still largely through prayer and personal action, that concerns the Christian. The point is not that Christians live a "better" life, but that they live a "different" one.[36] Mascall describes the duty of the Christian spiritual life as marked by three notes: those of "intensity," "vastness," and "permanence."[37] Mascall draws on accounts of the early Christians, and the first is the most obvious to human observance, that of a more intense observance of a religious discipline of life, centered upon a love of God and one's neighbor, of a kind of life that appears at times to be "imprudent, hazardous, and even downright ridiculous."[38] Such an intensity grows out of contemplation and of an intimacy with what Christians understand to be God, known in a secondary way through his angels and his saints. Second, Mascall identifies what he calls the "vastness" of the Christian conceptualization of the world in which he or she lives. The Christian, actively following Christ and attempting to be like unto him, is one whose horizon is not limited to the years of one's life on earth, nor of the material goods one might obtain during that sojourn. In fact, the Christian views such objects as fading joys, poor and fleeting goods that have no lasting greatness against the promise of a broad and vast terrain of discovery and goodness ahead. The spiritual life, which is not so distinct from the rest of one's life for the Christian, is motivated by the promise of seeing God "face to face." (1 Cor 13:12) The third note is "permanence," in which Mascall critiques

---

35. Mascall, *The Christian and the Next War*, 3.
36. Mascall, *Grace and Glory*, 75.
37. It is in *Grace and Glory* that Mascall most concisely explains these three notes; see especially 75–83.
38. Mascall, *Grace and Glory*, 78.

the world's utter failure to offer satisfaction, and grounds Christian hope in that which is lasting, joyful, and peaceful. It is because of this last note that the Christian says with a remarkable sureness, "Amen" and "Alleluia," trusting to God what only God can hold apart from finitude and fragility. The Christian spiritual life is that which struggles imperfectly against the temptations to turn back repeatedly to the finite and what cannot satisfy, re-discovering with an often daily renewal the beauty of a life that is intense, vast in its vision, and grounded in what might seem a bewildering sense of permanence.

In Mascall's three notes, one can identify great value in the notion of constancy in the spiritual life, which is often misunderstood as mere perseverance, as if faithfulness relied on a kind of illogical stamina. The vastness of the vision that captivates the Christian's gaze upon life and the world is a sustaining one, and tends towards replenishment and renewal. When considering the Christian fight against evil, Donald MacKinnon referred to the consolation of finding in the creative Word the One who "keeps company with those whom he has called his own."[39] The strength of such constancy is not derived from ourselves but shared by the one who calls us together in his body.

Conclusion

Eric Mascall leaves a legacy that has been neglected in recent decades. He was one of the most important critics of the New Approach in the twentieth century, of a step away from an integrated understanding of doctrine and faith, and of dogma and lived experience. His Chalcedonian defense of the weaving together of spirit and matter in the coherent logic of the Incarnation protects theological anthropology from excesses of extreme positions for contemporary scholars. Other schools of thought will find much sympathy in Mascall's work, such as the *Nouvelle Théologie* or *ressourcement* school, those of a Communio disposition, or even aspects of post-liberalism and Radical Orthodoxy, and in all of these a common interest will be Mascall's treatment of the mystery of the human person in light of Christian revelation. His contribution, utilizing a critical reading of Aquinas, may be seen as reviving an account of the human condition as a mystery to which the Christian contribution is profoundly positive and constructive. The achievement of a theological anthropology that is

---

39. MacKinnon, *Borderlands of Theology and Other Essays*, 93.

irreducibly theistic, and therefore fundamentally open to new knowledge and science, immersed within a sacramental vision alight with the frisson of glory, is itself a monumental achievement. Mascall's accomplishment was outside of narrow denominational lines, drawing on Western and Eastern Christian wisdom. It is a simple synthesis of the comprehensive account of orthodox Christian faith, which considers all the facts of the world and does not try to minimize or avoid the realities of fallen-ness, sin, or death.[40]

Moreover, Mascall deals with that most unpopular of tasks, explaining a robust Christian anthropology in a matter-of-fact way with reference to the unseen world of angels and spiritual warfare. Where the average preacher has been shy of travelling since the 1960s, Mascall boldly goes. The sowing together of the Thomistic with the poetic, of the glorious with the self-effacing, and of the creative with the traditional is a task in which Mascall proved himself a master, and in so doing he kept faith with his own vocation as an ordained minister of the Gospel. For this reason I conclude with words he shared not in a book but from the pulpit:

> And just as Christ's human nature was not destroyed by His Ascension, but transfigured and exalted to an unimaginable glory and dignity, so God's purpose for the world is not that it should be destroyed, but that it should be transfigured, through and through, from top to bottom, down to its humblest and most insignificant elements.[41]

Bibliography

Aquinas Thomas. *Summa Theologiae*. Translated by Thomas Gilby. 61 vols. London: Blackfriars & Eyre & Spottiswoode, 1964.
Berdyaev, Nikolai. "The Christian and the Social Order." *Sobornost* 9 (1937) 5–8.
Heidegger, Martin. *Being and Time*. Translated by John Macquarrie and Edward Robinson. London: SCM, 1962.
Jedin, Hubert. *Ecumenical Councils of the Catholic Church*. New York: Paulist, 1961.
MacKinnon, Donald M. *Borderlands of Theology and Other Essays*. London: Lutterworth, 1968.
Mascall, Eric, ed. *The Angels of Light and the Powers of Darkness: A Symposium by Members of the Fellowship of S. Alban and S. Sergius*. London: Faith, 1954.

40. Mascall, "In the Cunning of Nature" 19–20.

41. Mascall, "An Ascension Day Sermon," 6, preached before the University of Oxford.

———. "An Ascension-Day Sermon." *Laudate* 24.90 (1951) 2–7.

———. *Christ, the Christian, and the Church: A Study of the Incarnation and Its Consequences*. Peabody, MA: Hendrickson, 2017.

———. *The Christian and the Next War*. Westminster: Church Literature Association, 1939.

———. *The Christian Universe*. New York: Morehouse-Barlow, 1966.

———. *Compliments of the Season*. Worthing: Churchman, 1985.

———. *Grace and Glory*. New York: Morhouse-Barlow, 1961.

———. *A Guide to Mount Carmel: Being a Summary and an Analysis of the Ascent of Mount Carmel by St. John of the Cross, with Some Introductory Notes*. Westminster: Dacre, 1939.

———. *He Who Is: A Study in Traditional Theism*. Toronto: Longmans, Green & Co., 1943.

———. *The Importance of Being Human*. New York: Columbia University Press, 1958.

———. "In the Cunning of Nature." In *God and the Universe: A Course of Sermons Preached in the Chapel of Pusey House, Oxford*, 16–23. London: Mowbray & Co., 1960.

———. *The Openness of Being: Natural Theology Today (The Gifford Lectures)*. London: Darton, Longman & Todd, 1971.

———. *The Overarching Question: Divine Revelation or Human Invention?* Unpublished manuscript.

———. *Pi in the High*. London: Faith, 1959.

———. *The Recovery of Unity: A Theological Approach*. London: Longmans, Green, and Co., 1958.

———. *Saraband: The Memoirs of E. L. Mascall*. Trowbridge: Gracewing, 1992.

———. *The Secularisation of Christianity: An Analysis and a Critique*. London: Darton, Longman & Todd, 1965.

———. *Theology & the Gospel of Christ: An Essay in Reorientation*. London: SPCK, 1977.

———. *Whatever Happened to the Human Mind? Essays in Christian Orthodoxy*. London: SPCK, 1980.

———. "Wither Anglican Theology?" In *When Will Ye Be Wise? The State of the Church of England*, edited by A. A. C. Kilmister, 30–49. London: Blond & Briggs, 1983.

Nichols, Aidan. *The Panther and the Hind: A Theological History of Anglicanism*. Edinburgh: T. & T. Clark, 1993.

Prestige, G. L. *God in Patristic Thought*. London: Heinemann, 1936.

Robinson, J. A. T. *Honest to God*. Westminster: John Knox, 1963.

Sellers, Robert Victor. *The Council of Chalcedon*. London: SPCK, 1953.

———. *Two Ancient Christologies: A Study in the Christological Thought of the Schools of Alexandria and Antioch in the Early History of Christian Doctrine*. London: SPCK, 1940.

Van Buren, Paul. *The Secular Meaning of the Gospel: Based on an Analysis of Its Language*. New York: MacMillan, 1966.

4

Beyond Boethius

The Clarity and Capacity of Relational Personhood

SIMON R. WAYTE, MGL

Introduction

The theological quest to understand what it means to become "participants in the divine nature" (2 Pet 1:4) has a long history. Equally long is the history of the development and use of the concept of person in theology. Greater clarity regarding the divinization of the concrete human person may be gained by analyzing the concept of person from a relational perspective. With personhood understood as essentially a relational reality divinization can come to be recognized as the human person existing in Christ as *filii* in *Filio*. This understanding of divinization is often termed Christification. A clear understanding of Christification requires a precise delineation between person and nature. This delineation relies upon a clear distinction between person understood formally as a relational reality and person understood practically as a concrete reality. Therefore, the concept of person is analyzed to obtain this clear distinction between the inner core of personhood and the concrete person. The method chosen for this analysis is a retrieval of the tradition using a synthesis of the thought of Thomas Aquinas, Henry of Ghent, and Richard of St. Victor. This enables the concept of relational personhood already present in the tradition to be brought into clear relief. To ensure the rigorous nature of this synthesis it is necessary to concisely expound the development of the concept of person from the earliest times.

The Early History of Person

Etymologically the word person comes from the Latin *persona*. *Persona* in turn comes from the Etruscan *Phersu* which refers to the masks used in religious rites especially that of the important goddess Persephone.[1] These rites influenced the beginning of Roman theatre.[2] Later, in reference to the Roman theatre Gellius relates that Gavius Bassus connects *persona* with *personare* meaning "to sound through" because of the resonance caused by speaking through the theatrical masks.[3] Independently, the Greek word *prosopon* had developed from its Proto Indo-European origins, into a rich word that included the theatrical mask among its meanings.[4] Thus, it was natural that this word would come together with *phersu* and *personare* to contribute to the meaning of *persona*. On the surface, *prosopon* was not a philosophically deep word for the Greeks, but in combination with *phersu* and *personare* it developed into the richer word *persona*.[5]

In ancient poetry, rather than just narrating events, the writer creates characters that play dialogical roles "in order to give dramatic life to events."[6] These roles can be uncovered by later scholars using a method termed prosopographic exegesis. This method was employed by Christian writers in relation to scripture when it was noticed that here too events played out in dialogue between characters in their roles.[7] This is seen in interpreting the personification of Wisdom.[8] However, since scripture is

1. Rolnick, *Person*, 11.
2. Schmitz, "Geography of the Human Person," 29.
3. Gellius, *Attic Nights*, 5.7.
4. Rolnick, *Person*, 13.
5. Schmitz, "Geography of the Human Person," 31.
6. Ratzinger, "Concerning the Notion of Person," 441.
7. Ratzinger, "Concerning the Notion of Person," 441.
8. Schmitz, "Geography of the Human Person," 31.

not just poetry but the Word of God, the characters in these roles can really exist.[9] So *prosopon* moves from role to person as an existing reality with the layered texture added by reference to *personare* and *phersu*.

Thus, the concept of "person" became theologically important even before Tertullian's writing on the Trinity led to the famous formula "*una substantia—tres personae.*"[10] Tertullian's use of *persona* to present the faith regarding the Trinity opened up the possibility of a theologically more technical usage.[11] However, the use of *persona* in reference to the Trinity also opened up some difficulties. According to Basil of Caesarea, Sabellius speaks of one *hypostasis* or *ousia* and three *prosopa* which are like various masks through which God presents himself.[12] Basil and the Cappadocian fathers generally addressed this and other issues by making a distinction between *ousia* and *hypostasis* that allowed *ousia* to refer to the one common substance of divinity, while *hypostasis* became the proper or particular expression of the one substance.[13] Then three *prosopa* can be appropriate if the term moves away from the concept of mask towards the concept of a permanent proper subsistent—a *hypostasis*. Understood this way Basil and Gregory of Nazianzus find no fault with the western writers, but decry the poverty of Latin in not having enough words, so consequently they have to use *persona* instead of a word naturally equivalent to *hypostasis*.[14] In this way, *persona* developed as a theological term with ontological depth.

Following this theological vein, Gregory of Nazianzus "defined the *idia* [the particular expression] more neatly as unbegottenness, generation, and procession."[15] Thus, the person as the particular expression of the one common substance became identified with relational terms. Gregory of Nyssa also described the persons of the Trinity in terms of relations of origin and communion.[16] Like Basil and Gregory of Nazianzus, Augustine noted the lack of vocabulary in Latin, but used the word

9. Ratzinger, "Concerning the Notion of Person," 442.

10. Ratzinger, "Concerning the Notion of Person," 440. See Tertullian, "Adversus Praxean," 3, 12.

11. Hipp, *"Person" in Christian Tradition*, 93–94.

12. Sabellius appeals to the council of Nicaea where *ousia* and *hypostasis* are used as synonyms. Basil, "Epistolae," 214.3.

13. Basil, "Epistolae," 214.4; Lienhard, "*Ousia* and *Hypostasis*," 106.

14. Basil, "Epistolae," 214.4; Gregory of Nazianzus, "Oratio," 21.35.

15. Lienhard, "*Ousia* and *Hypostasis*," 106n30.

16. Turcescu, *Gregory of Nyssa*, 116–17.

persona due to prior use by important Latin authors.[17] However, he found the distinction between *ousia* and *hypostasis* unclear.[18] Nevertheless, by developing an understanding of the distinction in the Trinity by way of relative opposition, he went further than the Cappadocians in connecting person to relation.[19] For Augustine the persons are distinguished only according to relation, not substance, but because they do not change, these relations cannot be called accidents.[20]

Boethius also affirms that the category of relation brings about the distinction in the Trinity.[21] However, unlike Augustine, Boethius uses relation in a very weak sense and consequently his treatise on the Trinity is underdeveloped.[22] In his treatise on the Trinity, Boethius does speak about distinction in God being a difference of persons (*personarum*) while acknowledging the limitation of this word in interpreting the mystery of the Trinity.[23] He calls *persona* a "borrowed" term.[24] Boethius shows more confidence when he looks at a definition of person in general after explaining that "the proper definition of person is a matter of very great perplexity."[25] Boethius develops his definition, "the individual substance of a rational nature" in his argument against the Monophysitism of Eutyches.[26] This definition is developed by Boethius to make clear in Latin the distinction between person and nature, and align them, respectively, with *hypostasis* and *ousia* in the Greek. In his definition Boethius does not connect person to relation, since his interest is in making the distinction between *hypostasis* and *ousia* for the sake of an argument against Euytches, an eastern presbyter. Hence Boethius says that "person is properly predicated of substances" and no mention is made of relation.[27] This definition of person by Boethius became the classical definition of person that was received by the scholars of the middle ages.

---

17. Augustine, *De Trinitate*, 5.10.
18. Augustine, *De Trinitate*, 5.10.
19. Augustine, *De Trinitate*, 5.6, 5.7.
20. Cf. Augustine, *De Trinitate*, 5.6; Turcescu, *Gregory of Nyssa*, 387.
21. Boethius, *De Trinitate*, 6, lines 1–6.
22. Rolnick, *Person*, 43–44.
23. Boethius, *De Trinitate*, 5, lines 38–39.
24. Boethius, "Contra Eutychen," 3, line 8.
25. Boethius, "Contra Eutychen," 2, lines 1–2.
26. Boethius, "Contra Eutychen," 3, lines 4–5.
27. Boethius, "Contra Eutychen," 2, lines 19–20.

Relating Thomas Aquinas, Henry of Ghent, and Richard of St. Victor

Thomas Aquinas

Thomas Aquinas takes hold of Boethius's definition of person as an individual substance of a rational nature as a general definition. Aquinas understands Boethius's use of the phrase "individual substance" to mean an Aristotelian first substance—an existent "who"—a subject.[28] In Greek this translates not as *ousia*, but as *hypostasis*, as acknowledged by both Aquinas and Boethius. However, as something of a rational nature, it is a most excellent *hypostasis* and hence deserves the name *hypostasis* more surely than any other created thing.[29] It is also called a subsistence in that "it exists in itself and not in another."[30] "Person" thus designates the most excellent type of *hypostasis* and subsistence which occurs only in rational substances. This is a substantialist view of the person. However, such a substantialist understanding appears unhelpful for trinitarian theology today.[31]

Aquinas turns to a more inspiring theological vein when he moves from a general definition to a discussion of person in God. In his discussion of the Trinity, Aquinas effectively modifies the Aristotelian understanding of relation as the weakest type of being by equating relation in God to "the divine nature itself."[32] By this maneuver Aquinas radically strengthens relation so that it becomes suitable for understanding persons in the Trinity.

Aquinas finds that in God the word "person" signifies a relation, though he separates the understanding of person in general, as defined by Boethius, and person in God by making person in God a special case.[33] He separates the understanding of person in general from person in God by seeing a different principle of individuation in each case. In human persons the principle of individuation that makes a human person something individual and undivided in itself is matter. In the Godhead where

---

28. Aquinas, *Summa Theologiae*, I.29.2.co.

29. Boethius, "Contra Eutychen," 3, lines 75–76; Aquinas, *Summa Theologiae*, I.29.2.1.

30. Aquinas, *Summa Theologiae*, I.29.2.co.

31. Ratzinger, "Concerning the Notion of Person," 448.

32. Aquinas, *Summa Theologiae*, I.29.4.co.

33. Aquinas, *Summa Theologiae*, I.29.4.co.

there is no material or formal distinction, relation alone provides the principle of individuation. However, this relation is not accidental but constitutive of the divine nature itself, so Aquinas calls it subsistent. Thus, he uses the phrase "subsistent relation" to define person in God. This is a relation that is permanent, not an accident of a substance, but rather a *hypostasis* "subsisting in the divine nature" (*ousia*).[34]

The simplicity of God then shows why person has signified for some both relation and nature in varying degrees of primacy between relation and nature. Since there is no divine nature or substance or essence apart from the persons as subsistent relations, these terms, while separate for the purpose of discussion, are in reality united in the divine mystery when viewed from the perspective of the common nature.[35] Aquinas makes this clear when he notes that "since in the reality it has in God relation is identical with essence and essence with person, as is now clear, relation necessarily is the same as person."[36] Nevertheless, it is only relation that distinguishes the persons, and these relations in God are real and subsisting as the persons. Thus, Father, Son, and Holy Spirit are not just relational names, but the true personal reality of God.

Unfortunately, Aquinas limits this richer relational understanding of person to trinitarian persons. This is due to his use of differing principles of individuation for God and creatures. This use of differing principles of individuation then limits the analogy of being possible between human persons and divine persons. In human beings a person is an individual substance of a rational nature, while in God a person is a subsistent relation. Now Aquinas argues that the Boethian definition of person is a general definition that applies both to God and creatures, while the more specific definition of a subsistent relation applies only to God. Therefore, he argues that "person" is analogous between God and creatures. However, in this same article Aquinas also points out that in God person is a relative term while in humans it is an absolute term.[37] So even though Aquinas argues that person is analogous between God and creatures, any similarity in the analogy specifically excludes relation which is found in the definition of divine persons, but not in that of human persons. Given that the difference between the concept of being either absolute or

---

34. Aquinas, *Summa Theologiae*, I.29.4.co.
35. Aquinas, *Summa Theologiae*, I.39.1.co.
36. Aquinas, *Summa Theologiae*, I.40.1.co.
37. Aquinas, *Summa Theologiae*, I.29.4.

relative is so great, it appears that, in Aquinas's development of person, the analogy is quite weak as others have also noted.[38]

Henry of Ghent

Unlike Aquinas, Henry of Ghent, a thirteenth century member of the secular clergy at the University of Paris, uses analogy in a way that allows in general a greater likeness between God and creatures. Rather than making persons in the Trinity a special case, Henry begins with the Trinity and from there develops an understanding that also applies to creatures. Henry allows his theology to inform his philosophy as it gradually develops from an Aristotelian ontology to a real relational ontology.[39]

Henry draws from the emanationist position, found in the Franciscan tradition, to argue that distinction within the Trinity is based on origin. For Henry this distinction based on origin corresponds to God's intellect and will. The persons are hence distinguished by whether the person is ungenerated (the Father), generated according to intellect (the Son), or proceeding from the will (the Holy Spirit). Thus, for Henry, the distinction based on opposed relations is a secondary and unnecessary aspect. This is different from Aquinas who, while accepting the distinctions of origin, takes his lead from Augustine for whom there is only substance and relation in God.[40] For Aquinas the distinction of the persons comes about through the four mutually opposed relations (paternity, filiation, active and passive spiration). These opposed relations are the necessary aspect that give rise to the distinction of persons in the Trinity.

For Henry, the persons in the Trinity arise from the relations of origin in God reflecting the divine intellect and will. In analogous fashion he proposes that creatures are created by the divine intellect and will such that the essence of a creature arises from the eternal intellect of God in a relation of reason, while its non-eternal existence arises from the divine will by efficient causality.[41] Henry looks to the question of *how* there are creatures and finds a close analogy with his understanding of *how* there are three divine persons.

38. Gleeson, "Speaking of Persons," 54.
39. Decorte, "Relation and Substance," 14.
40. Friedman, *Medieval Trinitarian Thought*, 7.
41. Henninger, *Relations*, 46.

Synthesizing Aquinas and Henry with Richard of St. Victor

Richard of St. Victor gives us a definition of person in terms of existence. This definition can apply to both divine and created persons. For Richard, a person is an incommunicable existence of a spiritual (i.e., rational) nature. If this definition of Richard is used together with the method of Henry then we can come up with a more deeply analogous definition of person in creatures and God that is also in line with Aquinas's relational account of the Trinity.

For Aquinas, God is understood as *ipsum esse subsistens* the creature is correspondingly understood as *esse participatum*.[42] Thus, at the level of existence Aquinas has a strong analogy, like Henry, between God and creatures. In this understanding God communicates existence to creatures such that creatures can participate in being and hence really do exist. At the same time God's necessity of being is not communicated—it is incommunicable at its core. Thus, creatures subsist contingently not necessarily. Now, Henry provides a strong analogy not only between existence in God and the existence of creatures, but also between *how* there are three divine persons and *how* creatures exist. In so far as there is relation in God, shown forth in the persons, there is also relation between God and creatures such that creatures are able to subsist because of their relationship of dependence on God who creates by divine intellect and will. This relationship of creaturely dependence on God is essential to their existence.[43] So while creatures are contingent and do not necessarily exist, if they do exist then they must be constituted relationally. Thus, creatures can be termed subsistent relations (from Aquinas), since they are constituted by a relation with God that is analogous to the relational distinction between the divine persons (from Henry).[44] Thus, persons whether in God or in creatures can be termed subsistent relations of a spiritual nature. Aquinas gives us persons in God as subsistent relations, Henry gives us a stronger likeness between distinction in God and the existence of creatures, and Richard gives us a link between existence and person.

---

42. Henninger, *Relations*, 38.

43. Flores, *Henry of Ghent*, 185.

44. Note that characterizing creatures as subsistent relations does not exclude the reality that creatures are also absolute substances that can have internal and external categorical real relations in addition to their identity as subsistent relations.

Subsistent relation of a spiritual nature exhausts the idea of person with respect to the distinction of divine persons. With respect to the divine substance these relational distinctions disappear. In creatures, by contrast, the concept of a subsistent relation of a spiritual nature exhausts the relational aspect of personhood, but with respect to absolute substances the person does not fully disappear. Nevertheless, in both God and creatures Henry affirms that being-as-relation is equally strong as being-as-substance.[45] Hence, the absolute essence and the relational subsistence are equally important in both God and creatures. However, in creatures the relational subsistence is dependent on God as its transcendent origin.[46]

Thus, utilizing Henry's analogy of being whereby reality has an absolute and relative reality in both God and in creatures, and bringing this together with Aquinas's relational understanding of the persons of the Trinity, we can propose that creatures are also subsistent relations, but of a contingent type willed by God. Therefore, persons in general can be termed subsistent relations of a spiritual nature.

Person: Formal vs. Concrete

Since, in creatures, the concept of a subsistent relation of a spiritual nature only exhausts the relational aspect of personhood, not the concrete reality, a distinction is to be made between person formally defined as a relational reality and person actually discovered as a concrete reality. As something subsistent the person is not a relation inhering in an individual substance—not something added to or qualifying the substance.[47] Instead, it is a transcendental or *hypostatic* relation that constitutes the reality of the person.[48] This formally defines the person as a relational reality. However, the concrete reality of the person is not exhausted by this formal relational definition. In the concrete, the person retains the integrity of substance or nature. This means that, while the creature is primordially constituted through a relation with the creator, it comes about simultaneously as an integral substance. In the concrete, a person can

---

45. Henry of Ghent, *Summa*, art. 32, q. 5, p. 120, lines 39–44; Decorte, "Relation and Substance," 5.

46. Decorte, "Relation and Substance," 12.

47. Galot, *Who Is Christ?*, 299.

48. Gleeson, "Speaking of Persons," 56; Galot, *The Person of Christ*, 34.

never exist without a nature[49] and it is the unity of the person formally defined in relational terms together with the substantial nature that then constitutes the concrete person who actually exists. Persons with their intrinsic relational reality are not encountered in real life apart from a substance or nature. However, the person formally defined as a relational reality is distinct from any substance or nature that the person possesses.

The Triadic Structure of Being

The distinction between the person formally defined as a relational reality and the substance that the person possesses fits well with the triadic structure of existence (*esse-in*, *esse-ab*, and *esse-ad*) as discussed by Norris Clarke and David L. Schindler.[50] The neo-Thomist W. Norris Clarke presents a "creative retrieval and completion" of the thought of Aquinas regarding the person.[51] Clarke notes the lack of development in Aquinas's own thought on the dynamic, relational dimension of the person as discussed above regarding Aquinas's general definition of person, since in the Middle Ages the focus was more on what makes the person unique and incommunicable.[52] Clarke therefore seeks to join the idea of active relational being that he finds in Aquinas, though not strongly accentuated, with the idea of person to make explicit the relational dimension of the person.[53] From Aquinas, Clarke demonstrates that substance is active and self-communicating.[54] Being (*esse*) is not just static presence, but active presence so that, the first act of being expresses itself in action (*agere*), the second act of being, and because of this second act, beings "necessarily generate relations."[55] So being in its fullness can be described as "substance-in-relation" and this is the case for both God and creatures.[56] Thus, for Clarke substance and relation are equally primordial and of equal importance, even though relationality springs from the

49. This is analogous to the way Aristotle's prime matter cannot exist without some form.
50. Schindler, "Norris Clarke on Person," 87–88; Clarke, "Response," 593–96.
51. Clarke, *Person and Being*, 1.
52. Clarke, "To Be Is to Be Substance-in-Relation," 165.
53. Clarke, "Person," 603.
54. Clarke, "Person," 603.
55. Clarke, *Person and Being*, 14.
56. Clarke, "To Be Is to Be Substance-in-Relation," 166; Clarke, *Person and Being*, 14.

"second act" of being.⁵⁷ Clarke resists the thrust of postmodernism to turn away from substance altogether, which he attributes to the distorted view of substance as something self-enclosed and cut off from any relational dimension.⁵⁸ Postmodernism rightly turns away from this distortion of substance, but does not accept the classical understanding of substance, preferring to refer to things as mere bundles of relations. When Clarke applies "substance-in-relation" to the person, he finds in person a dyadic structure—"*presence in itself* and *presence to others*."⁵⁹ From here Clarke highlights communion which includes receptivity as the pinnacle of personal being.⁶⁰

David L. Schindler's responds to Clarke's presentation of *esse* and *agere* and affirms that his views are very much in harmony with those of Clarke. However, he would push further along the same line seeking to understand how in metaphysical terms receptivity can be a perfection of being.⁶¹ Schindler suggests therefore that relation must begin in the first rather than the second act of being, and that for creatures relation is primarily receptive in its meaning.⁶² Hence he proposes that being (*esse*) includes self-subsistence (*esse-in*), receptivity (*esse-ab*), and communication (*esse-ad*) in its very structure, and that the being of creatures mirrors analogously the being of God as Trinity.⁶³

In his response to Schindler, Clarke takes on board Schindler's helpful advance to a triadic structure of being—*esse-ab*, *esse-in*, and *esse-ad*.⁶⁴ As both Schindler and Clarke affirm, being has both a substantial (*esse-in*) and a relational (*esse-ab* and *esse-ad*) structure. The affirmation of the integrity of substance means that, while the creature is primordially constituted through a relation with the creator, it comes about simultaneously as an integral substance—a substance which is nevertheless always a "substance-in-relation."⁶⁵

---

57. Clarke insists that there must be some existent substance in the first act of being before it can be understood as relational in the second act. Clarke, *Person and Being*, 14–15.

58. Clarke, "To Be Is to Be Substance-in-Relation," 171, 174.

59. Clarke, *Person and Being*, 71.

60. Clarke, "Person," 613; Clarke, *Person and Being*, 75.

61. Schindler, "Norris Clarke on Person," 583, 585.

62. Schindler, "Norris Clarke on Person," 585.

63. Schindler, "Norris Clarke on Person," 587–88.

64. Clarke, "Response," 593, 596.

65. Clarke, "To Be Is to Be Substance-in-Relation," 166; Clarke, *Person and Being*, 14.

Subject, Individual, and Self

Due to this distinction between the person as formally defined in relational terms (*esse-ab, esse-ad*) and the substance or nature (*esse-in*) that the person possesses, there are consequences for what we mean by subject and individual. As formally defined a person can be distinguished from another person only by relation. In the case of the Trinity this distinguishes the divine persons as subjects, but only as relative to each other. In the case of human beings this distinguishes human persons similarly as relational subjects. No one person is constituted by relation in the same way as another person. The human person is unique, because the human person is constituted by a unique relation to God and carries a unique set of relations with all other persons. No other person can be or can have my unique set of relationships. This constitutes my unique subjectivity in relation to others. Now this subjectivity is only formal or relational. It expresses the *esse-ab, esse-ad*, not the *esse-in*. Thus, it does not distinguish individuals. Individuals are distinguished only in the concrete reality which includes the nature. In the case of God, the persons cannot be distinguished formally as individuals on the basis of their relational subjectivity. Nor can the persons be distinguished absolutely as individuals, since they share the one simple nature. Thus, the Trinity can be described as three relational subjects in one absolute individual. In the case of human beings, each concrete person has a substantial nature. This allows a concrete person to be distinguished as an individual from other concrete persons. This is the usual substantive way of describing the individuation of human beings. Thus, subject aligns with person as formally defined (*esse-ab, essa-ad*), and individual aligns with the nature or substance (*esse-in*). This agrees with normal usage. We can speak of an individual rock just as easily as we speak of an individual person, but we cannot speak of the rock as a subject. Only a person can be called a subject. Thus, a better term to use for the concrete person in modern usage is the personal individual. This personal individual comprises the relational subject (i.e., the person as formally defined) possessing an objective nature.

The term, "self," combines the idea of the subject and the individual into a single concept. Thus, the term "self" aligns with the concrete person.[66] Due to this, the term "self" can be ambiguous, since it can refer

---

66. The term "self" connects to "*autos*" in Greek. Henry, *Saint Augustine on Personality*, 6.

primarily to either the nature or to the formal person. From the point of view of nature the self is distinguished from others as an individual. In this context reference can be made to even inanimate objects; for instance, "the actual rock *itself*." However, from the view of the formal person, the self is distinguished from others as a subject. As a subject the self is distinguished from others by the unique set of relationships it possesses. However, it also grows in its own self-identity as those relationships increase and develop. In this way the more a person becomes connected and interrelated with others, the more the person becomes a unique identity distinguishable from others. In other words, the more I grow in communion with others, the more I become *myself*.

Person and Nature

This distinction between person formally defined in relational terms and person discovered in the concrete in which the person possesses a nature leads us to look even more closely at the distinction between person and nature. The distinction between person and nature clarifies not only our language, but also the dynamic of human growth. In human beings the person develops in their relational core at the same time as the nature of the concrete person grows. From the initial relation of creation by God, which constitutes the person's relational core, the person develops relations with others and with the world, as well as a volitional relation with God. This development happens at the same time as the concrete person grows in their human nature: from a child, through adolescence, to adulthood. The relational person and the substantial nature are connected in their growth, but they are not absolutely dependent on each other. Even in their growth, person and nature are to be distinguished.

In Christ, the person of the Son of God is fully developed.[67] However, at birth his human nature has little maturity, so the expression of his person in his nature is limited. As he grows in his human nature, the fully developed personal relations become progressively operational in his nature. Others also draw attention to this progressive expression of Christ's

---

67. When Thomas Aquinas calls Christ a composite person he makes clear that he is referring to the person of Christ subsisting in a nature. Since Christ has two natures, Aquinas calls the concrete person of Christ a composite person. However, Aquinas makes clear that in itself, the person of Christ is simple. Therefore, the person of Christ as formally defined in relational terms should be understood simply as the divine person of the Son of God. Aquinas, *Summa Theologiae*, III.2.4.co.

person in his human nature.[68] Some moments, like the baptism in the Jordan, can be seen as defining moments in this process of his person becoming progressively expressed in his nature. This distinction between person and nature helps us understand the way the divine person of the Son of God does not overwhelm his human nature. However, more needs to be said to describe the way the two natures of Christ come together in the one person.

The term "perichoresis" was first used by Gregory Nazianzen before the First Council of Constantinople and later by Maximus the Confessor to describe the hypostatic union. They use perichoresis to describe the interpenetration of the natures without confusion and without the natures being changed.[69] Maximus and later John of Damascus use the analogy of a red hot sword that can both burn and cut to describe the way in which divine and human natures are hypostatically united.[70] In coming to this analogy Maximus has in mind the activity of Christ, though he does not reduce the union to mere activity—it is a *hypostatic* union. It is a union at the level of being. However, remembering the earlier discussion of Clarke's work, we see that the relational structure of being (*esse*) is expressed in activity (*agere*). It is precisely the *hypostasis*, the subject of activity, which shows forth the relational structure of being. Since the divine and human natures come into relation, this relation itself must be expressed in the relational structure of being—in the *hypostasis*. Thus, the interpenetration of the divine and human nature in Christ cannot be understood as an interpenetration of substances which would result in mixture, confusion or change, but rather as an existential interpenetration through the relational structure of being. In other words, it is through the subsistent relation which is the *hypostasis* or person of the Son that the two natures interpenetrate. The union of the two natures in Christ is a *hypostatic* union not a substantial (*ousiatic*) union.[71]

The distinction between person and nature, which follows the structure of existence (*esse-in*, *esse-ab*, and *esse-ad*), indicates that while there is a unity of existence in Christ his human nature has a true, but

---

68. Coffey, *Deus Trinitas*, 76.

69. Harrison, "Perichoresis in the Greek Fathers," 54; Lawler, "*Perichoresis*," 50; Scalise, "Perichoresis," 75.

70. Maximus the Confessor, "Ambigua ad Thomam," 5.23; John of Damascus, "De Fide Orthodoxa," 3.19.

71. Cf. Augustine, *Sermones*, 186.1; Galot, *Who Is Christ?*, 292.

secondary existence.[72] Christ's human nature is created (*esse-in*) while Christ's person is uncreated (*esse-ab* and *esse-ad*). In God the divine nature is simple, so that the *esse-ab* and *esse-ad* of Christ's person always necessarily carries the divine *esse-in*. In contrast, humanity is not simple, so that there is not the same absolute requirement that the *esse-in* of his human nature has a corresponding human person (*esse-ab* and *esse-ad*). However, there is a requirement that some appropriate *esse-ab* and *esse-ad* completes the existence of Christ's human nature. The definition of the person as a subsistent relation, for both divine persons and analogously for human persons, ensures that the divine *esse-ab* and *esse-ad* is truly appropriate for the relational existence in his human nature.

With this existential structure Christ lives eternally in the divine communion, while at the same time he truly interacts within the human community. This interaction does not perfect him as a person, but it does affect him in his human nature. However, it is his relational person (the person of the Son of God) that *enables* his human nature to be affected. Thus, for instance, Christ can be moved to compassion and experience true human emotions in relationships with other human beings. Christ is truly a vital human individual, even though he is not a human person.

Divinization as *filii* in *Filio*

While Christ can truly experience human life as a vital human individual due to his divine person possessing a true human nature, the converse is also true. The human nature of Christ can participate in the dynamism of trinitarian life by means of the person of the Son who establishes his own relational existence in his human nature. Through this dynamism acting in his human nature he can not only be moved to compassion in his humanity, but also heal through the power of the divine life. Christ's human nature (*esse-in*) does not change into the divine nature (a different *esse-in*), rather his human nature shares in the divine life through the mystery of his person (*esse-ab*, *esse-ad*) through which his human nature is hypostatically united to his divine nature. In Christ "the infinite distance between God and man has been spanned by the relational being of the Word."[73]

---

72. Aquinas, *Quaestio disputata*, art. 4, co; Aquinas, *Summa Theologiae*, III.17.2.co. ad.2; Galot, *The Person of Christ*, 17–19.

73. Galot, *Who Is Christ?* 308.

The hypostatic union is unique to Christ. Human persons are not divine persons and so cannot be hypostatically united to the divine nature in exactly the same way as Christ. So how can the divinization of concrete human persons come about? We begin by examining the process of human beings becoming members of the church. Through faith and baptism members of the human race receive the Holy Spirit, become conformed to Christ, and enter into the communion of the church. This process of entering into the church and being conformed to Christ brings about a personal communion with Christ which is so intimate that Augustine refers to the whole Christ as "one man consisting of head and body."[74] In the act of incorporation into the whole Christ the unity achieved is not at the level of nature, but at the level of personal communion.[75] This unity is not an absolutely complete identification, for believers are not absorbed into Christ.[76] Even in the personal unity Augustine does not totally collapse the church into the person of Christ. He makes a distinction by speaking of Christ's own person and the person of the church.[77] In describing the church as a body Augustine identifies charity as the bond between Christ and his body.[78] This, in a sense, is the content of communion. Charity is not simply a moral connection, but an ontological one in which one part of the body shares the power of the whole through its incorporation into the whole.[79]

The Holy Spirit comes as the active agent of incorporation into this communion. The Holy Spirit who incorporates people into Christ in faith and charity is the same Holy Spirit who united the Son of God with his human nature in the hypostatic union.[80] The Holy Spirit engenders charity in those who choose to accept the life of Christ through faith. Thus, the active life of Christ is communicated by the Holy Spirit to members of the church. In this way, Christians are conformed to Christ by the Holy Spirit who incorporates them into the whole Christ, head and body. The process of being conformed to Christ is not a process by which human nature is simply changed to a new ecclesial nature. Rather, it is a process

---

74. Augustine, *Enarrationes in Psalmos*, 61.4.
75. Meconi, *The One Christ*, 212.
76. Meconi, *The One Christ*, 210, 213.
77. Augustine, *Enarrationes in Psalmos*, 61.4, 142.3.
78. Augustine, *Sermones*, 162A.5.
79. Augustine, *Sermones*, 162A.5.
80. Meconi, *The One Christ*, 197.

by which the relational structure of existence of the human person opens up to the power of the Holy Spirit who works to reorientate the *esse-ab, esse-ad* of the human person to the *esse-ab, esse-ad* of Christ.

However, Christ is not simply passive in this process. Christ makes himself available through the corporeality of his sacraments, and through the concrete church as the "universal sacrament of salvation."[81] In Christ himself, his divine person and his human nature are in harmony such that his personal power fully infuses his human nature, thus preventing his human nature from becoming an obstacle to the divine life. This is not the case for the unregenerate concrete human person where the nature (*esse-in*), caught in the law of sin, constrains the personal "I" (*the esse-ab, esse-ad*). The personal "I" may well desire the good, but cannot reach it (Rom 7:14–24). Christ breaks open the distorted nature of the unregenerate concrete human person by the mystery of his Cross. The hold of the law of sin on the nature which constrains the personal "I" is broken through the power of the divine perichoresis—the power of perfect love. When Jesus dies on the Cross he cries out "My God, my God, why have you abandoned me" (Matt 27:46). It is not because the Father has withdrawn his Spirit from the Son, but because he has given all to his Son—his entire Spirit—and there is nothing more to give. At this moment the perfect loving kenosis of the Father becomes manifest in the economy of salvation. Then through the human act of Christ's trusting acceptance as he dies upon the cross, allowing the Spirit of the Father to be his spirit/Spirit returning to the Father, the divine perichoretic unity breaks into the web of fallen human relationships and ruptures it. The kenosis of the Son lovingly responding to the total self-gift of the Father reveals the mystery of the divine perichoresis in the most perfect way possible within creation. This definitively opens the web of fallen human relationships to the communion of divine love and the personal activity of the Holy Spirit.[82] Through faith and baptism, concrete human persons open up to the power of Christ's Cross. This breaks the constraining power of the distorted human nature over the personal "I." This commences the lifelong process of sanctification whereby the Spirit, with human cooperation, progressively realigns the personal relations (the *esse-ab, esse-ad*) of the human person to those of Christ. The mystery of loving kenosis stands at the heart of this realignment.

81. Paul, *Lumen gentium*, no. 48.
82. See Coffey, "The Holy Spirit," 193, 228. Augustine's, mutual love model (Augustine, *De Trinitate*, 15.5.37) inspires Coffey's return model.

Divinization then flows from this as a flower comes forth from a plant. The process of sanctification leads to divinization in which the nature of the concrete human person becomes undistorted as the concrete person is Christified through the realignment of the relational reality of human persons (*filii*) to the relational reality of the person of Christ (*Filio*). Understood in this way divinization does not focus on a direct vision of the ineffable divine essence by the human being. Rather divinization as *filii* in *Filio* focuses on Christ as the eternal mediator with whom the human person in their relational core is united. This is not a mere moral union, but an ontological union through the relational dimension of existence (*esse-ab, esse-ad*). This then allows the integral human nature (*esse-in*) which the person possesses to fully become in Christ what it was created to be. This harmonizes with the thought of Sergi Bulgakov in a model of divinization focused on the personal subject, through which the nature possessed by the personal subject in the concrete human person reaches its fulfilment.[83] Divinization does not change human nature into the divine nature nor does the human person become a divine person. Rather, through the mediation of Christ and the action of the Spirit human persons in their relational core are taken up to share in the divine perichoretic unity that has definitively broken into the world through the cross of Christ. Then the unity of this divine life overflows into the human nature thereby perfecting it. In this way concrete human persons are enabled to "become participants in the divine nature" (2 Pet 1:4).

In divinization human persons share in the life of God through the Son of God and experience in their human nature the perichoresis manifest most perfectly in this world through Christ's death and resurrection. A foretaste of this permanent experience in heaven can be had on earth as St. Teresa says regarding the seventh mansion where the soul receives the infused knowledge to behold the presence of the Three in One—the divine perichoretic unity.[84] We are forever human, but we are raised to share in the perichoretic life of God where Christ is always our mediator and the Cross reveals itself as the tree of life eternally. We truly experience the self-giving of God within himself in the perfect kenosis found in the Triune perichoresis. So, just as Christ became a true human individual though he was never a human person so we truly share the life of the divine nature through Christ though we are never a divine person.

83. Ciraulo, "Divinization as Christification," 501.
84. Teresa of Avila, *Interior Castle*, 7.1.9.

In truth, he is the vine and we are the branches and the lesson we must learn is how to give all—how to enter the kenosis of the Cross.

Bibliography

Aquinas, Thomas. *Quaestio disputata de unione verbi incarnati (Disputed Question: Concerning the Union of the Word Incarnate)*. Translated by Jason Lewis Andrew West. https://hosted.desales.edu/w4/philtheo/loughlin/ATP/De_Unione/De_Unione4.html.

———. *Summa Theologiae*. Edited by Thomas Gilby and T. C. O'Brien. London: Blackfriars, 1964–81.

Augustine. *De Trinitate*. Edited by John E. Rotelle. Translated by Edmund Hill. Hyde Park, NY: New City, 1991.

———. "Enarrationes in Psalmos 61." In *Expositions of the Psalms (51–72)*, edited by John E. Rotelle, translated by Maria Boulding, 202–28. Works of Saint Augustine 3/17. Hyde Park, NY: New City, 2001.

———. "Enarrationes in Psalmos 142." In *Expositions of the Psalms (121–150)*, edited by Boniface Ramsey, translated by Maria Boulding, 344–59. Works of Saint Augustine 3/20. Hyde Park, NY: New City, 2004.

———. "Sermones 162A." In *Sermons: On the New Testament*, edited by John E. Rotelle, translated by Edmund Hill, 152–66. Works of Saint Augustine 3/5. New Rochelle, NY: New City, 1992.

———. "Sermones 186." In *Sermons: On the Liturgical Seasons*, edited by John E. Rotelle, translated by Edmund Hill, 24–26. Works of Saint Augustine 3/6. New Rochelle, NY: New City, 1993.

Basil of Caesarea. "Epistolae 214." In vol. 8 of *The Nicene and Post-Nicene Fathers: Second Series*, edited by Philip Schaff and Henry Wace, translated by Blomfield Jackson, 253–54. New York: Christian Literature, 1895.

Boethius. "Contra Eutychen." In *Theological Tractates: The Consolation of Philosophy*, translated by H. F. Stewart et al., 72–129. Loeb Classical Library 74. Cambridge: Harvard University Press, 1973.

———. "De Trinitate." In *Theological Tractates: The Consolation of Philosophy*, translated by H. F. Stewart et al., 2–31. Loeb Classical Library 74. Cambridge: Harvard University Press, 1973.

Ciraulo, Jonathan Martin. "Divinization as Christification in Erich Przywara and John Zizioulas." *Modern Theology* 32.4 (2016) 479–503.

Clarke, W. Norris. "Person, Being, and St. Thomas." *Communio* 19 (1992) 601–18.

———. *Person and Being*. Milwaukee: Marquette University Press, 1993.

———. "Response to David Schindler's Comments." *Communio* 20 (1993) 593–98.

———. "To Be Is to Be Substance-in-Relation." In *Metaphysics as Foundation: Essays in Honor of Ivor Leclerc*, edited by Paul A. Bogaard and Gordon Treash, 164–83. Albany: State University of New York Press, 1993.

Coffey, David. *Deus Trinitas: The Doctrine of the Triune God*. Oxford: Oxford University Press, 1999.

———. "The Holy Spirit as the Mutual Love of the Father and the Son." *Theological Studies* 51 (1990) 193–229.

Decorte, Jos. "Relation and Substance in Henry of Ghent's Metaphysics." In *Henry of Ghent and the Transformation of Scholastic Thought: Studies in Memory of Jos Decorte*, edited by Guy Guldentops and Carlos Steel, 3–14. Leuven: Leuven University Press, 2003.

Flores, Juan Carlos. *Henry of Ghent: Metaphysics and the Trinity*. Leuven: Leuven University Press, 2006.

Friedman, Russell L. *Medieval Trinitarian Thought from Aquinas to Ockham*. Cambridge: Cambridge University Press, 2010.

Galot, Jean. *The Person of Christ: Covenant between God and Man*. Rome: Gregorian University Press, 1981.

———. *Who Is Christ? A Theology of the Incarnation*. Translated by M. Angeline Bouchard. Chicago: Franciscan Herald, 1981.

Gellius, Aulus Cornelius. *The Attic Nights of Aulus Gellius*. Vol. 1. Translated by John C. Rolfe. Loeb Classical Library 195. Cambridge: Harvard University Press, 1946.

Gleeson, Gerald. "Speaking of Persons, Human and Divine." *Sophia* 43 (2004) 45–60.

Gregory of Nazianzus. "Oratio 21." In vol. 7 of *Nicene and Post-Nicene Fathers: Second Series*, edited by Philip Schaff and Henry Wace, translated by Charles Gordon Brown and James Edward Swallow, 269–80. New York: Christian Literature, 1894.

Harrison, Verna. "Perichoresis in the Greek Fathers." *St. Vladimir's Theological Quarterly* 35 (1991) 53–65.

Henninger, Mark G. *Relations: Medieval Theories, 1250–1325*. Oxford: Clarendon, 1989.

Henry of Ghent. *Summa (Quaestiones Ordinariae) Art. XXXI–XXXIV*. Edited by Raymond Macken. Leuven: Leuven University Press, 1991.

Henry, Paul. *Saint Augustine on Personality*. New York: Macmillan, 1960.

Hipp, Stephen A. *"Person" in Christian Tradition and the Conception of Saint Albert the Great: A Systematic Study of Its Concept as Illuminated by the Mysteries of the Trinity and the Incarnation*. Münster: Aschendorff, 2001.

John of Damascus. "De Fide Orthodoxa." In vol. 9 of *The Nicene and Post-Nicene Fathers: Second Series*, edited by Philip Schaff and Henry Wace, translated by Steward D. F. Salmond, 1–101. New York: Scribner's Sons, 1908.

Lawler, Michael G. "Perichoresis: New Theological Wine in an Old Theological Wineskin." *Horizons* 22 (1995) 49–66.

Lienhard, Joseph T. "*Ousia* and *Hypostasis*: The Cappadocian Settlement and the Theology of 'One *Hypostasis*.'" In *The Trinity: An Interdisciplinary Symposium on the Trinity*, edited by Stephen T. Davis et al., 99–121. Oxford: Oxford University Press, 1999.

Maximus the Confessor. "Ambigua ad Thomam." In *Ambigua ad Thomam una cum Epistula secunda ad eundem*, edited by B. Janssens, 45–74. Corpus Christianorum Series Graeca 48. Turnhout: Brepols, 2002.

Meconi, David Vincent. *The One Christ: St. Augustine's Theology of Deification*. Washington, DC: Catholic University of America Press, 2013.

Paul VI, Pope. *Lumen gentium*. In *Decrees of the Ecumenical Councils*, edited by Norman P. Tanner, 849–900. London: Sheed & Ward, 1990.

Ratzinger, Joseph. "Concerning the Notion of Person in Theology." *Communio* 17 (1990) 439–54.

Rolnick, Philip A. *Person, Grace, and God*. Grand Rapids: Eerdmans, 2007.

Scalise, Brian T. "Perichoresis in Gregory Nazianzen and Maximus the Confessor." *Eleutheria* 2.1 (2012) 58–76.

Schindler, David L. "Norris Clarke on Person, Being, and St. Thomas." *Communio* 20 (1993) 580–92.
Schmitz, Kenneth L. "The Geography of the Human Person." *Communio* 13 (1986) 27–48.
Teresa of Avila. The *Interior Castle or The Mansions*. Edited by Benedict Zimmerman. Translated by The Benedictines of Stanbrook. 3rd ed. London: Thomas Baker, 1921. http://www.ccel.org/ccel/teresa/castle2.html.
Tertullian. "Adversus Praxean." In vol. 3 of *The Ante-Nicene Fathers*, edited by Alexander Roberts and James Donaldson, translated by Peter Holmes, 597–627. New York: Christian Literature, 1885.
Turcescu, Lucian. *Gregory of Nyssa and the Concept of Divine Persons*. Oxford: Oxford University Press, 2005.

5

Rethinking the *Imago Dei*

Rationality and Relationality

THOMAS V. GOURLAY

Introduction

In his seminal catechetical work on human love in the divine plan, delivered as a series of addresses during the first five years of his pontificate, Pope John Paul II sought, amongst other things, to broaden an element of the tradition as it concerned the notion of the human person as *imago Dei*.[1] Popularly known as the Theology of the Body, the Polish pope's catechesis drew heavily on a phrase taken from the Vatican II document *Gaudium et Spes* which was to become a key feature of his teaching pontificate, namely that Jesus Christ fully reveals God to man, and man to man himself.[2] In this teaching, John Paul II found the chris-

---

1. John Paul II, *Man and Woman He Created Them*.

2. Second Vatican Council, *Gaudium et spes*, no. 22. The centrality of this text for the pastoral and theological vision of John Paul II is difficult to overstate. In his penultimate encyclical, *Fides et Ratio*, he wrote, "There is no doubt that the climactic section of the chapter [one of *Gaudium et spes*] is profoundly significant for philosophy; and it was this which I took up in my first Encyclical Letter *Redemptor hominis* and which serves as one of the constant reference-points of my teaching: 'The truth is that only in the mystery of the Incarnate Word does the mystery of man take on light. For Adam,

tological and anthropological resources with which to deepen his reflections on the notion of *imago Dei*, in a way which was considered by some to be a departure from at least elements of the tradition.

In this catechesis, John Paul II taught that the *imago Dei* is not to be found in man's rational faculty alone, but that it can also be found—perhaps even more perfectly found—in communion, of which the body (and therefore sexual difference), in its essentially symbolic quality, is a sign. He wrote that

> we can deduce that man became the image of God not only through his own humanity, but also through the communion of persons, which man and woman form from the very beginning. The function of the image is that of mirroring the one who is the model, of reproducing its own prototype. Man becomes an image of God not so much in the moment of solitude as in the moment of communion. He is, in fact, "from the beginning" not only an image in which the solitude of one Person, who rules the world, mirrors itself, but also and essentially the image of an inscrutable divine communion of Persons.[3]

According to John Paul II, the nuptial relationship of husband and wife can be understood as an analogy of the *communio personarum* of the Holy Trinity—and the analogy works both ways.[4] John Paul II's im-

---

the first man, was a type of him who was to come, Christ the Lord. Christ, the new Adam, in the very revelation of the mystery of the Father and of his love, fully reveals man to himself and brings to light his most high calling,'" John Paul II, *Fides et Ratio*, no. 12. For a masterful treatment of John Paul II's use of this text throughout his pontificate, as well as an account of the origin of the doctrine, see Newton, "John Paul II and *Gaudium et spes* no. 22," 375–412.

3. John Paul II, *Man and Woman He Created Them*, 163.

4. These insights have spawned a great deal of fruitful theological and pastoral work, but as alluded to above, they do not exist without criticism. Fergus Kerr, OP, for example, notes wryly that according to this new development, "it is not in our rationality but in sexual difference that we image God—in our genitalia, not our heads, so to speak." Kerr, *Twentieth Century Catholic Theologians*, 194. We will see, however, that those who, like John Paul II, affirm the nuptial image do not flippantly discard those traditional and compelling reasons that would caution against using nuptial and/or social images, nor do they merely *also* affirm the traditional one, but instead they see both ways of understanding the *imago* as implying and complementing each other. In that case, the Theology of the Body is (or at least ought to be) the first instantiation of a new reflection on how the rational soul is the form of the human body—all the way down. For an exposition regarding how so-called "nuptial mystery theology" can be read alongside as a compliment to the more traditional theology, see Scola, *The Nuptial Mystery*.

portant and significant work, however, is but one manifestation of this rediscovered understanding of the significance of relationality as constitutive, not only of uncreated persons (i.e., the persons of the Trinity), but for created human persons.

This notion of the human person as the image of God, *imago Dei*, is one that has inspired much reflection both on the nature of God and the human person. Traditional notions of where, in fact, the *imago Dei* resides in the human person have—particularly in the tradition of Western Christianity—followed St. Augustine, who has been commonly read to have posited that it is in his rational faculty, in his mind.[5] This understanding was solidified in the work of St. Thomas Aquinas, the great Dominican theologian of the thirteenth century, who taught that "since man is said to be to the image of God by reason of his intellectual nature, he is the most perfectly like God according to that in which he can best imitate God in his intellectual nature."[6] Thus, it came to be considered canonical in the tradition of Western Christianity that the *imago Dei* refers to man's rational faculty primarily, even solely.

There is a significant and growing body of literature that has developed over the past few decades, however, that has complicated this supposedly traditional account of a purely intellectual *imago* and which supports the work of John Paul II. Noteworthy in this field are the works of such figures as Rowan Williams, Lewis Ayres, Michel René Barnes, Michael Hanby, and more recently, Adrian Pabst.[7] The challenge which these scholars bring to the received narrative is not so much to deny the intellectual *imago*, but to show, first, that the notion of *imago Dei* is made more complex by a metaphysics of participation and of gift; and second, that this is not a merely novel perspective, but rather one which does have deep patristic, and even medieval roots.

Following the scholarship of Joseph Ratzinger, David L. Schindler, and others, this chapter will demonstrate the implications of the recovered and elevated status of relationality considered as constitutive of the human person as *imago Dei* and demonstrate the implications of this on the human faculty of knowing (and loving) God, and God's creation.

---

5. Augustine, *De Trinitate*, XIV.12.15.

6. See Aquinas, *Summa Theologiae*, I.93.4.c.

7. See, for example, Williams, "*Sapientia* and the Trinity"; Ayres, *Augustine and the Trinity*; Barnes, "Augustine in Contemporary Trinitarian Theology"; Hanby, *Augustine and Modernity*; Hanby, "Augustine on Human Being"; Pabst, *Metaphysics*.

Ratzinger on Relation and the Human Person

In an early and influential essay entitled *Concerning the Notion of the Person in Theology*, Joseph Ratzinger describes the philosophical notion of personhood itself as of uniquely Christian provenance.[8] While he acknowledges that Aristotelian substance metaphysics looms large over a great deal of the tradition in its definition of person (such as exhibited, for example, in the influential definition of Boethius, who defines the term "person" to mean, "an individual substance of a rational nature"), in this essay Ratzinger sought to bring the fruits of trinitarian theology and its understanding of the personhood of the Three to bear (analogically) on his developing theological anthropology.

According to Ratzinger, the element missing in much of the philosophical tradition of the Christian West in this regard was that of relationality, which he noted—somewhat disapprovingly—was neglected in Augustine's use of his famous psychological analogy to understand something of the Trinity. For Ratzinger, the psychological analogy emphasized an understanding of the persons of God as being "wholly closed into God's interior," and which, over time led to a loss in the sense of the dimension of the "we" in theology, and consequentially, what developed into a modern individualism.[9]

Ratzinger was later to recant an element of his critique of Augustine, as is seen in footnote 12 to the English translation.[10] And, as indicated above, his judgement has been vindicated by the more recent scholarship of persons such as Williams, Barnes, Ayres, Hanby, and Pabst who have, in myriad ways, demonstrated the importance of relations for Augustine and the Western tradition more broadly, refuting authoritatively any notion that Augustine was a crypto-individualist, or proto-modern.[11] It is

---

8. Ratzinger, "Concerning the Notion of Person in Theology." Originally published in German in 1973 and then in English in the journal *Communio* in 1990.

9. Ratzinger, "Concerning the Notion of Person in Theology," 118.

10. Ratzinger, "Concerning the Notion of Person in Theology," 118. "Today, of course, I would not judge as harshly as I did in the lecture above, because for Augustine, the 'psychological doctrine of the Trinity' remains an attempt to understand that is balanced by the factors of the tradition."

11. Those mentioned above as well as others who have contested the traditional understanding of Augustine's "psychological" analogy have done so on grounds that this traditional understanding misses, in Augustine, the very thing that Ratzinger was calling for. The very reason that the image is an *image*, and not the original, is that it exists in a relation of dependence, and is perfected in a relation of knowledge and

interesting to note, however, that in the same footnote (12) Ratzinger remarks that Aquinas's separation of the doctrine of the one God and the doctrine of the Trinity is particularly incisive in the development of a more individualized notion of the person, noting that "it led Thomas to consider the formula, 'God is one person' legitimate, although it had been considered heretical in the early Church."[12]

In this essay Ratzinger was seeking to develop the implications of trinitarian theology in an understanding of created human persons in order to counter the hyper-individualism of modernity.[13] In order to do so, Ratzinger needs to prioritize relations above mere accidental properties of personal being, and move them (at least) into, or alongside, substance itself.[14] He writes,

> In God, person means relation. Relation, being related, is not something superadded to the person, but it *is* the person itself. By definition, the person exists only *as* relation. . . . In God, person is the pure relativity of being turned toward the other; it does not lie on the level of substance—the substance is one—but on the level of dialogical reality, of relativity toward the other. . . . Relation here is recognized as a third specific fundamental category between substance and accident, the two great categorical forms of thought in Antiquity.[15]

Always careful to stay firmly within the bounds of the appropriate use of analogy,[16] Ratzinger argues that relationality becomes a fundamental element in one's understanding of created persons—such as

---

charity with the original who himself exists as substantively related. Thus, the *imago Dei* is an image of God in its very difference from him.

12. Here he cites Aquinas, *Summa Theologia*, III.3.3.ad1. Ratzinger, however, does not develop this critique of Aquinas at all, and it would seem that this reading of Aquinas might need some softening along much the same lines as his relaxing of his critique of Augustine. Adrian Pabst, for example, has shown how Aquinas can certainly be read as contributing to the relational narrative, albeit without addressing the citation provided by Ratzinger above. See here chapter 5 of Pabst, *Metaphysics*, 201–71.

13. See Pecknold, "'Man Is by Nature a Social and Political Animal,'" 894.

14. Whether Ratzinger in fact prioritizes relations *above* substance, and whether or how it is even possible or desirable to do so need not distract from our present argument. The situation of relations vis-à-vis substance is a point of ongoing debate. For Ratzinger, relations are at least coeval with, or constitutive of, substance.

15. Ratzinger, "Concerning the Notion of Person in Theology," 108.

16. The use of analogy is important to stress, lest some infer from this an implication that human persons are to be understood as subsistent relations.

humans—and we can extrapolate, again by way of analogy, of all of created reality.[17]

The question of relations is also taken up in one of Ratzinger's earlier works, *Introduction to Christianity*, where, reflecting on the doctrine of the Trinity, Ratzinger is eager to emphasize that the three-ness of God is not a mere accident of God's being/substance. The three-ness of God—the *relatio*—"stands beside the substance as an equally primordial form of being."[18] Ratzinger cites Augustine—"in God there are no accidents, only substance and relation,"—before commenting, "therein lies concealed a revolution in man's view of the world: the sole dominion of thinking in terms of substance is ended; relation is discovered as an equally valid primordial mode of reality."[19]

This interest in relations was not merely the academic interest of a young rising-star, but in fact it found its way into much of Ratzinger's later work, even in his role as pope. For example, in his encyclical *Caritas in veritate*, Pope Benedict XVI, highlighting the epistemic potential of this relational perspective, drew attention to the observation of his predecessor Pope Paul VI, who noted that "the world is in trouble because of the lack of thinking."[20] Benedict goes on to say that

> a new trajectory of thinking is needed in order to arrive at a better understanding of the implications of our being one family; interaction among the peoples of the world calls us to embark upon this new trajectory, so that integration can signify solidarity rather than marginalization. Thinking of this kind requires *a deeper critical evaluation of the category of relation*. This is a task that cannot be undertaken by the social sciences alone,

---

17. Speaking (analogously) of all of created reality as "personal," while having gained some philosophical credence in the writings of such figures as W. Norris Clarke, SJ, is not as novel within the tradition as it might seem at first blush. The Canticle of Daniel (Dan 3:57–88), for instance, calls on all of creation: sun, moon, stars, wind, rain, to engage in the personal act of praising God. Saint Francis of Assisi, also, makes use of this language in his own *Canticle of the Creatures*, famously cited in the opening of Pope Francis's encyclical on care for our common home, *Laudato si'*.

18. Ratzinger, *Introduction to Christianity*, 183. Stratford Caldecott notes that, "For Aristotle, *relation* belonged to the 'accidents,' the incidentals of circumstances of being (and in God there are no accidents), whereas substance was the real thing itself. But for Christianity, the "dialogue in God between Persons, the *relation* is 'an equally primordial form of being.'" Caldecott, *The Radiance of Being*, 107n10.

19. Ratzinger, *Introduction to Christianity*, 184.

20. Paul VI, *Populorum progressio*, no. 85, cited in Benedict XVI, *Caritas in veritate*, no. 53.

insofar as the contribution of disciplines such as metaphysics and theology is needed if man's transcendent dignity is to be properly understood.[21]

We now turn to a more sustained analysis of the category of relation, as it is developed in the thought of David L. Schindler.

Understanding Relations with David L. Schindler

The movement to recover the importance of relations as ontologically coeval with, constitutive of, or even above substance has been developed and argued by many people over the past few decades.[22] Along with Ratzinger, some key thinkers include Hans Urs von Balthasar, Kenneth Schmitz, W. Norris Clarke, SJ, and David L. Schindler.[23] Following the lead of Schindler as representative of this group,[24] we take a brief excursus to explore the notion of constitutive relationality as he presents it, before exploring the implications of this for the reasoning faculty of the human person.

Schindler's constitutive relations thesis is one that has been developed in conversation with the aforementioned theologians and philosophers,

---

21. Benedict XVI, *Caritas in veritate*, no. 53.

22. Significant centers where this thought is developing include: the English edition of the journal *Communio: International Catholic Review* (https://www.communio-icr.com/); the Relational Ontologies Research group, based at the Pontifical University of the Holy Cross, Santa Croce (http://ror.pusc.it/index2.html); Sophia University Institute, established and run by the new ecclesial movement "the Focolare," based in Loppiano, Italy (https://www.sophiauniversity.org/); The Centre for Theology and Philosophy at the University of Nottingham, UK (http://theologyphilosophycentre.co.uk/); and the New Trinitarian Ontologies Society, based at Cambridge University (https://www.newtrinitarianontologies.com/).

23. A sampling of key texts, which is by no means exhaustive would include Schmitz, *The Gift*; Balthasar, "On the Concept of Person"; Schmitz, "The Geography of the Human Person"; Schmitz, "Created Receptivity and the Philosophy of the Concrete"; Clarke, "To Be Is To Be Substance-in-Relation"; Clarke, *Person and Being*; Schindler, "Being, Gift, Self-Gift (Part One and Part Two)."

24. Schindler can be taken as perhaps being the thinker who has most comprehensively synthesized the work of the aforementioned, and as one who has demonstrated the most sustained development and defense of the notion of constitutive relationality of being. For a masterful presentation of the development of this metaphysical position (i.e., a metaphysics of the gift), and the concomitant relational ontology, as well as David L. Schindler's position within that tradition, see Taylor, *The Foundations of Nature*, 121–97.

as well as a great many others.²⁵ His thinking has generally taken shape in the task of responding to the many challenges to the Catholic-Christian faith in the context of modernity in its dominant liberal form, for which he takes America to be emblematic.

Schindler forcefully argues that liberal modernity—despite its putative neutrality on matters religious and metaphysical—harbors a hidden logic of being (onto-logic) that takes as given the radical independence of entities, whose interaction and relation he characterizes as extrinsic and mechanistic. "What the language of the machine brings out," Schindler argues, "is the preoccupation with power (understood in terms of physical force or displacement of physical bodies) and technique, and control or manipulation, which results from such externally conceived relations." As radically independent, entities within this order can only relate to one another externally and materially, "in the Cartesian sense of matter: things and persons are approached as though they only had an 'outside' as it were."²⁶

Further, Schindler understands that such a mechanistic view of the human person

> fails to take account of the receptivity implied in being-from-the-divine-Other, and thus slides ipso facto into a wrongly self-centered view of the person.... This self-centeredness is by definition a-theistic: not so much because of an explicit exclusion of God as of a (largely unintended) failure to integrate the constitutive relation to God into the first meaning of all creaturely being and action.²⁷

In seeking to demonstrate philosophically the constitutive relationality of being, Schindler has engaged in serious and prolonged dialogue with the aforementioned thinkers, and others. In a response to a programmatic essay by W. Norris Clarke, wherein Clarke argued for the importance of relations vis-à-vis substance,²⁸ Schindler argued that, rather than substantial forms being relational in a dyadic manner as Clarke had initially posited contending that substantial forms should instead be

---

25. For a thoroughgoing treatment of this, see Walker, "'Constitutive Relations.'"

26. Schindler, "Grace and the Form of Nature and Culture," 18. In adopting the language of mechanization and the machine he "follows von Balthasar, who in turn followed French writer Georges Bernanos." See Rowland, "Theology and Culture," 74.

27. Schindler, "Communio Ecclesiology and Liberalism," 776.

28. Clarke, *Person and Being*; Schindler, "Norris Clarke on Person, Being, and St. Thomas."

understood as being constituted with a triadic structure—a line of argumentation that Clarke accepted and subsequently adopted in his further discussions on this point. Clarke, following the prompts of Schindler conceded that "we should describe every created being as possessing its own existence *from another, in itself*, and oriented *towards others*."[29]

In demonstrating this point more phenomenologically and concretely, Schindler, in a very Balthasarian mode, develops a presentation of the ontological meaning of childhood. The child, whose existence is so obviously from another (*esse ab*), demonstrates in her or his very being the always anterior giftedness of being given.[30] This illustrates in a universal way that is at once phenomenological, metaphysical, and historical, the reality of being from and the priority of receptivity at the very core of human existence.

According to Schindler, "relationality is anchored already in the first act of the substance (*esse*); and . . . the first act of the substance is therefore already as a matter of principle open to the other (*ab* and *ad*), even as this first act simultaneously makes substance itself be (*in*)."[31] Receptivity, then, characterizes the basic structure of existence as act. This understanding of creaturely being is fundamental to Schindler's thinking, and also the relational project more broadly, however it is conceived.[32]

In an exposition of the doctrine of *creatio ex nihilo*, Schindler writes that in the act of creation, the creature (in this instance, the human person) is *wholly* given his or her creaturely being, and as such is therefore properly independent. Paradoxically he points out, this means that the creature owes everything, its whole being, to God, and is as such, radically *de*pendent. This is to be understood as a *relative* autonomy: an autonomy that is really constituted as it is, but is always-already in relation to God-in-Christ.[33]

---

29. Clarke, *Explorations in Metaphysics*, 119. Cf. Schindler, "Norris Clarke on Person, Being, and St. Thomas."

30. See Schindler, "We Are Not Our Own." Revised and republished as chapter 1 of his, *The Generosity of Creation*.

31. Schindler, "Norris Clarke on Person, Being, and St. Thomas," 587.

32. This project is developed under a variety of different names, including *communio* ontology, relational ontology, metaphysics of gift (and receptivity), Trinitarian ontology, metaphysics of sanctity, onto-logic of holiness. Notwithstanding different inflections and nuances in meaning, this triadic notion of being—*esse ab, esse in* and *esse ad*—is common.

33. This is how Schindler presents the teaching of the Vatican II Council (1962–65) on the legitimate autonomy of earthly affairs as it is encapsulated in Second Vatican

As gift, and therefore as given, the human person is then understood to be receptive not only chronologically but ontologically, prior to being creative. This is not, of course, to negate the importance of the human person as sharer in the creative activity of God, and by way of his or her work as participating in some way in God's creative action.[34] For modern liberal theorists however, the concept of givenness and creaturely dependence would leave the human person with little more than the illusion of freedom wherein being itself remains bound in a humiliating passively receptive relation to God and the givenness of things becomes an affront to the otherwise free human subject.

The human person's self-understanding of having been given to his or her self is therefore an acknowledgement of its having been given from an Other. Schindler writes,

> The generosity of the creative Giver takes original form in the creature as the *re-sponsive giving* properly called *gratitude*. Creation *ex nihilo*, in a word, implies that autonomy and gratitude in the creature can never be dissociated from each other—or can be dissociated only at the expense of distorting the integrity of the creature, thus rendering the creature unintelligible in his proper nature and dignity.[35]

Rather than being a source of humiliation for the human creature, receptivity—which as we argued earlier characterizes the basic structure of existence as act—manifests itself in a primary posture of active (non-passive) receptivity that is called gratitude. According to Schindler, gratitude is what allows the creature to then participate in the generative/creative gift giving that is proper to its nature. Schindler describes this receptivity as primarily and at once both christological (as in the case of Christ's *fiat* in the Garden of Gethsemane, see Matt 26:38) and Marian (he develops this with particular recourse to the *fiat* and subsequent *Magnificat* of the Blessed Mother).[36]

Council, *Gaudium et spes*, no. 36. See Schindler, "'Disenchantment' and the End of Modern Civilization.'" See also, Losinger, *Relative Autonomy*.

34. The importance and the dignity of human work as a significant aspect of human nature taken up and explored in particular in the great social encyclicals that have been written since Leo XIII's *Rerum novarum*.

35. Schindler, "Kenneth Schmitz on Creation Ex Nihilo," 7–8.

36. Schindler, *Heart of the World*, 92–93. See also Caldecott, "The Marian Dimension of Existence," 288.

Again, this acknowledgement of the human person as fundamentally receptive is not to posit an understanding of the human person as passive automaton, hence "non-passive." Here, Schindler points to the example of Mary the mother of Jesus who can be viewed as the icon of creaturely being *par excellence*. Her *fiat* is no mere passive acceptance of the inevitable, but a free and efficacious (non-passive) decision to accept and bear the Word within her.[37] It is in this sense that, in the active receptivity of her *fiat*, Mary becomes the archetype of all creation. Schindler writes that Mary, in her *fiat*, "reveals in all of its profundity what it means to be a creature." Furthermore, Schindler argues that "The *fiat* expresses the dependent relation on God that discloses the inner meaning of all of reality as gift, [and] which in turn disposes one towards service [i.e., in her *Magnificat*]. All that I am I have been given—by God in Jesus Christ; and what has been given is to be shared."[38] He writes,

> Man images the *creativity of God the Father and Creator only in and through the* receptivity of Jesus Christ and his mother Mary. The divine creativity of which human creativity is the image, in other words, is first that of Sonship and not that of Fatherhood. We are "sons in the Son": we represent the creativity of the Father only through the Son. (cf. Col. 1:15–16), and indeed through the archetypal creature, Mary—the freedom or love of both of whom consists first in receptive obedience.[39]

As gift—given—and therefore as received, the human person must be understood as being constituted by his or her relations. The human person exists, always and already, in every instance as related, primarily to God-in-Christ, who creates *ex nihilo*, holding everything in being, and who, in Christ the Son redeems. According to Hanby,

> this principle bears analogously on the [entire] order of creation. Substantiality in the etymological (and roughly Aristotelian) sense of standing in oneself is proportionally and not inversely related to receptivity. The greater a thing's capacity for receiving that which is not itself, the greater is its capacity for self-transcendence and the more distinct it is.[40]

---

37. On the notion of non-passive receptivity, see Schmitz, "Created Receptivity," 341.

38. Schindler, *Heart of the World*, 93.

39. Schindler, *Heart of the World*, 118.

40. Hanby, "Augustine on Human Being," 28.

This understanding of the human person, and indeed all of creation, significantly impacts on the human faculty of knowing, and on nature's knowability.

Wonder as the Cognitional Corollary to the Basic Structure of Being

As Ratzinger noted in his *Introduction to Christianity*, the modern era saw the development of a philosophical reduction of truth to facticity.[41] Ratzinger traces the various philosophical and theological developments that took place at the beginning of the modern era which led to this reduction, and describes its impact on human knowledge and understanding of the world generally, and also on the ascendant understanding of human nature itself.

In recovering the ontological importance of relations in the human person—and the concomitant non-passive receptive posture of gratitude proper to creatures—Ratzinger was hoping to overcome not only the (post-Kantian) individualism of the modern era, but also the notion of understanding that is prevalent in modern societies dominated by a mechanistic ontology. This mechanistic ontology is evidenced in the reduction of truth to function, and in the tacit assumption that things within the material order simply *are* "what they can do and what can be done with them."[42]

The creative retrieval of relationality achieved in the work of Ratzinger and Schindler as well as others is not an abandonment of the traditional intellectual *imago*, rather it shows the complexity of the human person as *imago Dei*, grounding the rational faculty of the human person within the context of relation. Commenting on this, C. C. Pecknold writes that, for Ratzinger,

> "Rationality" remains crucial to his understanding of the person, but he [Ratzinger] implicitly asks us, "rationality for what purpose?" Scripture and perennial philosophy alike can agree that human beings have a desire to know. We are rational animals. Yet this tells us too little. What, or whom, are we made to

---

41. Ratzinger, *Introduction to Christianity*, 57–69.
42. Dewey, *Reconstruction in Philosophy*, 115.

know? For biblical faith, Ratzinger thinks the answer is obvious: God creates us with a desire to know in relation.[43]

This relational anthropological vision understands the human person—as well as the rest of created reality—as gift (and therefore as given), and therefore as receptive (of being) on its most fundamentally basic ontological level. Such ontological receptivity structures the basic form of reason prior to any conscious or habitually formed disposition or posture in human persons. This is taken up into moral/volitional order in that it disposes the person to adopt a posture of receptivity and gratitude as exemplified most perfectly by the Son in his humanity, and then by the Blessed Mother, whose creaturely being stands as an icon of perfect creatureliness. This receptivity is not, as has been noted above, a mere passive acceptance, but a real, active, and potent acceptance of the word—one that impels Mary forward, to take the Word abroad, in service of her cousin Elizabeth (see Luke 1:46–55).

This receptive "letting be" exemplified in Mary is the voluntary corollary to the most basic structure of existence as act, and which has its cognitive equivalent in a contemplative mode of seeing the world and the things in the world (see Luke 2:19, 51) that is open to a fullness of reality that cannot otherwise be seen. Contemplation is not simply a habitual attitude to be piously adopted by the believer, it is the cognitive expression of the primitive structure of being itself as gift. As Hanby will remind us, "the world can only answer the questions we put to it. We pose these questions, moreover, on the basis of what interests us, that is, on the basis of desire which is in this and other ways an ingredient in all knowledge."[44] How human persons come to understand their own nature, its relation to God, to other human persons, and other objects or phenomena within the creation in fact determines the kinds of questions they will think will draw reasonable responses. If our point of departure is the simple acknowledgement of being's essential character as gift—and thus of being's constitutively relational character—then, and only then, it becomes possible to avoid the kind of reduction of reason's original capaciousness which necessarily accompanies the rise of modernity's mechanistic ontology.

Contrasting these two modes of being in the world—the modern, mechanistic, individualistic, and the Catholic-Christian, relational—and

---

43. Pecknold, "'Man Is by Nature a Social and Political Animal,'" 895.
44. Hanby, *No God, No Science*, 378.

their respective coincident epistemologies, Hanby goes on to state that, "A science commenced in wonder and love rather than a science predicated on control would yield profoundly different questions and answers, and perhaps even conceive of its subject matter differently."[45] Schindler, again making allusions to the Marian *fiat*, notes, "letting be and wonder . . . are but the *subjective-cognitional forms of participation in the objective nature of being as gift.*"[46]

If, as has been argued above, the human person is to be understood as gift and therefore as given, receptive prior to creative, and therefore constitutively relational, and if wonder/contemplation is the subjective/cognitional corollary to the most basic structure of being as such, then it is evident that the person's capacity for knowledge is significantly enlarged. The realm of what is considered knowable grows. Phenomena, as given, are approached as having an order and an intelligibility that exists prior to one's encounter with them that is to be sought and discovered—rather than being made or imposed upon it. Knowledge, then becomes a mode of seeing things in the light of their relations with the whole of creation and in turn, with the Creator. A recovery of this kind of contemplative science, which sits *contra* the dominating, manipulative, and technological science of modern secularized and mechanistic reason, would mean "recovering a more comprehensive conception of reason, on whose basis it would be possible, once again, to integrate the sciences into an order of wisdom."[47]

In fact, this seems to be precisely what Pope Francis is referring to, for example, in his encyclical *Laudato si'*, when he writes,

> Modern anthropocentrism [which excludes intrinsic relation to God] has paradoxically ended up prizing technical thought over reality, since "the technological mind sees nature as an insensate order, as a cold body of facts, as a mere 'given', as an object of utility, as raw material to be hammered into useful shape; it views the cosmos similarly as a mere 'space' into which objects can be thrown with complete indifference." The intrinsic dignity of the world is thus compromised. When human beings fail to find their true place in this world, they misunderstand themselves and end up acting against themselves.[48]

45. Hanby, *No God, No Science*, 378.
46. Schindler, *Ordering Love*, 412.
47. Hanby, *No God, No Science*, 379.
48. Francis, *Laudato si'*, no. 115, citing Guardini, *The End of the Modern World*, 55.

Conclusion

The trinitarian Christocentrism of the Second Vatican Council's pastoral constitution saw the flourishing of a great many developments in theological anthropology.[49] Noteworthy in this regard of course is the recovery of the constitutive role of relation in mainstream Catholic theological anthropology. This is not something that only comes to bear on the realm of sexual ethics, as some may reductively consider to be the main thrust of John Paul II's catechesis on human love in the Divine plan, nor is this renewed emphasis on relations purely a complete novelty within the tradition concerning the human person as *imago Dei*.

For thinkers such as Joseph Ratzinger and David L. Schindler, as well as others, the constitutively relational ontology of the human person does not ignore or usurp the intellectual *imago*, but instead deepens and complicates it. "For Ratzinger," writes Pecknold, the 'rationality' of the traditional notion of the *imago Dei* already implies its 'relationality.'"[50]

This relational logic of being marks the very structure of existence itself as act—as gift/given, and therefore as received—and is best exemplified on the ontological plane in the Marian posture of the *fiat* (which is an ontological posture before it is a volitional one). And it has a subjective-cognitional corollary, (and concomitant epistemology), best exemplified in the contemplative wonderment that she exhibited (see Luke 2:19, 51).

Because humans are constitutively relational, and because this (analogically) is the case for the entirety of the created order, a relational rationality is, in point of fact, more adequate to the task of coming to know reality as such. This saves the prioritization of man's rational faculty—the traditional seat of the *imago Dei*—and, overcomes the mechanistic and individualistic ontology of modernity, thereby affecting a certain broadening of reason,[51] a reason so capacious as to attend to reality according to the totality of its factors.[52]

---

49. Second Vatican Council, *Gaudium et spes*, no. 22.
50. Pecknold, "'Man Is by Nature a Social and Political Animal,'" 895.
51. See Benedict XVI, "Faith, Reason, and the University."
52. See Giussani et al., *Generating Traces in the History of the World*, 54.

Bibliography

Aquinas, Thomas. *Summa Theologiae*. Translated by the Fathers of the English Dominican Province. New York: Benzinger Brothers, 1947.

Augustine. *De Trinitate*. Edited by John E. Rotelle. Translated by Edmund Hill. Hyde Park, NY: New City, 1991.

Ayres, Lewis. *Augustine and the Trinity*. Cambridge: Cambridge University Press, 2010.

Balthasar, Hans Urs von. "On the Concept of Person." *Communio* 13.2 (1986) 18–26.

Barnes, Michel René. "Augustine in Contemporary Trinitarian Theology." *Theological Studies* 56.2 (1995) 237–50.

Benedict XVI, Pope. *Caritas in veritate: On Integral Human Development in Charity and Truth*. Vatican City: Libreria Editrice Vaticana, 2009.

———. "Faith, Reason, and the University: Memories and Reflections." http://w2.vatican.va/content/benedict-xvi/en/speeches/2006/september/documents/hf_ben-xvi_spe_20060912_university-regensburg.html.

Caldecott, Stratford. "The Marian Dimension of Existence." In *Being Holy in the World: Theology and Culture in the Thought of David L. Schindler*, edited by Nicholas J. Healy Jr. and D. C. Schindler, 281–94. Grand Rapids: Eerdmans, 2011.

———. *The Radiance of Being: Dimensions of Cosmic Christianity*. Tacoma, WA: Angelico, 2013.

Clarke, W. Norris. *Explorations in Metaphysics: Being-God-Person*. Notre Dame: University of Notre Dame Press, 1995.

———. *Person and Being*. Milwaukee: Marquette University Press, 1993.

———. "To Be Is to Be Substance-in-Relation." In *Metaphysics as Foundation: Essays in Honor of Ivor Leclerc*, edited by P. Bogaard and G. Treash, 164–83. Albany: State University of New York Press, 1993.

Dewey, John. *Reconstruction in Philosophy*. New York: Holt and Company, 1920.

Francis, Pope. *Laudato si': On Care for Our Common Home*. Vatican City: Libreria Editrice Vaticana, 2015.

Giussani, Luigi, et al. *Generating Traces in the History of the World: New Traces of the Christian Experience*. Montreal: McGill-Queen's, 2010.

Guardini, Romano. *The End of the Modern World*. Rev. ed. Wilmington, DE: ISI, 1998.

Hanby, Michael. *Augustine and Modernity*. London: Routledge, 2003.

———. "Augustine on Human Being." In *T&T Clark Companion to Augustine and Modern Theology*, edited by C. C. Pecknold and Tarmo Toom, 20–35. London: T. & T. Clark, 2013.

———. *No God, No Science: Theology, Cosmology, Biology*. Hoboken, NJ: Wiley-Blackwell, 2013.

John Paul II, Pope. *Fides et ratio: On the Relationship between Faith and Reason*. Vatican City: Libreria Editrice Vaticana, 1998.

———. *Man and Woman He Created Them: A Theology of the Body*. Translated by Michael Waldstein. Boston: Pauline Books & Media, 2006.

Kerr, Fergus. *Twentieth Century Catholic Theologians: From Neoscholasticism to Nuptial Mysticism*. Oxford: Blackwell, 2007.

Losinger, Anton. *Relative Autonomy: The Key to Understanding Vatican II*. New York: Lang, 1997.

Newton, William. "John Paul II and *Gaudium Et Spes* 22: His Use of the Text and His Involvement in Its Authorship." *Anthropotes* 24.2 (2008) 375–412.

Pabst, Adrian. *Metaphysics: The Creation of Hierarchy*. Grand Rapids: Eerdmans, 2012.

Paul VI, Pope. *Populorum progressio: On the Development of Peoples*. Vatican City: Libreria Editrice Vaticana, 1967.

Pecknold, C. C. "'Man Is by Nature a Social and Political Animal': Essential and Anti-Essentialist Relational Ontologies Revisited." *The Heythrop Journal* 57.6 (2016) 883–99.

Ratzinger, Joseph. "Concerning the Notion of Person in Theology." In *Joseph Ratzinger in Communio: Anthropology and Culture*, edited by David L. Schinder, translated by Michael Waldestein, 103–18. Grand Rapids: Eerdmans, 1990.

———. *Introduction to Christianity*. Translated by J. R. Foster. San Francisco: Ignatius, 2004.

Rowland, Tracey. "Theology and Culture." In *Being Holy in the World: Theology and Culture in the Thought of David L. Schindler*, edited by Nicholas J. Healy Jr. and D. C. Schindler, 55–88. Grand Rapids: Eerdmans, 2011.

Schindler, D. C. *Freedom from Reality: The Diabolical Character of Modern Liberty*. Notre Dame: University of Notre Dame Press, 2017.

Schindler, David L. "Being, Gift, Self-Gift: A Reply to Waldstein on Relationality and John Paul II's Theology of the Body (Part One)." *Communio* 42.2 (2015) 221–51.

———. "Being, Gift, Self-Gift: A Reply to Waldstein on Relationality and John Paul II's Theology of the Body (Part Two)." *Communio* 43.3 (2016) 409–83.

———. "Communio Ecclesiology and Liberalism." *The Review of Politics* 60.4 (1998) 775–86.

———. "'Disenchantment' and the End of Modern Civilization: The Symbolical, the Neutral, and the Diabolical." *New Polity* 1.2 (2020) 9–24.

———. *The Generosity of Creation*. Washington, DC: Humanum Academic, 2018.

———. "Grace and the Form of Nature and Culture." In *Catholicism and Secularization in America: Essays on Nature, Grace, and Culture*, edited by David L. Schindler, 10–30. Huntington, IN: Our Sunday Visitor, 1990.

———. *Heart of the World, Center of the Church: Communio Ecclesiology, Liberalism and Liberation*. Grand Rapids: Eerdmans, 1996.

———. "Kenneth Schmitz on Creation Ex Nihilo and the Metaphysics of Gift: A Reflection on the Occasion of His Becoming Emeritus Professor of Philosophy." https://www.johnpaulii.edu/files/Schindler_Presentation.pdf.

———. "Norris Clarke on Person, Being, and St. Thomas." *Communio: International Catholic Review* 20.3 (1993) 580–92.

———. *Ordering Love: Liberal Societies and the Memory of God*. Grand Rapids: Eerdmans, 2011.

———. "'We Are Not Our Own': Childhood and the Integrity of the Human in a Technological Age." https://humanumreview.com/articles/we-are-not-our-own-childhood-and-the-integrity-of-the-human-in-a-technological-age.

Schmitz, Kenneth L. "Created Receptivity and the Philosophy of the Concrete." *The Thomist* 61.3 (1997) 339–71.

———. *The Gift: Creation*. Milwaukee: Marquette University Press, 1982.

———. "The Geography of the Human Person." *Communio* 13.1 (1986) 27–48.

Second Vatican Council. *Gaudium et spes: Pastoral Constitution of the Church in the Modern World*. Vatican City: Libreria Editrice Vaticana, 1965.

Scola, Angelo. *The Nuptial Mystery*. Grand Rapids: Eerdmans, 2005.

Taylor, Michael. *The Foundations of Nature: Metaphysics of Gift for an Integral Ecological Ethic*. Euegene, OR: Cascade, 2020.

Walker, Adrian. "'Constitutive Relations': Towards a Spiritual Reading of *Physis*." In *Being Holy in the World: Theology and Culture in the Thought of David L. Schindler*, edited by Nicholas J. Healy Jr. and D. C. Schindler, 123–61. Grand Rapids: Eerdmans, 2011.

Williams, Rowan. "*Sapientia* and the Trinity: Reflections on the *De Trinitate*." *Augustiniana* 40.1/4 (1990) 317–32.

6

Dasein and Love

A Philosophical and Theological Reflection on Being and Anxiety

Lawrence Qummou

> "In him we live and move and have our being." (Acts 17:28)
>
> "In this love Being and *Dasein*, God and man, are one, wholly fused."
> (Hans Urs von Balthasar)

Martin Heidegger's attempt to recapture Being from its obscurity in Western philosophy and metaphysics more generally has intrigued theologians throughout the twentieth century and beyond.[1] Central to Heidegger's philosophical project is the rejection of the Cartesian subject—object dichotomy and a decisive move away from "substance

---

1. Beyond the works of famous twentieth century Catholic interlocutors such as Edith Stein, Erich Przywara, Karl Rahner, Edward Schillebeecx, Alasdair MacIntyre, Johann Baptist Metz, and Jean Luc-Marion, more recent engagements with Heidegger's thought include: Betz, "After Heidegger and Marion," 565–97; Orr, "Being and Timelessness," 114–31; Sweeney, *Sacramental Presence after Heidegger*; Wolfe, *Heidegger and Theology*; Fritz, "Catholic Theology and Heidegger," 850–61.

ontology," understood as any grounding of Being in a primordial category or essence prior to and separate from its existence. Heidegger's intention to analyze Being from within the historical and cultural condition of beings (as they find themselves) represents a move toward an existential understanding of what it means "to be." For theology to confront the radical historicity of "Being" espoused by Heidegger's thought, it must give an account of the relationship between concrete human experience and ontology, or as in the words of Joseph Ratzinger, it must answer the question: "How can history play a role in the moulding of being and when is it alien to being?"[2] Although recent Catholic interest in ontology has sought to revive a more dynamic understanding of Being patterned after the trinitarian relations,[3] this chapter will examine how contrasting theological and philosophical conceptions of Being result in divergent ways of interpreting concrete human experiences. It will do this by offering two distinct outlines: the hermeneutical ontology of Heidegger and the Christocentric understanding of Being present in the thought of Hans Urs von Balthasar. Following an outline of their respective ontologies, an insight into their interpretation of the experience of anxiety will be examined to discern the relationship between ontology and human experience. Notwithstanding their fundamental differences, both Heidegger and Balthasar share an affinity in philosophizing and theologizing from the vantage point of human experience and, as such, their reflection on human anxiety stems from a phenomenological construal of Being that opens up in the face of human finitude.

Heidegger: Hermeneutics and Ontology

Theological engagement with Martin Heidegger's philosophy has often centered upon his critique of metaphysics (onto-theology) and his influence on biblical hermeneutics more generally.[4] Heidegger's repositioning of hermeneutics from its classical definition as the interpretation of texts,

---

2. Ratzinger, *Principles of Catholic Theology*, 159. For an insight into the Christian influences on Heidegger's ontology see Baring, *Converts to the Real*, 85–116.

3. The recent translations of Ferdinand Ulrich's *Homo Abyssus* and Klaus Hemmerle's *Theses towards a Trinitarian Ontology*, have led to a recovery of interest in Trinitarian or relational conceptions of Being. A contemporary work in this vein is also to be found in Antonio Lopez's *Gift and the Unity of Being*.

4. For Heidegger's influence on biblical hermeneutics see Jeanrond, *Theological Hermeneutics*, 60–63.

language and symbols into a philosophical system aiming to explicate an understanding of Being more generally can be traced to his 1923 lecture series later published as *Ontology—The Hermeneutics of Facticity*. In this work, Heidegger outlines the fundamental ontology that will come to maturity in his 1927 magnum opus *Being and Time*. In his attempt to recover the meaning of "Being" from its obfuscation in the Western philosophical tradition, Heidegger employs a philosophical sensibility that rejects the Cartesian subject-object model of understanding human experience and instead seeks the analysis of concrete lived experience as the ground for ontological reflection. For Heidegger, the modern discipline of hermeneutics becomes deficient after its transformation into a strict methodological tool at the service of the human sciences. In contrast to the original meaning of Ἑρμηνείας (interpretation), which in its more classical usage referred to a more comprehensive notion of making known that which is concealed, modern hermeneutics, following the thought of Friedrich Schleiermacher and Wilhelm Dilthey, instead becomes reduced to what Heidegger calls an "art or technique of understanding."[5] In recentering and emphasizing the original meaning of hermeneutics, Heidegger attempts to demonstrate how interpretation itself is a primordial mode of Being. In this way, the human person does not connect meaning to experience in a deductive manner, but rather, the human person inhabits a world already replete with meaning and must seek to "disclose" that which is already there.[6] Thus existing in a world already furnished with meaning is one of the fundamental aspects of *Dasein*, Heidegger's term for existence as "being-there," a reference to the unique mode of existence tasked with understanding the Being of beings. In the introduction to *Being and Time*, Heidegger explains that, "*Dasein* is an entity which does not just occur among other entities. Rather it is ontically distinguished by the fact that, in its very Being, that Being is an issue for it."[7] In this way, *Dasein* can offer access into the nature of Being due to its "special distinctiveness" as having a pre-ontological familiarity, albeit vague, with Being itself that leads the fundamental inquiry.[8] Put

---

5. Heidegger, *Ontology*, 11.
6. Lafont, "Hermeneutics," 266.
7. Heidegger, *Being and Time*, 12.
8. Heidegger, *Being and Time*, 5. "If to interpret the meaning of Being becomes our task, Dasein is not only the primary entity to be interrogated; it is also that entity which already comports itself, in its Being towards what we are asking about when we ask this question. But in that case, the question of being is nothing other than the

another way, *Dasein's* intuitive understanding of the immediacy of Being from the outset propels it toward an authentic uncovering of what it means to be. Heidegger describes the basis for the priority of *Dasein* (as opposed to other entities) against the backdrop of the ontic/ontological distinction:[9]

> The first priority is an ontical one: Dasein is an entity whose Being has the determinate character of existence. The second priority is an ontological one: Dasein is in itself "ontological," because existence is thus determinative for it. But with equal primordiality, Dasein also possesses—as constitutive for its understanding of existence—an understanding of the Being of all entities as a character other than its own. Dasein has therefore a third priority over providing the ontic-ontological condition for the possibility of any ontologies.[10]

It is in virtue of this distinction that Heidegger's hermeneutical project is defined as an existential analysis of *Dasein*, understood as an inquiry into the fundamental way in which ordinary, everyday concrete life is experienced by the human person, understood as being-in-the-world.[11] The methodology for this analysis is a modification of the phenomenology made famous by Heidegger's teacher Edmund Husserl. Husserl's intention to go back to "the things themselves" centers upon the concept of intentionality, understood as the mental activity by which human consciousness is always directed towards objects of perception. The study of these intentional mental states is made possible by a "bracketing" of the world that lies beyond what is perceived in consciousness. Heidegger's critique of this particular phenomenological method rests upon his claim that Husserl's approach positions intentionality as prior to, in a transcendental sense, actual experiences of relation in the world.[12] In his judg-

---

radicalization of an essential tendency-of-being which belongs to Dasein itself—the pre ontological understanding of Being." Heidegger, *Being and Time*, 15.

9. What Heidegger refers to as *ontisch* (ontic) and *ontologisch* (ontological) can be understood as the necessary distinction between the concrete properties or characteristics of everyday life of entities (ontic) with the overarching reality of "Being." See Slaby, "Ontic," 542–46.

10. Heidegger, *Being and Time*, 14.

11. For a lucid description of *Dasein* see Barrett, *Irrational Man*, 218–19.

12. Richardson, *Heidegger*, 71–73; Carman, "The Principle of Phenomenology," 101. Heidegger famously notes in *Being and Time*, 249, that "the scandal of philosophy is not that a proof of the external world has never been given, but that such proofs are expected."

ment, Husserl's phenomenology lacks a necessary contextual reflexivity and attempts to formulate itself without regard to the mode of being of the entity.[13] Ultimately, Heidegger's charge is that Husserl's phenomenology still operates in the subject-object framework by prioritizing conscious mental states as separate and prior to concrete action in lived experience. Hubert Dreyfus notes that Heidegger's use of the word *Verhalten*, translated as "comportment," changes intentionality from its theoretical usage in Husserl to a more directed practical understanding of the way in which human beings relate to things in their everyday experiences.[14] Thus the basis for the human person's directedness towards things is not to be found exclusively in consciousness but rather in *Dasein*.[15]

With this modification of intentionality as grounded in concrete experience, Heidegger's phenomenology can be understood as an uncovering of Being itself, and as such phenomenology and ontology never gain a purely observational vantage point separate from one another in his thought:

> Ontology and phenomenology are not two distinct philosophical disciplines, among others. These terms characterise philosophy itself with regard to its object and its way of treating that object. Philosophy is universal phenomenological ontology, and takes its departure point from the hermeneutic of Dasein.[16]

Crucially, the analysis of *Dasein*, with its examination into the concrete experiences of the human person as already embedded in a web of meaningful signification, shapes Heidegger's understanding of the world. This can be seen in the notion of "Being-in-the-world," Heidegger's usage of "-in," refers not to the spatial location of entities in a place understood as "world" but rather the recognition that being itself entails sets of unavoidable relations with others and one's surroundings.[17] It is for this reason that Heidegger turns to the everyday actions of the human person, (including the examples of developing skills such as playing the piano or the use of equipment/tools), as a way to demonstrate the purposiveness that permeates existence prior to theoretical reflection. The notion of "towards-which," "in-order-to" and "for-the-sake-of" are technical

---

13. Dreyfus, *Being-in-the-World*, 52.
14. Dreyfus, *Being-in-the-World*, 51.
15. Dreyfus, *Being-in-the-World*, 52.
16. Heidegger, *Being and Time*, 38.
17. Dreyfus, *Being-in-the-World*, 40–41.

terms employed to articulate the structure of understanding that will enable disclosure or "uncovering" for *Dasein*.[18] This operates to negate the modern philosophical subject-object schema which Heidegger identifies as the chief culprit in the loss of a proper understanding of Being.[19] Since both "being-in" and "being-with" constitute a fundamental mode of being for *Dasein*, the notion of a transcendent subject able to ground Being in some principle or substance becomes redundant. For Heidegger then, the existence of a bare subject without a world is never given to us in phenomena and crucially, neither is the notion of an existent "I" without the presence of the "Other." Hence, human persons do not simply exist in the world as individual subjects. Rather, *Dasein's* mode as "being-in-the world" presupposes a world that Heidegger notes, "I share with Others."[20] Importantly, this interconnected world filled with significance is able to be shared by *Dasein* with the "other" not as the relation of subject to object but rather, as subject to subject by virtue of an understanding of language as that which enables the world to be disclosed.[21] This ability for language to be communicative implies an already shared contextual basis for meaning which further negates the subject-object paradigm by affirming that signification has already contextually been "deposited" prior to any concerted interpretation by either party.[22] Hence to see language as expressing this prior understanding of identity, Heidegger is able to frame the concept of understanding and interpretation as codetermining of the other, in the so called "hermeneutical circle."[23] Since all interpretation necessarily presupposes understanding, Heidegger introduces the notion of the threefold "fore-structure," consisting of "fore-having" (the general understanding of the whole or a grasp of its totality), "fore-sight" (a particular perspective which allows one to see in advance appropriate ways of interpretation), and "fore-conception" (a definite way of

---

18. Cooper, *Thinkers of Our Time*, 14.
19. Cooper, *Thinkers of Our Time*, 27–28.
20. Heidegger, *Being and Time*, 119.
21. Dreyfus, *Being-in-the-World*, 155.
22. Under the subheading "Idle Talk," Heidegger notes, "The way things have been expressed or spoken out is such that in the totality of contexts of signification into which it has been articulated, it preserves an understanding of the disclosed world and therewith, equiprimordially, an understanding of the Dasein-with of Others and of one's own Being-in." Heidegger, *Being and Time*, 168.
23. Jeanrond, *Theological Hermeneutics*, 5–6.

conceiving either fixed or with modifications) to undergird all interpretation.[24] Heidegger acknowledges the circularity of the nature of interpretation as outlined but notes that

> The "circle" in understanding belongs to the structure of meaning, and the latter phenomenon is rooted in the existential constitution of Dasein—that is, in the understanding which interprets. An entity for which, as Being-in-the-world, its Being is itself an issue, has, ontologically, a circular structure.[25]

Since *Dasein* always finds itself in a context shaped by temporality and culture, Heidegger must ground the fore-structure of interpretation and understanding in a fixed ontological concept capable of accounting for *Dasein's* mode of being as fundamentally self-interpreting. We will now see how this fundamental ontological concept will be crucial in Heidegger's understanding of anxiety.

Anxiety and Authentic Being

Heidegger identifies care (*Sorge*) as the way in which *Dasein* moves towards a unifying sense of meaning or wholeness in response to being "thrown" into the world.[26] Care in the ontological sense is the structure of totality that enables *Dasein* to authentically interpret Being and as such Heidegger speaks of care as "the being of *Dasein*."[27] Another way to express this is the fact that one's own finite existence is always looming in the background of everyday life, and as such *Dasein's* concern for the day when its own existence will end is inescapable. Hence the specter of death is the precondition for care. Finite existence encounters itself as determined by "facticity" (being bound up in its own destiny) and hence the range of possibilities available to select from are always in the service of this primordial understanding of care. As we have seen, in Heidegger's thought, existence is characterized as always already "in" a world full

---

24. Heidegger, *Being and Time*, 153: "In every understanding of the world, existence is understood with it, and vice versa. All interpretation, moreover, operates in the fore-structure, which we have already categorised. Any interpretation which is to contribute to understanding, must already have understood what is to be interpreted." See also Hoy, "Heidegger and the Hermeneutic Turn," 191; Dreyfus, *Being-in-the-World*, 199.

25. Heidegger, *Being and Time*, 154.

26. Richardson, *Heidegger*, 106.

27. Heidegger, *Being and Time*, 197.

of significance. In this way, meaning or significance in the ontological sense is to be found in the possibilities that confront *Dasein* in everyday existence and the movement towards becoming that one chooses, what Heidegger calls "Being-ahead-of-itself."[28] The reality that at some point, the very nature of existence as movement towards becoming will cease, results in the anxiety induced by the opening of "non-being" into Being.[29] Thus the object of dread that accompanies anxiety is nothing less than the absolute and inescapable awareness of finitude that haunts *Dasein*. Anxiety then points not to an entity-in-the-world but rather is the realization that

> The world can offer nothing more, and neither can *Dasein*-with of Others. Anxiety thus takes away from *Dasein* the possibility of understanding itself, as it falls, in terms of the "world" and the way things have been publicly interpreted.[30]

It is crucial to note that for Heidegger, this mood of anxiety, characterized by the "sinking away" of all the contextual facets of Being leaving nothing but one's bare existence provides the opportunity for the authenticity of Being, the individualization of *Dasein*.[31] In anticipating one's eventual death—what Heidegger claims is the only non-relational facet of Being—one is left with a clear path to gain a particular vantage point of the wholeness of one's life.[32] Anxiety then as a precondition for authentic Being is linked to the resoluteness with which one confronts the inevitability of death. Thus, in confronting the temporal nature of Being, that existence will one day end, the authentic self takes stock of their "wholeness" and then in a "moment of vision" is able to align itself with a sense of purpose and solidarity with others in the same situation by remembering the past.[33] For Heidegger then, the anxiety that accompanies the contingency of Being opens up the space for a continuous thread of past, present, and future meaning. In throwing into view the individuality of finite existence, anxiety enables *Dasein* to turn away from a "fleeing" of

---

28. Heidegger, *Being and Time*, 236.
29. Barrett, *Irrational Man*, 226.
30. Heidegger, *Being and Time*, 232. See also Richardson, *Heidegger*, 143.
31. Heidegger, *Being and Time*, 305–6.
32. Heidegger, *Being and Time*, 284. This mode of Being is described as "Being-towards-the-end."
33. Heidegger, *Being and Time*, 442–43. See also, Hoffman, "Death, Time, History," 234.

death and towards authentic existence by aligning oneself with others in the past who have found themselves in a similar situation. In light of Heidegger's temporal grounding of Being and its subsequent consequences for how human anxiety is to be understood, we now look at an alternate grounding of Being in Hans Urs von Balthasar's theology.

Being and Love: Von Balthasar

As Oliver Davies notes, traces of the notion *Seinsvergessenheit*—the term used by Heidegger to describe the "forgetfulness of Being"—can be found throughout the work of the Swiss theologian Hans Urs von Balthasar.[34] Like Heidegger, Balthasar acknowledges the centrality of the question posed by the relationship of Being in relation to beings and meditates upon this question throughout his theological *opus*. Although considered non-systematic in his methodology, Balthasar's theological approach can be described as a meditation on the transcendental properties of Being—at their core ultimately trinitarian—through the lens of Jesus Christ, who as the absolute singularity of all that is, manifests God's love in all of reality.[35] In this way, the biblical passages "God is love" (1 John 4:8), and "He is before all things, and in him all things hold together" (Col 1:17), can be seen as the scriptural pillars upon which Balthasar's theology is constructed. The implications of both passages in relation to an understanding of Being can be found in Balthasar's "trilogy," primarily the 1969 seven volume *Herrlichkeit*, translated in English as *The Glory of the Lord*.[36]

Before exploring his ontology, it is necessary to comment on Balthasar's understanding of the relationship between philosophy and theology. In an essay titled, *On the tasks of Catholic Philosophy in our Time*, Balthasar affirms the material separation between revelation (the light

---

34. Davies, "Von Balthasar and the Problem of Being" 11–17.

35. In reference to his work, Balthasar notes, "From first to last, the trilogy is keyed to the transcendental qualities of being, in particular to the analogy between their status and form in creaturely being, on the one hand, and in Divine Being, on the other." Balthasar, *Theo-Logic*, 1. See Oullet, "The Message of Balthasar's Theology to Modern Theology," 277. Oullet points to Balthasar's grounding of love as stemming "above all from the unsurpassable figure of Jesus Christ, who brings in himself the objective evidence of God's revelation as absolute love."

36. Balthasar's sixteen volume trilogy was published between 1961 and 1987 and consists of *Herrlichkeit* (Glory of the Lord Vols. I–VII), *Theodramatik* (Theo-Drama Vols. I–V), *Theologik* (Theo-Logic Vols. I–III) and *Epilogue*.

of faith) and human reason while underlining their symbiotic relationship and their shared objective of grasping ultimate meaning. Balthasar's claim is that any worldly thought system worthy to be called philosophy must of its nature be orientated towards that which is absolute and thus both theology and philosophy share a common "theological *eros*."[37] For Balthasar, any ultimate search towards a totality of meaning must by necessity break through "objects of philosophy and into the sphere of the divine Logos."[38] This is not to say that the integrity of each sphere is compromised, but rather that any philosophy that attempts to arrive at ultimate meaning outside of a connection with the divine Logos is impotent. This stance demonstrates Balthasar's shared understanding of the relationship between nature and grace expressed by Henri de Lubac.[39] The intrinsic relationship between nature and grace does not mean that philosophy as a distinct discipline has nothing to offer Christian thought. In reference to both Clement of Alexandria and Augustine, Balthasar notes that Christian thinking has always identified and utilized the latent theological and supernatural motifs in human wisdom to better explicate Christian teaching. Thus the purpose for the theologian is to identify how philosophical thought can be ordered towards the all-embracing totality of the Christ event.[40] Consistent with his emphasis upon the importance of love, Balthasar stresses that in order to identify any living fruit within systems of thought, one must genuinely seek to understand and approach philosophy with charity: "The will to understanding is love, and this is why no true and fruitful thinking is possible outside love."[41] From this we can glean both the totalizing incarnational foundation of Balthasar's thought and his emphasis upon love as the core in his theological articulation of Being.

Balthasar's notes that the wonder of Being is both the fundamental task of metaphysics and the beginning of all philosophical reflection.[42] This miracle of Being finds its basis in the impulse to answer the question of existence raised by the self-evident distinction between that which exists, "beings," and that anything should exist at all, Being. It is in grappling

---

37. Balthasar, "On the Tasks of Catholic Philosophy," 152.
38. Balthasar, "On the Tasks of Catholic Philosophy," 154.
39. Boersma, *Nouvelle Théologie and Sacramental Ontology*, 134.
40. Balthasar, "On the Tasks of Catholic Philosophy," 154–58.
41. Balthasar, "On the Tasks of Catholic Philosophy," 163.
42. Balthasar, *Glory of the Lord V*, 614.

with this distinction—articulated as the "real difference" between *esse* and *essentia* in Thomas Aquinas and later expressed in Heidegger's ontological difference—that Balthasar seeks to address in his Christian ontology. Balthasar's ontological reflections center upon two motifs: the relational character of the transcendental properties of Being—grounded above all in trinitarian love—and Christ as the concretization of the analogy of Being that unites the finite nature of created being with God.[43] As we will see, the hinge upon which this entire theological sensibility hangs is the unity between the divine and human natures in the God-man Jesus Christ. That the person of Christ is the focal point of any understanding of creaturely being leads Balthasar to question whether a better description for his understanding of Being is that of a "meta-anthropology" as opposed to a metaphysics.[44]

Balthasar's exposition begins with a four-fold experiential reflection that confronts the human person in relation to being.[45] The first of these four distinctions is the initial apprehension of existence itself. Balthasar refers to this as a "permitted entry" in that, we come to a realization of our being not immediately but rather only in a moment of contact with the "other" that in turn illuminates the self's own existence as distinct. This wonderous apprehension, understood as "non-necessity," leads to a questioning of existence in that one is aware that one's existence could have been otherwise: "Why it should have been me, I do not know."[46] The second experiential distinction is the acknowledgment of the shared relationship to existence common to other beings; that we all find ourselves in this particular predicament in relation to being, and that irrespective of how many different existents there are, being itself is inexhaustible:

---

43. Scola, *Hans Urs von Balthasar*, 26.

44. Balthasar, *My Work*, 92. See also Bieler, "Meta-Anthropology and Christology," 129–46; Scola, *Hans Urs von Balthasar*, 26.

45. Balthasar references this under the sub-heading "A. The Site of Glory in Metaphysics 1. The Miracle of Being and the Fourfold Distinction" in *The Glory of the Lord V*. He interchanges between "differences," "stages" and "distinctions" in his treatment of approaching being.

46. Balthasar refers to the awakening of the self via a relationship with the other: "Its 'I' [the child] awakens in the experience of a 'Thou': in its mother's smile through which it learns that it is contained, affirmed and loved in a relationship which is incomprehensively encompassing, already actual, sheltering and nourishing." Balthasar, *Glory of the Lord V*, 615–16. See also Schindler, "Metaphysics within the Limits of Phenomenology," 249.

> And then comes the second insight: we have all been permitted entry. Our mother too. And the animals with which I play. There is much that is real, and yet Being overarches everything, sublime and serene; nothing of all this had to be as it is.[47]

Following this, Balthasar's third stage is the notion that, given the fact that Being receives actuality exclusively in the existent, any account of the difference between essence and existence cannot find its derivation from Being itself.[48] Hence, to equate being as itself the source of all instantiations of itself in the existent, as a type of creator, would be to either relegate beings to simply a deficient expression of Being, or to locate the perfection of Being in the existents themselves, rendering being itself a projection of human thought devoid of any ontological content. As D. C. Schindler notes, the position one is left with is either to "absolutize being or absolutize beings."[49] Balthasar asks rhetorically, "Is the permission to be (existence), the being given entry, a beginning both for me and for Being?" It is here, in this third reflection, in this inability to ground any coherent absolutizing principle of Being, that Balthasar moves towards the necessity of the fourth difference, that between God and the world. The ontological dilemma is thus exposed to the kenotic nature of God's love as the key to unlocking this relationship between Being and beings. Thus, in contrast to philosophical systems that seek to "essentialize" Being, including Heidegger's project of grounding Being within itself, Balthasar notes that Christianity of necessity must reject any "essentializing of Being," but rather allow Being to oscillate or "hover" between non-existence and existence so as to preserve the absolute character of God's freedom to give being:

> The consequence is that the grounding in God of this Being which does not depend upon any necessity, points to an *ultimate freedom* which neither Being (as non-subsistent) could have, nor the existent entity (since it always finds itself as already

---

47. Balthasar, *Glory of the Lord* V, 635. See also Davies, "Von Balthasar and the Problem of Being," 12.

48. Balthasar, *Glory of the Lord* V, 623–24. "The *indifferentia* of the abundance which is characteristic of the Being of the existent fundamentally contradicts any form of planning, located within Being, in order to actualise itself in substance through a specific ascending sequence of stages of essential forms, which contain it first as 'vessels' and then (as Heidegger says) finally shepherd it. For the plans lie in the entity, not in Being, however true it may be that there are no entities which do not participate in Being."

49. Schindler, "Metaphysics within the Limits of Phenomenology," 250.

constituted in its own essentiality). And so on the one hand, the freedom of non-subsisting Being can be secured in its "glory" in the face of all that exists only if it is grounded in a subsisting freedom of absolute Being, which is God; and so, on the other hand, the dignity of an essential form evades being threatened by the encompassing act of Being and thus being swallowed up and devoured as an invalid "stage of Being" only if its valid contour can be referred back to a sovereign and absolute imagination or power of creation.[50]

The description of Being as secured by "glory" is in reference to fact that Balthasar, following in the thought of Ferdinand Ulrich, construes the very constitution of Being as the abundance or "ontological wealth" of God's Being freely emptied out in an act of love as pure gift.[51] In the free gifting of his infinite Being to beings, Being itself is thus both paradoxically "fullness" and also "poverty" in that "He knows no holding on to Himself."[52] Thus the implication of the pouring out of Being understood as a kenotic "gifting" extends to the reality of created being in the duality of "fullness" and "poverty." It is this paradoxical nature of God's donation of existence that is to be the paradigmatic lens through which creaturely being can live out Christ's exhortation: "For whoever would save his life will lose it, and whoever loses his life for my sake will find it" (Matt 16:25). Balthasar is able to characterize the fundamental aspect of Being as love in his affirmation of the "non-subsistence" of Being which in turn points to "gift and reception" as the primordial architecture of Being.[53] This is manifested firstly in the trinitarian relationship of love between the divine persons and, by extension, the created order. In other words, since Being itself is an expression of donation and reception in the Trinity, its manifestation in the created order culminates in the creature's love for both God and neighbor.[54]

---

50. Balthasar, *Glory of the Lord V*, 625.

51. Balthasar *Glory of the Lord V*, 625. An account of the influence of Ferdinand Ulrich on Balthasar's understanding of Being can be found in Betz's "Toward a More Catholic Metaphysics," 109–33.

52. Balthasar, *Glory of the Lord V*, 626; See also, Bieler, "*Analogia Entis* as an Expression of Love," 314–37.

53. Balthasar, *Epilogue*, 59. See also Bieler, "Meta-Anthropology and Christology," 143.

54. For a brief exposition of how Balthasar expresses the Trinitarian relationship of love between the divine persons, see Scola, *Hans Urs von Balthasar*, 63.

The archetype for this manifestation of love as central to Being is the person of Jesus Christ the God-man, understood by Balthasar as the "concrete" *analogia entis*. The analogy of Being as expressed by both Erich Przywara and Ulrich is appropriated by Balthasar to navigate the ontological difference without collapsing an understanding of Being into either univocity or equivocity.[55] In contrast to both univocity and equivocity, analogy points to a mode of thought able to express the distinction yet relation of the finite to the infinite, what can be seen as the seemingly unbridgeable abyss between the divine and created natures.[56] Far from being a philosophical abstraction however, Balthasar identifies Christ as the analogical bridge between God and creation. In Christ's person, the unification of the divine and human natures represents the coming together or "final proportion" between God and man.[57] The consequence of this is that Christ's entry into the analogy—as both particular in his Incarnation and universal as the Divine *Logos*—grounds the relationship between beings and Being and enables creaturely being to grasp God's love not in theoretical abstraction but in the intimacy of personal relation. In reference to Balthasar's appropriation of Christ as the concrete analogy, Schindler notes,

> The personal meaning he gives to the ontological difference is that of love. In other words, the revelation of Christ invites us, and indeed enables us, to view the reciprocity of principles that constitute worldly being as a dramatic image of the trinitarian exchange of love. When we do so, we come to see that the ultimate meaning of being is love, and therefore that love has an ontological weight, the density of reality.[58]

In this way, the appearance of trinitarian love in the person of Jesus Christ represents the very foundation on which Being as an inescapable mystery

55. Betz, "Toward a More Catholic Metaphysics," 111–12. Balthasar's understanding of Przywara's rendering of the *analogia entis* can be found in his work on Karl Barth, *The Theology of Karl Barth*. See also Balthasar, *A Theology of History*, 29.

56. Balthasar, *Theo-Drama III*, 136, 220. Adrian J. Walker notes that "The *analogia entis* is thus for Balthasar a relationship of creature to God such that the former is similar to the latter (both by way of an 'analogy of attribution' and an 'analogy of proportionality,' which are really two sides of the same analogical coin)—but within a greater dissimilarity that clearly underscores the creatureliness of the creature and the free transcendence of the Creator, *Hans Urs von Balthasar as Master of Theological Renewal*, 21.

57. Balthasar, *Theo-Drama III*, 137.

58. Schindler, "Ever Ancient, Ever New," 46.

becomes intelligible to creaturely existence. In his concretization and action in history, Christ manifests the giving away of God's love which can only be perceived and recognized according to Balthasar in the form of a "human spirit, as it is accomplished in man through God's loving grace."[59] Crucially, Christ as the channel to God's love and thus of the meaning of creaturely existence in its totality must never be separated from his Passion. Balthasar is emphatic in interpreting Christ as the paradigm of all existence only within the context of "the Hour" whereby Christ's obedience to the will of the Father in his death becomes the revelatory highpoint of the depth of God's love for creation.[60] This has implications in the way in which Balthasar will treat the existential reality of anxiety and death in relation to creaturely being.

Anxiety and Faith

In his short book *The Christian and Anxiety*, Balthasar notes that the identification of human anxiety begins in the inadequacy of human cognition to make sense of the ontological difference. Balthasar states that the same light (abstract thought) that enables us to grasp the notion of Being also "spreads to the same extent the night of meaninglessness and incomprehensibility."[61] Thus while anxiety is to be construed as the dread of "nothingness," starting from the difference between contingency and transcendence, its character is ultimately theological. For Balthasar, the root cause of anxiety is the space opened by the alienation of the human person from God.[62] In freely choosing to move away from God's love, Adam's disobedience heralds the permanent fixture of anxiety in the human condition. Strikingly however, the specter of anxiety that plagues the void of alienation is not extinguished with the coming of Christ into history. Balthasar notes that "God is present in the unfelt fullness, as fullness in the void."[63] This is not to say that God has not united himself to creation in the Incarnation but rather that the core of Christianity is precisely the interplay of the theological virtues of faith, hope, and love that is able to say "Yes" to God in his "invisibility" and thus to surrender human anxiety

---

59. Balthasar, *Love Alone Is Credible*, 42.
60. Balthasar, *Love Alone Is Credible*, 45–46.
61. Balthasar, *The Christian and Anxiety*, 71.
62. Balthasar, *The Christian and Anxiety*, 76.
63. Balthasar, *The Christian and Anxiety*, 76.

into the fullness of God's totality.[64] This can be interpreted as an offering of the reality of human anxiety into God's empowering love:

> When God bestows human suffering, including Christian anxiety, it is viewed from his perspective, fundamentally as an intensification of light and joy, a "darkness bright as day," because it is suffering out of joy, anxiety out of exultation: it is a sign of God's ever-greater confidence in the one who believes. And what experientially seems constricting and frightening to the believer is in truth enlarging, a fruitful *dilatatio* of the birth canal, an interior trembling that expands faith, hope and love.[65]

Christ as the central bridge between transcendence and contingency also comes to the fore in the finite character of Being. Balthasar notes that in death, the sense of human meaning seems to evaporate and the nature of our existence as unavoidably finite becomes clear.[66] Thus, the anxiety that comes to the surface in man's realization of the paradox between definitive meaning and transitory existence finds shelter in the person of Jesus through his salvific act. In this way, Christ's overcoming of death on the cross acts as the bridge between the inescapable shadow of anxiety hanging over human existence and the all-embracing concern of the Creator for his creation. Thus, the concrete human experience of anxiety solidifies the foundation of Being as love. That is, if creaturely Being is constituted primordially as the outpouring of God's love, the death and resurrection of Christ crystallizes the reality of trinitarian love in a concrete act of history which is thus able to transform creaturely death into what Balthasar calls a "parable of God" by imprinting trinitarian love (understood as self-abandonment) into worldly death.[67]

The Comfort of Being: Transcendence and Nothingness

Considering this, a further question arises: in what sense can Balthasar's theological reflection present a more coherent and comforting account of human anxiety than the approach offered by Heidegger? The logic of this comparison lies in the fact that, notwithstanding their fundamental differences in approach, both Heidegger and Balthasar locate the source

64. Balthasar, *The Christian and Anxiety*, 76.
65. Balthasar, *The Christian and Anxiety*, 78.
66. Balthasar, *Life out of Death*, 33.
67. Balthasar, *Life out of Death*, 71.

of anxiety in the suffocating presence of the ontological difference.⁶⁸ This seemingly unbridgeable gulf between the finite and contingent nature of beings on the one hand and the infinite and mysterious transcendent character of Being on the other, forces the human person into a deeper reflection about their own existence. Similarly, for both thinkers, anxiety exhibits a certain impulse towards movement, a thrust towards a greater understanding of what it means to be. For Heidegger specifically, it is only through the "unsettledness" induced by anxiety that one is able to step outside the "entangled absorption" in the world and realize the range of possibilities on offer that constitute *Dasein*'s potential to live authentically.⁶⁹ This can be understood as living life on one's own terms, rejecting conformism, and embracing choices for one's own life against the backdrop of the impending nothingness of non-existence. For Balthasar, the experience of alienation highlighted in anxiety points towards a void that can only be filled by faith in the outpouring of God's love in the person of Christ and his Passion. In both accounts, the experience of anxiety uncovers something profound yet often obscured about the human condition; a certain insight into a picture of the "wholeness" of one's existence that cannot be grasped by a strictly propositional conception of truth. Thus, Heidegger's retrieval of the Greek notion of *aletheia* (unconcealment) and Balthasar's understanding of analogy share a similar role in articulating the way in which the human person comes to understand Being.⁷⁰ An insight into the reality of Being is not attained by correspondence between propositions and fact but rather via the uncovering of hidden realities in human experience.

It is here, however, that Heidegger and Balthasar's differing conceptions of Being result in divergent readings of anxiety. Heidegger's fundamental ontology, while acknowledging the mysteriousness of Being, offers no fixed basis to its source beyond its immanence in *Dasein*. Anxiety then, while highlighting the chilling temporality of existence, may succeed in encouraging one to break free from an inauthentic life, in this

---

68. Balthasar, *The Christian and Anxiety*, 69. See also Cirelli, "Facing the Abyss," 706–8.

69. Heidegger, *Being and Time*, 343.

70. Wrathall, "Truth and the Essence of Truth," 242–43. Heidegger's use of the Greek *aletheia* describes the way in which the world is necessarily unconcealed or opened before us prior to any conception of truth understood as the correspondence between predicate and reality. Heidegger posits this "unconcealment" as the primordial basis for any derivative notion of truth. A comprehensive account of Heidegger's use of truth as unconcealment can be found in Dahlstrom, *Heidegger's Concept of Truth*.

sense a type of herd mentality distracted by "everydayness," yet it still fails to offer any compelling account for the meaning of existence, why is there something rather than nothing? What anxiety does offer, in Heidegger's thought, is confirmation that no single choice or project can provide any meaningful content in one's life overall. Rather, the resoluteness that anxiety cultivates in this confirmation provides a framework for *Dasein* to choose an authentic life consistent with the mode of being-towards-death. Only in grasping death as one's own, the only non-relational aspect of Being, can one understand how to live. In this way, what marks authenticity is simply the acceptance of the range of possibilities in any given situation. Dreyfus describes this in the following way:

> any possibility can provide a unique occasion on which to face anxiety and, having abandoned hope of "eternal" meaning or satisfaction, do whatever I do in the situation impeccably and passionately because it demands to be done.[71]

Thus, faced with the reality of finite existence, *Dasein*, in glimpsing the "nothingness" of Being, is forced to retreat inwards towards the shelter of an existence aware of its own mortality. This notion of Being's utter immanence, ultimately locked inside itself, relying upon beings to fill its contents, is specifically critiqued by Balthasar in *The Glory of the Lord*.[72]

In contrast to this, Balthasar's biblically informed understanding of the relationship between anxiety and sin and his understanding of the Christ as the concrete analogy of Being places the experience of anxiety within a metaphysical framework that accounts for the transcendence of Being. In this way, the connection between Being as "creatureliness" and the analogy of Being enables the human person to find comfort and dependence in the love of God as creator. Thus, by interpreting existence through the prism of "gift," the inescapable reality of anxiety on this side of the eschaton can be understood as a signpost pointing toward the font of all existence. Although in the fallen state, this yearning to comprehend God as the infinite source of all existence can only ever be partial, Christ's

---

71. Dreyfus, *Being-in-the-World*, 339.

72. Balthasar, *Glory of the Lord V*, 447–50. In Balthasar's estimation, Heidegger errs in rescinding the proper distinction between "limitless non-subsisting" and "limitless subsisting Being." In this way, Heidegger's ontology replaces the classical Christian understanding of God as the source of Being with a purely immanent preconceptual notion of Being that only illuminates itself in the existent. Being then as "nothingness" takes on the apophatic characteristics of the Christian doctrine of God and ultimately collapses the ontological distinction.

incarnation provides creaturely existence with the impetus to reach out toward the infinite. Thus, Balthasar notes,

> Whereas by venturing to let go of everything, the Christian takes a stand beyond finitude and comes into the limitlessness of God, Christ, in order to make this act possible and to be its source, has dared to emerge from the infinitude of the "form" of God and "did not think equality with God a thing to be grasped," has dared to set out into the limitation and emptiness of time.[73]

Ultimately, Balthasar's ontology and interpretation of anxiety, while affirming the tension between the finite and the infinite, offers the hope of encounter with the God-man Jesus Christ. In the sobering moments of anxiety, rather than lamenting on the nothingness of Being and retreating inwards to formulate meaning, Balthasar's theology offers an expression of Being grounded in the outpouring of God's infinite love, existence itself.

Conclusion

If the question of Being is fundamental for both philosophy and theology, it is by virtue of its position as the starting point of all human reflection into the meaning of existence. In the approach of Heidegger's existential analysis of *Dasein*, the rejection of any derivation of Being from an external or prior principle outside of existence forces his ontology of hermeneutics to ground the meaning of Being within the very constitution of Being itself. This ultimately groundless notion of Being interprets human anxiety as the necessary dread that enables human existence to move toward authenticity and resolutely view temporal existence as a connected thread of meaning tying the individual existent within the context of the world as given. In this way, the reality of death is not to be ignored or avoided but rather, kept in view as an emancipatory tool of Being, saving us from the obscurity of everyday existence. In contrast to this, Hans Urs von Balthasar presents the mystery of Being against the backdrop of two primordial moments: The notion of Being as the gift of love poured out from the very nature of God as creator and the further culmination of this outpouring of love in the Incarnation and Passion of Jesus Christ. Balthasar thus construes anxiety as the reality of human freedom but within the context of God's unification with creaturely being

---

73. Balthasar, *The Christian and Anxiety*, 77.

in the God-man Jesus Christ. In this way, the reality of anxiety is a moment of trust and dependence upon God who as the source of all Being and as "love" seeks to draw his creation back to his embrace.

Bibliography

Balthasar, Hans Urs von. *The Christian and Anxiety*. Translated by Dennis D. Martin and Michael J. Miller. San Francisco: Ignatius, 2000.

———. *Convergences: To the Source of Christian Mystery*. Translated by E. A. Nelson. San Francisco: Ignatius, 1983.

———. *Epilogue*. Translated by Edward T. Oakes. San Francisco: Ignatius, 2004.

———. *Glory of the Lord, a Theological Aesthetics*. Vol. 1, *Seeing the Form*. Edited by Joseph Fessio and John Riches. Translated by Erasmo Leiva-Merikakis. London: T. & T. Clark, 2001.

———. *Glory of the Lord, a Theological Aesthetics*. Vol. 5, *The Realm of Metaphysics in the Modern Age*. Edited by Brian McNeil and John Riches. Translated by Oliver Davies et al. London: T. & T. Clark, 1991.

———. *Life out of Death: Meditations on the Paschal Mystery*. Translated by Martina Stöckl. San Francisco: Ignatius, 2012.

———. *Love Alone Is Credible*. Translated by D. C. Schindler. San Francisco: Ignatius, 2004.

———. *My Work: In Retrospect*. San Francisco: Ignatius, 1993.

———. "On the Task of Christian Philosophy in our Time." *Communio* 20 (1993) 147–67.

———. *Theo-Drama: Theological Dramatic Theory*. Vol. 3, *Dramatis Personae: Persons in Christ*. Translated by Graham Harrison. San Francisco: Ignatius, 1992.

———. *Theo-Logic: Truth of the World: Theological Logical Theory*. Vol. 1. Translated by Adrian J. Walker. San Francisco: Ignatius, 2000.

———. *A Theological Anthropology*. New York: Sheed and Ward, 1967.

———. *A Theology of History*. San Francisco: Ignatius, 1994.

———. *The Theology of Karl Barth: Exposition and Interpretation*. Translated by Edward T. Oakes. San Francisco: Ignatius, 1992.

Baring, Edward. *Converts to the Real: Catholicism and the Making of Continental Philosophy*. Cambridge: Harvard University Press, 2019.

Barrett, William. *Irrational Man: A Study in Existential Philosophy*. New York: Anchor, 1962.

Betz, John, R. "After Heidegger and Marion: The Task of Christian Metaphysics Today." *Modern Theology* 34.4 (2018) 565–97.

———. "The *Analogia Entis* in Erich Przywara and Ferdinand Ulrich: Towards a More Catholic Metaphysics." *Communio* 46 (2019) 109–33.

Bieler, Martin. "*Analogia Entis* as an Expression of Love According to Ferdinand Ulrich." In *The Analogy of Being: Invention of the Antichrist or the Wisdom of God*, edited by Thomas Joseph White, 314–37. Grand Rapids: Eerdmans, 2011.

———. "Meta-Anthropology and Christology: On the Philosophy of Hans Urs von Balthasar." *Communio* 20 (1993) 129–46.

Boersma, Hans. *Nouvelle Théologie and Sacramental Ontology: A Return to Mystery*. Oxford: Oxford University Press, 2009.

Carman, Taylor. "The Principle of Phenomenology." In *The Cambridge Companion to Heidegger*, edited by Charles B. Guignon, 97–119. New York: Cambridge University Press, 2006.

Cirelli, Anthony. "Facing the Abyss: Hans Urs von Balthasar's Reading of Anxiety." *New Blackfriars* 92.1042 (2011) 705–23.

Cooper, David, E. *Thinkers of Our Time: Heidegger*. London: Claridge, 1996.

Dahlstrom, Daniel, O. *Heidegger's Concept of Truth*. Cambridge: Cambridge University Press, 2009.

Davies, Oliver. "Von Balthasar and the Problem of Being." *New Blackfriars* 79.923 (1998) 11–17.

Dreyfus, Hubert, L. *Being-in-the-World: A Commentary on Heidegger's Being and Time: Division I*. Cambridge: MIT Press, 1991.

Dupré, Louis. "The Glory of the Lord: Hans Urs von Balthasar's Theological Aesthetic." In *Hans Urs von Balthasar: His Life and Work*, edited by David L. Schindler, 182–206. San Francisco: Ignatius, 1992.

Fritz, Peter Joseph. "Catholic Theology and Heidegger." In *The Oxford Handbook of Catholic Theology*, edited by Lewis Ayres and Medi Ann Vlope, 850–61. Oxford: Oxford University Press, 2019.

Heidegger, Martin. *Being and Time*. Translated by John Macquarie and Edward Robinson. New York: Harper and Row, 1962.

———. *Ontology—The Hermeneutics of Facticity*. Translated by John van Buren. Bloomington: Indiana University Press, 1999.

Hoffman, Piotr. "Death, Time, History: Division II of *Being and Time*." In *The Cambridge Companion to Heidegger*, edited by Charles B. Guignon, 222–40. New York: Cambridge University Press, 2006.

Hoy, David Couzens. "Heidegger and the Hermeneutic Turn." In *The Cambridge Companion to Heidegger*, edited by Charles B. Guignon, 170–94. New York: Cambridge University Press, 2006.

Jeanrond, Werner. *Theological Hermeneutics: Development and Significance*. London: SCM, 1991.

Lafont, Cristina. "Hermeneutics." In *A Companion to Heidegger*, edited by Hubert L. Dreyfus and Mark Wrathall, 265–84. Hoboken, NJ: Wiley and Son, 2007.

Lopez, Antonio. *Gift and the Unity of Being*. Cambridge: Clarke & Co., 2014.

Nichols, Aidan. *Say It Is Pentecost: A Guide Through Balthasar's Logic*. Washington, DC: Catholic University of America Press, 2001.

Orr, James. "Being and Timelessness: Edith Stein's Critique of Heideggerian Temporality." *Modern Theology* 30.1 (2014) 114–31.

Ouellet, Marc. "The Message of Balthasar's Theology to Modern Theology." *Communio* 23 (1996) 270–99.

Ratzinger, Joseph. *Principles of Catholic Theology: Building Stones for a Fundamental Ontology*. Translated by Sister Mary Frances McCarthy. San Francisco: Ignatius, 1987.

Richardson, John. *Heidegger*. New York: Routledge, 2012.

Schindler, D. C. "Ever Ancient, Ever New: Jesus Christ as the Concrete Analogy of Being." *Communio* 39 (2012) 33–47.

———. "Metaphysics within the Limits of Phenomenology: Balthasar and Husserl on the Nature of the Philosophical Act." *Teología y Vida* 50 (2009) 243–58.

Scola, Angelo. *Hans Urs von Balthasar: A Theological Style*. Grand Rapids: Eerdmans, 1995.
Slaby, Jan. "Ontic *(Ontisch)*." In *The Cambridge Heidegger Lexicon*, edited by Mark A. Wrathall, 542–46. Cambridge: Cambridge University Press, 2021.
Sweeney, Conor. *Sacramental Presence after Heidegger: Onto-Theology, Sacraments, and the Mother's Smile*. Eugene, OR: Cascade, 2015.
Walker, Adrian J. "Love Alone: Hans Urs von Balthasar as a Master of Theological Renewal." In *Love Alone Is Credible: Hans Urs von Balthasar as Interpreter of the Catholic Tradition*, edited by David L. Schindler, 16–38. Grand Rapids: Eerdmans, 2005.
Wolfe, Judith. *Heidegger and Theology*. London: Bloomsbury T. & T. Clarke, 2014.
Wrathall, Mark. A. "Truth and the Essence of Truth in Heidegger's Thought." In *The Cambridge Companion to Heidegger*, edited by Charles B. Guignon, 241–68. New York: Cambridge University Press, 2006.

7

Anthropology of the Image

The Human Person as Mirror

Helenka Mannering

This chapter seeks to understand the human person, who today is situated within a culture saturated with images of the consumer economy, as the image and likeness of God. Recourse is made to the anthropology of St. Augustine, as well as to contemporary image studies. It is claimed that while the human person is made in the image and likeness of God, and intended to grow in and perfect this image, other loves, desires, or manners of perceiving can sway the person off this path, deforming the image of God within them. In order to undertake this analysis, the first section of this chapter focuses on the meaning of "image," and different ways that images are images. Recourse is made to the distinction between the idolatrous, aniconic, and iconic. Augustine's thought is then used to provide a framework to evaluate the human person's constitutive relationality not only to others, but also to the images we consume. Ultimately, it is suggested that there is a fundamental difference between the kind of gaze elicited by the consumer economy and the kind of gaze required for growth in the image of God.

The Image

Before any exploration regarding the nature of the human being created in the image and likeness of God is conducted, it is first necessary to answer the question, "what is an image?" In his essay under the same title, picture theorist and father of the "pictorial turn,"[1] W. J. T. Mitchell, wrote,

> It is a commonplace of modern cultural criticism that images have a power in our world undreamt of by the ancient idolaters.[2]
> ... [L]anguage and imagery are no longer what they promised to be for critics and philosophers of the Enlightenment—perfect, transparent media through which reality may be represented to the understanding. For modern criticism, language and imagery have become enigmas, problems to be explained, prison houses which lock the understanding away from the world. The commonplace of modern studies of images, in fact, is that they must be understood as a kind of language; instead of providing a transparent window on the world, images are now regarded as the sort of sign that presents a deceptive appearance of naturalness and transparence concealing an opaque, distorting, arbitrary mechanism of representation, a process of ideological mystification.[3]

Mitchell here articulates one side of the problem of images, which is that today their sign-value is questioned and they are recognized as opaque, bearing a significance of their own. Others have stated that there has been a movement in understanding images from *representation* to *presentation*.[4] It is claimed that "the visual object [is] invested with an animating power of its own,"[5] and is not a token of a reality it merely signifies.[6] Natalie Carnes explains that this defense of the image against a purely

---

1. Mitchell, *Picture Theory*, 11.

2. Some sources that Mitchell refers to here are Sontag, *On Photography*; Benjamin, *The Work of Art*; Boorstin and Rushkoff, *The Image*.

3. Mitchell, "What Is an Image?," 503–4.

4. Moxey, "Visual Studies and the Iconic Turn," 132–33.

5. Moxey, "Visual Studies and the Iconic Turn," 139.

6. While this view has become increasingly prevalent among picture theorists, it is by no means universal. For example, Nicholas Mirzoeff claims images are primarily signs or political and cultural representations, often with "ideological potential," as explained by Moxey, "Visual Studies and the Iconic Turn," 139. See Mirzoeff, *An Introduction to Visual Culture*.

utilitarian approach is a reaction against a Platonic, Kantian, or Hegalian approach to the image "that reduces the image to meaning—to how, that is, the image points beyond itself to a significance located elsewhere."[7]

However, in response to Mitchell, it remains clear that not all images are devoid of signification. Carnes writes that that which distinguishes an image from a picture is precisely its signification. She gives the example of a child drawing a picture with a yellow crayon, delighting in the color the crayon leaves on the paper. An adult who sees the picture asks the child whether they were drawing the sun. At that moment, the picture becomes "negotiated in a new relationship, one that overlaps with but remains distinct from pictures. It has become for the child an image."[8] The difference between the picture and the image lies in the child's gaze: when perceiving the former, the child does not perceive something pointing beyond itself, when perceiving the latter, the yellow crayon on paper was signifying the sun.[9] Against theorists such as Mitchell, Carnes contends that recognizing the signification of images does not necessitate devaluing their particular, immanent value. It is possible to hold the value both of the image as that which has value in-and-of itself, as well as that which valuably signifies something beyond itself. As claimed by Douglas Hedley in *The Iconic Imagination*, upholding the Platonic recognition of transcendence does not necessarily denigrate the image.[10]

However, it is useful to distinguish between the type of signification found in an image and other types of signs. Images are not arbitrary signs which signify purely extrinsic cultural conventions. If this were the case, the image in itself would indeed be disposable and inessential, and any other image could be instituted in its place to signify that which the first image signified. In other words, images cannot be interpreted as participating in a nominalist ontology; otherwise, Mitchell's qualms about the denigration of images would be realized. Rather, images are intimately connected with that which they signify. Carnes expresses this by claiming that images have a likeness to that which they signify: "Likeness to the signified is the essential and distinctive feature of images, distinguishing

---

7. Carnes, *Image and Presence*, 60. See, Mitchell, *What Do Pictures Want?*; Mitchell, "Idolatry"; Mitchell, *Picture Theory*.

8. Carnes, *Image and Presence*, 4.

9. Carnes, *Image and* Presence, 5.

10. Hedley, *The Iconic Imagination*, 29–30.

them from all other species of signs, including words and symbols."[11] Such a concept of image is also present in the thought of St. Augustine, who wrote, "When there is an image there is necessarily a likeness but not necessarily equality."[12] Therefore, according to this reasoning, images do signify, but they are also neither disposable nor interchangeable in the face of the transcendent reality they point to.

Further clarification may be gained from the distinction between sign and symbol proposed by Paul Evdokimov. According to Evdokimov, images should be properly interpreted as symbolic rather than as signs. Signs inform and teach and are "empty of any presence."[13] Examples of signs include road signs, algebraic signs and chemical formulas: in all of these, "there is no relation of communion or presence between the *significant*, the physical symbol and the *signifié*, the thing and content symbolized."[14] Evdokimov also places allegories into this category of signs whose aim is primarily "didactic illustration."[15] In contrast to signs and allegories, symbols contain an epiphanic content, or, in other words, "the presence of what is symbolized."[16] In other words, a symbol

> fulfils the function of revealing a meaning and at the same time it becomes an expressive and effective container of the "presence." Symbolic knowledge is always indirect. It appeals to the contemplative faculty of the mind, to the real imagination, both evocative and invocative. In this way, symbolic knowledge decodes the meaning and message of the symbol and grasps its epiphanic character, a character which shows forth a figured, symbolized but very real presence of the transcendent.[17]

Being able to gaze at images as symbols ensures that both their integrity is respected, and that they are interpreted as icons, open to a transcendent reality. However, Evdokimov claims that with the rise of modernity, it has become increasingly difficult for us to view images as symbolic.[18] Both changes in the style of thinking (e.g., the movement from the "reasonable"

---

11. Carnes, *Image and Presence*, 5.
12. Augustine, *Responses to Miscellaneous Questions*, 137.
13. Evdokimov, *The Art of the Icon*, 166.
14. Evdokimov, *The Art of the Icon*, 166.
15. Evdokimov, *The Art of the Icon*, 166.
16. Evdokimov, *The Art of the Icon*, 167.
17. Evdokimov, *The Art of the Icon*, 167. See Alleau, *De La Nature Des Symboles*.
18. Evdokimov, *The Art of the Icon*, 168.

to the "rational")[19] and in the style of art (e.g., the slide towards perspective realism)[20] have contributed to the loss of a symbolic gaze, and the widespread dichotomization of images as either signs (purely pointing to the transcendent) or as closed off from any further meaning or transcendence, that is, fully sufficient in themselves.

Although all images are, by their very nature, symbolic, they can be structured to encourage a reading which denies transcendence (idol), or which looks over the immanent (aniconic). By ignoring the true nature of the image and reading it as either a sign devoid of any immanent value or as a picture devoid of a signification which transcends it, we close our perception to what is the essential nature of the image. However, the way that the image is read and interpreted depends not only upon the image itself, but also on the gaze of the viewer of the image, and on the medium through which the image is presented. In fact, each influences the other, operating in a circular dynamic. Thus, the operative intentionality of the person conditions the gaze and influences what is perceived and how it is received.[21] The image that is perceived, however, together with its medium, produces or elicits particular desires in the subject.[22] These desires, in turn, influence and mold the *habitus* of the person and his or her operative intentionality, and hence the perception of future images.

---

19. Evdokimov, *The Art of the Icon*, 171.

20. Evdokimov, *The Art of the Icon*, 169.

21. The term "operative intentionality" is here used in the sense that Maurice Merleau-Ponty defines it: "[Operative intentionality is] the intentionality that establishes the natural and pre-predicative unity of the world and of our life, the intentionality that appears in our desires, our evaluations, and our landscape more clearly than it does in objective knowledge. Operative intentionality is the one that provides the text that our various forms of knowledge attempt to translate into precise language." Merleau-Ponty, *Phenomenology of Perception*, lxxxii.

22. Mitchell writes, "Pictures . . . have a tendency to swallow us up, or (as the expression goes) take us in. But images are also, notoriously, a drink that fails to satisfy our thirst. Their main function is to awaken desire; to create, not gratify thirst; to provoke a sense of lack and cravings by giving us the apparent presence of something and taking it away in the same gesture." Mitchell, *What Do Pictures Want?*, 80.

FIGURE 1

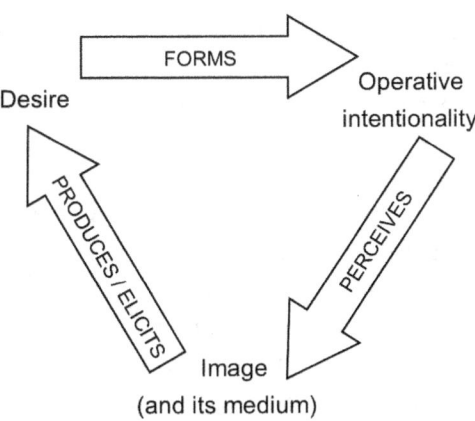

Figure 1: Relation of desire, operative intentionality, and image

In this way, the ability to perceive rightly[23] is influenced by: (a) the operative intentionality which can be deliberately shaped and formed in a particular way; (b) the desires which one cultivates and which are elicited by external stimuli, and (c) the types of images one perceives, which elicit particular desires. In what follows, we will focus mostly on (c), examining the way different types of images elicit different desires. As we proceed with this analysis, it may be helpful to keep in mind that, although particular images are intended to evoke particular desires, the success in accomplishing this is dependent not only on the image, but also on the prior operative intentionality of the subject. Ultimately, we will weave this analysis into a reflection about what it means to be a human person made in the image of God.

Idol

Images have been traditionally divided into two categories: idols and icons.[24] To these two categories, some, such as Carnes, have added a third, namely, the aniconic image. In this section we will analyze idols, aniconic

---

23. This has bearing on moral theology for, as Joseph Pieper argues, the ability to perceive rightly is intimately connected with the ability to act rightly. Pieper, *Only the Lover Sings*, 35.

24. See Pattison, "Idol or Icon?"

images, and icons, seeking to uncover the kinds of desires they elicit and the operative intentionality that is in turn formed by these desires, commencing with an analysis of the idol. The idol has sometimes been presented as an image which is read as total presence, and which negates any desire to go beyond it to reach the prototype. The idolatrous image represents "the arrogance of the image,"[25] which pretends to be more than it actually is.[26] Jean-Luc Marion has claimed that there is nothing in the idol that calls forth a transformation or elicits an ecstatic movement of love: rather, the idol functions within the bounds of immanence, merely confirming what is already known. Because it is not open to any further transcendence, Marion writes that the idol is "closed off to its original" and thus "no longer has any reality other than itself."[27] Thinkers as diverse as Baudrillard and Ratzinger have suggested that most images today fall into this category. Ratzinger states, "our world of images no longer surpasses the bounds of sense and appearance, and the flood of images that surrounds us really means the end of the image."[28]

However, articulating the idol in this way is problematic. As we have seen, if an image refuses to point to a reality beyond itself, it is no longer an image, but a mere picture. Every image, by its very nature, has to be open in some measure to something which transcends the presence of the image: it must symbolize something beyond. Some scholars have tapped into this reality and have criticized Marion for claiming that idolatrous images are closed off to any further meaning, an approach which, they would claim, is inherently contradictory. These scholars include Yves De Maeseener,[29] Thomas A. Carlson,[30] and Mark C. Taylor.[31] Maeseener claims that images always function as icons, that is, as "constitutive image[s],"[32] even when they seem to be idols. Similarly, Carlson

---

25. Marion, *The Crossing of the Visible*, 47.
26. Boersma, *Augustine's Early Theology of Image*, 189.
27. Marion, *The Crossing of the Visible*, 49. Similarly, Evdokimov writes, "an idol is the expression of what is non-existent, fiction, simulacre, nothingness." Evdokimov, *The Art of the Icon*, 200.
28. Ratzinger, *The Spirit of the Liturgy*, 131. See Evdokimov, *The Art of the Icon*, 171–72.
29. Maeseneer, "Saint Francis versus Mcdonald's?"
30. Carlson, "Consuming Desire's Deferral."
31. Taylor, *Hiding*.
32. Maeseneer, "Saint Francis versus Mcdonald's?," 33.

writes that, although it is easy to claim that the televisual image has an idol structure, it in fact bears some aspects of an icon as well.

Both Maeseener and Marion touch upon fundamental truths when it comes to images, albeit accessing these truths from different angles. It is possible to agree with both Maeseener, that every image functions in a symbolic manner and with Marion that some images are not icons, but idols, by incorporating the work of Carnes. Carnes suggests that idols are images which provoke *desires* which are closed off from the symbolic dimension. An idolatrous image always maintains a symbolic structure but provokes idolatrous desires. Therefore, on the one hand, Marion focuses on the desires which images provoke, claiming that this represents the structure of images, while on the other Maeseener focuses on the structure of the images, while neglecting the different desires images provoke. By making this distinction, the images themselves retain their identity as symbolic depictions, but the distinction between idol and icon is also maintained.

Carnes's distinction between the desire elicited by the idol and by the icon is very illuminative. She explains that desire can be literal, literalized, and non-literal. Literal desires are morally neutral desires which occur on the level of nature, such as the desire for pleasure and honor. These desires, as they stand, are neither morally good nor evil, rather, they just form an essential part of our nature. Any philosophy of life which seeks to deny or repress literal desires does not accept the fullness of our human condition and thus lacks wholesomeness, corresponding to the aniconic gaze analyzed below. Occasionally, however, literal desires are evoked or cultivated in such a way that their fulfillment seems to become the sole purpose of our existence. When this happens, literal desires become literalized. Literalized desires are always vicious, according to Carnes.[33] They can be seen as a minimized kind of desire: a desire which plays it safe by remaining within the bounds of literal desire.[34] An example of literalized desire can be found in Augustine's analysis of lust. Cavadini writes,

> It is not itself a "natural" desire, oriented to any particular good of human nature. It is, rather, oriented towards a pleasure which, if it has any orientation to any natural good, is only accidental and circumstantial. If it can be spoken of as "ordered" at all, it is an ordering only towards its own gratification, and the field of

---

33. Carnes, *Image and Presence*, 22–23.
34. Carnes, *Image and Presence*, 49.

that gratification has no limit and is ever expanding. In other words, there is no "reason" or "rationale" evident in this desire.[35]

Literal desire does not prohibit an openness to non-literal desire, whereas literalized desire denies desire for anything other than itself.[36] In other words, idols, according to Carnes, minimize desire and harm it by literalizing it.[37]

FIGURE 2

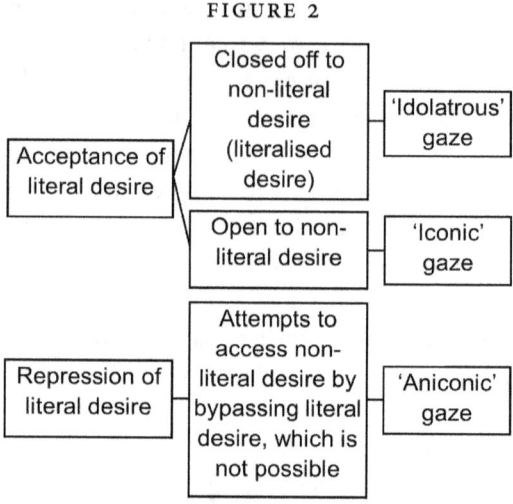

Figure 2: Types of desire and perception

Idols, therefore, elicit literalized desire. Such images do not reach to anything beyond the desiring subject but merely confirm his or her literal desires, acting as a mirror, "in which the consuming subject finds only a reflection and satisfaction of self."[38] In this economy of literalized desire, the subject is a voyeur, consuming images according to how they meet his or her desires. Marion elaborates,

> A "viewer": thus is defined the one who, under the most neutral names of "spectator" or "consumer," undergoes, governs, and defines the image—all under the pretexts of access to information, the opening of the world, and "connecting" on (albeit

35. Cavadini, "Reconsidering Augustine on Marriage and Concupiscence," 187.
36. Carnes, *Image and Presence*, 172.
37. Carnes, *Image and Presence*, 40.
38. Carlson, "Consuming Desire's Deferral," 42.

poor) coverage of current events of situations even more trivial and yet more restrictive.³⁹

In fact, literalized desire and the economy of the idol is one kind of image dynamic cultivated by consumerism, where images must constantly seek to conform to the literal desires of the viewer or otherwise risk not being seen. In a culture saturated with images, only those which promise the greatest intensity of literal satisfaction, and hence provoke the greatest intensity of literalized desire, are the ones that end up being sought after, cultivated, and consumed.

A further intensification of this economy of literalized desire occurs when images are mediated through technological mediums. According to Carlson, "In its most fundamental aim . . . the rule of technological reproduction excludes the emergence of anything that might disrupt, whether by disappointment or surprise, the desirous gaze of the subject—which means anything radically new or unforeseen."⁴⁰ Similarly, Jean-Luc Marion claims that the televisual images we consume on a daily basis elicit an idolatrous gaze.⁴¹ In a powerful passage, he explains the dynamic of the televisual image (which also applies to digital images consumed on our smartphones and other devices), connecting such images with the literalized desire they provoke and the voyeuristic attitude of the consumer:

> The viewer watches for the sole pleasure of seeing: thanks to technology, he is finally able to succumb without limit or restriction to the fascination of the *libido vivendi*, which was always denounced by the Fathers: a pleasure [*jouissance*] of seeing, of seeing all, especially what I do not have the right or strength to see; the pleasure also of seeing without being seen—that is, of mastering by the view [*vue*] what does not return to me without exposing me to the gaze of another. The viewer thus maintains a perverse and impotent relationship with the world that it both flees and possesses at one and the same time in the image.⁴²

---

39. Marion, *The Crossing of the Visible*, 50.
40. Carlson, "Consuming Desire's Deferral," 42.
41. Marion, *The Crossing of the Visible*, 50.
42. Marion, *The Crossing of the Visible*, 50.

Images which conform precisely to the desires of the viewer are ultimately, for Marion, "prostituted images."[43] They always exist primarily to satisfy the literal desires of the viewer.[44]

In the digital world, there is also a reversal of voyeur/"shameful subject" which occurs when the self is presented as image. Here the self is staged as an aesthetic image and this self-as-image becomes the "shameful subject" which must conform to the desires of the viewers if it is to be seen at all.[45] Marion explains,

> I must constitute myself as an image, no longer first an image of me, but rather an image of the idol expected by the viewers—an idol, the image of a desire, thus of a voyeuristic gaze; I must, in order to be, give myself up, twice: to the gaze and to the desire of the viewers. My own desire to be seen demands, in the end, that I let myself be seen as an approximate image of the idol desired by those who, in order to be, see. The ambition to dominate, in whatever field it might be, paradoxically requires being reduced to the rank of an idol—thus an idol of viewers.[46]

Marion refers to this movement as a prostitution—a reduction of the self to correspond precisely to the desires of the viewers.[47]

Images which function according to the economy of the idol and provoke literalized desire, whether they be images of objects seen voyeuristically or images of the self conformed to other's literal desires, are archetypically exemplified by pornographic or advertising images. The pornographic image does not encourage a participation in non-visual, spiritual desire, but rather mirrors back the voyeur's own desire and presents to the voyeur what he or she desires to see.[48] It closes itself off "from transformation beyond itself."[49] Furthermore, for Carnes, advertising is "pornography's kin,"[50] participating in the same idolatrous economy. She writes,

---

43. Marion, *The Crossing of the Visible*, 53–54.
44. Marion, *The Crossing of the Visible*, 50–51.
45. Marion, *The Crossing of the Visible*, 52.
46. Marion, *The Crossing of the Visible*, 52–53.
47. Marion, *The Crossing of the Visible*, 53.
48. Marion, *La Croisée Du Visible*, 92.
49. Carnes, *Image and Presence*, 50.
50. Carnes, *Image and Presence*, 50.

> Both pornographic and advertising images' desires terminate in the assimilation of the image to the beholder. . . . The pornographic image controls desire by consuming the cause of that desire. It contains desire by assimilating the desired object to the desiring one.[51]

Ultimately, both pornography and advertising promote the same kind of literalized desire in the subject.

Although the perception of images as idols through the voyeuristic gaze is closed off from transcendence, the gazing subject becomes nonetheless transformed by the act of viewing and consumption. The transformation occurs, not through an opening up to non-literal desire, but rather through the intensification of an insatiable literal desire, which comes to increasingly characterize the operative intentionality of the subject. Furthermore, this operative intentionality drives the perception of the subject, so that what is seen is only that which participates within the idolatrous economy: the iconic and the aniconic is no longer perceived. The dynamic created by digital images is an archetypical example of how the viewer is transformed towards increasing voyeurism and consumerism, and away from iconic perception. The digital world, apart from drawing and provoking literal desire in a literalized manner, also alters the categories of perception such as space and time, in this way changing the consumer's operative intentionality to view more, desire more and thus consume more.[52] Marion writes that, through the televisual image, "space and time no longer constitute the *a priori* structures of experience but instead constitute the *a priori* conditions of the impossibility of any real experience—of the impossibility of moving back from images to their conditional [*éventuel*] original."[53]

Aniconic

The opposite approach to images from the idolatrous gaze is not iconophilia—rather, it is the aniconic gaze. Within this structure, the image becomes worth nothing in itself, and all value is placed on the transcendent reality it signifies. Literal desire is denied for the sake of the non-literal.[54]

---

51. Carnes, *Image and Presence*, 45.
52. Marion, *The Crossing of the Visible*, 48.
53. Marion, *The Crossing of the Visible*, 49.
54. Carnes, *Image and Presence*, 40.

This denial of literal desire enacts what Carnes refers to as an "iconoclasm of temptation,"[55] or what other writers simply refer to as iconoclasm.[56] The aniconic, iconoclastic gaze is present in some traditions of Western Christianity which critique the existence of all images, particularly some Protestant traditions. For example, the sermon "Against Peril of Idolatry" in the Elizabethan *Book of Homilies* suggests that image and idol "are merely two words for the same thing."[57] Some (but not all) allegorical art can also incline towards aniconism, as it consists of using images to point towards a non-literal meaning and evoke non-literal desire, but also of cultivating a gaze which sees beyond the image, thus potentially rendering the image itself invisible. Pattison explains that, in such art, "the visual image has become a cipher, a convention,"[58] and, furthermore, that in such a picture "the important thing about the picture is what is signifies,"[59] and not the actual image itself.

The problem with the aniconic gaze is that it ignores what is particularly distinctive about an image. Thus, although images have meaning, the aniconic gaze forgets that "this meaning defies translation into the clarity of prose, not because it is vacuous, but because it is inexhaustible."[60] Within the aniconic economy, images become mere signs, not symbols.[61] Ultimately, this kind of gaze, according to Ratzinger, is "a denial of the Incarnation, as the summation of all heresies."[62] He explains,

> Iconoclasm rests ultimately on a one-sided apophatic theology, which recognizes only the Wholly Other-ness of the God beyond all images and words, a theology that in the final analysis regards revelation as the inadequate human reflection of what is eternally imperceptible.[63]

Regarding the world aniconically, therefore, is simply "not a Christian option."[64]

---

55. Carnes, *Image and Presence*, 25.
56. See Ratzinger, *The Spirit of the Liturgy*, 122.
57. Pattison, "Idol or Icon?," 1.
58. Pattison, "Idol or Icon?," 2.
59. Pattison, "Idol or Icon?," 2.
60. Nichols, *The Art of God Incarnate*, 93.
61. Evdokimov, *The Art of the Icon*, 219.
62. Ratzinger, *The Spirit of the Liturgy*, 122.
63. Ratzinger, *The Spirit of the Liturgy*, 123–24.
64. Ratzinger, *The Spirit of the Liturgy*, 132.

It is essential to note that the gaze which sees images in an aniconic way is not necessarily incompatible with the idolatrous gaze. In fact, both the idolatrous and the aniconic may be discerned as being present within the consumer economy. To explain, let us imagine a Coca Cola advertisement. While on one level, it could be evoking literalized desires by portraying an image of friendship or love, on another level it is linking these desires to an arbitrary sign—a Coke bottle—which bears no intrinsic relationship to the literal desire of friendship, happiness, or sexual fulfillment. The Coke bottle becomes the desired transcendent through which one's literal desires may be fulfilled. However, simultaneously, the literal desires themselves are being rewritten: they become linked to the arbitrary transcendent sign, and hence they lose their "literalness," their naturalness. The gaze, thus, becomes an aniconic gaze, focused on the attainment of the object of non-literal desire (the transcendent good symbolized by the Coke bottle), through which is promised the attainment of literal desires which are no longer quite literal, because they are divorced from their true origins and attached to an arbitrary sign. These "literal" desires, it could be said, are simulacra of true literal desires: externally manifesting a similar image, but in reality, being founded on a non-literal "abstraction."[65] Hence, while it may initially seem that the aniconic is the inverse of the idolatrous, in reality they may both be present simultaneously, on different levels.

In addition, aniconism and idolatry share some foundational assumptions. Both are, in the words of Carnes, "failures of sight that are also failures of desire."[66] They participate in an ontology which fails to recognize the simultaneous presence of literal and non-literal desire: they function within an either/or mentality rather than recognizing the depth and complexity of both/and.[67] In other words, they are both firmly situated within an ontology of univocity and are therefore structures of sight which are deeply embedded within the modern, post-Enlightenment social imaginary. And these failures of sight, which lead to failure of desire, also lead to failure in moral action: for when one's desires are literalized, then one acts in such a way as to pursue only temporal goods and pleasures, and when one's desires deny the literal, then one falls into angelism and a perverted attitude towards human flesh. However, due to the

---

65. Baudrillard, *The Consumer Society*, 134.
66. Carnes, *Image and Presence*, 171.
67. Barron, *Vibrant Paradoxes*.

common ontology undergirding both extremes, in the modern Western world we struggle to see an alternative: "Modern Westerns are trained by our institutions to relate to images as either images of consumption or images of critique—with either literalized desire or no desire."[68] Only by opening up to the possibility of an iconic gaze, which operates within an ontology of participation or analogy, and which recognizes the essentialness of both literal and non-literal desire, can this false dichotomy be avoided.

Icon

The iconophilic gaze should not be thought of as a compromise between the two extremes outlined above. Rather, it participates in a radically alternate economy and therefore is not situated on the same plane as idolatry or aniconism. The gaze which sees images as icons is open to both the image in itself and to the prototype which the image represents; it is also open to both literal and non-literal desire. In fact, the primary gaze is not of the subject but of the prototype through the image, but unlike aniconism or idolatry, this gaze is not objectifying nor voyeuristic, but rather intensely personal and relational.[69] Hence the response of the subject is not shame, but an ecstatic transfiguration in a relation of love between the subject and the prototype mediated by the image. Marion writes, "Before the icon, if I continue to look, I feel myself seen. . . . Thus the image no longer creates a screen (or, as in the case of the idol, a mirror), since through it and under its features another gaze—invisible like all gazes—envisages me."[70] The gaze of the icon is a loving gaze towards the subject, which transfigures the subject, who, feeling himself or herself gazed at and loved, awakens to the reality of unconditional love. Marion writes,

> The gaze looks at the one who, in prayer . . . raises his gaze toward the icon: the painted gaze invisibly responds to the invisible gaze of the one in prayer, and transfigures its own visibility by including it in the commerce of two invisible gazes—the one from a praying man, taken through the painted icon, to look upon an invisible saint, the other the gaze of the invisible saint

---

68. Carnes, *Image and Presence*, 45.
69. Marion, *La Croisée Du Visible*, 103.
70. Marion, *The Crossing of the Visible*, 59.

covered with benevolence, visible through the painted icon, looking upon the one in prayer.[71]

Thus, the voyeuristic gaze of the "objective" economy is radically different here, being the loving gaze permeating through an icon, which seeks personal involvement and relation, rather than to be permanently masked and exert power over the subject. The image becomes like a stained-glass window depicting the lover, beautiful in itself, but through which the gaze of the lover can also penetrate.

The iconic gaze bears a similarity to the idolatrous gaze only in that it recognizes the full beauty of literal desire and does not see in it a cause for shame. Nonetheless, it differs from idolatry by refusing to literalize desire but allowing it to lie open to a transfiguring beyond. As Evdokimov emphasizes, "The very word *icon* suppresses any identification and underlines the *difference of nature* between the image and its prototype."[72] The icon does not seek to appropriate the status of prototype to itself, as does the idol, but faithfully points beyond itself to the prototype. Hence, we can speak of icons as *kenotic* images in contrast to both idols (arrogant images) and the aniconic (self-destructive images).[73] Furthermore, in the sharing of loving gazes which occurs through an icon, the viewer is transfigured, although not in the same way as one who cultivates an idolatrous gaze. Whereas in the latter the transformation enlarges the capacity of literal desire, the former enlarges the capacity of non-literal desire while simultaneously respecting the integrity of the literal. Because non-literal desire is for that which is not fully known or grasped, but rather loved as good, it transforms the person through the ecstatic movement of love, not the controlling movement of knowledge.[74] The viewer's operative intentionality is transfigured through the piercing through of another intentionality which causes a drastic reconfiguration of vision. The icon leads to a "new kind of seeing."[75] Hence the icon has the power to both reconfigure perception and desire and transform the subject.[76]

---

71. Marion, *The Crossing of the Visible*, 20.
72. Evdokimov, *The Art of the Icon*, 195.
73. Marion, *The Crossing of the Visible*, 63.
74. Sheen, *Three to Get Married*, 41.
75. Ratzinger, *The Spirit of the Liturgy*, 121.
76. Marion, *The Crossing of the Visible*, 33. See Carnes, *Image and Presence*, 176; Gregory of Nyssa, *The Life of Moses*, 114.

Finally, because the iconophilic gaze is dependent on the transformational perception of the gaze of the loving Other, it is really the loving Other that enables the subject or teaches the subject to develop and deepen this gaze. When the icon touches upon the fundamental ground of reality, and acts as a window for the gaze of the wholly Other, God, it is the Holy Spirit who enables us to develop an iconophilic gaze.[77] This is because, as Evdokimov explains,

> Our natural faculties are not sufficient to allow us to perceive the spiritual. This is why Christ united human energy to divine and deifying energy. The senses are spiritualised and become like the object they are sensing: "He who participates in the light becomes himself light."[78]

Without our natural senses and desires being overridden, repressed, or denied[79]—this would be aniconism—the Holy Spirit enables us to open to non-literal desire, to perceive the spiritual reality which exists in-and-beyond the physical and the natural.

Whereas as a result of original sin we are inclined to limit desire to the literal and seek for ever stronger stimulations of literal desire (a seeking traditionally referred to as concupiscence), or to react in desperation against literal desire, seeking unnaturally to repress it (movements such as Gnosticism and Manichaeism are good illustrative examples), the Holy Spirit pierces through this closed circle of literal desire by enabling a properly "analogical" vision, and hence "symbolic" action. He does this without denigrating or destroying the literal, for it, too, is his creation; rather, through opening it up to the spiritual, He situates it within his original plan and its true potential. Evdokimov summarizes, "In the final analysis, we are talking of the ascetical rehabilitation of matter as the substratum of the resurrection and the medium in which all epiphanies take place."[80]

---

77. Ratzinger, *The Spirit of the Liturgy*, 122.

78. Evdokimov, *The Art of the Icon*, 28. Original citation unacknowledged.

79. Ratzinger, *The Spirit of the Liturgy*, 123. See Evdokimov, *The Art of the Icon*, 27–28.

80. Evdokimov, *The Art of the Icon*, 28.

The Image and Likeness of God

Our analysis of the three different modes in which an image may be perceived—the idolatrous, the aniconic, and the iconic—will enable us to now turn to an anthropological account of the human person as image and likeness of God. In Christian theology, the discussion of the meaning of image has taken on different contours throughout the centuries. The theme of image came to be central in many Patristic discussions concerning the identity of Christ and of the human person, as Vladimir Lossky claims,

> The theme of the *image*, in the knowledge of God and man, is of such importance for Christian thought that I think we are justified in speaking of a "theology of the image" in the New Testament or in the work of a particular Christian writer without fear of magnifying a doctrinal element of secondary value out of all due proportion.[81]

Although reflections on the meaning of image and likeness were present in the early centuries of Christianity, a significant focus on the precise meaning of these words occurred in reaction to the Arian heresy. As St. Paul writes in his letter to the Colossians that Christ is "the image of the invisible God" (Col 1:15), some church Fathers came to interpret image as denoting equality of substance or nature, in order to uphold Christ's divinity against the Arians.[82] For these church Fathers, such as Hilary of Poitiers, the human person is not *made in* the image of God, but *ordered to* the image of God: not *imago Dei*, but *ad imaginem*. Image was interpreted theologically as denoting a personal relationship within a consubstantial nature. According to these thinkers, that which is an image shares the nature of the archetype.[83]

However, an image is not identical with its archetype—otherwise it would not be an "image" but be the archetype itself. Therefore, there must be some difference between image and archetype. Within God, this difference cannot be that of nature: Christ the Image has the same nature as Father. The only distinction between them, rather, is the difference of personal relations: the Father relates to the Son in a different way than the Son relates to the Father. Therefore, within the Trinity, image can

---

81. Lossky, *In the Image and Likeness of God*, 125.
82. Boersma, *Augustine's Early Theology of Image*, 2–3.
83. Lossky, *In the Image and Likeness of God*, 134.

only refer to personal relation between the divine persons.[84] The Son is Image because he relates to the Father in the manner of an Image. For Lossy, therefore, rather than substantial unity, which does not sufficiently differentiate between "prototype" and "image," what lies at the heart of a theological understanding of image is a shared personal relationship between "prototype" and "image." This is true of Christ imaging the Father, and it is also true of the human person imaging God. This is why, for Lossky, trying to place the "image of God" in a particular human faculty is ultimately doomed to fail.[85]

Lossky's analysis is complemented by Augustine's theology on this topic. Augustine clearly distinguishes between image, equality, and likeness, claiming that image implies likeness but not necessarily equality; equality implies likeness but not necessarily image; and likeness does not necessarily imply either image or equality.[86] Therefore, Augustine diverges from the earlier church Fathers by claiming that image does not necessarily have to be consubstantial with the "prototype."[87] This allows for humans to be properly referred to as *imago Dei*, and not only *ad imaginem*. Christ is the image with the perfect likeness, whereas human persons have an imperfect likeness which improves the closer we draw to Christ.[88] Likeness is, therefore, as Lossky claimed, based on a personal relationship, and is possible both with and without the existence of equality. Ultimately, Christ, by opening the possibility of a personal relationship with God, opened up a new way for humanity to image God, too. In the words of Carnes, "This way that the Son images the Father sustains, in the incarnation, a new form of imaging—a new way that humanity can image divinity. In Christ, humanity reveals divinity by expressing the divine life of God."[89]

---

84. Lossky, *In the Image and Likeness of God*, 138.

85. Lossky, *In the Image and Likeness of God*, 139.

86. Augustine, *Responses to Miscellaneous Questions*, 137.

87. In this, and in his overall analysis of the *imago Dei*, Augustine presents some strikingly original ideas. Edmund Hill writes, "In his treatment of the image of God in man, I think Augustine was breaking wholly new ground, and owed little or nothing to the tradition." Hill, Introduction to Augustine, *The Trinity*, 58. However, intimations of Augustine's dynamic approach to the *imago Dei* can be discerned in the thought of Ambrose of Milan. For example, for Ambrose, as Boersma writes, "To follow one's true nature as image of God, it is necessary to perfect a spirit of detachment with regard to material and temporal goods." Boersma, *Augustine's Early Theology of Image*, 114.

88. Boersma, *Augustine's Early Theology of Image*, 261.

89. Carnes, *Image and Presence*, 13.

Placing the "image and likeness" of the human person within the context of relation, rather than in a static human faculty, such as intellect or will, further allows for the articulation of the essential dynamism or plasticity of the image structure in human persons. Intimations of such a plasticity can be found in Augustine and other patristic writers.[90] For Augustine, sin leads to a deformation and discoloration of the image.[91] It is reformed and renovated when, through grace, the human person turns from sin and grows in remembrance, understanding, and love of God.[92] Hence, when one's loves turn one away from God and towards other created things, the soul, although still capable of imaging God, comes to image those things which it loves more than God, essentially disfiguring itself and frustrating its true vocation and identity. It seems that, although there is an essential image structure within the human person which is there for the purpose of the human person imaging God, that which the image structure comes to actually image is dependent on the moral life of the subject: if the person chooses to strengthen their relation with God, they will come to image God more fully; but, if instead of pursuing God they pursue objects of literalized desire, their soul will come to image these things.[93] Hence, the kind of image the human person becomes—an idol, aniconic, or an icon—is dependent on the gaze that person cultivates, for the way one views images in the world bears on how one views the self, which is an essential image structure.[94]

It is important here to emphasize that, according to Augustine, the image of God in the human person is essentially dynamic and found in the acts of remembering, understanding, and loving, rather than in the faculties of the memory, reason, and will.[95] Placing it in the latter rather than in the former has led to claims which posit him as a precursor to Cartesian rationalism and individualism.[96] Edmund Hill notes

90. Gregory of Nyssa, *Song of Songs*, 92.

91. Augustine, *The Trinity*, 389.

92. These three acts constitute the image of God according to Augustine. See Augustine, *The Trinity*, 384–89; Drever, "The Self before God?," 240; Augustine, *On Genesis*, 234–35.

93. Miles, "Vision," 126–29. See Drever, "Sightings," 4.

94. Evdokimov, *The Art of the Icon*, 45.

95. Williams, "*Sapientia* and the Trinity," 319. See Sullivan, *The Image of God*.

96. Notable scholars who have proposed Cartesian interpretations of Augustine's philosophy of the self include Philip Cary, Wayne Hankey, Brian Stock, and Charles Taylor.

that this serious misunderstanding of Augustine's thought has significant consequences for the moral life: it "deprives the whole doctrine of the divine image in man of any effective application to the spiritual life of the Christian."[97] Furthermore, while Augustine discerns an image of the Trinity in the acts of the mind remembering, understanding, and loving itself in book X of *De Trinitate*,[98] in book XIV he modifies his claim by stating that the image of the Trinity exists more clearly when the mind remembers, understands, and loves God: "This trinity of the mind is not really the image of God because the mind remembers and understands and loves itself, but because it is also able to remember and understand and love him by whom it was made. And when it does this it becomes wise."[99] In fact, by stopping short and remembering, understanding, and loving only oneself, and not God, the image of God is distorted in the human person. Hill explains,

> It is by stopping at these acts at a self-directed level that Everyman in fact falls, and defaces the image. The true self is open to God; by closing itself to God the self-centred self loses its real self-possession, all its coherence, and tumbles down and outward, like Humpty Dumpty, scattering itself in pieces in the world of sensible material things. It practices a kind of parody of the divine missions, by the higher contemplative function of the mind sending the lower active function out into the world on lawless tasks of exploitation, in all the kinds of sin with which we are familiar.[100]

Hence, Augustine's understanding of the *interior homo* is diametrically opposed to the self-sufficient and autonomous self, as it is sometimes interpreted.[101]

Finally, it must be noted that the image structure of the human person exists in a volatile state, more easily coming to image literalized desires rather than God. Because the human person was created *ex nihilo* but given the lofty vocation, through grace, to become a child of God, he or she exists always within a tension between nothingness and the fullness of being. Drever claims that because of the creation *ex nihilo* "there is a fundamental potential for (moral and ontological) instability

---

97. Hill, Introduction to Augustine, *The Trinity*, 26.
98. See Augustine, *The Trinity*, 300–302.
99. Augustine, *The Trinity*, 384.
100. Hill, Introduction to Augustine, *The Trinity*, 58.
101. Drever, "The Self before God?," 331.

or mutability in human existence, exacerbated all the more by sin."[102] The human soul, therefore, is easily malleable to image the objects of its desires and loves. As Margaret Miles puts it, the Augustinian self is "primarily a partially centred energy, initially barely distinguishable from its cosmic, physical, and spiritual environment, which comes to be cumulatively distinguished and defined by the objects of its attention and affection."[103] As we shall see in the following sections, the kind of gaze that is cultivated by the operative intentionality of the subject, his or her desires, and the images he or she consumes, can deeply influence the kind of image the person becomes. Ultimately, the gaze with which we view the world is also the gaze with which we view ourselves, actively molding our image structure in idolatrous, aniconic, or iconic ways.

Human Person as Idol

We can combine our preceding definition of an idol with Augustine's analysis of people who remember, understand, and love themselves without loving God, and come to the conclusion that such people become idols to themselves. Idols, which, as explained previously, negate any desire to reach beyond the prototype, fail to recognize that which they image. In a like manner, a human person as an idol fails to recognize God who is the source of his or her existence. Augustine claims that such people are foolish[104] and deformed by worldly lusts.[105] They are also unfortunate[106] and, ultimately, lacking in true self-love. He writes,

> So the man who knows how to love himself loves God; and the man who does not love God, even though he loves himself, which is innate in him by nature, can still be said quite reasonably to hate himself when he does what is against his own interest, and stalks himself as if he were his own enemy. It is indeed a dreadful derangement that while everyone wants to do himself good, many people do nothing but what is absolutely destructive of themselves.[107]

---

102. Drever, "The Self before God?," 238.
103. Miles, "Vision," 129.
104. Augustine, *The Trinity*, 384.
105. Augustine, *The Trinity*, 389.
106. Augustine, *The Trinity*, 385.
107. Augustine, *The Trinity*, 386.

The human person is inclined to this molding of the image structure into an idol of self in the fallen world apart from grace. Suspended, as it were, between "nothingness and goodness,"[108] the human person seeks for stability, perfection, and control. We seek to love that which is immutable, and in seeking to control it, we situate it within ourselves rather than within our Creator. This, ultimately, is a self-delusional position, for, as Adam Ployd writes, "The changeableness of created existence means that we cannot sufficiently, on our own, know and love our own minds with the necessary stability and perfection to be truly the image of God."[109] Hence, the self-idolatrous person is lacking in wisdom and truth. For Augustine, another important shortcoming that such people manifest is a lack of justice, which consists in failing to recognize one's true state.[110]

The self as idol, in positing a radical autonomy, also gives free rein to his or her literalized desires. There seems to be nothing—or nobody—to draw one beyond literal desire into the realm of the non-literal. With the self as idol, nothing stands in the way of an operative intentionality which is increasingly conditioned to seek out and satisfy an insatiable concupiscence. This restless insatiability is most characteristic, Evdokimov writes, of the demons, whom he contrasts with the angels who serve God unceasingly, and who remain iconic.[111] Yet it is also characteristic of the postmodern human person inhabiting today's hypervisual world. In fact, Baudrillard claims that one of the characteristics of postmodernity is "the effect of the sign" where signs no longer "refer to any sort of 'reality' or 'referent' or 'signified' whatsoever."[112] Marion states, "For what one calls, very often without thinking about it, an 'audiovisual civilization,' thus a 'world of images,' presupposes precisely this self-idolatry."[113] The requirement that the digital images we consume mold our literal desires already sets us up as idols viewing idols within a voyeuristic economy. Hence, even as "The image becomes the idol of man—'man is the original of his idol' (Feuerbach)," Marion claims, "man is self-idolised in the visible that

---

108. Drever, "The Self before God?," 237.

109. Ployd, "Inseparable Virtue and the *Imago Dei* in Augustine," 162.

110. Augustine, *The Trinity*, 389.

111. Evdokimov, *The Art of the Icon*, 189. See Exod 25:1, 17–22; Num 7:88–89; Ezek 1. See also Maeseneer, "Saint Francis versus Mcdonald's?," 10.

112. Baudrillard, *Baudrillard Live*, 141.

113. Marion, *The Crossing of the Visible*, 62.

he chooses himself in a spectacle. Thus the inversion of Platonism does not put an end to metaphysical iconoclasm; it radicalizes it."[114]

Yet simultaneously, and seemingly contradictorily, as soon as the human person, who has become an idol unto him or herself, seeks to become an idol to others, a reversal of gazes occurs which leaves the self within the more powerful voyeuristic gaze of the Other. As explained above, the staged self, or the image of the idol that the self becomes in the digital image world, must conform to the literalized desires of his or her viewers, thus effecting a reduction of the self. Therefore, the person whose image structure becomes that of an idol may very easily oscillate between a restless seeking to fulfill one's own literalized desires, and a demeaning attempt to conform oneself to the literalized desires of others. However, these two are not the only two options: rather it is possible to move beyond the "objective gaze" and for the person to become neither objectivizing nor objectivized, but an icon of God.

The Aniconic Person

On the other hand, there can also be an aniconic movement within the image structure of the human person. Within this dynamic, the human person becomes a mere sign or allegory pointing towards a transcendent reality while at the same time failing to recognize the inherent symbolism present within the body. For Baudrillard, this occurs within the structures of the consumer society, where the person seeks to signify and trade in signs which participate in the consumer economy, often seeking to skip over literal desire in accessing non-literal desire. Here the human person, as image, becomes a sign divorced from any inherent meaning; ultimately becoming a simulacrum.[115] In *The Consumer Society*, Baudrillard offers three examples of how this happens within the structure of the human person, namely, first, through cultivating a particular relationship to the body; second, through the aesthetics promoted within current society; and third, through the functional eroticism of consumerism.

Baudrillard claims that within consumer society, the body has replaced the soul as the object of salvation.[116] It has become the most

---

114. Marion, *The Crossing of the Visible*, 81.
115. Tiqqun, *Preliminary Materials*, 99.
116. Baudrillard, *The Consumer Society*, 129.

cherished object[117] because salvation seems to be achievable through a managed narcissism and correct cultivation of the body.[118] However, the main point here is that this narcissism is precisely *managed*. There can be no free giving in to the literal desire of the body once the body is discovered or "liberated"; rather, there must be a careful manipulation and pruning of desire so that the body comes to signify the object of salvation that it is believed to be. However, because the body seeks to participate in the signification not of its own literal meaning, which can then become opened up to a transcendent, non-literal meaning, but in the signification of the exchange-value of the consumer society, it itself becomes disposable. There is nothing intrinsic to the body that participates within this economy of signification—the body is merely chosen as the most preferred object.[119] But it is treated as an object nonetheless, and "any other object can, by the same fetishistic logic, play [the same] role."[120] It is raw matter, devoid of its own intrinsic signification, "a deposit to be mined in order to extract from it the visible signs of happiness, health, beauty, and the animality which triumphs in the marketplace of fashion."[121]

Such a treatment of the body is unmistakably aniconic. There is a suppression of the natural signification of the body and the literal desires of the person as the body is formed into the perfect object through which one attains salvation. Hence what is perceived as the "liberation" of the body is in reality the enslavement to a foreign system of signification. The body, which images the person, is obscured in its primordial signification, becoming worth nothing in itself and acting as a mere screen which displays the signification of the consumer society. One basic example of how this happens is through the wearing of logos (e.g., Nike, Adidas), or the tattooing of logos onto one's body.[122] However, even more insidiously, within this structure, the body itself becomes manipulated to signify happiness, health, and salvation. This happens particularly within the aesthetic economy.

---

117. Baudrillard, *The Consumer Society*, 131.
118. Baudrillard, *The Consumer Society*, 136.
119. Baudrillard, *The Consumer Society*, 131.
120. Baudrillard, *The Consumer Society*, 131.
121. Baudrillard, *The Consumer Society*, 131.
122. See also Klein, *No Logo*, 148.

Baudrillard claims that the cultivation of beauty or aesthetics of the body and even the functional eroticism of consumerism participates in this same dynamic. The ethics of beauty, Baudrillard writes,

> which is the very ethics of fashion, may be defined as the reduction of all concrete values—the "use-values" of the body (energetic, gestural, sexual)—to a single functional "exchange-value," which itself alone, in its abstraction, encapsulates the *idea* of the glorious, fulfilled body, the *idea* of desire and pleasure [*jouissance*], and of course thereby also denies and forgets them in their reality and in the end simply peters out into an exchange of signs.[123]

Beauty, therefore, functions as a sign with no real grounding, and is therefore disjoined from any association with truth and goodness.[124] The beautiful person signifies that they are one of the elect.[125] But what signifies beauty is governed by the consumer economy and "subjected to a *labour of investment*":[126] it is a face that has been "invested" in with carefully applied make-up, false eyelashes, colored and styled hair which signifies beauty,[127] or a figure that has been visibly "invested" in with a regimen of exercising and dieting. Ultimately, this is because, as Baudrillard writes, "beauty is nothing more than sign material being exchanged. It *functions* as sign-value."[128]

Finally, and perhaps most surprisingly, the eroticism present in the presentation of the body, including in fashion and advertising, is itself also aniconic. Rather than being a "liberating" expression of literal desire, it consists of a particular presentation of the "eroticized" body which also participates in the consumer economy.[129] Baudrillard insightfully distinguishes between literal (sexual) desire and the erotic body, writing,

> We have to distinguish the erotic body—substrate of the exchanged signs of desire—from the body as site of fantasy and abode of desire. In the drive/body, the fantasy/body, the individual structure of desire predominates. In the "eroticized"

---

123. Baudrillard, *The Consumer Society*, 132.
124. Tiqqun, *Preliminary Materials*, 46.
125. Baudrillard, *The Consumer Society*, 132.
126. Baudrillard, *The Consumer Society*, 132.
127. Baudrillard, *The Consumer Society*, 135. See Tiqqun, *Preliminary Materials*, 79.
128. Baudrillard, *The Consumer Society*, 132.
129. Baudrillard, *The Consumer Society*, 137.

body, it is the social function of exchange which predominates. In this sense, the erotic imperative—which, like courtesy or so many other social rituals, is mediated by an instrumental code of signs—is merely (like the aesthetic imperative in beauty) a variant or metaphor of the functional imperative.[130]

Hence, the erotic body seen in advertisements, in fashion, and the media, is not the expression of literal desire, but an aniconic expression of a kind of transcendent or non-literal signification which ultimately does not permit the realization of literal desire but masks and twists it.[131] Within such a structure, with the body's ontological meaning, as well as literal desire being denied, neither the true idolatrous gaze of literalized desire, nor the iconic gaze of literal desire opening up to the non-literal is possible. Baudrillard writes that what remains is an "abstraction";[132] what we would term, within the context of this chapter, as aniconic non-literal desire. Because non-literal desire dominates and is not grounded in literal desire, signs take on a life of their own, unmoored from any inherent meaning of the signified. Baudrillard writes, "the whole of advertising and modern erotics are made up of signs, not of meaning."[133] This also opens the path to ideology and manipulation.

While Baudrillard insightfully presents the aniconic anthropology which operates within the consumer society, particularly within fashion and advertising, he fails to propose any adequate solution. In fact, he seems to believe that this unmooring of signs from meaning, this unreality, and what he terms "seduction" of the world, is inevitable. His views, as he himself articulated on a number of occasions,[134] align him with a classical Manichean position.[135] He writes, "My position . . . is evil because it contradicts all possibility of rebuilding the world."[136] Ultimately, Baudrillard is working out of an iconoclastic paradigm which, although he critiques it, he simultaneously claims is unavoidable. However, the preceding analysis of the image opens up another option—rather than an iconoclastic decrying of the aniconic understanding of the person,

130. Baudrillard, *The Consumer Society*, 133.
131. Baudrillard, *The Consumer Society*, 133.
132. Baudrillard, *The Consumer Society*, 134.
133. Baudrillard, *The Consumer Society*, 132; see also 145–46.
134. Baudrillard, *Baudrillard Live*, 176.
135. Baudrillard, *Baudrillard Live*, 139.
136. Baudrillard, *Baudrillard Live*, 177.

the person can also become an icon, openly and freely imaging a reality which is above and beyond themselves. To this final way in which a person can be said to be an "image" we will now turn.

Person as Icon

To image iconically, we must see the world and ourselves with an iconic gaze, that is, to accept both literal desire and be open to non-literal desire. This iconic gaze may also be referred to as participating in a sacramental ontology.[137] A human being who is an icon is able to perceive the beauty of both the physical world and be open to the transcendence of the spiritual, recognizing that neither necessarily contradicts nor cancels each other out. For such a person, as St. Maximus the Confessor wrote, the world reveals itself as an "image and appearing of the invisible light, a very pure mirror, clear, showing a true reflection, immaculate, undarkened, welcoming, if it is proper to speak so: all the splendor of the primal beauty."[138] Other persons, too, are recognized as unique human beings with strengths and weaknesses on the natural plane, but simultaneously as graced children of God, gifted with immortal souls and called to eternal beatitude. Here both the literal and non-literal are present and shown to be in synergy rather than competition with each other.

Furthermore, just like any other iconic image, the iconic person seeks to "let all God's glory through,"[139] that is, he or she does not seek to attribute truth, beauty, and goodness to their own attainments, but to recognize them as a gift from God. As Marion wrote, "The icon . . . is derived from the kenosis of the image."[140] He or she exhibits neither the arrogance of an idolatrous image functioning according to literalized desire, nor the shame of an aniconic image seeking to completely suppress or manipulate literal desire. Instead, in being open to the divine through non-literal desire, he or she simultaneously sees the goodness in literal desire, which is recognized as a gift of God's creation and a potential tool for sanctification and a preparation for heavenly beatitude. This has at least two

---

137. See Boersma, *Heavenly Participation*; Boersma, *Nouvelle Théologie and Sacramental Ontology*.

138. St. Maximus the Confessor, *Myst.* 23, PG 91, 701C, as cited in Evdokimov, *The Art of the Icon*, 14.

139. Hopkins, "The Blessed Virgin."

140. Marion, *The Crossing of the Visible*, 62.

implications. First, it means that being a true icon means remembering, understanding, and loving God, as is presented in Augustine's definition of the image of God outlined above.[141] One cannot "let all God's glory through" if one does not turn to God in one's mind, heart, and actions. To use Balthasar's manner of expression: only through attunement and contemplation[142] can one be transformed into the Christ-form.[143] Once again we see here the necessity of cultivating habitual actions which form our operative intentionality and mold us into the kind of persons, or the type of images, we become.

The second implication is that such a person operates according to justice, a key virtue in Augustine's conception of goodness. Just as the person as idol lacks justice because they fail to acknowledge one's true state (particularly the recognition of one's radical dependence on God), so an iconic person, by not seeking to attribute glory to him or herself, operates according to the basic principle of justice. In other words, one recognizes and accepts one's creaturely status. As Williams writes,

> Growing into the image of God, then, is not a matter of perfecting our possession of certain qualities held in common with God, nor even simply . . . coming to have God as the formal object of our mental activity. It is for us to be at home with our created selves (our selves as produced, derived), and so to be at home with the action of a creator.[144]

The true image of God is not self-referential, according to Augustine, but acknowledges the essential relation between the human person and God.[145] Boersma explains that therefore, for Augustine, "an account of 'human nature' must transcend the human person; it finds intelligibility in its exemplar, the Holy Trinity."[146] This recognition of the essential relation to God further enables one to relate to others in a just way: having restored the relationship with God and with oneself, one is able now to love others as they should be loved. Augustine writes,

141. Williams, "*Sapientia* and the Trinity," 326.

142. Balthasar, *Prayer*, 19.

143. Nichols, *The Word Has Been Abroad*, 81. See Steck, *The Ethical Thought of Hans Urs Von Balthasar*, 157.

144. Williams, "*Sapientia* and the Trinity," 321.

145. Boersma, *Augustine's Early Theology of Image*, 256. See Williams, "*Sapientia* and the Trinity," 324.

146. Boersma, *Augustine's Early Theology of Image*, 256. See Williams, "*Sapientia* and the Trinity," 320.

> But when the mind loves God, and consequently as has been said remembers and understands him, it can rightly be commanded to love its neighbour as itself. For now it loves itself with a straight, not a twisted love, now that it loves God; for sharing in him results not merely in its being that image, but in its being made new and fresh and happy after being old and worn and miserable.[147]

However, the iconic imaging of God by the human person is not a static accomplishment. One must seek to make "steady progress in the renewal of this image"[148] following one's conversion from an idolatrous and aniconic manner of being. This means that we are able to continue growing in the image of God throughout the entirety of life, a quest which is accomplished through the moral life and seeking to grow in holiness. Central to this growth is to resist falling into either an idolatrous or aniconic gaze. Augustine writes,

> So then the man who is being renewed in the recognition of God and in justice and holiness of truth by making progress day by day, is transferring his love from temporal things to eternal, from visible to intelligible, from carnal to spiritual things; he is industriously applying himself to checking and lessening his greed for the one sort and binding himself with charity to the other. But his success in this depends on divine assistance; it is after all God who declares, *Without me you can do nothing* (Jn 15.5).[149]

Furthermore, the image will only become truly a fully iconic image of God with the beatific vision of God in heaven: "For only when it comes to the perfect vision of God will this image bear God's perfect likeness."[150]

It is possible to refer to a kind of "branding" which occurs when the human person becomes an iconic image of God. Maeseneer draws on the thought of Balthasar, who claims that the process of stigmatization—or what could be referred to as being branded with "Christ"—is the ultimate model for every Christian. Yet while this branding, just as the commercial branding with a company logo, signifies "total surrender to an alterity,"[151] nevertheless there is a radical difference between the two.

147. Augustine, *The Trinity*, 386.
148. Augustine, *The Trinity*, 391.
149. Augustine, *The Trinity*, 391.
150. Augustine, *The Trinity*, 391.
151. Maeseneer, "Saint Francis versus Mcdonald's?," 9.

The Christian who comes to be an iconic image of God and is "branded" with Christ does not seek to destroy nor malign literal desire, but understands Christ's presence as elevating, transforming, and ultimately fulfilling the literal plane. On the other hand, the person who is branded with a company logo enters into an alterity which is foreign to literal desire: "the body disappears behind the brand"[152] in an aniconic manner, and the literal is denied for the sake of the non-literal. Hence, as Maeseneer explains, "the branding logo . . . strikes us by its shiny appearance, in which nothing reminds us of materiality, mortality, and vulnerability."[153] Here the distinction between the aniconic, iconic, and idolatrous gaze allows once again for clarification between what may, superficially, seem like two very similar processes.

The saints demonstrate in the fullest way possible what it means to be an iconic image of God.[154] Saints are "irresistible icons of meaningful living aligned and rooted within Scripture, Sacrament, and the Church,"[155] who recognize that the entirety of their being is a gift from God and seek to "let all God's glory through."[156] They are able to perceive iconically, that is, sacramentally or liturgically,[157] and recognize the goodness in literal desire while simultaneously maintaining its essential openness to non-literal desire. Of all the saints, Mary, the Mother of God, is the purest icon of the divine. In the Litany of Loreto, she is referred to as the "Mirror of Justice," a title which both refers to her iconicity as well as to her deep virtue of justice, which, as we have seen, is a central quality of the iconic person. In his first encyclical, John Paul II wrote that "among all believers she is like a 'mirror' in which are reflected in the most profound and limpid ways 'the mighty works of God.' (Acts 2:11)."[158] Likewise, the reference of "letting all God's glory through," which has been used throughout to refer to the primary disposition of the person who is an iconic image of God, originates from a poem by Gerard Manley Hopkins which is devoted to the Blessed Virgin Mary.[159]

---

152. Maeseneer, "Saint Francis versus Mcdonald's?," 11.

153. Maeseneer, "Saint Francis versus Mcdonald's?," 11.

154. Evdokimov, *The Art of the Icon*, 17.

155. Klein, "The Strange Witness of the Saints," iv.

156. Hopkins, "The Blessed Virgin."

157. Evdokimov writes, "A Saint is not a superman but someone who lives his truth as a liturgical being." Evdokimov, *The Art of the Icon*, 15.

158. John Paul II, *Redemptor hominis*, no. 25.

159. Hopkins, "The Blessed Virgin."

In our analysis of the image and the image structure of the human person, the anthropology of the consumer has been shown to oscillate between the poles of an idolatrous and an aniconic gaze, which contrasts with the anthropology of the Christian, who is awakened to an iconic gaze through grace, and enabled to become an iconic image of God. The difference between the idolatrous, aniconic, and iconic has been claimed to lie in the kinds of desire they promote or elicit: the idolatrous promotes literal desire while denying the non-literal, the aniconic promotes non-literal desire while denying or subverting the literal, while the iconic is able to hold the two together in an analogical or sacramental manner. Augustine's insights on the human person as image and likeness of God have been used throughout the chapter, and provided a useful framework to evaluate the human person's constitutive relationality to the images we consume.[160] To conclude, the following quote from Evdokimov summarizes both the ability of the iconic to hold the literal and non-literal together in a fruitful interrelationship, as well as the necessity of undergoing a process of conversion to be able to perceive iconically and become an iconic image of God:

> There is no ontological dualism between the Church and the world, between the sacred and the profane. There is an ethical dualism, however, between "the old man" and the "new man" between the redeemed sacred and the demonized profane.[161]

---

160. Hanby, "Desire," 112; Maeseneer, "Saint Francis versus Mcdonald's?"
161. Evdokimov, *The Art of the Icon*, 53.

Bibliography

Alleau, Rene. *De La Nature Des Symboles: Introduction a La Symbolique Generale*. Paris: Payot, 2006.

Augustine. *On Genesis*. Edited by John E. Rotelle. Translated by Edmund Hill and Matthew O'Connell. Hyde Park, NY: New City, 2002.

———. *Responses to Miscellaneous Questions: Miscellany of Eighty-Three Questions, Miscellany of Questions in Response to Simplician and Eight Questions of Dulcitius*. Edited by John E. Rotelle. Translated by Boniface Ramsey. Hyde Park, NY: New City, 2008.

———. *Teaching Christianity: De Doctrina Christiana*. Edited by John E. Rotelle. Translated by Edmund Hill. Vol. I/11, Hyde Park, NY: New City, 1996.

———. *The Trinity*. Edited by John E. Rotelle. Translated by Edmund Hill. Hyde Park, NY: New City, 1991.

Balthasar, Hans Urs von. *Prayer*. Translated by A. V. Littledale. London: Chapman, 1961.

Barron, Robert. *Vibrant Paradoxes: The Both/And of Catholicism*. Skokie, IL: Word on Fire, 2016.

Baudrillard, Jean. *Baudrillard Live: Selected Interviews*. New York: Routledge, 1993.

———. *The Consumer Society: Myths and Structures*. London: SAGE, 1998.

Belting, Hans. *Das Echte Bild: Bildfragen Als Glaubensfragen*. Munich: Beck, 2005.

———. "Image, Medium, Body: A New Approach to Iconology." *Critical inquiry* 31.2 (2005) 302–19.

Benjamin, Walter. *The Work of Art in the Age of Mechanical Reproduction*. London: Penguin, 2008.

Boehm, Gottfried. "Die Wiederkehr Der Bilder." In *Was Ist Ein Bild?*, 11–38. Munich: Fink, 1994.

Boersma, Gerald P. *Augustine's Early Theology of Image: A Study in the Development of Pro-Nicene Theology*. New York: Oxford University Press, 2016.

Boersma, Hans. *Heavenly Participation: The Weaving of a Sacramental Tapestry*. Grand Rapids: Eerdmans, 2011.

———. *Nouvelle Théologie and Sacramental Ontology: A Return to Mystery*. Oxford: Oxford University Press, 2009.

Boorstin, Daniel J., and Douglas Rushkoff. *The Image: A Guide to Pseudo-Events in America*. New York: Vintage, 2012.

Bredekamp, Horst. *Darwins Korallen: Die Frühen Evolutionsdiagramme und Die Tradition Der Naturgeschichte*. Vol. 73, Berlin: Wagenbach, 2005.

———. "Drehmomente-Merkmale und Ansprüche Des Iconic Turn." In *Iconic Turn: Die Neue Macht Der Bilder*, edited by Christa Maar and Hubert Burda, 15–26. Cologne: Du Mont, 2004.

Bredekamp, Horst, and Gabriele Werner. "Editorial." In *Bilder in Prozessen. Die Fruhen Evolutionsdiagramme und Die Tradition Der Neturgeschichte*, 7–8. Berlin: Oldenbourg, 2003.

Carlson, Thomas A. "Consuming Desire's Deferral: A Theological Shadow in the Culture of Image." *Parallax* 5.1 (1999) 39–55.

Carnes, Natalie. *Image and Presence: A Christological Reflection on Iconoclasm and Iconophilia*. Stanford: Stanford University Press, 2018.

Cary, Philip. *Augustine's Invention of the Inner Self: The Legacy of a Christian Platonist*. Oxford: Oxford University Press, 2000.

Cavadini, John C. "Reconsidering Augustine on Marriage and Concupiscence." *Augustinian Studies* 48.1–2 (2017) 183–99.

Drever, Matthew. "The Self before God? Rethinking Augustine's Trinitarian Thought." *Harvard Theological Review* 100.2 (2007) 233–42.

———. "Sightings." In *Image, Identity, and the Forming of the Augustinian Soul*, 1–41. New York: Oxford University Press, 2013.

Elkins, James. *The Domain of Images*. Ithaca: Cornell University Press, 2001.

———. "Visual Practices across the University." Paper presented at the Beyond Mimesis and Convention, 2010.

———. *Visual Studies: A Skeptical Introduction*. New York: Routledge, 2003.

Evdokimov, Paul. *The Art of the Icon: A Theology of Beauty*. Redondo Beach, CA: Oakwood, 1990.

Ferretter, Luke. "The Trace of the Trinity: Christ and Difference in Saint Augustine's Theory of Language." *Literature and Theology* 12.3 (1998) 256–67.

Gregory of Nyssa. *The Life of Moses*. Translated by Everett Ferguson and Abraham Johannes Malherbe. New York: Paulist, 1978.

———. *Song of Songs*. Translated by Casimir McCambley. Brookline, MA: Hellenic College Press, 1987.

Hanby, Michael. "Desire: Augustine beyond Western Subjectivity." In *Radical Orthodoxy: A New Theology*, edited by John Milbank et al., 121–38. New York: Routledge, 1998.

Hankey, Wayne. "Between and beyond Augustine and Descartes: More Than a Source of the Self." *Augustinian Studies* 32,.1 (2001) 65–88.

———. "The Postmodern Retrieval of Neoplatonism in Jean-Luc Marion and John Milbank and the Origins of Western Subjectivity in Augustine and Eriugena." *Hermathena* 165 (1998) 9–70.

———. "Re-Christianizing Augustine Postmodern Style: Readings by Jacques Derrida, Robert Dodaro, Jean-Luc Marion, Rowan Williams, Lewis Ayres and John Milbank." *Animus* 3 (1998) 387–415.

———. "Stephen Menn's Cartesian Augustine: Metaphysically and Ahistorically Modern." *Animus* 3 (1998) 1–28.

Hedley, Douglas. *The Iconic Imagination*. New York: Bloomsbury, 2016.

Hopkins, Gerard Manley. "The Blessed Virgin Compared to the Air We Breathe." https://hopkinspoetry.com/poem/the-blessed-virgin/.

John Paul II, Pope. *Redemptor hominis*. Roma: Libreria Editrice Vaticana, 1979.

Klein, Carmel. "The Strange Witness of the Saints: Hans Urs Von Balthasar's Embodied Theology of Mission." PhD diss., University of Dayton, 2017.

Klein, Naomi. *No Logo: No Space, No Choice, No Jobs*. London: Flamingo, 2001.

Lossky, Vladimir. *In the Image and Likeness of God*. New York: St. Vladimir's Seminary, 1974.

Maeseneer, Yves de. "Saint Francis versus McDonald's? Contemporary Globalization Critique and Hans Urs Von Balthasar's Theological Aesthetics." *Heythrop Journal* 44.1 (2003) 1–14.

Marion, Jean-Luc. *The Crossing of the Visible*. Edited by Mieke Bal and Hent de Vries. Translated by James K. A. Smith. Cultural Memory in the Present. Stanford: Stanford University Press, 2004.

———. *La Croisée Du Visible*. Paris: Presses Universitaires de France, 1991.
Merleau-Ponty, Maurice. *Phenomenology of Perception*. Translated by Donald A. Landes. New York: Routledge, 2012.
Miles, Margaret. "Vision: The Eye of the Body and the Eye of the Mind in Saint Augustine's *De Trinitate* and *Confessions*." *Journal of Religion* 63.2 (1983) 125–42.
Mirzoeff, Nicholas. *An Introduction to Visual Culture*. London: Routledge, 1999.
Mitchell, William John Thomas. "Idolatry: Nietzsche, Blake, and Poussin." *Things* (2011) 112–26.
———. *Picture Theory: Essays on Verbal and Visual Representation*. Chicago: University of Chicago Press, 1995.
———. *What Do Pictures Want? The Lives and Loves of Images*. Chicago: University of Chicago Press, 2005.
———. "What Is an Image?" *New Literary History* 15.3 (1984) 503–37.
Moxey, Keith. "Visual Studies and the Iconic Turn." *Journal of Visual Culture* 7.2 (2008) 131–46.
Nichols, Aidan. *The Art of God Incarnate: Theology and Image in Christian Tradition*. Eugene, OR: Wipf & Stock, 2016.
———. *The Word Has Been Abroad: A Guide through Balthasar's Aesthetics*. Vol. 1. Washington, DC: Catholic University of America Press, 1998.
Pattison, George. "Idol or Icon? Some Principles of an Aesthetic Christology." *Literature and Theology* 3.1 (1989) 1–15.
Pieper, Josef. *Only the Lover Sings: Art and Contemplation*. Translated by Lothar Krauth. San Francisco: Ignatius, 1990.
Ployd, Adam. "Inseparable Virtue and the *Imago Dei* in Augustine: A Speculative Interpretation of *De Trinitate* 6.4." *Scottish Journal of Theology* 72.2 (2019) 146–65.
Ratzinger, Joseph. *The Spirit of the Liturgy*. Translated by John Saward. San Francisco: Ignatius, 2000.
Sheen, Fulton J. *Three to Get Married*. New York: Scepter, 1996.
Sontag, Susan. *On Photography*. Harmondsworth: Penguin, 2019.
Steck, Christopher. *The Ethical Thought of Hans Urs von Balthasar*. New York: Crossroad, 2001.
Stock, Brian. *Augustine the Reader*. Cambridge: Harvard University Press, 1996.
Sullivan, John E. *The Image of God: The Doctrine of St. Augustine and Its Influence*. Dubuqe, IA: Priory, 1963.
Taylor, Charles. *Sources of the Self: The Making of the Modern Identity*. Cambridge: Cambridge University Press, 1989.
Taylor, Mark C. *Hiding*. Chicago: University of Chicago Press, 1997.
Ticciati, Susannah. "The Human Being as Sign in Augustine's *De Doctrina Christiana*." *Neue Zeitschrift für systematische Theologie und Religionsphilosophie* 55.1 (2013) 20–32.
Tiqqun. *Preliminary Materials for a Theory of the Young-Girl*. Translated by Ariana Reines. Los Angeles: Semiotext(e), 2012.
Williams, Rowan. "*Sapientia* and Trinity: Reflections on the *De Trinitate*." *Augustiniana* 40.1/4 (1990) 317–32.

8

Becoming a Social Human Being

Communal Life as a Path to Deification in the Ascetical Works of Basil of Caesarea

Kevin Wagner

Basil of Caesarea is renowned both as a theologian and as a key figure in the history of coenobitical monasticism. His doctrine of deification—which is far less developed than that of his fellow Cappadocians—relies particularly on the imitation (*mimesis*) of Christ. For Basil, this requires asceticism and the working of the Holy Spirit. The asceticism Basil has in mind is that which is practiced by the community of monks who seek sanctification through the common or social life. In this chapter we will begin by setting out briefly Basil's doctrine of deification. Next, we will examine some key Basilian texts in order to determine what he means by the term κοινωνικὸς ἄνθρωπος. Finally, we will show that Basil's *Long Rules* is written for the end that every monk should become a social human being and thus, deified.

Basil of Caesarea was born around AD 330 and died on January 1, 379. His early years were spent on family estates in Cappadocia, Pontus, and Annisa (modern Turkey) and it was here that his education began. At the age of fourteen Basil ventured to Caesarea to begin his formal studies. From there he moved to Constantinople and then Athens in order to soak up the best *paideia* the Greek world had to offer. From the outset it can be seen that Basil was given every opportunity to attain some level of prestige. What set him apart for true greatness, however, was his family, which contained a number of saints and martyrs. It could be reasonably argued, especially on the basis of his brother Gregory's work on the life of their sister Macrina, that it was the human formation provided through the family that made Basil a saint. Furthermore, it could be contended that this familial formation enabled Basil to integrate effectively his theology and his pastoral practice.

We will begin this chapter with a short summary of three types or categories of deification—the nominal, realistic, and ethical—that have been proposed by modern scholars. Next, we will look closely at Basil's theology of deification, focusing first on his understanding of image and likeness, then on the place of baptism and asceticism in the process of deification. Following this, we will consider Basil's teaching on the social dimension of personhood and the necessity of becoming a social human being in order to be deified. Finally, we will draw some examples from Basil's *Long Rules* for monastic life (the *Great Asketikon*) that serve to demonstrate how the life of practical asceticism is helpful for making one a social human being and thus for restoring one to likeness with God.

Types of Deification

Deification may be defined as the process by which created human persons "become," "participate in," or "partake of" God, such that each "fulfill[s] that divine image and likeness originally implanted deep within every human soul."[1] There has been a resurgence of interest in the West in the doctrine of deification since the late nineteenth century.[2] With this

---

1. Meconi and Olsen, "Introduction," in Meconi and Olson, *Called to Be the Children of God*, 13.

2. Rowland, "Vatican II, John Paul II, and Postconciliar Theology," in Meconi and Olson, *Called to Be the Children of God*, 245.

renewed focus has come an awareness that there are different types or categories of deification and the language which is used to describe it. In a 2015 article, Daniel Keating helpfully analyzed various attempts to define these categories, examining the works of Norman Russell, Gösta Hallonsten, and Paul Gavrilyuk.[3] A year later, in a book chapter on deification in the Greek Fathers, Keating addressed the issue of categorization again. In this work, we find that Keating settles on three categories of deification: the nominal, realistic, and ethical.[4]

For Keating, the nominal type is *merely* or *simply* "honorific and occurs when the title 'god' is given to humans as a way to honor their status."[5] An example might be Ps 82:6,[6] where the psalmist declares men to be gods, a sentiment repeated by Jesus himself in John 10:34–35.[7] Keating points out that this type of language is "somewhat rare" in the works of the Greek Fathers.[8] More interesting for our purpose are the realistic and ethical categories, which, Keating (following Russell) notes, are dependent on one another.[9]

The realistic category refers to "the idea that human beings are somehow transformed and participate in God."[10] This notion is rooted in the fact that baptism makes one a Christian; that is, an adopted son or daughter of the Father and "a dwelling place of the Spirit."[11] As we shall soon see, while Basil does not typically use "realistic" language, he does attribute to the Spirit—which is given in a definitive manner in baptism—a transformative power that deifies.

---

3. Keating, "Typologies of Deification," 267–83.

4. Keating, "Deification in the Greek Fathers," in Meconi and Olson, *Called to Be the Children of God*, 57. We note here that Keating is basing his work heavily on that of Norman Russell, particularly his monograph *The Doctrine of Deification in the Greek Patristic Tradition*.

5. Keating, "Deification in the Greek Fathers," 56–57.

6. "I say, 'You are gods, sons of the Most High, all of you.'" (RSV).

7. "Jesus answered them, 'Is it not written in your law, "I said, you are gods"? If he called them gods to whom the word of God came (and scripture cannot be broken)'" (RSV).

8. Keating, "Deification in the Greek Fathers," 57.

9. Keating, "Deification in the Greek Fathers," 57.

10. Keating, "Deification in the Greek Fathers," 56. See also 2 Pet 1:4, "Through these, he has bestowed on us the precious and very great promises, so that through them you may come to share in the divine nature, after escaping from the corruption that is in the world because of evil desire" (NABRE).

11. Keating, "Typologies of Deification," 282.

In contrast to the realistic category of divinization, the ethical refers to "the ascetic effort to attain likeness to God by imitation of him."[12] Keating declares the mutuality of the realistic and ethical categories and the pre-eminence of the realistic as he states,

> the ethical needs to *follow in principle* upon the realistic, for if Christ has not redeemed our nature in himself and granted to us a share in that redeemed nature through the Spirit in baptism, we have no ability to exert ourselves and so grow into the fullness of the divine likeness.[13]

What is at play here is the working out of the faith and works question that has raged since Paul and James wrote their epistles. Faith, the gift received by the individual in baptism, incorporates the recipient into the Body of Christ. Asceticism, on the other hand, keeps the Body from rejecting the new member, builds unity amongst the members of the Body, and causes the member to attain likeness to the Head of the Body, Christ.

In short, these three key categories of deification highlight the gratuitous gift of God's Son who, in assuming human nature, redeemed it, and welcomed human beings to actively participate in the work of becoming like God.

Deification in the Works of St. Basil

Image and Likeness

Central to the concept of deification is the question of what it means for man to be created in the image *and* likeness of God (Gen 1:26). In patristic theologies of deification this question is approached in different ways. *Contra* Athanasius, Cyril of Alexandria, and his own brother Gregory of Nyssa, who deem image and likeness to be equivalent terms, Basil believes Gen 1:26 points to two separate actions, one divine and the other

---

12. Keating, "Deification in the Greek Fathers," 56.

13. Keating, "Deification in the Greek Fathers," 57. See also Keating, "Typologies of Deification," 272–73.

human.[14] In a homily on Genesis 1, perhaps dated late in his life,[15] Basil expounds on the difference between man's image and his likeness to God;

> "Let us make the human being according to our image and according to our likeness." . . . By our creation we have the first, and by our free choice we build the second. In our initial structure co-originates and exists our coming into being according to the image of God. By free choice we are conformed to that which is according to the likeness of God. And this is what is according to free choice: the power exists in us but we bring it about by our activity.[16]

Basil holds, therefore, that God himself, through our very creation by him, makes us into his image. We are made in God's image, he believes, as we share with God a rational nature;[17] that is, we possess intellect, "a mind capable of understanding."[18] Additionally, like God, we have the capacity to love both God and his creatures, and this capacity is given to each person from the first moment of his or her creation.[19] These capacities for rational thought and love are instrumental in enabling persons to return to God's likeness, a likeness which was lost in the Garden. Further to this, Basil states that God "placed in man some share of His own grace, in order that he might recognize likeness through likeness."[20] Not only are we blessed with the ability to think and love, but God has given his people the gift of being naturally "desirous of the beautiful" and the good.[21] Sin, however, "marred the beauty of the image by dragging the soul down to

---

14. Keating, "Typologies of Deification," 276. We should be wary of presuming a Pelagian influence on Basil here. It should be noted that Basil recognizes that the very possibility of human persons being able to act to restore their likeness is only possible as God has given each the power to do this. Indeed, likeness is restored, on Basil's view, through adherence to Gospel teaching and baptism. Basil, *On the Origin of Humanity, Discourse 1*, 17, in Basil, *On the Human Condition*, 45.

15. On the question of dating and authorship, see Harrison, "Introduction," in Basil, *On the Human Condition*, 15.

16. Basil, *On the Origin of Humanity, Discourse 1*, 16, in Basil, *On the Human Condition*, 43–44.

17. Basil, *Long Rules* 1, in Basil, *Ascetical Works*, 237.

18. Basil, *Give Heed to Thyself*, in Basil, *Ascetical Works*, 435, 441.

19. Basil, *Long Rules* 2, in Basil, *Ascetical Works*, 234.

20. Basil, *Homily* 19.8, in Basil, *Exegetical Homilies*, 325.

21. Indeed, for Basil, "all creatures desire God." Basil, *Long Rules* 2, in Basil, *Ascetical Works*, 234–35.

passionate desires" and this caused man to lose "his likeness to God."[22] Likeness to God is thus lost through original sin, and by our failure to act rationally and in accordance with the natural desire for God that we have been given. Basil contrasts this failure on our part with the natural urges of animals who show gratitude to their human masters and of babies who cling to their mothers.[23] Acting against this God-given desire is a key sign that one is falling short in the battle to conform to the likeness of God.

On Basil's view then, human persons have been given by God, at the moment of their creation, the means by which they might work out their salvation and attain likeness to God. So, how does Basil imagine this likeness is restored? The short answer is by submission to baptism and the embracing of asceticism.

Baptism as Restoration to Likeness

In his work *Concerning Baptism*, Basil offers in quick succession two compelling images to illustrate how the human person may be restored to the likeness of God. The first of these images is that of a shattered statue of a king, the image of which is "no longer discernable."[24] This statue, Basil believes, is analogous to fallen humanity, beastly, senseless, and unlike its Creator in whose image it is fashioned. Mercifully, the statue is restored by the "wise artificer and skilled craftsman" who, "seeking to regain the beauty of his work, shapes it anew and restores it to its former splendor."[25] This, Basil declares, is the end of those who turn to "that form of doctrine [τύπον διαδοχῆς] into which [we] were delivered" (Rom 6:17) and are thus "recalled to . . . original glory as the image of God."[26] But what is this "form of doctrine" and how can adherence to this doctrine restore one to prelapsarian glory?

To answer these questions adequately it is necessary to clarify an important textual anomaly in Basil's quotation here of Rom 6:17. The issue concerns the fact that Basil records Paul's text as "τύπον διαδοχῆς,"[27] while the text of the New Testament (Nestle-Aland 28) here

22. Basil, *Sermo 13*, in Basil, *Ascetical Works*, 207.
23. Basil, *Long Rules 2*, in Basil, *Ascetical Works*, 236.
24. Basil, *Concerning Baptism* 1.2, in Basil, *Ascetical Works*, 358.
25. Basil, *Concerning Baptism* 1.2, in Basil, *Ascetical Works*, 358.
26. Basil, *Concerning Baptism* 1.2, in Basil, *Ascetical Works*, 358.
27. Basil. *De baptismo libri duo* 1.2.7, in Migne, *PG* 31, 1537.

is "τύπον διδαχῆς."²⁸ A proximity search of the words τύπον, διαδοχῆς and their cognates in the *Thesaurus Linguae Graecae* reveals that this rendering of the text of Rom 6:17 is unique in extant Greek literature.²⁹ So, what can we make of this difference between Basil's text and that found in the NT?

The NT text (τύπον διδαχῆς) has been translated as a pattern, form, or standard of teaching.³⁰ Brendan Byrne presumes this "refers to some kind of catechetical compendium given to new converts" that Paul assumes his readers are aware of.³¹ This view that the τύπον διδαχῆς of Rom 6:17 constitutes a set of teachings used for baptismal instruction goes back at least to Alfred Seeberg (d. 1915) and his seminal work on early catechetical texts.³² There is, however, much debate regarding Seeberg's argumentation and the veracity of his conclusions, particularly those concerning the content of this teaching. One suspects that Byrne's reluctance to declare his position more assertively is due to this ongoing disputation.³³ In the absence of a definitive solution to this question, we can say at least that this διδαχῆς was liberating teaching of some sort, probably transmitted by Paul and his companions, to which commitment and obedience was expected of the recipients.

Basil's text (τύπον διαδοχῆς) is translated by M. Monica Wagner as "form of doctrine."³⁴ On the face of it, this translation seems poor as διαδοχή means "succession" not "doctrine." Further investigation, however, reveals that, among other possibilities, patristic usage of the term διαδοχή could refer to a succession of (episcopal) office or to a "succession of pupils and teachers, hence of transmission of tradition of teaching."³⁵ It could be argued, then, that the discrepancy in Basil's text—be it the result of Basil's faulty memory, a scribal error in the text Basil used, or a corruption of the Basilian text—is a happy fault, for διαδοχή conveys

28. https://www.academic-bible.com/en/online-bibles/novum-testamentum-graece-na-28/read-the-bible-text/bibelstelle/rom%206%3A17/bibel/text/lesen/ch/50 c96ed7ee90091e7489cdaa42d86b78/.

29. TLG, http://stephanus.tlg.uci.edu/Iris/indiv/tsearch.jsp#s=2.

30. See, for example, the following translations: "pattern of teaching" (NABRE, NIV, NET); "form of teaching" (NRSV, NKJV); "standard of teaching" (RSV).

31. Byrne, *Romans*, 206.

32. Edsall, "Kerygma," 412. See the Bibliography for these seminal works.

33. Edsall's article traces the history of scholarly engagement with Seeberg's work.

34. Basil, *Concerning Baptism* 1.2, in Basil, *Ascetical Works*, 358.

35. Lampe, *A Patristic Greek Lexicon*, s.v. "διαδοχή."

strongly the sense of traditional instruction passed from the apostles to their successors. Given that the New Testament text appears to refer to teaching handed on by Paul and his co-workers, it seems that this form of διαδοχή is essentially equivalent to the pattern of διδαχή; that is, the form of διαδοχῆς may be understood as some type of catechesis.

Having established what the form of doctrine is, we are still left to determine how this catechesis has the power to restore one to the likeness of God. The second image Basil offers in this section of *Concerning Baptism* suggests an answer. He writes,

> Just as wax applied *to the form of a carving* [τῷ τύπῳ τῆς γλυφῆς] is *formed exactly according to the form impressed upon the carved surface* [μορφοῦται πρὸς ἀκρίβειαν τὴν ἐγκειμένην τῇ γλυφῇ μορφὴν], so we, *having handed ourselves over to the form of the teaching according to the Gospel* [παραδόντες ἑαυτοὺς τῷ τύπῳ τῆς κατὰ τὸ Εὐαγγέλιον διδασκαλίας], *are formed as regards the inner man* [μορφωθῶμεν τὸν ἔσω ἄνθρωπον].[36]

We see here that the carved surface is analogous to Gospel teaching, the Εὐαγγέλιον, and that the Christian is the one who has submitted to this teaching. This submission leads to the stripping away of the old man and his deeds, and the putting on of the new man, "who is renewed unto knowledge according to the image of him that created him."[37] Given the context of Basil's text—which is immediately followed by a reference to "being born anew of water"—we may well assume that both "the form of teaching according to the Gospel" and the τύπον διαδοχῆς constitute some form of teaching to which the catechumen submits before baptism.[38]

It is not, however, this teaching itself that causes the soul to be returned to the likeness of God. Rather, whole-hearted devotion to pre-baptismal catechesis leads one to strip off the old man and to submit to baptism, and baptism—which is the sacramental means by which one puts on the new man—restores one's likeness to God. This restoration through baptism enables those "who are born of the Spirit [to] become

---

36. Basil, *Concerning Baptism* 1.2, in Basil, *Ascetical Works*, 358, with my own changes made to the translation. Note that I have intentionally translated this passage very literally from Basil, *De baptismo libri duo* 1.2.7, in Migne, *PG* 31, 1537. Unless otherwise indicated, italics are used to indicate the text translated from the supplied Greek text.

37. Basil, *Concerning Baptism* 1.2, in Basil, *Ascetical Works*, 359.

38. Basil, *Concerning Baptism* 1.2, in Basil, *Ascetical Works*, 359.

spirit [πνεῦμα γενέσθαι]."[39] And this is achieved by the working of the Holy Spirit who "illuminates those who have been cleansed from every stain and *makes them spiritual* [πνευματικοὺς ἀποδείκνυσι] by means of communion with himself."[40] Made "spirit (πνεῦμα)" or "spiritual (πνευματικός)" by baptism, the neophyte is endowed with the gifts of "foreknowledge of the future, understanding of mysteries, apprehension of secrets, distribution of graces, heavenly citizenship, the chorus with angels, unending joy, remaining in God, kinship with God, and the highest object of desire, becoming God."[41] In short, the rite of baptism—which is received as a free response to one's submission to pre-baptismal catechesis—opens the possibility for the transformation of a person to become like God and a god; that is, to be deified.

Asceticism as Restoration to Likeness

In the first paragraph of a short work on asceticism (*Sermo 13*), Basil argues that the taming of the passions—that is, *apatheia*—is effective for restoring likeness to God. It is worth quoting in full:

> Man was made after the image and likeness of God; but sin marred the beauty of the image by dragging the soul down to passionate desires. Now, God, who made man, is the true life. Therefore, when man lost his likeness to God, he lost his participation in the true life; separated and estranged from God as he is, it is impossible for him to enjoy the blessedness of the divine life. Let us return, then, to the grace [which was ours] in the beginning and from which we have alienated ourselves by sin, and let us again adorn ourselves with the beauty of God's image, *being made like to our Creator through the quieting of our passions* [διὰ τῆς ἀπαθείας ὁμοιωθέντες τῷ κτίσαντι]. He

---

39. τοὺς γεννηθέντας ἐκ πνεύματος πνεῦμα γενέσθαι. Basil, *De baptismo libri duo* 1.2.21, in Migne, *PG* 31, 1561.

40. Italics added for emphasis. "Τοῦτο τοῖς ἀπὸ πάσης κηλῖδος κεκαθαρμένοις ἐλλάμπον, τῇ πρὸς ἑαυτὸ κοινωνίᾳ πνευματικοὺς ἀποδείκνυσι." Basil, *Liber de Spiritu Sancto* 9.23, in Migne, *PG* 32, 109; Basil, *On the Holy Spirit* 9.23, 54. We note here that "making spiritual" here could be understood in a number of different ways. According to the *Liddell-Scott-Jones Greek-English Lexicon* (LSJ), the verb ἀποδείκνῡμι means, among other possible options, to "show forth a person or thing as so and so." It could indicate then that the Spirit "appoints, proclaims, creates, makes, renders, represents as, ordains, dedicates, or consecrates" the illuminated one to be spiritual (πνευματικοὺς). *LSJ Greek-English Lexicon*, in *TLG*, http://stephanus.tlg.uci.edu/lsj/#eid=12753.

41. Basil, *On the Holy Spirit* 9.23, 54.

> who, *to the best of his ability* [καθώς ἐστι δυνατὸν], *copies within himself* [ἐφ' ἑαυτοῦ μιμησάμενος] *the tranquility of the divine nature* [τὸ ἀπαθὲς τῆς θείας φύσεως] attains to a likeness with the very soul of God; and, being made like to God in the manner aforesaid, he also achieves in full a semblance to the divine life and abides continually in unending blessedness. If, then, *by overcoming our passions* [διὰ τῆς ἀπαθείας] we regain the image of God and if the likeness of God bestows upon us everlasting life, let us devote ourselves to this pursuit in preference to all others, so that our soul may never again be enslaved by any vice, but that our understanding may remain firm and unconquerable under the assaults of temptation, to the end that we may become sharers in the divine beatitude.[42]

Here it is necessary to point out that the *apatheia* of God and the *apatheia* of the creature are related, but fundamentally different due to the fact that God is divine, and humans are not. The *apatheia* (or tranquility) of God's nature is due to the simplicity, uniformity, and incomposite nature of the Godhead, which cannot allow for the multiplicity of contrary passions.[43] On the other hand, for the creature, *apatheia* is an active and life-long struggle that leads one to "an independence from passions."[44] It should be understood, therefore, that Basil is not saying that the individual can become simple, uniform and incomposite as God is, but rather, one is to work *as he is able* [καθώς ἐστι δυνατὸν][45] to imitate, represent, or portray in himself God's tranquil nature. This is, according to Basil, "a spiritual mode of life" and "the way of the angels."[46] Now for Basil, the angelic live free of marriage, undistracted by created beauty, and are constantly

---

42. Basil, *Sermo 13*, in Basil, *Ascetical Works*, 207.

43. Pelikan, *Christianity and Classical Culture*, 86.

44. "'Impassibility,' the ἀπάθεια of the Greeks, is in general poorly understood and interpreted. It is not an indifference, not a cold insensibility of the heart. On the contrary, it is an active state, a state of spiritual activity, which is acquired only after struggles and ordeals. It is rather an independence from passions. Each person's own 'I' is finally regained, freeing oneself from fatal bondage. But one can regain oneself only in God. True 'impassibility' is achieved only in an encounter with the Living God. The path which leads there is the path of obedience, even of servitude to God, but this servitude engenders true freedom, a concrete freedom, the real freedom of the adopted sons of God. In evil the human personality is absorbed by the impersonal milieu, even though the sinner may pretend to be free. In God the personality is restored and reintegrated in the Holy Spirit, although a severe discipline is imposed on the individual." Florovsky, *Creation and Redemption*, 88.

45. Translated above as "to the best of his ability."

46. Basil, *Sermo 13*, in Basil, *Ascetical Works*, 209.

focused on God's face.⁴⁷ To those who wish to undertake this angelic mode of life, Basil recommends cenobitic monasticism; for Basil this means communal living in groups of ten or more, guided by a worthy leader.⁴⁸ Let us now examine how this mode of life can both form the individual into a social human being such that he or she may be divinized.

The "Social Human Being" (κοινωνικὸς ἄνθρωπος)

In the lengthy introduction of his translation of a number of Basil's works on wealth and poverty, C. Paul Schroeder coins the term "social human being" (κοινωνικὸς ἄνθρωπος). Schroeder makes the claim that "according to Basil, God is calling every person to become a κοινωνικὸς ἄνθρωπος, a "social human being," one who understands his or her social obligations and lives in proper relationship to his or her neighbour."⁴⁹ A search of the *Theosaurus Linguae Graecae* (*TLG*) indicates that this term is indeed a construct of Schroeder's rather than one used by Basil.⁵⁰ This search identified one instance where Basil uses the related term ὁ κοινὸς ἄνθρωπος (the common man), in his work on the Holy Spirit, but this is not used in the sense that Schroeder is referring to.⁵¹ A second, somewhat more relevant, occurrence of the term κοινὸς ἄνθρωπος is found in Basil's commentary on the Prophet Isaiah. Here Basil describes the common man alone as being elevated above other creatures by virtue of his common human nature, a nature which may, nevertheless, be diminished by one's failure to guard oneself against the whims of the passions.⁵² So the question must be asked, on what basis does Schroeder coin this term κοινωνικὸς ἄνθρωπος? To answer this question, we will focus on Basil's homily on Luke 12:16–21, which addresses the parable of the rich

47. Basil, *Sermo 13*, in Basil, *Ascetical Works*, 209.
48. Basil, *Sermo 13*, in Basil, *Ascetical Works*, 210.
49. Schroeder, "Introduction," in Basil, *On Social Justice*, 32.
50. *TLG*, http://stephanus.tlg.uci.edu/Iris/indiv/tsearch.jsp#s=2.
51. Here Basil refers to the common man in order to highlight that if the humans are glorified by God, then it is absurd not to glorify the Holy Spirit. Basil, *On the Holy Spirit*, 55, 93.
52. Ὁ μὲν γὰρ κοινὸς ἄνθρωπος, ὁ μόνοις τοῖς κοινοῖς τῆς φύσεως πλεονεκτήμασιν ἐπηρμένος, μὴ ζῶν κατὰ τὴν ἐνυπάρχουσαν αὐτῷ ἐκ τῆς πρώτης κατασκευῆς δύναμιν, ταπεινοῦται· ὁ δὲ ἤδη καὶ ἐν προκοπῇ τινι γενόμενος καὶ ἄξιος ἤδη τοῦ ἀνὴρ χρηματίζειν, ἐπειδὰν καταμαλακισθεὶς ἐνδῷ πρὸς τὰ πάθη, ἀτιμασθήσεται. Basil, *Enarratio in prophetam Isaiam* 167.5–11, in Migne, *PG* 30, 393.

man who wished to tear down his barns in order to store up for himself material wealth.[53]

Near the beginning of this homily, Basil notes that the man was already rich before God blessed him with abundant crops.[54] Basil's explanation for the benevolence of God to one who was already wealthy is intriguing:

> As the lover of humankind, God did not immediately judge [the rich man] for the ingratitude of his ways, but rather attempted to satisfy him by adding even more wealth to what he already had, thus inviting his soul to a more sociable and civilized demeanor.[55]

What does Basil mean here by a "more sociable and civilized demeanor"? It seems clear that this demeanor is in contrast to that which is displayed by the rich man of the parable, an attitude which leads Jesus to label him a fool. For Basil, the sociable and civilized person is to treat possessions as though they belong to others.[56] The rich man, however, "enjoys what is offered for the benefit of all in common," like a person who "take[s] the first seat in the theatre [and] then bar[s] everyone else from attending."[57] Basil believes that such an action denies the fact that no-one can claim to have brought any goods into this life and that all things are therefore given to serve the common good.[58] Rather than being a consumer and hoarder of these common goods (τὰ κοινὰ), the sociable and civilized man is to be a steward of all he has received.[59] For instance, in times of famine (which may have been occurring at the time Basil gave this homily), one ought never to seek to profit from the misery of others by making "common need a means of private gain."[60] The "more sociable and civilized demeanor" expected of the rich is thus characterized by a

---

53. *Homilia in illud: Destruam horrea mea* (English: *I will tear down my barns*).

54. Basil, *I Will Tear Down My Barns* 1, in Basil, *On Social Justice*, 59.

55. Basil, *I Will Tear Down My Barns* 1, in Basil, *On Social Justice*, 59–60. τοῦ φιλανθρώπου Θεοῦ ἐξ ἀρχῆς αὐτὸν ἐπὶ τῇ ἀγνωμοσύνῃ τῶν τρόπων μὴ κατακρίναντος, ἀλλ' ἀεὶ τῷ προϋπάρχοντι πλούτῳ πλουτονέτερον προστιθέντος, εἴ πως αὐτῷ κόρον ἐμποιήσας ποτὲ, πρὸς τὸ κοινωνικὸν καὶ ἥμερον τὴν ψυχὴν αὐτοῦ ἐκκαλέσαιτο. Basil, *Destruam horrea mea* 1.13–16, in Migne, *PG* 31, 261.

56. Basil, *I Will Tear Down My Barns* 2, in Basil, *On Social Justice*, 61.

57. Basil, *I Will Tear Down My Barns* 7, in Basil, *On Social Justice*, 69.

58. Basil, *I Will Tear Down My Barns* 7, in Basil, *On Social Justice*, 69.

59. Basil, *I Will Tear Down My Barns* 7, in Basil, *On Social Justice*, 69.

60. Basil, *I Will Tear Down My Barns* 3, in Basil, *On Social Justice*, 64.

concern for the needy, a detachment from personal possessions, and a recognition that all good things come from God.

This demeanor is not, however, simply an expectation. Rather, it is an obligation or a debt for the rich to pay. In his *Moralia*, a collection of rules for life based on the New Testament,[61] Basil declares, "That whatever a man may possess over and above what is necessary for life, he is obliged to do good with [ὀφειλέτης ἐστὶν ἐκεῖνον εὐεργετῆσαι], according to the command of the Lord who has bestowed on us the things we possess."[62] The term ὀφειλέτης, used here to signify obligation, literally means "debtor." A scan of the New Testament (the primary source for Basil's *Moralia*) reveals that this word is found in three of the four gospels and in two of Paul's epistles. In the synoptics, we find it used in various parables about debtors, as well as in the Lord's Prayer, where it refers to those whose debts we are to forgive (cf. Matt 6:12; 18:24; Luke 7:14; 16:5). In the account of the washing of the feet, John uses the word to stress the seriousness of the apostle's obligation to repay the generous gift of service rendered by Jesus by the extending of this service to others (cf. John 13:14). Within the Pauline corpus the term appears most frequently in the Epistle to the Romans. Here Paul utilizes ὀφειλέτης to highlight: the debt of love owed to others; the debt owed to God for the gift of sonship; Paul's obligation to preach the gospel to Greeks and barbarians; and the debt owed by the Greeks to the Jews (cf. Rom 13:8; 8:12; 1:14; 15:27). With this New Testament usage in mind, we see that Basil's rule is more a moral imperative than a mere expectation. Grasping onto excess is not simply a matter of charity or social justice, but rather, it constitutes a failure to repay a debt owed to God that will be reckoned at the moment of judgement.

The link between the repayment of debt and union with God is made even more explicit by Basil. In a homily given during a period of famine, the Cappadocian exhorts his listeners to "[g]ive but a little, and you will gain much; undo the primal sin by sharing your food. Just as Adam transmitted sin by eating wrongfully, so we wipe away the treacherous food when we remedy the need and hunger of our brothers and sisters."[63] Undoing the primal sin means precisely to imitate Christ, the New Adam, who untied the knots that were bound by the sin of the first

---

61. Basil, *Concerning Faith*, in Basil, *Ascetical Works*, 68. Note that this is one of two prologues to the *The Morals (Moralia)*.

62. Basil, *The Morals* 48. Cap 1, in Basil, *Ascetical Works*, 125.

63. Basil, *In Time of Famine and Drought* 7, in Basil, *On Social Justice*, 86.

Adam. Ever the pragmatist, Basil attributes the loosing of the bonds formed by the first sin to the unitive capacity of the common meal. In this aforementioned homily, Basil notes first that beasts share the plants of the wilderness for food.[64] He then points out that even the pagan Greeks exercised philanthropy in their example of common meals.[65] Finally, Basil puts before his hearers the example of the early Christian community (cf. Acts 2:41–47), who had a common "life, soul, concord," as well as "a common table" and "indivisible kinship."[66] Such expressions of unity may be attributed, Basil opines, to love, which "constituted many bodies as one and joined many souls into a single harmonious whole."[67] The common meal shared between rich and poor alike establishes communion within the body of Christ and conforms the body to its head. In short, treating one's goods as common and opening one's hands to share them with the needy is a means by which one may be integrated into the body of Christ and made fit to share in his work of undoing the sin of Adam.

Let us return to the question of the legitimacy of Schroeder's coining of the term "social human being" (κοινωνικὸς ἄνθρωπος). In the first instance we recognize that Basil urged the rich not to appropriate common goods (τὰ κοινά) as their own (ἴδια).[68] Next, he declared that those who hold common goods back from the needy poor are robbers and thieves.[69] Finally, Basil states plainly that those who commit this sin of omission (not sharing with the needy poor) will suffer the fate of those described in Matt 25:31–46 who are condemned for failing to perform the corporal works of mercy.[70] The *anti*-social human being thus excommunicates him or herself from the society of the saved by virtue of the fact that she or he has misappropriated common goods. In contrast, the social human being undoes the bonds of sin and is blessed by God at the time of judgement by virtue of his or her generosity.

Rightly understood, Basil's teaching on common goods is not founded on a nascent socialist ideology. Rather, it is based on an orthodox soteriology and a sound understanding of charity. These foundations, we

---

64. Basil, *In Time of Famine and Drought* 8, in Basil, *On Social Justice*, 86.
65. Basil, *In Time of Famine and Drought* 8, in Basil, *On Social Justice*, 86.
66. Basil, *In Time of Famine and Drought* 8, in Basil, *On Social Justice*, 86.
67. Basil, *In Time of Famine and Drought* 8, in Basil, *On Social Justice*, 86.
68. Basil, *I Will Tear Down My Barns* 7, in Basil, *On Social Justice*, 69–70.
69. Basil, *I Will Tear Down My Barns* 7, in Basil, *On Social Justice*, 69–70.
70. Basil, *I Will Tear Down My Barns* 8, in Basil, *On Social Justice*, 70.

The Long Rules

We move now to consider the *Long Rules* of Basil and their practical instructions on how to live so as to become like God. Before we do this, however, we will look briefly at one of Basil's short ascetical works, entitled *Prologus* 5, in order to pinpoint some key requirements for living the ascetical life.

In the first line of *Prologus* 5, Basil states plainly that the *telos* of the ascetical life is the salvation of the soul.[71] In light of this *telos*, Basil sets out a number of key features of rightly constituted cenobitic life. First, the ascetic is to rid him or herself "of the varied and diverse movements of the passions toward evil whereby the soul is defiled."[72] Second, the ascetic is to renounce worldly possessions due to the fact that they cause the soul undue anxiety and thus, distraction.[73] Third, collectively dispossessed, the community of ascetics is to work on being of "one heart, one will, [and] one desire"; in short, "one body consisting of divers members."[74] Fourth, in order "to avoid confusion resulting from each person's conducting himself according to his private whim," there ought to be a well-suited superior chosen, towards whom each can look for good example.[75] Fifth and finally, ascetics "should have the same mutual charity, equal in degree, for one another, as a man naturally feels for the members of his body."[76] This precludes one, for instance, from loving one member more than the others, as exclusivity breeds enmity within the community.[77]

Having established some key requirements for living the ascetical life, what specific directives are there in the *Long Rules* that are particularly useful for making the ascetic a social human being and setting him

---

71. Basil, *Prologus* 5, in Basil, *Ascetical Works*, 217.
72. Basil, *Prologus* 5, in Basil, *Ascetical Works*, 217.
73. Basil, *Prologus* 5, in Basil, *Ascetical Works*, 217.
74. Basil, *Prologus* 5, in Basil, *Ascetical Works*, 217.
75. Basil, *Prologus* 5, in Basil, *Ascetical Works*, 218.
76. Basil, *Prologus* 5, in Basil, *Ascetical Works*, 219.
77. Basil, *Prologus* 5, in Basil, *Ascetical Works*, 219.

or her on the path to deification? Here we will focus on three of the more relevant rules, offered as replies to Questions 7, 8, and 20.[78]

Basil's reply to Question 7, which serves to guide the ascetic on the path of growing in likeness to God, deals with the necessity of living the common, rather than solitary, life. Basil gives a number of reasons for his preference. For instance, he holds that "a life passed in solitude is concerned only with the private service of individual needs," and thus, the solitary is unable to fulfill the law of love which requires that one seeks what is profitable "to many that they might be saved."[79] On the contrary, communal living allows one to practice all the commandments, particularly the law of love. Basil offers a useful and highly relevant example:

> When [a solitary ascetic] is visiting the sick, he cannot show hospitality to the stranger and, in the imparting and sharing of necessities (especially when the ministrations are prolonged), he is prevented from giving zealous attention to [other] tasks. As a result, the greatest commandment and the one especially conducive to salvation is not observed, since the hungry are not fed nor the naked clothed.[80]

Basil thus believes solitary asceticism to be an imperfect means for attaining salvation, of becoming like God, due to the fact that it not only makes it more difficult to practice all the commandments, but that it makes it impossible, at least at times, to practice the corporal works of mercy.

Basil provides other reasons for preferring communal monasticism to the solitary life in his response to Question 7. These include: the difficulty the solitary can have in discerning his or her own defects,[81] especially the defect of self-satisfaction;[82] the benefit one can receive from the censure of one's sin by the community;[83] and the fact that no one individual can possess all the spiritual gifts, but the body of community members can collectively possess more of these graces.[84] In sum, communal life "is an arena for the combat, a good path of progress, continual

---

78. Space prohibits us from examining other rules.
79. Basil, *Long Rules* 7, in Basil, *Ascetical Works*, 249.
80. Basil, *Long Rules* 7, in Basil, *Ascetical Works*, 249.
81. Basil, *Long Rules* 7, in Basil, *Ascetical Works*, 248.
82. Basil, *Long Rules* 7, in Basil, *Ascetical Works*, 251.
83. Basil, *Long Rules* 7, in Basil, *Ascetical Works*, 248–49.
84. Basil, *Long Rules* 7, in Basil, *Ascetical Works*, 250.

discipline, and a practicing of the Lord's commandments."[85] We could add, that this life enables one to better care for the needy, which is a trait of one with a sociable and civilized demeanor.

Basil's reply to Question 8 deals with renouncing everything. Along with the renunciation of material goods, Basil points out other things that one must renounce in order to live the Gospel call: "Above all, we renounce the Devil and carnal affections, in having given up the things of our secret shame, ties of physical relationship, human friendships, and a mode of life that is inimical to the perfection of the Gospel of salvation."[86] While the cenobite *can* fail to renounce every one of these things, there is little doubt that the cenobitic life is conducive to helping one commit her or himself fully in this regard. For example, handing over to the superior concern for the food one is to eat and the clothes one is to wear is a means for attaining detachment from wealth and "the riches and pleasures" of the world.[87] Furthermore, the renunciation of ties to friends and family is made easier when one steps into the cenobitic community. Of course, the cenobite may well become attached to his or her fellow community members, but at the very least external ties are cut. Ultimately, abiding by the directives of Rule 8 leads the cenobite to detach from personal possessions and therefore assists in making him or her a social human being. As a result of renouncing these possessions, one is made "more fit to set out upon the road leading to God," and the individual's heart is transferred "to a heavenly mode of life," which is "the first step toward the likeness to Christ."[88]

Basil's reply to Question 20 concerns the serving of meals to guests. Here Basil highlights that in showing this form of hospitality there is a great danger of falling into vainglory, which he describes as "the desire to please men, and acting for display."[89] He is anxious to avoid the trap of putting on too fancy a fare for guests. For Basil, the provision of a meal for a fellow ascetic ought to lead that guest to appreciate the simplicity of what is provided. Feeding secular guests on the other hand, should give them the experience of "frugal sufficiency."[90] In both instances, the

---

85. Basil, *Long Rules* 7, in Basil, *Ascetical Works*, 252.
86. Basil, *Long Rules* 8, in Basil, *Ascetical Works*, 253.
87. Basil, *Long Rules* 8, in Basil, *Ascetical Works*, 257.
88. Basil, *Long Rules* 8, in Basil, *Ascetical Works*, 256.
89. Basil, *Long Rules* 20, in Basil, *Ascetical Works*, 277.
90. Basil, *Long Rules* 20, in Basil, *Ascetical Works*, 278.

provision of hospitality is an opportunity to witness to and model a sober disposition towards food. One may ask, however, why this is important for helping the ascetic to become like Christ? Basil gives three key reasons. First, such sobriety in the preparation of the meal allows one to put off the worldly garment of ostentatiousness and sensuality and to put on the glory of the Lord.[91] Second, in providing only what is sufficient to each guest, one assumes the role of Mary, who, seeing her sister Martha worry about serving, preferred to rest at the feet of Jesus.[92] Third and finally, giving only what is necessary to the guest enables the ascetic to avoid wasting God-given food on the rich, which has the two-fold effect of saving the poor from hunger and saving the rich from indulgence.[93]

Central to Basil's argument here is the idea that sufficiency—as opposed to both poverty and its opposite, satiety—is all that is necessary for physical health.[94] Poverty is obviously to be avoided as it can lead to vices such as theft, and riches are to be shunned as these prevent one from entering heaven.[95] A sufficient fare, on the other hand, helps the one who partakes to see that there is only one thing truly necessary; that is, putting on the glory of God.[96] We see then, that a sufficient fare at table can help one to recognize that God's glory, rather than fine and luxurious food, is the true good, and that God is the source of all that is good.

This brief survey of the *Long Rules* has shown that, among other things, Basil has laid out a wonderful, practical set of instructions for making his cenobitic followers social human beings. The common life enables one to better care for the needy. Renunciation of everything—which is a prerequisite of the monastic life—helps one to detach from personal possessions. And eating a sufficient fare helps one to appreciate that all good things are God-given. So formed into social human beings, the cenobite is fashioned into the likeness of God.

---

91. Basil, *Long Rules* 20, in Basil, *Ascetical Works*, 279.
92. Basil, *Long Rules* 20, in Basil, *Ascetical Works*, 279.
93. Basil, *Long Rules* 20, in Basil, *Ascetical Works*, 280.
94. Basil, *Long Rules* 20, in Basil, *Ascetical Works*, 280.
95. Basil, *Long Rules* 20, in Basil, *Ascetical Works*, 278.
96. Basil, *Long Rules* 20, in Basil, *Ascetical Works*, 279.

Our overview of Basil's theology of deification, his teaching on common and private goods, and the *Long Rules* has possibly provoked more questions than provided answers. We have not, for instance, considered why Basil had a different position to his brother Gregory on the equivalence or otherwise of the words "likeness" and "image." Furthermore, we have not examined Basil's theology of grace to determine precisely the link between what is provided to human nature at the beginning and what is offered to man as he seeks to attain likeness to God. Regarding the social nature of the human person, we have only scratched the surface in identifying what constitutes social and anti-social behavior. Finally, our look at the *Long Rules* has not yet provided an exhaustive analysis of the means offered to the ascetic for becoming like God.

On the positive side, what we have discovered is not inconsequential. First, we have discovered that Basil has a very positive view of the human person, who is, by nature made in God's image, and who, by grace, is able to work towards assuming likeness to God. Next, we have learnt that Basil's position on common and private goods was, and remains, challenging for all, particularly the rich. Further to this, we have discovered that Basil was no early socialist, but rather, a lover of Christ, who saw that a correct disposition towards material goods was literally the key to undoing the bonds of sin and leading the Christian to eternal life. Finally, we have been able to show that the *Long Rules* of Basil are useful for helping the ascetic to become a "social human being" and thus, to attain likeness to God.

Bibliography

Basil. *Ascetical Works*. Translated by M. Monica Wagner. Washington, DC: Catholic University of America Press, 1962.

———. *Exegetical Homilies*. Translated by Agnes Clare Way. Washington, DC: Catholic University of America Press, 1963.

———. *On Social Justice*. Translation, introduction, and commentary by C. Paul Schroeder. Crestwood, NY: St. Vladimir's Seminary, 2009.

———. *On the Holy Spirit*. Translation and introduction by Stephen Hildebrand. Yonkers, NY: St. Vladimir's Seminary, 2011.

———. *On the Human Condition*. Translated by N. V. Harrison. Crestwood, NY: St. Vladimir's Seminary, 2005.

Byrne, Brendan. *Romans*. Sacra Pagina 6. Collegeville, MN: Liturgical, 1996.

Edsall, Benjamin. "Kerygma, Catechesis, and Other Things We Used to Find: Twentieth-Century Research on Early Christian Teaching since Alfred Seeberg (1903)." *Currents in Biblical Research* 10 (2012) 410–41.

Florovsky, Georges. *Creation and Redemption*. Belmont, MA: Nordland, 1976.

Keating, Daniel A. "Typologies of Deification." *International Journal of Systematic Theology* 17.3 (2015) 267–83.

Lampe, G. W. H. *A Patristic Greek Lexicon*. Oxford: Clarendon, 1961.

Meconi, David, and Carl E. Olson, eds. *Called to Be the Children of God: The Catholic Theology of Human Deification*. San Francisco: Ignatius, 2016.

Migne, J.-P. *Patrologiae cursus completus: Series Graeca*. Vols. 30–32. Paris: Garnier, 1857–66.

Novum Testamentum Graece (Nestle-Aland). 28th ed. Stuttgart: Deutsche Bibelgesellschaft, 2012. https://www.academic-bible.com/en/online-bibles/novum-testamentum-graece-na-28/read-the-bible-text/.

Pelikan, Jaroslav. *Christianity and Classical Culture: The Metamorphosis of Natural Theology in the Christian Encounter with Hellenism*. New Haven: Yale University Press, 1993.

Russell, Norman. *The Doctrine of Deification in the Greek Patristic Tradition*. Oxford: Oxford University Press, 2005.

Seeberg, Alfred. *Die beiden Wege und das Apostheldekret*. Leipzig: Deichert, 1906.

———. *Die Didache des Judentums und der Urchristenheit*. Leipzig: Deichert, 1908.

———. *Das Evangelium Christi*. Leipzig: Deichert, 1905.

———. *Der Katechismus der Urchristenheit*. Leipzig: Deichert, 1903.

Thesaurus Linguae Graecae Digital Library (TLG). Edited by Maria C. Pantelia. Irvine, CA: University of California. http://www.tlg.uci.edu.

9

A "New Creation in Christ" (2 Cor 5:17)

Mary, the Immaculata, as Anthropological Model

M. Isabell Naumann, ISSM

The *Immaculata*, as the fully redeemed person, is significant for the view of human identity and Christian personality. The theological-anthropological aspects of the *Immaculata* presented here presume a fundamental understanding of the dogma of the Immaculate Conception, the stages of its historical development, and the related magisterial teaching on the *Intemerata*.[1] The horizon of engagement will be the truth

---

1. Definition of the dogma of the Immaculate Conception of Mary: "We declare, pronounce, and define: that the doctrine that maintains that the Most Blessed Virgin Mary at the first instant of her conception, by the singular grace and privilege of almighty God and in view of the merits of Jesus Christ, the Savior of the human race, was preserved immune from all stain of original sin, is revealed by God and, therefore, firmly and constantly to be believed by all the faithful." Pius IX, *Ineffabilis Deus*, 2803. Due to the scope of this chapter, I will not discuss the dogma of the Immaculate Conception as such. For additional references regarding the dogma of the *Immaculata* and the related teaching on the *Intemerata*—not listed in here in the footnotes—see Pius X, *Ad diem illum laetissimum*, 3370; Council of Trent, *Decretum de peccato originali*, 1516; Calloway, *The Virgin Mary and Theology of the Body*; Cecchin, *L'Immacolata Concezione*; Gambero, *Mary and the Fathers of the Church*; Jelly, "The Roman Catholic

and the beauty of the Christian as a "new creation in Christ" (2 Cor 5:17) exemplified most concretely in the *Immaculata*.

In a homily given on the Feast of the Immaculate Conception, Pope Benedict XVI said, "In Mary, the Immaculate, we find the essence of the Church without distortion. We ourselves must learn from her to become 'ecclesial souls', as the Fathers said, so that we too may be able, in accordance with St. Paul's words, to present ourselves 'blameless' in the sight of the Lord, as he wanted us from the very beginning (Col 1:21; Eph 1:4)."[2] Here, Pope Benedict reaffirms Vatican II's teaching on the interwovenness of Mary and the church[3] by pointing out the important connection between the Immaculata and the essence of the church, hence his appeal that we are to become "ecclesial souls," or as he wrote on another occasion, "only in being Marian do we become Church."[4]

Further, Pope Benedict refers to Mary's scriptural portrayal from the Annunciation to Pentecost to express in more theological-anthropological terms the interwovenness of Mary and the church. He points to her as "someone whose freedom is completely open to God's will. Her immaculate conception is revealed precisely in her unconditional docility to God's word. Obedient faith in response to God's work shapes her life at every moment . . . (Lk 2:19, 51). . . . This mystery deepens as she becomes completely involved in the redemptive mission of Jesus."[5] From

---

Dogma of Mary's Immaculate Conception"; Lohfink, *Maria-nicht ohne Israel*; Mullaney, "Mary Immaculate in the Writings of St. Thomas," 433–68; O'Connor, *The Dogma of the Immaculate Conception*; Macquarrie, *Mary for All Christians*.

2. Benedict XVI, "Homily," 15–16. See in this context Marshner's "ontological correlation," in Marshner, "The Dogma of the Immaculate Conception in Modern Ecclesiology: Prolegomena," 145.

3. "Mary is so interwoven in the great mystery of the Church that she and the Church are inseparable, just as she and Christ are inseparable. Mary mirrors the Church, anticipates the Church in her person." Benedict XVI, "Homily," 15–16. See also Paul VI, *Lumen gentium*; Lubac, *The Splendor of the Church*; Balthasar, *Theo-Drama*.

4. Ratzinger, "The Ecclesiology of Vatican II." The full text is as follows: "the Church is not an apparatus; she is not simply an institution; she is not even one among many social entities; she is a person. She is a woman. She is mother. She is living. The Marian comprehension of the Church most decisively counters a merely bureaucratic concept of the Church. We cannot make the Church, we must be her. And only to the extent that faith, by our doings, moulds our being, are we Church, is the Church within us. Only in being Marian do we become Church. Even in the beginning, the Church was not made, but generated. She was generated when in the soul of Mary there awakened the *fiat*."

5. Benedict XVI, *Sacramentum caritatis*, no. 33.

these texts, we begin to see the significance of Mary, the *Immaculata*, as anthropological model.

Importantly, the framework of the topic takes as its starting point the true identity of the human person, who, created in "the image and likeness of God, is called to the fullness of immediate communion with God."[6] This theological-anthropological starting point provides the parameters of the approach used to consider the texts from Pope Benedict, and assist in facilitating a distinct exposition.

Ratzinger, speaking of the essence of an *image*, specifies the fact that it points to something beyond itself. The *image* manifests something that it itself is not. Consequently, in view of the human person, the image of God cannot be closed in him—or herself—it implies relationality, that dynamic that sets the human being in motion toward the totally Other; it is the human capacity for God,[7] the capability "of manifesting God in the extent to which his nature allows itself to be penetrated by deifying grace."[8]

Here, one cannot fail to also recognize the contribution of Yannaras, a Greek theologian, who writes that the human person has his/her face toward someone or something: he/she is *opposite* (in relation to or in connection with someone or something); in other words, we exist as reference and relation to God.[9]

Consequently, Ratzinger points out, human beings are "most profoundly human when they step out of themselves and become capable of addressing God on familiar terms . . . and moving toward Another, oriented to giving themselves to the Other and only truly receiving themselves back in real self-giving."[10]

---

6. Sakharov, *I Love, Therefore I Am*, 213. See further Lossky, *The Mystical Theology of the Eastern Church*, 115–16.

7. Ratzinger, *In the Beginning*, 47–48.

8. Lossky, *In the Image and Likeness of God*, 139. In Christian theological anthropology, "resemblance to God can never be thought of otherwise than by grace coming from God" (138). For the concept of image and likeness, see Lossky, *In the Image and Likeness of God*, 125–39; Bulgakov, *The Bride of the Lamb*, 134–45; Staniloae, "Image," 64–83.

9. Yannaras, *The Freedom of Morality*, 20–22. Lossky makes a similar point: "Personhood belongs to every human being by virtue of a singular and unique relation to God who created him [/her] in His image." Lossky, *In the Image and Likeness of God*, 137. See also Balthasar's exposition of "Answer" and "Face," in Balthasar, *Theo-Drama*, 284–87.

10. Ratzinger, *In the Beginning*, 47–48. Sakharov writes, "Mankind is modelled

Put differently, we are "given" in that we receive the ontological substance of our existence from divine love and our creation is an act of God's love: not of God's "kindly disposition," but of God's love which *constitutes* being as an existential event of personal communion *and* relationship. We are created to become partakers in the personal mode of existence—which is the life of God; we are created to become partakers in the freedom of love—which is true life.[11]

Created in the Image and Likeness of the Trinity

In our Christian faith we confess that Father, Son, and Holy Spirit together imprint their image on human nature. Thus, each human person is a unique, distinct, and unrepeatable living reflection of the trinitarian God;[12] he and she is an existential distinctiveness. The common nature, or essence, that all human beings share has no existence except as personal distinctiveness—that is, freedom and transcendence of our own natural predeterminations and natural necessity.[13] Further, this divine image, which is both of the divine nature and of the communion of the divine Persons,[14] is in its more perfect form that of *conformity*.[15]

Through the Paschal mystery, Christ makes possible for every human person to image God precisely as a Trinity of Persons. That which is only potentially and aptitudinally an image of the divine Persons by

---

upon the prototype of the Trinity. As such mankind is to imitate trinitarian life, and this was manifested in and by Christ." Sakharov, *I Love, Therefore I Am*, 214.

11. Yannaras, *The Freedom of Morality*, 19. See also Bulgakov's notion of "call to being" and "creaturely freedom," in Bulgakov, *The Bride of the Lamb*, 115, 127.

12. Bulgakov, *The Bride of the Lamb*, 115.

13. "This mode of existence which is personal distinctiveness forms the image of God in man, making man a partaker in being. It is not as nature that man constitutes an image of God: it is not because he has natural attributes in common with God, or analogous to Him. Man constitutes an image of God as an ontological hypostasis free from space, time and natural necessity. The reason for this is that human existence derives its ontological substance from the fact of divine love, the only love which gives substance to being." Yannaras, *Freedom of Morality*, 19.

14. The *Trinitarian* image. Cessario, *Christian Faith and the Theological Life*, 41.

15. "The natural image of conformity exists in the human person, for whom God is in some way an object of contemplation and love." Cessario, *Christian Faith and the Theological Life*, 46.

nature—due to human defectiveness and sinfulness—becomes actually an image of God only by the *conformity that grace bestows*.[16]

Thus, by establishing the person within a communion of friendship with God, divine grace personally and ontologically shapes human nature, so that those who enjoy the *koinonia* of divine friendship begin to act in a distinctive fashion.[17] Only through grace can this transformation of human nature occur originally and pre-eminently in the Incarnation of the divine Word (Eph 4:7).[18] It is within this graced image of conformity that the Christian believer enjoys the full measure of God's favor. He/she knows God by faith and loves God "in the same way by hope and charity as the supreme Friend."[19]

Therefore, "knowing," with its specific characteristic nature of love, transfers the existence of the person who loves into the beloved. Knowing assimilates the life of the loved one.[20] This integration of the beloved presupposes assumption in one's being of that person's manifestations, and especially his or her will. The Russian Orthodox theologian Sophrony speaks here of the "principle of obedience" which is exemplified in the relationship between Christ and his followers (John 4:15, 14:31).[21]

Obedience then, in its true and positive sense, is an "opening up" to the realization of essential potential in the human person.[22] In obedience, the manifestations of one persona—its will, mentality, aspirations, and experiences—are taken into oneself by another persona, imitating thereby the relationship of the divine personae in the Trinity—the divine

---

16. Cessario, *Christian Faith and the Theological Life*, 46. Pesch refers to this grace in the following sense: "'Die Gnade' ist ein Verhalten, ein Verhältnis Gottes zum Menschen, das, weil *Gottes* Verhalten, nicht ohne eine reale Auswirkung im Geschöpf gedacht werden kann und *insofern* dem Menschen innerlich wird-ansonsten aber 'äußeres Prinzip' bleibt, eben jene 'besondere Liebe,' in der Gott sich selbst dem Menschen schenkt und die identisch ist mit der göttlichen Vorherbestimmung." Pesch and Peters, *Einführung in die Lehre von Gnade und Rechtfertigung*, 85.

17. According to Aquinas, Christ reveals the difference that grace makes for human life. Participation through grace in the inner-Trinitarian life of God completes the image of *conformity*. Cessario, *Christian Faith and the Theological Life*, 47.

18. Cessario, *Christian Faith and the Theological Life*, 48.

19. Cessario, *Christian Faith and the Theological Life*, 47.

20. Sophrony, *La félicité de connaître la voie*, 21, cited in Sakharov, *I Love, Therefore I Am*, 214.

21. Sophrony, *La félicité de connaître la voie*, 21, cited in Sakharov, *I Love, Therefore I Am*, 214.

22. Lossky, *The Mystical Theology of the Eastern Church*, 121.

perichoresis.²³ By progressing in obedience—to God and to neighbor—we progress in charity.²⁴

Hence, the human person, created in the image and likeness of the trinitarian God, represents the possibility of summing up the whole in a distinctiveness of relationship, in an act of self-transcendence toward God and others.²⁵ Through our personal distinctiveness the personal mode of existence enables us to either realize or reject the true life of love.²⁶

From the above it becomes clear that the human person is indeed called and gifted to reflect the divine image impressed on him/her as a true manifestation of God. Having set the scene within these parameters of theological anthropology, we now direct our focus to Mary, the *Immaculata*, the fully redeemed person, as a manifestation of God and as a model for the followers of Christ.

Mary—The Fully Redeemed Person²⁷

Lossky, citing a homily of Gregory of Palamas, highlights the fact that Mary as

> a created person bring[s] together in herself all perfections, both created and uncreated, the complete realization of the beauty of creation. "Wishing to create," he says "an image of all beauty, and to manifest clearly . . . the power of His art, God truly created Mary all-beautiful. In her He has brought together all the partial

---

23. Sakharov, *I Love, Therefore I Am*, 215.

24. Sophrony, *Birth into the Kingdom Which Cannot Be Moved*, 138, in Sakharov, *I Love, Therefore I Am*, 216. See also Slesinski, *Pavel Florensky*, 222; Bulgakov, *The Comforter*, 320–21.

25. Yannaras, *The Freedom of Morality*, 20–22.

26. Yannaras, *The Freedom of Morality*, 24.

27. Rahner, pointing to Mary's unique salvation-historical role, refers to the *Immaculata* as the most perfectly Redeemed. He explains, "Redemption takes place as the reception of Christ in the act of faith, which is itself grace and—for faith—establishes itself as something historically tangible in the world. Then the most perfect redemption is the conception of Christ in faith and in the body for the salvation of all in the holiest act of freedom, which is grace. Because Mary stands at that point of saving history at which through her freedom the world's salvation takes place definitively and irrevocably as God's act, she is most perfectly redeemed." Rahner, "The Fundamental Principle of Marian Theology," 89. See also Rahner, "Immaculate Conception," 201–13; Rahner, "The Dogma of the Immaculate Conception," 129–40.

beauties which he distributed amongst other creatures, and has made her the ornament of all beings.[28] . . . He has made her a blending of all perfections—divine, angelic, and human; [a] sublime beauty."[29]

This passage describes Mary's unique place and role at the center of salvation history. The mystery of the incarnation and the redemption cannot be thought of without reference to Mary, the *Immaculata*.

It is through her unique role in the drama of salvation, that Mary becomes the exemplary model of the human person and for the human person before God. In her active co-operation she exemplifies the perfect case of free response to God and God's covenant. God's law, *Deus operatur per causas secundas liberas*, is indicative of the relational characteristics: receptivity and response toward God and the divine. The *Immaculata*, as the fully redeemed person, not only personifies and exemplifies this receptivity and total free response of creation and of humanity toward God but also represents that attitude in its *lasting* effectiveness.

The actuality of Mary's participation and cooperation in the mystery of Christ becomes exemplary for the ecclesial community and for the individual person before God.

Mary's position in the history and order of salvation demonstrates a twofold relevance for a Christian anthropology: First, the *incarnational relevance*. By Mary's participation into the mystery of the incarnation, she witnesses to the *concrete-ness of Christ's incarnation* against rationalistic and ideological tendencies.[30] And second, in her election and active cooperation with God's will, as the *prototype of the human person and the ecclesial community*. Within the ecclesial community, Mary, as the truly free person, is indeed the "first" *new creation in Christ* and thus the *new person* in Christ, who guides the faithful toward the true freedom of the children of God.[31] As she points beyond herself, she both connects and brings together.[32]

---

28. Florensky calls Mary, the Mother of God, the one "true ornament of human being," Slesinski, *Pavel Florensky*, 182–83.

29. Gregory of Palamas, *In Dormitionem*, PG, CLI, 468, cited in Lossky, *The Mystical Theology of the Eastern Church*, 194.

30. Kentenich, *Daß neue Menschen werden*, 95–97; Kentenich, *Das Lebensgeheimnis Schönstatts*, 99–100.

31. Kentenich, *Kampf um die wahre Freiheit*, 249–50.

32. Roten, "Marian Light on Our Human Mystery," 112–39.

What is said of the graced human person, as shown in the above, is most sublimely visible in Mary, particularly in the gift of her being the *Immaculata* and what this endowment of her stands for.[33] Thus, Mary can be distinguished not only as "actor in the event and process of salvation history" but also as the

> recipient of salvation, and thus as a redeemed creature. This fully graced person is indeed both a "fully and perfectly redeemed person"[34] and the "ideal of faith," and thus is justly acclaimed as the "personal summit of the faithful." All of these aspects—personal redemption, ideal of faith and hence model for all faithful—highlight Mary's personal identity. . . . Her personal identity clearly states that she is creature before God and in need of salvation. Redeeming grace was given to her in abundance, but it needed to be received in faith and lived out in obedience patterned on the Fiat of the Annunciation.[35]

Earlier we pointed to the human person representing the possibility of summing up the whole in a distinctiveness of relationship, in an act of self-transcendence, and that in this we either realize or reject the true life of love. Mary, as the fully and perfectly redeemed person in Christ, as the *Immaculata*, and thus as the anthropological model of the human person, in particular of Christian personality, illustrates this truth.[36] Her freedom from original sin points to the intended distinctive relatedness of the human person to the You because "the essence of sin can only be understood in an anthropology of relation, not by looking at an isolated human being."[37] Original sin then, in the words of Ratzinger, can be described "as a statement about God's evaluation of man; evaluation not as something external, but as a revealing of the very depths of his interior being. It is the collapse of what man is, both in his origin from God and in himself, the contradiction between the will of the Creator and man's empirical being."[38]

---

33. Roten, "Marian Light on Our Human Mystery," 112–39.

34. See Rahner, "The Immaculate Conception," 206–7; Rahner, "The Fundamental Principle of Marian Theology," 102; Rahner, *Mary, Mother of the Lord*, 44–47.

35. Roten, "Marian Devotion for the New Millennium," 61–62. See in this context Naumann, "Mary as the Anthropological Model," 31–47.

36. Rahner, "The Fundamental Principle of Marian Theology," 120–21.

37. Ratzinger, *Daughter Zion*, 69.

38. Ratzinger, *Daughter Zion*, 69–70. See further Lohfink, *Maria*, 298–312; Bulgakov, *The Bride of the Lamb*, 191–92.

In Mary the reverse is testified in that, "this contradiction between God's 'is' and man's 'is not' is lacking in the case of Mary," hence

> God's judgment about her is pure "Yes," just as she herself stands before him as a pure "Yes." This correspondence of God's "Yes" with Mary's being "Yes" is the freedom from original sin. Preservation from original sin, therefore, signifies no exceptional proficiency, no exceptional achievement; on the contrary, it denotes that Mary reserves no area of being, life, and will for herself as a private possession: instead, precisely in the total dispossession of self, in giving herself to God, she comes to the true possession of self. Grace as dispossession becomes response as appropriation.[39]

Accordingly, in the words of the same author, the *Immaculata* testifies, "that God's grace was powerful enough to awaken a response, that grace and freedom, grace and being oneself, renunciation and fulfillment are only apparent contradictories; in reality one conditions the other and grants it its very existence."[40]

The *Immaculata* not only points to a beautiful beginning that originates from God who is faithful but a beginning with the end in view (in Mary's case the Assumption). God always envisages the whole—from the graced beginning to the eschatological fulfilment, the *visio beata*.[41]

As a personal individual, Mary shows us how to relate to God and to others. From the Annunciation to Pentecost every reference to Mary in the New Testament is relational. By virtue of the *donum integritatis* her relationality reflects harmony, it is ordered and just. Her portrait from her first Yes to the You until her presence in the Upper Room gives evidence to a profound development in her dialoguing with her You: through creative interaction, passive transformation (pondering), active transformation (Cana); receiving and giving. She reaches her self-fulfilment in self-giving on Golgotha and at Pentecost. Mary's self-determination is realized in the dependence and inter-dependence of a creature to her

---

39. Ratzinger, *Daughter Zion*, 70. "From another viewpoint the mystery of barren fruitfulness, the paradox of the barren mother, the mystery of virginity, becomes intelligible once more: dispossession as belonging, as the locus of new life." Ratzinger, *Daughter Zion*, 70.

40. Ratzinger, *Daughter Zion*, 71.

41. Rahner, *Mary, Mother of the Lord*, 47–50.

creator. Through the progressive emptying-assimilation of her mission, she reaches her ultimate vocation.[42]

In this, her continuous integrated co-operation with God is the ultimate example of that *synergy* that characterizes the true notion of being "created in the image and likeness of God,"[43] of the *theological* person.[44] A central text to illustrate the God-human relation and co-operation is Luke's account of the Annunciation to Mary (Luke 1:26–38).[45]

Indeed, the creature finds its truth in Mary: to be called into existence as one whose being is to welcome and to respond to God's call and to become fruitful in that gratuitous response. Mary, the *Immaculata*, then guarantees the ontological independence of creation, but she does so as woman. To deny or reject this feminine-Marian aspect of creatureliness would entail, as Ratzinger states, "the negation of creation and the invalidation of grace" and would lead "to a picture of God's omnipotence that reduces the creature to a mere masquerade and that also completely fails to understand the God of the Bible."[46]

Later, as Pope Benedict XVI, the same author urges the followers of Christ to learn from the *Immaculata*, that the person "who abandons himself totally in God's hands does not become God's puppet, a boring 'yes man'; he does not lose his freedom," but

> finds true freedom, the great, creative immensity of the freedom of good. The person who turns to God does not become smaller but greater . . . he becomes divine, he becomes truly himself. The person who puts himself in God's hands does not distance himself from others, withdrawing into his private salvation; on the contrary, it is only then that his heart truly awakens and he becomes a sensitive, and hence, benevolent and open person.[47]

In view of this creative receptivity, Martin alerts us to the *feminine* dimension in the inner life of the Trinity:

---

42. Roten, "Marian Light on Our Human Mystery," 112–39.

43. Bulgakov, *The Comforter*, 247. Also, Bulgakov, *The Bride of the Lamb*, 411–12.

44. Novotny, "Making Mary's Yes Our Own," 101–22.

45. Within the scope of this chapter it is not possible to elaborate on this text and its theological implications. See La Potterie, *Mary in the Mystery of the Covenant*.

46. Ratzinger, *Daughter Zion*, 28; López, "Mary, Certainty of Our Hope," 197. See further Balthasar, *Theo-Drama*, 298–99; Balthasar, *You Crown the Year*, 191; Novotny, "Making Mary's Yes Our Own," 101–22.

47. Benedict XVI, "Homily," 15–16.

> The Word and the Spirit within the Trinity have a feminine dimension in that they are receptive—the Word in regard to the Father and the Spirit in regard to both the Father and the Son. ... What is asserted here of the Trinity ... is our essential state as creatures, what is intrinsic in our act of knowing, what is our glory as receivers of the grace of God, what is in fact, the feminine dimension of all human beings.[48]

The centrality of "Mary's *fiat* reveals what is at stake in man's dialogue with God: what it is to be a person, that is, 'to be a fit habitation for God.'"[49] It is a gradual discovering of the dialogue of love that constitutes the very divine nature.

Conclusion

In the light of the above, Mary's place and role, as the fully redeemed person in Christ, as the *Immaculata*, in the history of salvation and as representative of humanity (when we think of her role in the Incarnation and Redemption) does not really advocate purely partial aspects in describing her in her relationship with God.

The theological-anthropological approach, as has been shown, allows for a focus on Mary, who in the authenticity of her feminine, personal self, "created in the image and likeness of God" gives that perfect human response to God's unique call.[50] In the gift of grace Mary conforms to the love of God in a friendship with God that leads her progressively into the ever-wider horizon of the fullness of God's favor. Thus, the form of her own existence becomes that of the Triune God.

Through love's assimilating and uniting power, Mary's being and acting are transformed in the God-human relationship: the integral beauty of her personality and her femininity in the distinctiveness of her being make her the exemplary model—in the words of Görres, the "unsullied

---

48. Martin, "Feminist Theology," 372–73. See in this context also Boff, *The Maternal Face of God*, 18–21, 61–104.

49. López "Mary, Certainty of Our Hope," 178–79.

50. It is not the intent to engage here in a gender polemic—in favoring femininity over masculinity and in playing one off against the other. A true interpretation of being "created in the image and likeness of God" presupposes an approach of complementarity and not confrontation.

concept" of every human person, man and woman, in the God-intended divine-human relationship.[51]

Bibliography

Balthasar, Hans Urs von. *Theo-Drama: Theological Dramatic Theory*. Vol. 3, *Dramatis Personae: Persons in Christ*. San Francisco: Ignatius, 1992.
———. *You Crown the Year with Your Goodness: Radio Sermons*. Translated by Graham Harrison. San Francisco, Ignatius, 1989.
Benedict XVI, Pope. *Homily: Solemnity of the Immaculate Conception of the Blessed Virgin Mary*. Vatican website. December 8, 2005. https://www.vatican.va/content/benedict-xvi/en/homilies/2005/documents/hf_ben-xvi_hom_20051208_anniv-vat-council.html.
———. *In the Beginning: A Catholic Understanding of Creation and the Fall*. London: T. & T. Clark, 1995.
———.*Sacramentum caritatis*. Post–Synodal Apostolic Exhortation. Vatican website. February 22, 2007. https://www.vatican.va/content/benedict-xvi/en/apost_exhortations/documents/hf_ben-xvi_exh_20070222_sacramentum-caritatis.html.
Boff, Leonardo. *The Maternal Face of God*. San Francisco: Harper & Row, 1987.
Bulgakov, Sergei. *The Bride of the Lamb*. Translated by B. Jakim. Grand Rapids: Eerdmans, 2002.
———. *The Comforter*. Translated by B. Jakim. Grand Rapids: Eerdmans, 2004.
Calloway, Donald H, ed. *The Virgin Mary and Theology of the Body*. West Chester, PA: Ascension, 2007.
Cecchin, St. *L'Immacolata Concezione*. Rome: Pontificia Academia Mariana, 2005.
Cessario, Romanus. *Christian Faith and the Theological Life*. Washington, DC: Catholic University of America Press, 1996.
Council of Trent. *Decretum de peccato originali*.The Council of Trent website. June 17, 1546. http://www.thecounciloftrent.com/ch5.htm.
Denzinger, Heinrich, ed. *Enchiridion Symbolorum: Compendium of Creeds, Definitions, and Matters of Faith and Morals*. 43rd ed. San Francisco: Ignatius, 2012.
Gambero, Luigi. *Mary and the Fathers of the Church: The Blessed Virgin Mary in Patristic Thought*. San Francisco: Ignatius, 1999.
Görres, Ida F. *Maria, das unverdorbene Konzept*. Meitingen: Kyrios, 1968.
Jelly, Frederick. "The Roman Catholic Dogma of Mary's Immaculate Conception." In *The One Mediator, the Saints, and Mary*, edited by H. Anderson, 263–78. Minneapolis: Fortress, 1992.
Kentenich, Josef. *Daß neue Menschen werden: Eine pädagogische Religionspsychologie*. Vallendar: Schönstatt, 1971.
———. *Forming the New Person: Paedagogical Conference 1951*. Waukesha, WI: Schoenstatt Editions USA, 2003.
———. *Kampf um die wahre Freiheit, Priesterexerzitien 1946*. Unpublished manuscript.
———. *Das Lebensgeheimnis Schönstatts*. 2 vols. Vallendar: Schönstatt, 1971.

---

51. Görres, *Maria*; King, *Joseph Kentenich*; Lohfink, *Maria*, 383–95.

———. *With Mary into the New Millennium. Selected Texts about the Mission of the Blessed Mother*. Edited by G. Boll et al. Vallendar: Schoenstatt, 1993.

King, Herbert, ed. *Joseph Kentenich–Collected Texts: Free and Wholly Human*. Translated by M. Cole. Vallendar: Patris, 1998.

La Potterie, Ignace de. *Mary in the Mystery of the Covenant*. New York: Alba, 1992.

Lohfink, Ludwig Weimer. *Maria—nicht ohne Israel: Eine neue Sicht der Lehre von der Unbefleckten Empfängnis*. Freiburg: Herder, 2008.

López, Antonio. "Mary, Certainty of Our Hope." *Communio* 35 (2008) 174–99.

Lossky, Vladimir. *In the Image and Likeness of God*. Crestwood, NY: St. Vladimir's Seminary, 1985.

———. *The Mystical Theology of the Eastern Church*. Crestwood, NY: St. Vladimir's Seminary, 1998.

Lubac, Henri de. *The Splendor of the Church*. San Francisco: Ignatius, 1986.

Macquarrie, John. *Mary for All Christians*. London: T. & T. Clark, 2001.

Marshner, William H. "The Dogma of the Immaculate Conception in Modern Ecclesiology: Prolegomena." *Marian Studies* 33 (1982) 124–46.

Martin, Francis. "Feminist Theology: A Proposal." *Communio* 20 (1993) 334–76.

McGregor, Bede, and Thomas Norris. *The Beauty of Christ: An Introduction to the Theology of Hans Urs von Balthasar*. Edinburgh: T. & T. Clark, 1994.

Mullaney, Thomas U. "Mary Immaculate in the Writings of St. Thomas." *The Thomist* 17.4 (1954) 433–68.

Naumann, Isabell. "Mary as the Anthropological Model in the Thought of J. Kentenich." *Ephemerides Mariologicae* 59.1 (2009) 31–47.

Novotny, Ronald. "Making Mary's Yes Our Own: A Study of Theological Personhood." *Marian Studies* 56 (2005) 101–22.

O'Connor, Edward Dennis. *The Dogma of the Immaculate Conception: History and Significance*. Notre Dame: University of Notre Dame Press, 1958.

Pesch, Otto, and Albrecht Peters. *Einführung in die Lehre von Gnade und Rechtfertigung*. Darmstadt: Wissenschaft-liche Buchgesellschaft, 1989.

Pius IX, Pope. *Ineffabilis Deus*. In *Enchiridion Symbolorum: Compendium of Creeds, Definitions, and Matters of Faith and Morals*, edited by Heinrich Denzinger. 43rd ed. San Francisco: Ignatius, 2012.

Pius X, Pope. *Ad diem illum laetissimum*.Encyclical Letter. Vatican website. February 2, 1904. https://www.vatican.va/content/pius-x/en/encyclicals/documents/hf_p-x_enc_02021904_ad-diem-illum-laetissimum.html.

Rahner, Karl. "The Dogma of the Immaculate Conception in Our Spiritual Life." In *Theological Investigations*. Vol 3, *The Theology of the Spiritual Life*, translated by Boniface Kruger, 129–40. Boston: Helicon, 1967.

———. "The Fundamental Principle of Marian Theology." *Maria* 1 (2000) 86–122.

———. "The Immaculate Conception." In *Theological Investigations*. Vol. 1, *God, Christ, Mary and Grace*, translated by Cornelius Ernst, 201–13. London: Darton Longman & Todd, 1963.

———. *Mary, Mother of the Lord: Theological Meditations*. New York: Herder, 1963.

Ratzinger, Joseph. *Daughter Zion: Meditations on the Church's Marian Belief*. San Francisco: Ignatius, 1983.

———. "The Ecclesiology of Vatican II." Paper presented at the opening of the Pastoral Conference of the Diocese of Aversa, Italy. https://www.ewtn.com/catholicism/library/ecclesiology-of-vatican-ii-2069.

---. *In the Beginning: A Catholic Understanding of the Story of Creation and the Fall.* Translated by Boniface Ramsey. Grand Rapids: Eerdmans, 1995.

Roten, Johann. "Marian Devotion for the New Devotion." *Marian Studies* 51.7 (2000) 52–95.

---. "Marian Light on Our Human Mystery." In *The Beauty of Christ: A Introduction to the Theology of Hans Urs von Balthasar*, edited by Bede McGregor and Thomas Norris, 112–39. Edinburgh: T. & T. Clark, 1994.

Sakharov, Nicholas V. *I Love, Therefore I Am: The Theological Legacy of Archimandrite Sophrony.* Crestwood, NY: St. Vladimir's Seminary, 2002.

Second Vatican Council. "Dogmatic Constitution on the Church, *Lumen gentium*, 21 November, 1964." In Vatican Council II: The Conciliar and Post Conciliar Documents, edited by Austin Flannery, 350-426. Collegeville, MN: Liturgical Press, 1975.

Slesinski, Robert. *Pavel Florensky: A Metaphysics of Love.* Crestwood, NY: St. Vladimir's Seminary, 1984.

Staniloae, Dumitru. "Image, Likeness, and Deification in the Human Person." *Communio* 13.1 (1986) 64–83.

Yannaras, Christos. *The Freedom of Morality.* Translated by Elizabeth Briere. Crestwood, NY: St. Vladimir's Seminary, 1984.

10

Theological Anthropology and Evolutionary Science at the Beginning of the Third Millennium

An Overview

COLIN PATTERSON

Introduction

A challenge which has significantly impacted theological anthropology in recent times has been that posed by those areas of science which draw upon evolutionary theory. Questions arising from developments in these fields of enquiry have prompted theologians, in their response, to find new language and concepts with which to express the Catholic truth about humanity. One need only compare the language of the Tridentine and 1997 Catechisms in their respective treatments of the creation of the world including mankind to be assured that notable adjustments have been made in this regard.[1]

---

1. Note the manner in which the doctrine of creation is expressed in the Roman Catechism of 1566, Article 1, Chapter 2, para. 18 (*Catechismus Ex Decreto Concilii Tridentini*, 17): "The earth also God commanded to stand in the midst of the world. ... Lastly, He formed man from the slime of the earth. ... By referring to the sacred

This chapter will consider three key questions in the conversation conducted between theological anthropology and evolution-based sciences. The ones I have chosen are: (1) is mankind fundamentally different from other species? (2) can the mechanisms of evolution be understood as compatible with the Christian faith? and (3) are the manifestations of the human religious impulse reducible to non-rational evolutionary processes?

It must be noted that the science-theology engagement I refer to has not been a monologue spoken by the sciences *to* theology since theologians have had some significant things to say to their scientific interlocuters. In this chapter, however, we will focus particularly on what the sciences have had to contribute to the discussion.

1. Is Mankind Fundamentally Different from Other Living Creatures?

Evolutionary science has been able to describe, at least in broad terms, the development of aspects of the created order in ways which do not draw upon any notion of divine intervention. According to this account, for living beings, change and growth appear to proceed without the necessity of causes external to nature. Admittedly, there are still difficulties that arise in the question of origins—how did life actually emerge on earth?—but this is not seen as an unanswerable problem.[2] As it touches the central affirmations of theological anthropology, the study of evolutionary processes has led many to conclude that we humans can no longer view ourselves as occupying a fundamentally unique position within nature. In this frame, our apparent differences from other living species are now seen as just variations on the *continua* observable in the myriad forms of living creatures.

The dominant name in the field is, of course, Charles Darwin. He proposed the mechanism of natural selection by which species better

---

history of Genesis the pastor will easily make himself familiar with these things for the instruction of the faithful." This may be compared with the similar section in the 1997 *Catechism of the Catholic Church*, para. 283: "The question about the origins of the world and of man has been the object of many scientific studies which have splendidly enriched our knowledge of the age and dimensions of the cosmos, the development of life-forms and the appearance of man."

2. For a recent review of efforts to solve this problem, see Walker, "Origins of Life," 92601.

adapted to their environment were more likely to survive and reproduce than those less well adapted.³ Only after his time was there a clarification of the means by which variation within species was accomplished; that is, through Mendelian inheritance of genes from one generation to the next. Darwin's work inaugurated a process of theoretical elucidation and maturation that continues today. At the same time, it must be acknowledged that evolutionary explanation is almost entirely a process of investigating past events; it has not yet been able to articulate laws by which pre-specified species could be expected to emerge under a given set of boundary conditions. Thus, it cannot yet predict the outcomes of natural processes in the way some other sciences can.

Yet, even given this limitation, evolutionary theory—and here I use the term to embrace the main outlines of the theory as set out in its "modern synthesis"—has demonstrated its compelling power to narrate the development and demise of species including humans in such a way as to seriously call into question traditional Christian teaching about the special character of mankind.⁴

For seventy years after the publication of Darwin's *The Origin of Species* in 1859, popes made no official pronouncements on the theory it expounded even though, during that period, it was exercising a profound and often disturbing impact on Western culture. Judging from this, one might have assumed that the attitude of the Vatican to evolutionary theory was, if not benign, then at least not opposed. Yet more was going on beneath the surface than was widely apparent. In 2002, following the opening up of the relevant Vatican archives, Artigas, Glick, and Martinez, in their work *Negotiating Darwin: The Vatican Confronts Evolution, 1877–1902*, exposed the strongly conflicted attitudes towards Darwinism in Rome during the early period of its diffusion.⁵ While no high-level official rejection of evolution was forthcoming, some theologians who ventured into the area were silenced, others were warned off broaching the subject, and a note of unwelcome pervaded the whole area for several decades.

---

3. Darwin, *On the Origin of Species*, ch. 4.

4. The so-called modern synthesis was first articulated as such by Julian Huxley and has formed the framework for a general understanding of evolutionary theory. See Huxley, *Evolution*.

5. See also Brundell, "Catholic Church Politics and Evolution Theory," 81–95; Martínez, "El Vaticano y la evolución," 529–49.

This changed after World War II. The first authoritative document to address the question of evolution was that of Pius XII's encyclical *Humani generis* which was published in 1950, almost a century after Darwin first propounded his theory. Paragraph 35 first draws a distinction between the "clearly proven facts" of science and "hypotheses having some sort of scientific foundation" and what follows suggests that evolutionary theory belongs to the latter category. We note that the document's interest is not in the general notion of the evolution of living species, but more specifically in the origins of humans. The encyclical then goes on to affirm that the Magisterium "does not forbid . . . research and discussion . . . on the doctrine of evolution, insofar as it inquires into the origin of the human body as coming from pre-existing and living matter."[6] Before moving immediately on to the next qualifying clause of the text, it is worth pausing to reflect on the significance of this statement.

Here we have a cautious acceptance of evolutionary theory as part of biological science. In the background is an anxiety about the authoritativeness of the scientific endeavor and its potential to undermine or contradict church teaching. This text seems to raise a number of important questions. Does Darwinism necessarily oppose the Genesis accounts of creation? Does the church teach that the emergence of humans occurred six days after the creation of the universe? Does the idea that, in the development of the plant and animal world, more complex species appear to have (spontaneously!) arisen from the less complex—something that the church's preferred philosophy of the time, Aristotelianism, believed could not happen—present problems for Catholic faith? *Humani generis* would seem to answer at least an implicit 'no' to each of these questions and in doing so, it presents itself as at least willing to listen to what science might say on the question of the origins of life. For instance, it still uses the language of magisterial authority—"does not forbid"—over scientific activity. Furthermore, it seems that its author(s) had not yet reached the point of accepting that it does not fall within the competence of the church's Magisterium to make judgments on questions of an empirical nature.

The clause following the one we have examined contains an important limitation on how evolutionary theory is to be interpreted in relation to the origin of human beings: "for the Catholic faith obliges us to hold

---

6. Pius XII, *Humani generis*, no. 36.

that souls are immediately created by God."[7] Whatever science might venture to affirm about the differences between human and non-human creatures, it is a matter of faith that the difference is of a qualitative, or better, ontological nature, one upheld by the fact that for each individual human being, the soul is created immediately by God.

Interestingly, reading further through paragraph 36, we realize that the teaching about the immediate creation of souls is almost parenthetical, for the text resumes consideration of the main question of the church's relation to science.[8] It continues the discussion by noting that, in the weighing up of the evidence for and against any theory of evolution, all must submit to the judgement of the church; that none may rashly ignore what divine revelation might have to say about the matter; and that it would seem that polygenism, the idea that not all humans have their origins in one couple, is not an option for faith.[9]

Overall, we see in *Humani generis* a carefully circumspect engagement with the theory of evolution insofar as it relates to Catholic faith. On the question of man's place in the order of living beings, it is clear: though sharing bodily life with all other creatures, the distinctiveness of each human being is so profound that his or her soul requires a separate act of creation on God's part.

Although ground-breaking in the area it addressed, *Humani generis* was not to initiate a period of more intensive magisterial teaching on evolutionary theory, for it was not until 1996 that the matter was again directly considered. Pope St. John Paul II in an address to the Pontifical Academy of Sciences noted that "some new findings lead us toward the recognition of evolution as more than an hypothesis.... The convergence in the results of these independent studies—which was neither planned nor sought—constitutes, in itself, a significant argument in favor of the theory."[10] Here the pope moves beyond his predecessor's rather cautious openness to a consideration of the merits of evolutionary theory and now wishes to acknowledge its status as a well-supported scientific theory.

---

7. Pius XII, *Humani generis*, no. 36.

8. Given the complexities associated with the question of the nature of the soul, the matter cannot be addressed here. But see below for brief comments on the relation of the immaterial soul to its expression in the material world.

9. Pius XII, *Humani generis*, no. 37.

10. John Paul II, *Message to the Pontifical Academy of Science on Evolution*, no. 4. An English translation of the address, originally in French, appeared in *L'Osservatore Romano* (English edition) 23rd October 1996.

Later in the address, the Polish pontiff re-affirms Pius XII's distinction between the bodily and spiritual origins of man:

> It is by virtue of his eternal soul that the whole person, including his body, possesses such great dignity. Pius XII underlined the essential point: if the origin of the human body comes through living matter which existed previously, the spiritual soul is created directly by God.[11]

At what point might theories of evolution go wrong, the pope asks? "The theories of evolution which . . . regard the spirit either as emerging from the forces of living matter, or as a simple epiphenomenon of that matter, are incompatible with the truth about man. They are therefore unable to serve as the basis for the dignity of the human person."[12]

Here the teaching makes truth claims which are more clearly on the theological side of the theology/science divide. The spiritual soul is divinely created and is not to be understood as merely the product of impersonal, material processes.

Since the time of John Paul II, there has been little further magisterial comment on evolutionary theory, though in October 2014 Pope Francis, in an address to the Pontifical Academy of Science, made the following comment:

> The Big Bang theory, which is proposed today as the origin of the world, does not contradict the intervention of a divine creator but depends on it. Evolution in nature does not conflict with the notion of Creation, because evolution presupposes the creation of beings that evolve.[13]

Though not touching on the key theological issues relating to mankind, the address taken as a whole can be understood as further normalizing the place of evolution in church's understanding of faith.

In relation to our question, Pope Francis's address affirms the *fundamental* differences between humans and other animals, a position in line with the comments of John Paul II which located those differences within the theological rather than in the empirical domain. Of course, this teaching leaves much work for theologians since the question remains: how can mankind's distinctiveness be explained?

---

11. John Paul II, *Message to the Pontifical Academy of Science on Evolution*, no. 5.
12. John Paul II, *Message to the Pontifical Academy of Science on Evolution*, no. 5.
13. Francis, *Address to the Pontifical Academy of Science*.

The most common response has been to follow the traditional Aristotelian-Thomistic hylomorphism with its twin notions of the soul as immaterial and the soul as the form of the body. This approach has the advantage that it aims to remove the soul from direct empirical scrutiny while at the same time preserving the sense of human identity as something singular and distinctive. It must be acknowledged, however, that it has come under challenge in light of contemporary neuroscience.[14] For this and for other reasons, alternative foundations for human distinctiveness have been sought. One such approach, proposed by Hans Urs von Balthasar and Joseph Ratzinger, looks to the distinction between person and nature as articulated in the trinitarian and christological dogmas of the early church councils as providing a basis for the distinctiveness of mankind vis-à-vis non-human species. Such work, however, is only in its infancy.[15]

While the magisterial teaching on evolution has focused upon the affirmation of mankind's special place within creation, broader challenges relating to the theorized processes of evolutionary development have also exercised theologians. We will now consider some of them.

2. Can the Mechanisms of Evolution Be Understood as Compatible with Christian Faith?

Two key aspects of this question which arise from a theological reflection upon the processes by which biological evolution is understood to proceed are: (a) how we are to conceive of the purpose and order of God's actions in the world in the face of the seeming purposelessness and disorder of the emergence, development and disappearance of living species? and (b) how can the central claims of evolutionary theory (e.g., the

---

14. This is not to say that hylomorphism does not have the resources to respond to these challenges. It is simply to indicate that more than a few scholars have observed that, with advances in understanding the science of cognition, emotion, intention and other mental processes, such a notion of the soul, insofar as it makes claims about the soul's impact on the real world, has become a "soul of the gaps." That is, it is less and less required to understand human actions. Whether this impression reflects the truth is not my interest here. It is just that this "difficulty" has prompted theologians to consider alternative ways of understanding the human soul. For an example of recent reflection on these matters, see Crisp et al., *Neuroscience and the Soul*.

15. Balthasar, "On the Concept of Person," 18–26; Ratzinger, "Concerning the Notion of Person in Theology," 439–54; Galot, "La Definition de la personne, relation et sujet," 281–99; Rolnick, *Person, Grace, and God*; Patterson, *Chalcedonian Personalism*.

appearance of novel species, the common origin of all species) be related to the chief elements of the metaphysical frameworks which Christian theologians have traditionally relied upon?

a) How Does God Act in Relation to the Evolution of Species?

A feature of contemporary evolutionary biology is its description of the emergence and disappearance of species as occurring in remarkably contingent and almost random ways without any discernible large-scale patterns.[16] Underlying these phenomena are the process of genetic mutation, the ever dynamic and varied environments in which species undergo natural selection and, not least, the catastrophic mass extinctions which have dramatically shaken up life on earth.[17] How could it be that the Creator God could be said to have planned and guided all of this? Two broad types of response have been offered by theologians. Some, like Robert John Russell and Thomas Tracy, have proposed that the indeterminacy of quantum mechanics could serve as the medium by which divine action is effected in the biological realm. These authors argue that, although physical processes operating at the quantum level cannot be predicted, this does not result in chaos at higher levels of reality. Such a principle, they suggest, might underlie the observation that, while there is much seeming randomness in the history of terrestrial evolution, this has not compromised the obvious ordering which has led to the emergence of human beings.[18]

The second approach sees recourse to quantum theory as having the undesirable effect of placing God's work in the world on the same level as natural causes. It is better, so this approach argues, to draw upon Aquinas's distinction between God as the primary transcendent cause and natural processes as secondary causes. From this perspective, under

---

16. This is illustrated by the discussion of the notion of complexity. In 1991, Daniel McShea argued in his article, "Complexity and Evolution," 303–24, that there was no evidence for trends towards increasing complexity across large-scale evolutionary history and scholars have been hard put to contradict this claim by offering examples. But see Jones et al., "Stepwise Shifts Underlie Evolutionary Trends," 1–13.

17. The current scientific literature speaks of five mass extinction events with a possible sixth now being produced by humankind. For an account of the last prehuman event, see Stanley and Yang, "A Double Mass Extinction at the End of the Paleozoic Era," 1340–44.

18. Russell, "Special Providence and Genetic Mutation," 191–224; Tracy, "Special Divine Action and the Laws of Nature," 249–83.

normal circumstances, God's actions do not compete with nature but work *through* nature in a manner which is not analyzable by empirical means.[19] As John Callaghan remarks, "God's causality in creation is not a causality that competes with natural causes, or even cooperates with them. It is best thought of as enabling natural causes to be what they are."[20] So, despite the apparent convoluted and meandering paths taken by evolution, according to this understanding, Christian faith can still recognize the endpoint of humankind, and more particularly Jesus Christ, the perfect man, as evidence of purpose within seeming randomness. It is as if the Creator is in a kind of conversation with the natural world to which He allows a manner of "freedom" from which still emerges his providential ends. As the scientist-theologian Nicanor Austriaco argues, creation of mankind via evolutionary processes better reveals God's glory than does special creation of the kind envisaged by adherents of intelligent design theory.[21]

b) How Are We to Deal with the Apparent Clash of Metaphysics with Evolutionary Theory?

Evoking Aquinas on these questions reminds us of another more extensive discussion concerning the question of compatibility of evolutionary theory with Aristotelian-Thomist metaphysics. Does not a commitment to this philosophical framework actually preclude a theological coming-to-terms with evolutionary theory?

Aquinas begins his treatment of creation by drawing upon Augustine's account in *De Genesi ad litteram* which, rather than accepting Genesis's six days, preferred to think of creation as occurring all at once. The Bishop of Hippo viewed the appearance of natural realities as taking place over indeterminate periods of time but always according to the form of the *rationes seminales*, seed-principles which existed at the beginning of creation.[22] "Yes, within the categories of the various kinds of thing which [God] set up at first, he manifestly makes many new things which he did not make then. But he cannot rightly be thought to set up any new

---

19. See, for example, Moreno, "Some Philosophical Considerations on Biological Evolution," 417–54; Austriaco, "In Defense of Double Agency in Evolution," 947–66.
20. O'Callaghan, "Evolution and Catholic Faith," 277.
21. Austriaco, "A Theological Fittingness Argument," 539–50.
22. See, for example, Augustine, *The Trinity*, 3, 7, 13.

kind, since he did then complete them all."²³ Aquinas follows this line of thought but feels bound to de-Platonize it somewhat so that instead of these seed-principles existing in the mode of Ideal Forms at creation, he understandings them as existing *ab initio* either visibly expressed, e.g., as lions, elephants, dogs, etc. or else in potency (within the heavenly bodies) for those creatures which, according to the Aristotelian science of his time, emerged not from generation but rather from the process of putrefaction.²⁴ When it comes to humans, Aquinas affirms that the first human body could only have been formed immediately and in its full maturity by God, and furthermore that the first and all subsequent souls "cannot come to be except by creation; this is not the case with other forms."²⁵

Several problems emerge in comparing Aquinas on these matters with evolutionary biology. Certainly, Thomistic scholars today do not feel bound to follow Aquinas in his adherence to the science of Aristotle; the Angelic Doctor was simply drawing upon the best knowledge available to him. Yet, even setting that to one side, we still have questions of a metaphysical nature relating to contemporary evolutionary theories that hold to the emergence of truly new species. The very possibility of such new species seems incompatible with the idea of the existence from the beginning of all creatures, either actually or as potentially existing. This raises the further point that in modern biology, species are thought of as continually changing and transitioning into what later come to be recognized as new species. It is difficult to account for this with a static notion of substantial forms.

Moreover, according to Thomas's metaphysics, one is hard pressed to explain how it is that more complex or "perfect" creatures have emerged from those of less complexity or perfection.²⁶ Given the metaphysical principle that an effect cannot be greater than its cause, how could it be that there should exist animals as complex as cats or dolphins which are the result of evolutionary processes beginning from a single-celled creature? In fact, this principle undergirded the key arguments by which several nineteenth century Catholic theologians opposed the whole idea

---

23. Augustine, *On Genesis*, 5, 20, 41.

24. Aquinas, *Commentary on the Metaphysics*, 7.6. Among Aristotle's examples are the generation of flies from rotting material.

25. Aquinas, *Summa Theologiae*, I.90.2.

26. The idea of the proportionality of causes appears at several points in Aquinas's writings. For an account of his nuanced treatment, see Carl, "Thomas Aquinas on the Proportionate Causes of Living Species," 223–48.

of evolution as Darwin described it. The story of the emergence of amazingly complex life forms via purely material means was, on this understanding, simply impossible.[27]

During the past twenty years, original and sophisticated attempts have been made to tackle these and several related questions. For example, Marius Tabaczek and Antonio Moreno have offered theistic accounts of evolution, and in particular, of how one substantial form could emerge from another in ways which, though their explanations move beyond Thomas, are broadly consistent with his metaphysics.[28] Space does not allow a discussion of the details but let one example suffice. Tabaczek develops his argument from the basic hylomorphic principle that the matter of any substantial form must be suited to or proportioned to it. Bronze is suitable or proportioned for use in a sculpture whereas water is not.[29] He then goes on to propose that with enough accidental changes to the underlying matter of a substantial form (here broadly equivalent to a biological species), the groundwork can be set for a new form to come into existence and this could be a more developed form.[30] Tabaczek quotes Aquinas in support of the direction taken by this idea: "From the fact that matter is known to have a certain substantial mode of existing, matter can be understood to receive accidents by which it is disposed to a higher perfection, so far as it is fittingly disposed to receive that higher perfection."[31] Provision is therefore made, within this scheme, for the evolution of higher species.

Opposed to this theory of theistic evolution is that which sees attempts to find convergences between Thomas and evolutionary theory

---

27. This was the case particularly among the Roman Jesuits linked to publication *La Civiltà Cattolica*. For further details, see Brundell, "Catholic Church Politics." An early example of this writing is that of Piancini, "Della origine e della unità della specie humana," 165–87. The author argues that species cannot change through accidental processes (171) and that while humans develop towards perfection, ("Distinctive of man is his indefinite perfectibility," 173) the species of apes show the opposite trend ("The apes most like man appear to deteriorate . . . rather than grow towards perfection," 174) (My translations).

28. Moreno, "Some Philosophical Considerations on Biological Evolution"; Tabaczek, "Thomistic Response to the Theory of Evolution," 325–44; Tabaczek, "The Metaphysics of Evolution," 945–72.

29. Tabaczek, "Metaphysics of Evolution," 966.

30. Tabaczek, "Metaphysics of Evolution," 966–68.

31. Thomas Aquinas, *Quaestio disputata de anima*, q.9, quoted in Tabaczek, "The Metaphysics of Evolution," 966.

as unworkable and prefers to call into question the very foundations of neo-Darwinian evolution. Some of the proponents of this approach have drawn inspiration from the work of evangelical scholars.[32] This approach proposes the model of intelligent design according to which the observed complexities in nature are viewed as truly inexplicable and could only have arisen through the direct mode of divine intervention. For example, Logan Paul Gage criticizes theistic evolution as espoused by Thomist writers for not being true to the Angelic Doctor's essentialism with its implication of discrete and fixed species boundaries.[33] He argues against theistic evolution's account of fuzzy species transitions and its acceptance of the notion of the common descent of all species from a single source that is central to evolutionary theory, and insists instead upon intelligent design as a necessary element in any faith-based account of the natural order.[34] It must be said that this approach has not found much support within Catholic circles where a theistic evolutionary approach dominates. Perhaps its main weakness as an alternative to theistic evolution is that it is essentially unscientific since it posits something that is outside the scope of science, that is, instantaneous divine intervention. For example, intelligent design proponents see the existence of the human eye as a clear instance of divine intervention in natural processes, since, they argue, it could not have evolved in a stepwise manner but must have been formed as a complete working mechanism.[35] The assumption of science, that empirical processes occur over periods of time, however brief, rather than instantaneously, places this explanation outside of the scientific framework (although this is not to say that it could not be true).

From a quite different perspective, another alternative to that which might be called standard theistic evolution is, the approach that looks to process theology[36] to provide a basis for reflection on evolutionary theory as it touches on theological matters. Prominent among supporters of this approach is the American Jesuit, John Haught. His influences include

---

32. For a collection of essays demonstrating the connections between these groups, see Richards, *God and Evolution*.

33. Gage, "Can a Thomist be a Darwinist?," 87–202.

34. Gage, "Can a Thomist be a Darwinist?," 188.

35. Behe, "Evidence for Intelligent Design from Biochemistry," 27–40.

36. Process theology emerged in the twentieth century and developed from the work of the U.S. philosopher, Alfred North Whitehead. A key idea of this theology is that God is involved in his creation to the point of being affected and indeed limited by its processes and history. This stands in marked contrast to orthodox Christian belief.

Teilhard de Chardin and A. N. Whitehead, but also Karl Rahner, Jürgen Moltmann and Wolfhart Pannenberg. His writings are extensive and widely recognized as being instrumental in assisting many believers to come to terms theologically with the issues raised by evolutionary theory.[37] Only a few pointers to the tenor of his thought can be offered here.

Haught sees nature as future-oriented, as possessing purpose (but not design) and as heading towards increasing complexity, diversity and beauty. God, through kenotic self-limitation, allows incredible openness to nature—a fact we observe in the processes of evolutionary novelty—and his working *for* (not *in*) nature is directed towards an eschatological future to which we can look forward in hope.[38] Indeed, the Incarnation is a sign of divine self-emptying which takes the form of compassionate, persuasive love (rather than coercion). This is an essential event not only for the repair of human failure (sin), but more profoundly as an acknowledgement of the tragic suffering within nature which has been part of its movement towards becoming a perfect creation. As Haught notes, "redemption, if it means anything at all, must mean—perhaps above everything else—the healing of the tragedy (and not just the consequences of human sin) that accompanies a universe in via."[39]

Haught preempts criticism that such an approach seems to sacrifice—and thus de-value—the earlier participants in the history of evolution for the sake of those who come later and who benefit from the increase in complexity and beauty. He does so by affirming God's complete remembrance of every moment and every experience, including suffering and apparent meaninglessness, within his evolving creation. As Haught expresses it:

> Everything whatsoever that occurs in evolution—all the suffering and tragedy as well as the emergence of new life and intense beauty—is "saved" by being taken eternally into God's own feeling of the world. Even though all events and achievements in evolution are temporal and perishable, they still abide permanently within the everlasting compassion of God.[40]

---

37. Among Haught's most recent writings are *God after Darwin: A Theology of Evolution*; *Deeper than Darwin: The Prospect for Religion in the Age of Evolution*; *Resting on the Future: Catholic Theology for an Unfinished Universe*.

38. Haught, *God after Darwin*, 142.

39. Haught, *Deeper than Darwin*, 169.

40. Haught, *God after Darwin*, 43.

Critics of Haught have noted that, while he has sought to take account of the major signposts within Catholic theology in attempting to relate it to contemporary science, certain imbalances have found their way into his work.[41] While fully attuned to the problem of the wastefulness, catastrophe and suffering in nature, his God, like that of many who follow a form of process theology, verges in the direction of being less than omnipotent. And along with this distortion, Haught is seen to go lightly on the idea of sin as a falling away from God (emphasizing rather sin as failure) and thus of the Cross as a genuinely sacrificial death *pro nobis*. Underlying these positions would appear to be a difficulty in making sense of the genuine distinctiveness of mankind. The main theological problem for him would seem to be suffering across species rather than sin in the particular species which is mankind.[42] More generally, we might note that this confusion looks to be a problem with not a few attempts to bring theological anthropology into juxtaposition with an evolutionary understanding.

The questions I have considered so far, that is, mankind's distinctiveness and the compatibility of evolutionary processes with the Christian understanding of God's creation, arose within the first decades of the publication of *The Origin of the Species*. Theologians have had plenty of time to reflect upon them and to offer their responses. The next question deals with a more recent encounter between evolutionary science and theological anthropology which has been generated by the study of religion considered from an evolutionary point of view.

3. Are the Manifestations of the Human Religious Impulse Reducible to Non-rational Evolutionary Processes?

This last challenge is one which raises doubts about the very basis of theological anthropology within a broader questioning of the rationality of religion. That is, it raises questions for any Catholic theological anthropology that rests upon the foundational concept that humans are rationally inclined towards the true and the good and that these capacities are not bound by or necessarily controlled by non-intellectual appetites.

The remote antecedents of this challenge are found in Ludwig Feuerbach's *Essence of Christianity*, with its core proposal that religious

---

41. For an insightful critique, see Conradie, "John Haught on Original Sin," 1–10.
42. Haught, *God after Darwin*, 56.

notions about God correspond to and, in fact, are driven by various human desires and needs.[43] Perhaps more influential was the seismic shift in the Western understanding of the human mind initiated by the Austrian neurologist/psychoanalyst Sigmund Freud. His view of the unconscious as the driver of much that had hitherto been considered the preserve of rationality was developed in several of his works which dealt with religion.[44] Common to them was the idea that religion, though perhaps one of the most important psychological constituents of civilization, was nevertheless merely an illusion.[45]

Whereas Freud's work in this area was mostly of a speculative nature, recent approaches have sought to provide a more evidentiary foundation to the idea that religion has its roots in non-rational evolutionary mechanisms. In 1980, the U.S. anthropologist, Stewart Guthrie and colleagues published a seminal paper entitled "A Cognitive Theory of Religion" which argued that religious behavior among humans was the *by-product* of evolved cognitive capacities and modes of thought which emerged because they served important survival needs.[46] The idea articulated in the paper is that our tendency to find human characteristics in the nonhuman world—that is, person-like gods—stems from a deep-seated perceptual strategy; in the face of pervasive uncertainty about what we see, we bet on the most meaningful interpretation we can. For example, if we are in the woods and see a dark shape that might be either a bear or a boulder, for example, it is good policy to think it is a bear. If we are mistaken, we lose little, and if we are right, we gain much. The U.S. psychologist, Justin Barrett, took up this insight of Guthrie's group and refined it in proposing a Hyperactive Agent Detection Device in humans. In a nutshell, "the high cost of failing to detect agents and the low cost of wrongly detecting them has led researchers to suggest that people possess a Hyperactive Agent Detection Device, a cognitive module that readily

---

43. Feuerbach, *The Essence of Christianity*. Summary statements of this nature are found in ch. 2: The Essence of Religion in General.

44. Freud wrote extensively on religion. The infantile and thus irrational nature of religion is well brought out in his 1930 essay, "Civilization and Its Discontents," in *The Major Words of Sigmund Freud*, 767–802. There he writes, "The derivation of a need for religion from the child's feeling of helplessness and the longing it evokes for a father seems to me incontrovertible" (770).

45. Cf. Freud, *The Future of an Illusion*, 55: "If after this survey we turn again to religious doctrines, we may reiterate that they are all illusions."

46. Guthrie et al., "A Cognitive Theory of Religion," 181–203.

ascribes events in the environment to the behavior of agents."[47] Thus, it is argued, the idea of invisible spirits and gods emerged in our early history.

Further developments in the field of the Cognitive Science of Religion (CSR), have led researchers to suggest other evolved cognitive mechanisms that underlie the phenomenon of religion among humans. An example would be *minimally counter-intuitive concepts*, by which is meant the prevalence of slightly counter-intuitive and even counter-factual religious beliefs (e.g., ghosts, goblins, gods) which, it is proposed, develop a life of their own because they are more arresting and memorable than ideas better in line with reality. Another such mechanism is that of *costly signaling*, which refers to practices among humans that, because of their inherent cost, are typically relied upon by observers to provide an honest signal regarding the intentions of the agent, e.g., celibacy among priests, believers who are willing to be martyred, systems of sacrifice, the commitment to love strangers. A final example would be those cognitive mechanisms that help humans *cope with anxiety*, e.g., evolved defense mechanisms which protect against the existential anxiety resulting from a fundamental conflict between the desire to live and the realization that death is inevitable.[48]

A major difficulty for CSR is the fact that, even taken together, the biologically evolved cognitive mechanisms proposed as explanatory of religious belief and practice appear to capture only a small part of the religious terrain; much is left unaccounted for. This has led other scholars to look beyond biology to cultural processes for explanations. Just as something like the widespread adoption of the skill of reading is not the result of specific human genetic adaptions but rather of what is called cultural evolution, so too, it would seem that many of the core elements of religion derive from this latter form of adaptation. Thus, for example, religious ritual, and the movement and rhythm associated with it, appears to serve the adaptive purpose of binding together communities at the local level and in so doing enhance survival. So too, belief in moralizing "big gods," it is argued, provides the behavioral norms which serve as the glue to hold together large-scale civilizations, again leading to greater chances of survival for their citizens.[49]

---

47. Gray and Wegner, "Blaming God for Our Pain," 7–16.

48. See, for example, Atran and Norenzayan, "Religion's Evolutionary Landscape," 713–30.

49. Sosis, "The Adaptive Value of Religious Ritual," 166–72.

In sum, then, the rather narrow approach to the study of religion that was committed to the assumption that religion was merely the by-product of biological adaptations of more general cognitive capacities among humans—a kind of sideways development in human evolution, as it were—is increasingly seen as too limited in its explanatory power and, it is argued, requires the addition of the much wider sweep of cultural evolutionary theories to give a fuller picture of religion as a natural phenomenon.

Where, then, does that leave Catholic theological anthropology? How has theological reflection responded to the CSR and research into the evolution of religion more generally? At first glance, much of the CSR work looks to be a threat to the reasonableness of religious belief. What might seem rational to the religious believer, so it is argued, is really the result of non-rational processes. Yet, while several key players in this field come to it with skeptical attitudes towards religion, this is not always the case. Justin Barrett, for example, has written of the value such work has for believing Christians. He writes,

> Rather than seeing cognitive and evolutionary explanations as hostile to Christianity, I see much promise in the cognitive sciences to enrich our understanding of how humans might be "fearfully and wonderfully made" (Ps 139:14) to readily (though not inevitably) understand God sufficiently to enjoy a relationship with Him.[50]

Despite Barrett's optimistic view of the cognitive evolutionary approach, it allows little scope for the rational content of belief to play a role in shaping religious phenomena. In view of such a limitation, it is typically the alternative, cultural evolutionary mode of explanation which is viewed as more amenable to faith and more in line with religious self-understanding. As proponents of cultural evolution argue, evolved cultural practices and beliefs—the rough equivalent of genes in biological evolution—can include ideas and beliefs. That is, there can be sound, rationally based "causes" for the wider adoption and spread of some beliefs—including religious beliefs—rather than others; such beliefs are not simply at the mercy of non-rational evolutionary forces.[51] Understandably, theologians addressing these matters tend to favor the cultural evolution approach. A common theological argument is that a naturalistic explanation for

---

50. Barrett, "Cognitive Science, Religion, and Theology," 77.
51. Henrich et al., "Five Misunderstandings about Cultural Evolution," 119–37.

religious phenomena does not preclude their ordering and execution by God so that, for example, the text of the Genesis creation accounts finds its antecedents in Babylonian literature, and the forms of Old Testament worship owe much to that of the surrounding cultures. The particularities of the Judeo-Christian salvation history can comfortably accommodate such understandings through the distinction between primary and secondary causes that we met with above.

A common element in CSR is a focus upon non-rational aspects of the origin and practice of religion in all its forms. At first glance, this would appear to sit uneasily with traditional forms of theological anthropology which emphasize instead the rational foundations of faith. Yet, more recent theological engagement with this work has accepted the passions and, more generally, the non-intellectual aspects of our make-up, as significant dimensions of religious belief and practice, a move which is reflected, for example, in the following passage from *Gaudium et spes*:

> It is in regard to death that man's condition is most shrouded in doubt. Man is tormented not only by pain and by the gradual breaking-up of his body but also, and even more, by the dread of forever ceasing to be. But a deep instinct leads him rightly to shrink from and to reject the utter ruin and total loss of his personality. . . . While the mind is at a loss before the mystery of death, the Church, taught by divine Revelation, declares that God has created man in view of a blessed destiny that lies beyond the limits of his sad state on earth.[52]

Of course, it is one thing to affirm this expanded understanding, one that more fully incorporates non-intellectual factors into explanations of the various forms of religious belief, and yet another thing to develop it into a coherent theological account. The theological response requires further elaboration.

Work in the field of CSR has stimulated a lively science-theology discussion which has been helpful in prompting a deeper understanding of the human elements contributing to our religious faith and practice. Thus, we might even acknowledge the contribution of Freud to this process. Admittedly, the habit of CSR researchers to treat "religion" as a unitary human phenomenon and religions as sharing common characteristics (rather than "family resemblances") places limits on the value of their efforts since it cannot take account of the overwhelming variety

---

52. Second Vatican Council, *Gaudium et spes*, no. 18.

among religions. Yet, if what Christians believe is true—that the Lord God has made us so that the grace of a living faith heals, elevates and perfects our nature—then the study of the biological, cultural and historical origins of religions as such need not be seen as contraposed to the specificity and unicity of the faith "once for all delivered to the saints."

Conclusion

For centuries prior to the period covered by this review, theology has both taken advantage of and been challenged by what scientists have been able to discover about the natural world. For example, Aquinas, on the one hand, drew upon Aristotelian science to develop his account of souls during the formation of the human being. On the other hand, he had to deal with the apparent mismatch between the Christian belief that human life was sacred from its very beginning of life and the "science" which told him that the rational soul of a human only came into existence after about forty days. The past century has seen continuing questioning of Christian faith arising from a deeper understanding of the natural world and humans as part of that world, but also a robust response to this questioning among theologians. Central to that response has been the conviction that the *imago Dei* in man (and his call to blessedness) is at the foundation of the belief that man "is the only creature on earth which God has wanted for its own sake."[53] Since at this point in the life of the church, the language of science has become a virtual *lingua franca* in Western societies where scientific literacy is widely disseminated especially within the more educated segments of society, it behooves theologians to deepen their engagement with science so that they might be able to offer well-reasoned answers to the questions posed by that key aspect of human endeavor.

Bibliography

Aquinas, Thomas. *Commentary on the Metaphysics of Aristotle*. Vol. 2. Translated by John P. Rowan. Chicago: Regnery, 1961.
———. *Summa Theologiae*. Vol. 13. Translated by Edmund Hill. London: Blackfriars, 1964.
Artigas, Mariano, et al. *Negotiating Darwin: The Vatican Confronts Evolution, 1877–1902*. Baltimore: Johns Hopkins University Press, 2006.

53. Second Vatican Council, *Gaudium et spes*, no. 24.

Atran, Scott, and Ara Norenzayan. "Religion's Evolutionary Landscape: Counterintuition, Commitment, Compassion, Communion." *Behavioral and Brain Sciences* 27 (2004) 713–30.

Augustine. *On Genesis*. Translated by Edmund Hill. New York: New City, 2002.

———. *The Trinity*. Translated by Edmund Hill. New York: New City, 1991.

Austriaco, Nicanor Pier Giorgio. "In Defense of Double Agency in Evolution: A Response to Five Modern Critics." *Angelicum* 80 (2003) 947–66.

———. "A Theological Fittingness Argument for the Evolution of Homo Sapiens." *Theology and Science* 17 (2019) 539–50.

Balthasar, Hans Urs von. "On the Concept of Person." *Communio* 13 (1986) 18–26.

Barrett, Justin L. "Cognitive Science, Religion and Theology." In *The Believing Primate: Scientific, Philosophical, and Theological Reflections on the Origin of Religion*, edited by Jeffrey Schloss and Michael Murray, 76–99. Oxford: Oxford University Press, 2009.

———. "Exploring the Natural Foundations of Religion." *Trends in Cognitive Sciences* 4 (2000) 29–34.

Behe, Michael. "Evidence for Intelligent Design from Biochemistry." *Think* 4.11 (2005) 27–40.

Brundell, Barry. "Catholic Church Politics and Evolution Theory, 1894–1902." *The British Journal for the History of Science* 34 (2001) 81–95.

Carl, Brian T. "Thomas Aquinas on the Proportionate Causes of Living Species." *Scientia et Fides* 8.2 (2020) 223–48.

Catechism of the Catholic Church. Strathfield: St. Paul's, 1997.

Catechismus Ex Decreto Concilii Tridentini: Ad Parochos Pii Quintii. Rome: Typis Sacrae Congregationis de Propaganda Fide, 1845.

Conradie, Ernst M. "John Haught on Original Sin: A Conversation." *HTS Theological Studies* 72 (2016) 1–10.

Crisp, Thomas M. et al., eds. *Neuroscience and the Soul: The Human Person in Philosophy, Science, and Theology*. Grand Rapids: Eerdmans, 2016.

Darwin, Charles. *On the Origin of Species by Means of Natural Selection*. London: Collins, 1910.

Feuerbach, Ludwig. *The Essence of Christianity*. Translated by George Eliot. New York: Harper, 1957.

Francis, Pope. *Address to the Pontifical Academy of Science on the Occasion of the Inauguration of a Bust in Honour of Pope Benedict XVI*. http://www.vatican.va/content/francesco/en/speeches/2014/october/documents/papa-francesco_20141027_plenaria-accademia-scienze.html.

Freud, Sigmund. *The Future of an Illusion*. Translated by W. D. Robson-Scott. London: Hogarth, 1928.

———. *The Major Works of Sigmund Freud*. Chicago: Encyclopedia Britannica, 1952.

Gage, Logan Paul. "Can a Thomist Be a Darwinist?" In *God and Evolution*, edited by Jay Richards, 87–202. Seattle: Discovery Institute, 2010.

Galot, Jean. "La Definition de la personne, relation et sujet." *Gregorianum* 75.2 (1994) 281–99.

Gray, Kurt, and Daniel Wegner. "Blaming God for Our Pain: Human Suffering and the Divine Mind." *Personality and Social Psychology Review* 14 (2010) 7–16.

Guthrie, Stewart, et al. "A Cognitive Theory of Religion [and Comments and Reply]." *Current Anthropology* 21 (1980) 181–203.

Haught. John F. *Deeper than Darwin: The Prospect for Religion in the Age of Evolution.* Boulder, CO: Westview, 2003.

———. *God after Darwin: A Theology of Evolution.* Boulder, CO: Westview, 2000.

———. *Resting on the Future: Catholic Theology for an Unfinished Universe.* New York: Bloomsbury, 2015.

Henrich, Joseph, et al. "Five Misunderstandings about Cultural Evolution." *Human Nature* 19.2 (2008) 119–37.

Huxley, Julian. *Evolution: The Modern Synthesis.* London: Allen & Unwin, 1942.

John Paul II, Pope. *Message to the Pontifical Academy of Science on Evolution.* https://www.ewtn.com/catholicism/library/message-to-the-pontifical-academy-of-science-on-evolution-8825.

Jones, Katrina E., et al. "Stepwise Shifts Underlie Evolutionary Trends in Morphological Complexity of the Mammalian Vertebral Column." *Nature Communications* 10.1 (2019) 1–13.

Martínez, Rafael A. "El Vaticano y la evolución. La recepción del darwinismo en el Archivo del Índice." *Scripta Theologica* 39 (2007) 529–49.

McShea, Daniel W. "Complexity and Evolution: What Everyone Knows." *Biology and Philosophy* 6.3 (1991) 303–24.

Moreno, Antonio. "Some Philosophical Considerations on Biological Evolution." *The Thomist* 37 (1973) 417–54.

O'Callaghan, John. "Evolution and Catholic Faith." In *Darwin in the Twenty-First Century: Nature, Humanity, and God*, edited by Phillip Sloan et al., 269–98. Notre Dame: University of Notre Dame Press, 2015.

Patterson, Colin. *Chalcedonian Personalism: Rethinking the Human.* Oxford: Lang, 2016.

Piancini, Giovanni Battista. "Della origine e della unità della specie humana." *Civiltà Cattolica* 9 (1861) 165–87.

Pius XII, Pope. *Humani generis.* https://www.vatican.va/content/pius-xii/en/encyclicals/documents/hf_p-xii_enc_12081950_humani-generis.html.

Ratzinger, Joseph. "Concerning the Notion of Person in Theology." *Communio* 17 (1990) 439–54.

Richards, Jay W., ed. *God and Evolution.* Seattle: Discovery Institute, 2010.

Rolnick, Philip A. *Person, Grace, and God.* Grand Rapids: Eerdmans, 2007.

Russell, Robert John. "Special Providence and Genetic Mutation: A New Defense of Theistic Evolution." In *Evolutionary and Molecular Biology: Scientific Perspectives on Divine Action*, edited by Robert John Russell et al., 191–224. Berkeley: Center for Theology and the Natural Sciences, 1998.

Sosis, Richard. "The Adaptive Value of Religious Ritual: Rituals Promote Group Cohesion by Requiring Members to Engage in Behavior That Is Too Costly to Fake." *American Scientist* 92 (2004) 166–72.

Stanley, Steven M., and Xiangling Yang. "A Double Mass Extinction at the End of the Paleozoic Era." *Science* 266.5189 (1994) 1340–44.

Tabaczek, Mariusz. "The Metaphysics of Evolution: From Aquinas's Interpretation of Augustine's Concept of Rationes Seminales to the Contemporary Thomistic Account of Species Transformism." *Nova et Vetera* 18 (2020) 945–72.

———. "Thomistic Response to the Theory of Evolution: Aquinas on Natural Selection and the Perfection of the Universe." *Theology and Science* 13 (2015) 325–44.

Tracy, Thomas F. "Special Divine Action and the Laws of Nature." In *Scientific Perspectives on Divine Action: Twenty Years of Challenge and Progress*, edited by Robert John Russell et al., 249–83. Berkeley: Center for Theology and the Natural Sciences, 2008.

Second Vatican Council. *Gaudium et spes*. In *Vatican Council II: The Conciliar and Post-Conciliar Documents*, edited by Austin Flannery, 903–1001. New York: Costello, 1988.

Walker, Sara Imari. "Origins of Life: A Problem for Physics, a Key Issues Review." *Reports on Progress in Physics* 80.9 (2017) 92601.

11

More Than a Mind

4E Cognition and Eastern Christian Liturgical Experience

Antonios Kaldas

> He took upon Him your denser nature,
> having converse with Flesh by means of Mind.[1]

A fascinating convergence has emerged between the ancient Eastern[2] Christian liturgical tradition and a contemporary field of cognitive

---

1. Gregory of Nazianzus, "Select Orations," 29.19. I would like to acknowledge the contribution of Fr. Daniel Fanous, Samuel Kaldas, Ramez Mikhail, and the editor of this volume, Kevin Wagner, who provided valuable feedback on aspects of this chapter. I would like to thank the participants at the Theological Anthropology Conference at Notre Dame University, Sydney, Australia for their feedback on a presentation form of this chapter.

2. I use the term "Eastern Christian" rather than "Orthodox Christian" in order to avoid debate over who qualifies as genuinely Orthodox and who does not—the debate over Chalcedonian versus non-Chalcedonian claims to Orthodoxy. In this context, all I have to say about the holistic view of human cognition in "Eastern Christianity" applies equally (with some nuances) to Eastern Orthodox, Oriental Orthodox, and the Church of the East. I hasten to add that many of the Eastern liturgical features

science.³ "4E Cognition"—the view that human cognition is intrinsically Embedded, Embodied, Enacted, and Extended—overlaps surprisingly well with the Eastern Christian emphasis on praying and participating with body, mind, and spirit as an integrated part of a community in the physical world and in communion with the divine. The goal of this chapter is to introduce readers to both these approaches to understanding the nature of the interaction of the human mind with the body and the environment and to draw some interesting and mutually beneficial connections between them. More broadly, this is an exercise in stepping outside rigid disciplinary boundaries, bringing the disciplines of liturgical theology and philosophy of cognitive science into conversation with each other, and thereby enriching and advancing our knowledge and understanding by seeing familiar things in new ways.

To that end, I begin by briefly sketching the 4E Cognition approach and Eastern Christian theological anthropology, before bringing the two together to bear upon the rich tradition of the Coptic Orthodox eucharistic liturgy. I conclude with some reflections on the value of this kind of approach.

4E Cognition Described

Is the web part of the spider, or just something that the spider made?⁴ Richard Menary's illustration highlights a difficulty in how we "carve up" the world. On the one hand, we tend to think of organisms as being *physically* delimited by their integuments—by their skin, or in the case of a spider, their exoskeleton. But on the other hand, when considered *functionally*, the spider and web seem to form a single indivisible system—the web is merely an extension of the one physical system that senses the

---

discussed here are also found in some form in the liturgical traditions within Roman Catholicism, and certain strains of Protestantism. But I focus on the Eastern tradition I know best from long personal experience and draw my illustrations from the Coptic tradition I live daily.

3. "Cognition" here refers to all those functions generally ascribed to minds, such as memory, perception, imagination, calculation, contemplation, reasoning, etc. "Cognitive science" is an umbrella term for the multidisciplinary project of understanding the mind and brain. It encompasses disciplines including (but not limited to) computer science, linguistics, neurobiology, neurology, neuroscience, philosophy, psychology, and psychiatry. For a brief history, see Simon, "Cognitive Science"; Bechtel et al., "Cognitive Science."

4. Menary, *Cognitive Integration*, 1–2.

presence of food, traps it, and consumes it.[5] Turning from spiders to human beings, where exactly is the boundary between "self" and "non-self"? Is it the skin of the body? Or is the body itself merely a "tool," mere clothing worn by the immaterial mind or soul?

Physical answers to these questions turn out to be conventional rather than analytical—an amputated hand does not therefore produce two Captain Hooks (like a worm), nor does it cause the body of Captain Hook to cease being Captain Hook. Philosophers argue over whether your brain, excised from your cranium and preserved fully functional in a jar in a laboratory, would still be "you." These are complex questions and I do not intend to address them here—I mention them only to point out that the heuristic physical criteria we use in our daily lives to delineate the boundaries of our personhood are not as clear cut as we might think.

Functional criteria are perhaps even more problematic. Your memory is the "storehouse" of useful information you need to navigate life, and on some accounts (e.g., Locke),[6] it is your memory that identifies you *as you* over time. But an increasing proportion of this store no longer resides within the human skull, but on electronic devices, where it is accessed and utilized just as efficiently—in many more ways, far more efficiently—than the information stored in your brain. Of course, this is nothing new. From the first prehistoric cave paintings, to the advent of writing, the abacus, and through to modern electronic devices, this process of "outsourcing" cognitive functions has been gathering pace exponentially. It is, perhaps, the growing functional intimacy between human and device—and its increasing seamlessness—that has made this ambiguity in how we 'carve up' the world all the more obvious.

The predominant approach in modern times has been what Menary calls the *cognitivist internalist* view of cognition.[7] He defines *cognitivism* as the view that cognition "is simply defined as the processing of representations" and *internalism* as the view that "cognitive processes, whether computational or otherwise, occur inside the head." In other words, this is the view that cognition is nothing other, nothing more or less than, the manipulation of representations in the brain, period. Perhaps some of the content of those representations is derived from the environment via the senses, perhaps these manipulations result in the body performing

---

5. Japyassú and Laland, "Extended Spider Cognition."
6. Locke, *An Essay concerning Human Understanding*, 2.27.
7. Menary, *Cognitive Integration*, 10.

motor actions, but the picture here is of the brain as very much a tightly enclosed black box, with inputs and outputs (via the peripheral nervous system), but with internal operations that are completely independent of the body or the environment around that body. Whereas the Behaviorist philosophers of the first half of the twentieth century ignored anything going on *inside* the black box, the cognitive internalists of the second half of the same century and until today consider whatever is going on *outside* the black box to be of very limited relevance and focus instead almost completely on unpicking the secrets of the black box's inner workings.

4E Cognition takes a more holistic view.[8] There are non-representational kinds of cognition. And the environment, the input and output channels, and the internal workings of the black box are all part of a single and holistic integrated and interacting system. One cannot fully understand the function of any component—including the brain—without paying attention to the whole system. 4E Cognition, then, presents an alternative to both cognitivism and internalism.

The four Es of 4E Cognition stand for cognition that is Embedded, Embodied, Enacted, and Extended. An example will help to illustrate the features of 4E Cognition. Consider young student Charlotte, trying diligently to weave an answer to a difficult mathematical problem the teacher has written on the board.

Charlotte's mind is *Embedded* in an environment. There are constant interactions between things in that environment and what goes on in her mind. Each is constantly changing the other. She *sees* numbers on the board, which causes certain *thoughts* in her head, which cause certain *actions* of her hand, which *change* the numbers on the board, which she *sees*, and the cycle goes on until a satisfactory solution to the problem is reached. This is a single integrated causal system, composed of Charlotte's brain and body and the board and marker. We might also include the helpful suggestions and conversations Charlotte has with her teacher and fellow students—there is more learning occurring in the room than just that which is in Charlotte's head.

Charlotte's mind is *Embodied*. We tend to think of the neurons of the brain as existing and operating in a vacuum, but in fact we are discovering just how intimate are the interactions between those neurons and the rest of the body. Of course, the sensory receptor organs (eyes, ears,

---

8. There are a number of expressions of this approach to cognition, but Menary's *Cognitive Integration* is an excellent introduction to the particular expression I employ here.

skin, etc.) play a vital role in producing the inputs to cognition. Within the brain, the chemical environment and supporting tissue cells play a substantial role in what neurons do,[9] as do the circumstances of other organs of the body such as the hormonal glands, and even the stomach,[10] and perhaps even the microorganisms in our digestive systems.[11] There is now a considerable body of research that shows that bodily movements relate to cognitions in both directions: a thought can cause an action, but an action can cause a thought. For example, the mere act of saying the words "I really like you" out loud while looking at the face of a stranger actually makes you like that stranger.[12]

Charlotte's mind is *Enactive* in that it does far more than merely "think." It interacts with its environment. There is a constant interaction between body and environment that heavily influences cognition, and most of the time we are completely unaware of it. Charlotte moves closer to the board when she wants to adjust a detail or further from the board when she wants to take a "broader" perspective on the problem. Her eyeballs make constant small but rapid eye movements (*saccades*) necessary for her vision to function optimally and produce the right input for her cognitions. And of course, every change she makes on the board cascades into changes in her pattern of thought, and vice versa.

And Charlotte's mind is *Extended* in that it carries out many of its operations by utilizing objects in the world as an integral component of the problem-solving system. Not only does she use the board and marker to represent and extend the steps of the calculations in her head, but she might also whip out her handheld calculator or smartphone to perform certain calculations too difficult for mental arithmetic, or turn to her mathematics textbook to remind herself of an equation or mathematical law she has forgotten. The objects outside her skin work seamlessly together with her body and brain as a single system to solve the problem.

The point here is that cognitivist internalism—approaching the brain as nothing more than a self-enclosed system for manipulating representations, independent of the body or the environment—is a seriously incomplete and unsatisfactory approach. The 4E Cognition kind

---

9. Fields, *The Other Brain*.
10. Danziger et al., "Extraneous Factors in Judicial Decisions."
11. Winter et al., "Gut Microbiome and Depression."
12. Collins, "I Really Like You."

of approach remedies that lack in important ways, and thus opens to us richer ways of understanding human cognition.

> Its cash value is that the co-ordination of bodily processes of the organism with salient features of the environment, often created or maintained by the organism, allows it to perform cognitive functions that it otherwise would be unable to; or allows it to perform functions in a way that is distinctively different and is an improvement upon the way that the organism performs those functions via bodily processes alone. If we studied the spider's ability to catch prey without taking account of its web, we would not have much of an explanation at all. If we were to take away the spider's ability to create and manipulate its webs, we would severely curtail its ability to catch prey. Similarly, I suggest, studying the cognitive abilities of the human organism without taking account of its bodily manipulations of environmental vehicles is not much of an explanation at all, and if we were to take away the human organism's abilities to bodily manipulate its environment, we would severely curtail its cognitive abilities.[13]

If we wish, then to properly understand cognition, including all those things that make us human—the solution of a mathematical problem, the genesis of a poem, the creation of sculpture, the discovery of a profound truth about the universe, or even the love of a mother for her child—we cannot treat the human agent as an island, independent of either body or environment.

Eastern Christian Anthropology

It should come as no surprise that this is no less true of religious cognition.[14] I argue that in many ways the 4E approach is more in harmony with Eastern Christian spirituality (based on its soteriology and anthropology) than cognitivist internalist approaches are. Patristic anthropology, while differing on some points from one author to another, is by and large inherently and deeply holistic. Human beings are not to be understood (or treated) as self-contained islands, but as indivisible components of a much larger entity. And the human soul cannot be considered apart from its body—the two form an essentially single entity. Two

---

13. Menary, *Cognitive Integration*, 3, 6–7.
14. Krueger, "Extended Mind and Religious Cognition."

specific patristic concepts will serve to illustrate this view: the human being as microcosm and the cosmos as macranthropos; and salvation as applying not just to the soul, but also to the body (and indeed, to the whole cosmos). The natural harmony with 4E cognition accounts should soon become apparent.

Long before 4E Cognition was a glint in the eye of the modern philosophers, the Greek philosophers and—following them—the church Fathers spoke of the human as a *microcosm*, a small cosmos, and the cosmos as *macranthropos*, a large human, and of the two as an inseparably intertwined single whole.[15] It is not hard to find 4E language in Eastern Christian theology, e.g., "In this second creation story [Gen 2–3], the human being appears as the *hypostasis* of the earthly cosmos: *terrestrial nature extends his body.*"[16] Note that this is not a merely *functional* account of human existence (and therefore also of the human cognition it subsumes) but essentially an *ontological* account, which again, subsumes the functional.

While humanity is inextricably embedded in its physical environment, it is also more than that. The human being is "Plac'd on this isthmus of a middle state. . . . In doubt to deem himself a god, or beast; In doubt his mind or body to prefer."[17] In patristic Christian thought, human nature is the "bond of the cosmos, *syndesmos tou kosmou*,"[18] the nexus or bridge between the heavenly and the earthly, the eternal and the temporal, the spiritual and the physical. Human beings embody the creative and divine love of God and divinize the material creation. This universal human vocation flows from the nature of the True Human, Jesus Christ, of whom it is said, "the middle wall you have broken down and the old enmity You have abolished. You have reconciled the earthly with the heavenly and made the two into one, and fulfilled the economy in the flesh."[19]

Salvation, then, in Eastern Christianity, has as one of its central features this idea of healing the divisions in the world and restoring a harmonious holism, grounded in God, at the center of which is humanity. As such, the states of humanity and the cosmos are connected: if

15. Lossky, *Dogmatic Theology*, 85.
16. Lossky, *Dogmatic Theology*, 83. Italics added for the last phrase.
17. Pope, *An Essay on Man*, 2.1.
18. Louth, *Introducing Eastern Orthodox Theology*, 42.
19. *Prayer of Reconciliation* of the Coptic Liturgy of St. Gregory, in *The Divine Liturgies*, 220. Cf. Eph 2:14.

humanity falls, the cosmos falls; and if humanity is healed, the cosmos is healed. But this also means that the whole human being is, *a fortiori*, healed—body, mind, and soul.

> For that which He has not assumed He has not healed; but that which is united to His Godhead is also saved. If only half Adam fell, then that which Christ assumes and saves may be half also; but if the whole of his nature fell, it must be united to the whole nature of Him that was begotten, and so be saved as a whole.... Keep then the whole man, and mingle Godhead therewith, that you may benefit me in my completeness.[20]

This understanding of human salvation as encompassing the whole-person-in-the-world is itself based on a certain theological anthropology—a metaphysical account of the nature of the human being—that contradicts more dualistic accounts. Traditional Eastern Christian theology is open-minded about the metaphysical nature of the mind/soul-body relationship. The church Fathers held a variety of philosophical views,[21] but they insisted upon a *physical* resurrection,[22] for even in eternity, a human soul without a human body (albeit a spiritual body, a *soma pneumatikon*)[23] is not fully human. What is relevant here is that strict Cartesian dualism—which tends to the strict division of mind/soul from body—is by no means the only option for the Christian, and in fact, in some important ways diminishes the truth and beauty of the holistic Eastern Christian view of human nature. I am not *just* my mind (as per Cartesianism), nor am I *just* my body (as per modern physicalism); rather, I am necessarily the seamless union of those two, and am therefore only fully saved by the divine assuming them both, together, and healing them both, together: "Now, spiritual men shall not be incorporeal spirits; but our substance, that is, the union of flesh and spirit, receiving the Spirit of God, makes up the spiritual man."[24] If liturgy is the living out of this healing salvific process, then, the liturgical encounter with God *must* involve both body and mind/soul, together.

---

20. Gregory of Nazianzus, "Select Letters," Epistle CI, 440.
21. Karamanolis, *The Philosophy of Early Christianity*, 181–213.
22. Hall, *Learning Theology with the Church Fathers*, 246–73.
23. 1 Cor 15:44.
24. Irenaeus, *Against Heresies*, 5.8.2.

4E Cognition Applied

Given the remarkable similarities between ancient Eastern Christian theological anthropology and the contemporary 4E Cognition account on the level of *theory*, it will come as no surprise that we can trace 4E cognition principles extensively in Eastern Christian liturgical *practice*. In this section, I illustrate with a few examples (by no means exhaustive) the fecund possibilities of exploring this connection for each of the four E's in turn as they are expressed in different aspects of the Coptic Orthodox liturgical tradition.[25] This holistic mindset is by no means restricted to liturgical worship—it pervades every aspect of Eastern Christian thought and life. But since we are most human—closest to the image and likeness of God and in closest communion with him—in liturgical worship, it is no surprise that liturgy is one of the clearest expressions of this holistic mindset.

Embedded

Consider now, Pachomius, a faithful Eastern Christian participating in the Eucharistic liturgy at his local parish.[26] There is a reason liturgies are prayed in carefully designed church buildings. The environment such structures provide allows for a constant and fruitful interplay between Pachomius (mind/soul and body) and his environment.[27] The fixed environment reliably molds his experience: the rectangular church building is an ark of safety from the billows of this chaotic world; the gradual narrowing of spaces from capacious nave to smaller choir to mysterious inner sanctuary focuses his attention upon the altar, the throne of God incarnate; and the colorful icons flood his vision with a window to heavenly mysteries no words can utter. There are also more fleeting

---

25. For a classic introduction the Coptic Eucharistic rite, see Burmester, *The Egyptian or Coptic Church*. For a thoughtful description of the Coptic eucharistic liturgical rite with patristic commentary, see Malaty, *Christ in the Eucharist*. For an overview of Coptic Liturgical Studies, see Youssef, "Liturgy in the Coptic Church."

26. Pachomius is conveniently both the name of the fourth century monastic and father of coenobitism and, like Charlotte above, a famous spider (in this case, a Central American genus of spiders). I use the name here to denote an imaginary person who illustrates the concepts I wish to discuss.

27. For accounts of the theology of church building environments from a Coptic perspective, see Malaty, *The Church*; and from an Eastern Orthodox perspective, see Alfeyev, *Orthodox Christianity*.

aspects of the environment interacting with Pachomius. The melodies of a hundred voices singing age-old hymns in unison unite Pachomius not only to those present around him in this church today, not only to the Body of Christ spread throughout time and space "from generation to generation and unto the age of ages,"[28] but thereby also to God through Christ himself. And the clouds of scented incense soothe the soul and turn his thoughts to the kenotic self-giving of Christ's self-sacrifice which became "a sweet aroma before the Father on Golgotha."[29] The very smell of the incense is demonstrably changing his inner experience. Modern science would seem to support this claim. One study found that pleasant aromas—in this case the aroma of cinnamon buns—increases the proportion of women performing benevolent acts from 17 percent to 61 percent.[30]

The physical environment of the church molds the experience of each worshipper in the present, but of course, the worshippers themselves have molded the design of the church and its contents over the centuries with the express goal of creating these kinds of effects on worshippers. Pachomius's religious cognitions are clearly not just in his head, but in a very real sense they are part of a single integrated causal system, composed of Pachomius's brain and body (and those of all the others who have worshipped in churches) and the physical constituents of the church around him.

Embodied

The integration of the body's senses and actions in worship can be traced back to Scripture. We need only consider the elaborate instructions for the Old Testament tabernacle.[31] Or consider how impoverished the tale of the repentant sinful woman would be without the washing of Jesus' feet with tears and wiping with the hair of her head.[32] Without the body,

---

28. Coptic Liturgy of St. Basil, in *The Divine Liturgies*, 185.

29. From the hymn, *Fai etaf-enf* (*This is He* . . .), which is prayed during the Holy Week and Feasts of the Cross in the Coptic rite. For a study of the role of the sense of smell in ancient worship, see Harvey, *Scenting Salvation*.

30. Baron, "The Sweet Smell," discussed in Miller, *The Character Gap*, 148–49.

31. See Exod 25–31 and 35–40.

32. Luke 7:36–50.

the soul loses an essential medium for instantiating and experiencing divine love.

> In essence, my body is my relationship to the world, to others; it is my life as communion and as mutual relationship. Without exception, everything in the body, the human organism, is created for this relationship, for this communion, for this coming out of oneself. It is not an accident, of course, that love, the highest form of communion, finds its incarnation in the body; the body is that which sees, hears, feels, and thereby leads me out of the isolation of my I. . . . [T]he body is the soul as love, the soul as communion, the soul as life, the soul as movement.[33]

If the body instantiates the soul's love, it thereby also connects and unites the soul to Love himself. In Christ's incarnation, the ineffable mystery of divinity became in some limited way accessible to humanity, and the body's senses and actions play a central role in this revelation:

> God who rests in His saints
> was incarnate from the Virgin for the sake of our salvation.
> Come, gaze and wonder, praise and rejoice in jubilation
> at this mystery which has been revealed to us.
> For the Bodiless was incarnate and the Logos was embodied
> the Beginningless began and the Timeless entered time.
> The Ineffable has been touched, The Invisible, seen,
> the Son of the living God became a Son of Man in truth.[34]

> And perhaps, as the Apostle says, *for those who have their senses exercised to the discerning of good and evil*, Christ becomes each of these things in turn, to suit the several senses of the soul. He is called the true Light, therefore, so that the soul's eyes may have something to lighten them. He is the Word, so that her ears may have something to hear. Again, He is the Bread of life, so that the soul's palate may have something to taste. And in the same way, He is called the spikenard or ointment, that the soul's sense of smell may apprehend the fragrance of the Word. For the same reason He is said also to be able to be felt and handled, and is called the Word made flesh, so that the hand of the interior soul may touch concerning the Word of life. But all these things are the One, Same Word of God, who adapts Himself to the sundry

---

33. Schmemann, *O Death Where Is Thy Sting?*, 42–43.

34. Coptic *Theotokia* for Wednesday, 7, in *The Holy Psalmody*, 178–80. Compare Gregory of Nazianzus, "Select Orations," 38.

tempers of prayer according to these several guises, and so leaves none of the soul's faculties empty of his grace.[35]

Eastern Christian *liturgical* experience is therefore very much *bodily* experience. Every possible aspect of the body is involved: sensation-mind/soul-action form a single seamless system. Each of the five classical senses is involved: Pachomius *sees* the icons and clouds of incense and the rubrics being performed; he *hears* the hymns and the bells; he *smells* the incense; he *tastes* the Body and Blood of Christ; and he *feels* the warmth and friction of other's hands in the apostolic greeting, and the hardness of the floor as he kneels. Even senses other than these five are engaged: for example, in bowing and standing the sense of joint *proprioception* is involved, and the chemical sensation of hunger from fasting before communion is another sense engaged. The whole congregation performs liturgical actions such as bowing and rising, lifting up the hands in prayer, exchanging the kiss of peace, processing reverently to partake of the Body and Blood, and making the sign of the cross, while the celebrant performs a host of symbolically rich rubrics. Pachomius's cognitions influence body movements, and his body movements influence his cognitions.

Enacted

Enactivism about cognition is an alternative to *cognitivist internalism* (see above), which holds that our cognitions are neither more nor less than the processing of representations inside our heads. The *enactivist* view of cognition holds instead that actions and interactions between the person and the environment are not just causes or consequences of cognitions, but constituents of cognitions. Applied to liturgical practice, this would suggest that the rubrics and liturgical actions are themselves constituent of (although not exhaustive of) religious cognition. To put it more simply, prayer is not just thoughts *in the head*, but the evolving state of the whole world-body-mind/soul system. To pray is to soar like a kite caught up by the winds of divinity and become one with divinity—moving and being moved as one.[36]

---

35. Origen, *The Song of Songs*, 2.9. For a succinct account of Origen's five "spiritual senses," see Louth, *The Origins of the Christian Mystical Tradition*, 66–68.

36. A beautiful sentiment captured in Peter Morten's poem, "The Winds of Cape Elizabeth."

The very names we give to liturgical prayer are essentially about action. *Eucharist* is the act of giving thanks for the good (Greek, *eu-*) gift (*-charizomai*) we receive constantly from God in our lives. *Liturgy* is the work (*ergon*) of the people (*laos*). And even in the West, *mass* is the act or mission (Latin, *missa*, from *mittere*: to let go, send) of taking Christ out into the world. Liturgical prayer by its nature cannot be restricted to the head, to merely *internal* emotions or abstract thoughts or language. There is a constant dance within the single environment-body-mind/soul system, a dance of the Charites, of eternal mutual giving and taking and gratitude, enriching all its components and making the whole system spiritually fertile.

There is a constant interaction amongst the components of Pachomius's environment-body-mind/soul system that together constitutes his religious cognition. For example, the physical turning of Pachomius's body orients it to be face-to-face with his neighboring worshipper and allows each to look upon the other's face, to communicate via body language and facial expressions, and to exchange the kiss of peace. This in turn mediates internal feelings of love and connection for each other. In the Coptic tradition, the kiss of peace is exchanged by forming what I like to call a "love sandwich"—Pachomius's two hands take one of his neighbor's hands between them, while his neighbor's two hands do the same to one of Pachomius's hands. Each then slides his own two hands out of the sandwich and raises them to his lips to kiss them. The symbolism is profound: our lives, like our hands, are intertwined together, for "our life and our death is with our neighbor."[37] Pachomius's smooth palm caresses the weather-beaten skin of the back of his neighbor's hand because they support each other through the rough and the smooth of life. And this relationship is immensely precious, such that Pachomius must kiss the hands that held those of his beloved brother. Similarly, in the act of communal singing, Pachomius and his fellow worshippers enter into a relationship of mutual listening—or else they will fall out of musical harmony. The act of singing melds together many larynxes into a single instrument, and thereby, many individuals into a single body. None of this need be representational, in the sense of mental propositions or even sensory images held in the minds of the participants. The act *itself* constitutes the cognition.

---

37. Ward, *The Desert Christian*, Anthony the Great, 9.

There is a temporal dimension to this enacted religious cognition that extends beyond the time of the liturgy. Exchanges such as the kiss of peace have the power to mold the ongoing behavior of the participants. Past grievances are let go and forgotten; future relations are set upon a more affectionate footing. The liturgical action becomes an inflection point, a moment in time that alters our character as individuals and as community, and therefore, alters the direction of our lives.

Extended

There are some obvious and rather quotidian ways in which liturgical practice is extended. For example, the use of a hymnal or eucharistic missal represents the shared memory of the community for the words of the prayers they intone together. This is particularly important for long prayers or rarely used ones, which are difficult to memorize. But there are even more aspects of extended cognition involved.

Consider this analogy: in the Olympic sport of rhythmic gymnastics, the dancer and the apparatus—a hoop, a ball, clubs, a ribbon, or a rope—seem to become one. The apparatus is moved with exactly the same control, precision, and elegance as the arms and the legs of the gymnast. Even when the apparatus is flying through the air—physically separated from the organic body of the gymnast—this implies no diminution in this union between gymnast and apparatus. In a very similar way, in a liturgical setting, Pachomius might shift a prayer bead with each *Kyrie eleison* ("Lord have mercy") he prays, subcontracting the task of counting them to the beads in much the same manner as Charlotte, above, subcontracts the more complex mathematical tasks to her calculator.

This extension of cognition to incorporate objects external to the body applies even more obviously to the liturgical celebrants, who have a broader range of apparatus available to them than the congregation. I have seen priests manipulating their censors, and deacons their cymbals and triangles, in ways perhaps just marginally less artistic than the art of the rhythmic gymnast. Napkins, spoons, candles, fans—and in the Ethiopian tradition, drums and umbrellas—all manner of inanimate objects are co-opted into the liturgical act. For example, in the second half of the Coptic Prayer of Reconciliation, the priest holds a square altar napkin folded into two triangular halves above his head as he stands facing the East at the altar. The two connected triangles symbolize the heavenly

Holy Trinity united with the earthly trinitarian human nature of body, soul, and spirit. From behind the priest, the congregation sees a triangle that looks like the wings of an angel (if held just right) directly below the large icon of Christ the Pantocrator in the apse to the East of the altar. If the architecture is correctly aligned, the six-sided wing-shaped napkin symbolizes that Cherubim upon which sits God-with-us, a physical extension of the spiritual truth that through Christ, heaven and earth have become one.

Again, there is something more going on here than mere abstract representation. The inanimate objects are not just being *used*, they are being drawn in, enveloped, encompassed, and imbued with significance no less than the internal wiring and the display screen of the hand-held calculator. In fact, what is happening here is that the human being—the bridge of realities—is drawing inanimate earthly objects into the rational heavenly song of praise. Through the human worshipper, the cosmos finds a voice with which to worship its Creator and is thereby sanctified and sacramentalized. The reality of the divine presence in this little piece of the cosmos is unveiled.

I have tried to illustrate as far as possible the profound coherence between the ancient Christian approach to holistic liturgical practice and the modern secular concept of 4E cognition. There is so much more that might be said, but not here.

But I do wish to tentatively point out one difference between the two approaches. The 4E Cognition approach is chiefly an *objectively descriptive* project—it seeks to describe the inherent nature of situated and embodied human cognition. In the case of liturgical practice, on the other hand, description is very low on the list of priorities. Liturgy is about *subjective experience*, about personal relationship, about life, essence, transformation, ways of being. It is about being a being who loves Goodness and is being united to Goodness. When Pachomius prays, the last thing he wants to be thinking about is *how* his body is involved, and *what* role his environment is playing. He wants to just *be* prayer. Nonetheless, there is no reason why the objective description cannot elucidate the 'mechanics,' as it were, that underlie the subjective experience. Philosophers and scientists—even the most secular—often find very practical applications to their models. There is no reason to think the application of 4E Cognition to liturgical practice should be any less valuable.

Some Final Reflections

I have described some interesting connections between an ancient Eastern Christian liturgical tradition and 4E Cognition, a modern trend in philosophy of mind and cognitive science. These are not generally thought of as natural bedfellows, but I believe they should be. In this final section, I make three points that illustrate how these connections can enrich both the liturgical practice and the inquiry into the nature of human cognition.

Understanding the World

First, exploring these connections represents an instance of the kind of holistic inquiry that liberates us from some of the more egregious isolationist trends in modern western thought and life. This tendency to divide and isolate manifests in at least two ways relevant here: the division of fields of knowledge, and the division of the person.

One can observe extreme forms of the division of knowledge fields equally in Young Earth Creationism and the New Atheism. Both see science and faith as being in harsh conflict; Creationists therefore disdain science while New Atheists therefore disdain faith. This is not the place to argue why both are sadly mistaken, but I mention them to make the point that the discussion above is part of a more general project of finding an approach to knowledge and understanding that respects the potential—but also the boundaries—of both faith and science. The synthesis of Eastern Christian liturgy with 4E Cognition is proof of concept that faith and science not only need not be enemies, but that it is possible for them to complement each other so far as to provide together a richer and clearer picture of reality.

Similarly, approaches such as cognitivist internalism tend to deepen the Cartesian divisions—between mind and body, or mind and world—in ways that hinder our understanding of human nature and experience. 4E Cognition may be motivated, at least in part, by a sense of dissatisfaction with a purely and intensely reductionist attitude to human experience—a sense that such an approach is missing something and incomplete. Likewise, the Eastern Christian liturgical experience is motivated by a desire and yearning for a more accurate and more complete engagement with the reality of our existence. Indeed, the Eastern Christian would argue that liturgy pursues this yearning and extends it further than the essentially descriptive 4E Cognition can. By living the liturgy, Pachomius not only experiences the dissolution of boundaries between mind and body; body and world; self and other—he also begins to experience the dissolution of the boundary between the temporal and the eternal, the heavenly and the earthly, *through* the dissolution of the former boundaries. As Lossky points out, the sacramental Christian experience necessarily *remains* rooted in earthly realities, even as it raises its exponents to participate in a transcendent reality:

> The Christian mystery opens itself to understanding and to experience, the most concrete experience: eating bread, drinking wine, but neither experience nor an understanding can ever exhaust it.[38]

Worship

Second, then, it is of value to worshippers, because the holistic approach here described opens the door to a more authentic experience of communal worship, and 4E Cognition confirms and illuminates that experience. There may be other ramifications. For example, a recent Pew study[39] found that only one third of Catholics understood and believed in the doctrine of the real presence of Christ in the Body and Blood, while about half of the respondents held them to be just "symbols."[40] Anecdotally, I would estimate the vast majority of Eastern Christians, certainly in the Coptic Church, accept the real presence. One wonders whether the relative fading of 4E practices in Western worship—as opposed to their steadfast preservation in the East—might have helped to facilitate such theological shifts. Might there be a causal connection between bodily and environmental immersion in communal liturgical worship and strength of faith in the theological doctrine of real presence? Is it a coincidence that the Protestant reformers jettisoned both 4E liturgical practices and the doctrine of real presence? An approach that divides things into *solas* is in some ways antithetical to an approach that integrates the whole

---

38. Lossky, *Dogmatic Theology*, 157.

39. Pew Research Center, "What Americans Know about Religion." Note however that this finding has been challenged, for example, by Dailey, "How Accurate Is the Pew Survey on the Eucharist?"

40. In the modern sense of the word, of course, not the ancient, on which see Schmemann, *For the Life of the World*, 135–51.

world as together *sacramental*. Perhaps, what we *do* influences what we *believe* just as much as our beliefs influence what we do.

There are, of course, limits as to how far 4E Cognition can contribute to liturgical theology. There have been some attempts to apply 4E Cognition to more practical uses, such as ethics,[41] but in a field such as liturgical theology, one must be very wary of the limits of a merely philosophical or scientific approach. Pointing us to the importance of a holistic approach, elucidating how such an approach functions—all of these are helpful, but they are no substitute for the actual living experience of liturgy, any more than reading SparkNotes is a substitute for an actual Shakespeare play. While it would be a mistake to think that accounts like 4E Cognition have nothing to offer liturgical practice, it would be equally mistaken to think liturgical practice can be reduced to nothing more than a 4E Cognition account.

Research

Third, this synthesis of theology and cognitive science is of value to researchers, not only in theological circles, but also in philosophical and scientific circles. Recent decades have seen a surge in interdisciplinarity, the close cooperation between what have hitherto been islands of inquiry as diverse, in the case of "cognitive science," as biochemistry, philosophy, and history. Religious fields have not been excluded. Philosophers of mind in recent times have engaged with Eastern traditions, particularly Indian philosophy and Buddhism.[42] Yet, I have not been able to uncover any such engagement between philosophy of mind and cognitive science and the rich Eastern Christian tradition.

There is much scope for fruitful inquiry here. Christian theologians have a long and rich tradition of addressing metaphysical questions about unity and plurality, mereology, and interacting "systems." The concept of human beings as *microcosm* mentioned above is not the only concept relevant to 4E Cognition. Two other examples (among many) that deal with 'systems' that are seamlessly integrated are the concept of *perichoresis*— "the exchange of being by which each Person [of the Trinity] exists only

---

41. Levy, "Rethinking Neuroethics"; Swallow, "Sharing the Blame."

42. See for example, Chadha, "Perceptual Experience"; Ricard and Singer, *Beyond the Self*; Menon et al., *Interdisciplinary Perspectives*. This influence can be traced back even as far as David Hume in the seventeenth century; see Gopnik, "Could David Hume Have Known."

in virtue of his relationship with the others,"[43] and the formula describing the union of the divine and the human in the incarnate Christ as being "without mingling, without confusion, and without alteration."[44]

Eastern Christian liturgy and 4E Cognition converge upon a view of reality that is complementary and mutually illuminating, a view that not only reveals our being in the cosmos as profoundly integrated and holistic, relieving to some degree our lonely isolation, but also lifting us into union with the transcendent divine.

Bibliography

Alfeyev, Hilarion. *Orthodox Christianity*. Vol. 3, *The Architecture, Icons, and Music of the Orthodox Church*. Yonkers, NY: St. Vladimir's Seminary Press, 2014.

Baron, Robert A. "The Sweet Smell of . . . Helping: Effects of Pleasant Ambient Fragrance on Prosocial Behavior in Shopping Malls." *Personality and Social Psychology Bulletin* 23.5 (1997) 498–503.

Bechtel, William, et al. "Cognitive Science: History." In *International Encyclopedia of the Social and Behavioral Sciences*, edited by N. J. Smelser and P. B. Baltes, 2154–58. Amsterdam: Elsevier, 2001.

Burmester, O. H. E. *The Egyptian or Coptic Church; A Detailed Description of Her Liturgical Services and the Rites and Ceremonies Observed in the Administration of Her Sacraments*. Publications de La Societe d'archeologie Copte. Textes et Documents. Cairo: Print Office of the French Institute of Oriental Archaeology, 1967.

Chadha, Monima. "Perceptual Experience and Concepts in Classical Indian Philosophy." In *The Stanford Encyclopedia of Philosophy*, edited by Edward N. Zalta. https://plato.stanford.edu/archives/spr2016/entries/perception-india/.

Clément, Olivier. *The Roots of Christian Mysticism: Texts from the Patristic Era with Commentary*. Translated by Theodore Berkeley and Jeremy Hummerstone. 2nd ed. New York: New City, 1993.

Collins, Nathan. "I Really Like You." *Scientific American Mind* 23.1 (2012) 6.

Dailey, Thomas. "How Accurate Is the Pew Survey on the Eucharist?" https://media.ascensionpress.com/2019/08/16/how-accurate-is-the-pew-survey-on-the-eucharist/.

Danziger, Shai, et al. "Extraneous Factors in Judicial Decisions." *Proceedings of the National Academy of Sciences* 108.17 (2011) 6889–92.

The Divine Liturgies of Saints Basil, Gregory, and Cyril. Tallahassee, FL: St. Mary & St. George Coptic Orthodox Church, Coptic Orthodox Diocese of the Southern United States, 2001.

Fields, R. Douglas. *The Other Brain: From Dementia to Schizophrenia, How New Discoveries about the Brain Are Revolutionizing Medicine and Science*. New York: Simon & Schuster, 2009.

---

43. Clément, *The Roots of Christian Mysticism*, 67.
44. Coptic Liturgy of St. Basil, *The Confession*, in *The Divine Liturgies*, 199.

Gopnik, Alison. "Could David Hume Have Known about Buddhism? Charles Francois Dolu, the Royal College of La Flèche, and the Global Jesuit Intellectual Network." *Hume Studies* 35.1–2 (2009) 5–28.

Gregory of Nazianzus. "Select Letters." In vol. 7 of *Nicene and Post Nicene Fathers, Series II*, edited by Peter Schaff and Henry Wace, 435–82. Grand Rapids: Eerdmans, 1893.

Gregory of Nazianzus. "Select Orations." In vol. 7 of *Nicene and Post Nicene Fathers, Series II*, edited by Peter Schaff and Henry Wace, 185–434. Grand Rapids: Eerdmans, 1893.

Hall, Christopher A. *Learning Theology with the Church Fathers*. Downers Grove, IL: IVP Academic, 2002.

Harvey, Susan Ashbrook. *Scenting Salvation*. 1st ed. Berkeley: University of California Press, 2006.

The Holy Psalmody. Tallahassee, FL: St. Mary & St. George Coptic Orthodox Church, Coptic Orthodox Diocese of the Southern United States, 1996.

Irenaeus of Lyon. *Against Heresies*. In vol. 1 of *Ante-Nicene Fathers*, edited by Alexander Roberts et al., 309–567. Grand Rapids: Eerdmans, 1885.

Japyassú, Hilton F., and Kevin N. Laland. "Extended Spider Cognition." *Animal Cognition* 20.3 (2017) 375–95.

Karamanolis, George. *The Philosophy of Early Christianity*. New York: Routledge, 2014.

Krueger, Joel. "Extended Mind and Religious Cognition." In *Religion: Mental Religion*, edited by Niki Kasumi Clements, 237–54. Farmington Hills, MI: MacMillan Reference, 2016.

Levy, Neil. "Rethinking Neuroethics in the Light of the Extended Mind Thesis." *The American Journal of Bioethics* 7.9 (2007) 3–11.

Locke, John. *An Essay concerning Human Understanding*. Edited by Kenneth P. Winkler. Indianapolis: Hackett, 1996.

Lossky, Vladimir. *Dogmatic Theology: Creation, God's Image in Man, & the Redeeming Work of the Trinity*. 2nd ed. Yonkers, NY: St. Vladimir's Seminary Press, 2017.

Louth, Andrew. *Introducing Eastern Orthodox Theology*. Downers Grove, IL: IVP Academic, 2013.

———. *The Origins of the Christian Mystical Tradition: From Plato to Denys*. 2nd ed. Oxford: Oxford University Press, 2007.

Malaty, Tadros Yacoub. *Christ in the Eucharist*. Alexandria: St. George Coptic Orthodox Church, 1986.

———. *The Church, the House of God*. Translated by Nabieh Fanous et al. Alexandria: St. George Coptic Orthodox Church, 1994.

Menary, Richard. *Cognitive Integration: Mind and Cognition Unbounded*. Basingstoke: Palgrave Macmillan, 2007.

Menon, Sangeetha, et al., eds. *Interdisciplinary Perspectives on Consciousness and the Self*. New Delhi: Springer India, 2014.

Miller, Christian B. *The Character Gap: How Good Are We?* New York: Oxford University Press, 2017.

Morton, Peter. "The Winds of Cape Elizabeth." https://www.poemhunter.com/poem/the-winds-of-cape-elizabeth/.

Origen. *Origen: The Song of Songs, Commentary and Homilies*. Translated by R. P. Lawson. Ancient Christian Writers: The Works of the Fathers in Translation 26. London: Longmans, Green, & Co., 1957.

Pew Research Center. "What Americans Know about Religion," 2019. *Pew Research Center*, July 23, 2019. https://www.pewforum.org/2019/07/23/what-americans-know-about-religion/.

Pope, Alexander. *An Essay on Man*. Edited by Mark Pattison. Oxford: Clarendon, 1892.

Ricard, Matthieu, and Wolf Singer. *Beyond the Self: Conversations between Buddhism and Neuroscience*. Cambridge: MIT Press, 2017.

Schmemann, Alexander. *For the Life of the World*. Yonkers, NY: St. Vladimir's Seminary Press, 1973.

———. *O Death Where Is Thy Sting?* Yonkers, NY: St. Vladimir's Seminary Press, 2003.

Simon, Herbert A. "Cognitive Science: The Newest Science of the Artificial." *Cognitive Science* 4.1 (1980) 33–46.

Swallow, Jessica. "Sharing the Blame: Implications of the Hypothesis of Extended Cognition for Personal Identity and Ethics." PhD diss., University of Exeter, 2013.

Ward, Benedicta, ed. *The Desert Christian: The Sayings of the Desert Fathers*. Translated by Benedicta Ward. New York: MacMillan, 1975.

Winter, Gal, et al. "Gut Microbiome and Depression: What We Know and What We Need to Know." *Reviews in the Neurosciences* 29.6 (2018) 629–43.

Youssef, Youhanna Nessim. "Liturgy in the Coptic Church." In *Coptic Civilization: Two Thousand Years of Christianity in Egypt*, edited by Gawdat Gabra, 55–65. Cairo: American University in Cairo Press, 2014.

12

Resources for a Theological Anthropology of the Heart

PETER JOHN MCGREGOR

In everyday speech we often use the term "heart." It can be used to describe someone's personality or disposition: one can have a soft, hard, warm, or cold heart. To indicate love or affection: I love you with all my heart. To indicate courage: take heart. To describe a person's character: he is a man after my own heart. To indicate knowledge: I knew in my heart. To indicate memory: I know it by heart. And so on. The term is also used frequently in Sacred Scripture. As shall be seen, therein it is used to indicate knowing, believing, willing, conscience, the passions, imagination, and memory. It is the place of relationships with other persons, the place which God searches and knows, the place of revelation and the refusal of revelation, and the place of God's indwelling.

In examining this term, we should seek to answer two fundamental questions. First, can the term "heart" be used clearly in theological anthropology, or must it remain forever vague, ambiguous, indeterminate? Second, can the term be used fruitfully in theological anthropology, can it be used in a way that helps us to understand the mystery of ourselves and the mystery of our relationship with God? This chapter will focus mainly on the first question. After beginning with the contemporary search for a theological anthropology of the heart, it will engage in a chronological examination of two main "traditions" of understanding the heart. These are the "analytic" tradition which treats the heart as a particular faculty of the human person, and the "synthetic" tradition which treats it as in some way transcending a particular faculty. The chapter will conclude with a few thoughts on the importance of answering the second question.

The Contemporary Search for a Theological Anthropology of the Heart

In his 1965 work, *The Sacred Heart: An Analysis of Human and Divine Affectivity*, Dietrich von Hildebrand writes,

> The affective sphere, and the heart as its center, have been more or less under a cloud in the entire course of the history of philosophy. It has had a role in poetry, in literature, in the private prayers of great souls, and above all in the Old Testament, in the Gospel, and in the Liturgy, but not in the area of philosophy proper.[1]

He goes on to claim that, not only has the nature of the heart generally been ignored, but that when a question of its nature has arisen, that nature has been misunderstood. Moreover, he states that "[t]he affective sphere, and with it the heart, has been excluded from the spiritual realm" also.[2] According to von Hildebrand, for Plato, the affective sphere did not possess a rank comparable to that of the intellect.[3] For Aristotle, this sphere is consigned to the irrational, animalistic part of the human being.[4] This attitude has remained as "a more or less noncontroversial part of our philosophical heritage. The entire affective sphere was for the most part subsumed under the heading of passions, and as long as one dealt with it expressly under this title, its irrational and nonspiritual character was emphasized."[5]

---

1. Von Hildebrand, *The Sacred Heart*, 25.
2. Von Hildebrand, *The Sacred Heart*, 25.
3. Von Hildebrand, *The Sacred Heart*, 25.
4. Von Hildebrand, *The Sacred Heart*, 25–26.
5. Von Hildebrand, *The Sacred Heart*, 26.

The Hungarian theologian Beáta Tóth also addresses the philosophical neglect of the heart, but points out that this neglect is, even more so, theological in nature.

> For too long, theology has abandoned the project of exploring the human heart and has left the problematic job of mapping the domain of human emotionality to secular philosophy. Even philosophy has been oblivious of the issue of the emotions for a long time and has only recently regained a lively interest in the subject.[6]

Tóth recognizes the need for a contemporary theological anthropology of the heart. According to her,

> the rich notion of the biblical heart—the unifying centre of human knowing and feeling—has gradually waned into the thin concept of the seat of mystical emotionality, pietist religious feeling, or unearthly biblical sentiment. It is as if the biblical heart, which originally comprised reason together with volition and sensibility, forming an indivisible unity, broke up and gave way to independent self-supporting modern reason and the juxtaposed modern and emancipated, purely emotional heart.[7]

Tóth maintains that one of the consequences of the Enlightenment is that current theology, in its struggle to deal with the consequences of rationalism,

> is much more ignorant of its own tradition regarding human emotionality and is therefore practically unequipped against the dangers of irrational sentimentalism, on the one hand, and an emotionally deficient rationalism, on the other. Such neglect affects the entire shape of the Christian stance towards faith, revelation, and the theology of love.[8]

According to Tóth, in the wake of "the regrettable disappearance of the theme of the biblical heart after the Enlightenment," we are now in a situation where even theology based on the heart is "incapable of developing a 'Christian logic of affectivity.'"[9] Tóth accepts the diagnosis:

---

6. Tóth, *The Heart Has Its Reasons*, 14.
7. Tóth, *The Heart Has Its Reasons*, 11.
8. Tóth, *The Heart Has Its Reasons*, x.
9. Tóth, *The Heart Has Its Reasons*, x.

> That reason and sensibility suffer from an unwholesome disassociation in our world, hence intellect and affectivity are in disharmony. The head and the heart are set in opposition and one usually opts for one at the expense of the other; the two are hardly ever considered as a unified whole and the interaction between them is not conceptualized.[10]

Tóth admits that there are currently "numerous attempts at the exploration of the passional character of reason or the rationality of emotion."[11] However, she regards these as inadequate since,

> these accounts are typically written from a philosophical perspective and so they do not reckon in a systematic manner with the particularities of the Christian theological tradition; and ... they mostly seek to overcome the dichotomy by leveling out differences between the two sides: either reason is integrated into a concept of emotion, or emotion is made an integral part of reason.[12]

Tóth herself wishes to find "a median zone where affectivity and reason, love and logos coincide and, without losing their distinctive identities, interact in multiple mediations."[13] Furthermore, she holds that, despite the piecemeal way in which discourse on the emotions "has traditionally been scattered throughout various fields of moral and dogmatic theology," the solution is not to be found in treating of the emotions in isolation, but by investigating them as an aspect of theological anthropology, where they can be looked at in the context of "the human condition with reference to God and creation, and reflection on the human person viewed in his relation to God, the Creator."[14] Thus Tóth holds that the "theological logic of affectivity coincides with a larger logic that views the human person as being created in the image of God, recreated through Christ's redemption, and destined to eschatological beatitude in the eternal life of the Triune God."[15]

---

10. Tóth, *The Heart Has Its Reasons*, x.
11. Tóth, *The Heart Has Its Reasons*, x.
12. Tóth, *The Heart Has Its Reasons*, x–xi.
13. Tóth, *The Heart Has Its Reasons*, xi.
14. Tóth, *The Heart Has Its Reasons*, xi.
15. Tóth, *The Heart Has Its Reasons*, xii.

Following Paul Ricoeur, Tóth points out that, in *The Republic*, there is another understanding of the heart that differs from that normally associated with Plato. Thus,

> Plato's description of the soul is dominated by the idea of unstable movement and a system of tensions that culminate in the median power of the *thumos*, which is not so much a mean, but rather a mixture or *"melange"* of reason and desire: it sides both with reason (in the form of indignation and endurance) and it also sides with desire (in the form of irritation and fury). . . . What is missing from the static political symbol of the soul is the dynamism of the soul, that is, its unity in movement towards the Ideas and the Good. By contrast, in the dynamic *thumos*, Ricoeur welcomes a versatile force that occupies a middle position between sensible desire (*epithumia*) and reason's specific desire (*erōs*) and, in this manner, forms a kind of "affective node," constituting the field of human feeling *par excellence*. Therefore, Ricoeur's key contention is to transpose Plato's intuition into the mode of philosophical reflection by working out a modern theory of feeling where *thumos* as the "heart" assumes a pivotal role.[16]

From this starting point, Tóth goes on to develop a theological anthropology of the heart in dialogue with the Ricoeur and Karol Wojtyła/ John Paul II. In Ricoeur's philosophical anthropology she discerns an understanding of the heart as a "median zone," a "dynamic site" where affectivity unites the sensible and spiritual polarities of the human person.[17] In John Paul II's catechesis on conjugal love she sees a break from "the intellectual versus body dichotomy [that] makes the biblically understood heart the centre of what is 'spiritual' in man, while, however, not setting the heart over against the body, but making it the body's spiritual dimension."[18] Tóth concludes that "what is distinctively human is not so much the abstracted intellect [which we share with the angels] as the symbolic heart, the seat of complex mediation between rationality, emotionality, and will and the site of relationality with regard to fellow humans and God."[19]

---

16. Tóth, *The Heart Has Its Reasons*, 44–45. See Ricoeur, *Fallible Man*, 161–63.
17. Tóth, *The Heart Has Its Reasons*, 232.
18. Tóth, *The Heart Has Its Reasons*, 234.
19. Tóth, *The Heart Has Its Reasons*, 237.

Robert Sokolowski is another scholar engaged in developing such an anthropology. As Tracey Rowland points out, a "theological anthropology which pays due regard to the intellectual and affective dimensions of human action is now in the course of development."[20] She states that,

> the contemporary work of Robert Sokolowski has also drawn attention to this neglected element in presentations of the natural law. With reference to the notion of the law being written on the hearts of the gentiles, Sokolowski has argued that the word *kardia* in the passage from St. Paul's *Letter to the Romans* . . . does not connote the separation of heart and head that we take for granted in a world shaped by Descartes. He concurs with Robert Spaemann's claim that in the New Testament the heart is taken to be a deeper recipient of truth than even the mind or intellect in Greek philosophy since it deals with the person's willingness to accept the truth.[21]

We see here that both Sokolowski and Spaemann ground their understanding of the heart in the New Testament. At the contemporary zenith of this understanding stands Joseph Ratzinger/Benedict XVI, who, beginning from the biblical understanding of the heart, most simply defines it as "the wholeness of man."[22]

So, there have been two different ways of understanding what is meant by the term "heart." They could be called the analytic and the synthetic ways. The first is an analysis of the human faculties, one that needs to be synthesized. The second is a synthesis of the human heart, one that needs to be analyzed. The first is based on how we think about being human, while the second is based on how we experience being human.

The Analytic Tradition

The analytic tradition distinguishes between the individual faculties of the human person. Thus, in *The Republic*, Plato divides the soul into three parts: the logical, symbolized by the head; the spirited, symbolized by the heart; and the appetitive, symbolized by the entrails. Here Plato likens the soul to the three orders of the city, the guardians, the auxiliaries, and the

---

20. Rowland, "The Role of Natural Law and Natural Right," 164–65.
21. Rowland, "The Role of Natural Law and Natural Right," 164–65.
22. Ratzinger, *From the Baptism*, 93. For more on Ratzinger's theological anthropology of the heart, see McGregor, *Heart to Heart*, 279–310.

producers.²³ In *Timaeus*, he divides the human person into the immortal rational soul, the body, and the two parts of the mortal soul. The immortal rational soul resides in the head, and the two parts of the mortal soul reside in the body, the spirited part in the chest and the appetitive part in the guts.²⁴ These Platonic schemata provide the basis for this tradition. Yet we find these schemata are adapted in various ways in order to account for the place of the heart. The first adaption is found amongst the Greek Fathers.

The heart lies at the center of Eastern Christian spirituality. As Tomas Spidlik points out in his classic study of the spirituality of the Christian East, the spiritual writers of the East "speak of custody of the heart, of attentiveness to the heart, of purity of heart, of the thoughts, desires, and resolutions of the heart, of prayer of the heart, of the divine presence in the heart, and so on."²⁵ Faced with the fact that, in Sacred Scripture, "the heart contains the fullness of the spiritual life, which involves the whole person, with all his faculties and all his activities," the Fathers were faced with the dilemma of how to express this in a way comprehensible to a Greek mind.²⁶ Since the mind occupied pride of place for the Greeks, the patristic response was to identify the heart with the mind. As Spidlik continues, "[s]peculative by nature, the Greeks certainly did not by mere chance substitute *nous* (reason, mind) for the Hebraic *lev, levav* (heart). According to Gregory Nazianzus the 'clean heart' of Ps. 50:2 was the *dianoētikon* (mind)."²⁷

With Thomas Aquinas, we find that his view of the heart seems to combine Platonic and Aristotelian understandings, depending upon the particular sense in which he is using the term. Thus, he sometimes uses it to mean the principle of animal life and movement (Aristotelian).²⁸ He also "thinks of the heart as the organ of the passions, in the sense that the motions and affections of the sensitive part of the soul are joined with a powerful motion (*commotio*) of the body, and in particular of the heart. In this way love produces a *dilatatio cordis* [an enlargement of the heart]

---

23. Plato, *The Republic*, 435–42.
24. Plato, *Timaeus*, 69b–72d.
25. Spidlik, *The Spirituality of the Christian East*, 103. See also Spidlik, *Prayer*.
26. Spidlik, *The Spirituality of the Christian East*, 104.
27. Spidlik, *The Spirituality of the Christian East*, 104, referring to Gregory of Nazianzus, *Orationes* 40.39.
28. See Elders, "The Inner Life of Jesus," 79, where he refers the reader to St. Thomas Aquinas, *Summa Theologicae*, I.20.1.ad.1; III.90.3.ad.3; and *In IV Sent.*, 14.1.ad.2.

(Platonic)."²⁹ When speaking of the heart in its biblical sense he equates *cor* with *spiritus*.³⁰ Furthermore, when commenting on the use of the term in the evangelical counsel to love God with all one's heart (cf. Luke 10:27) he says that it indicates an *actus voluntatis quae hic significatur per cor* (an act of the will, which is indicated here by heart).³¹ Yet, in prayers attributed to him, one can sometimes find a more "biblical" understanding of the term "heart." For example, in a Prayer for a Priestly Heart we read:

> Give me, O Lord, an ever watchful heart which no subtle speculation may ever lure from you. Give me a noble heart that no unworthy affection shall ever draw downwards to earth. Give me a heart of honesty that no insincerity shall warp. Give me a heart of courage that no distress shall ever crush or quench. Give me a heart so free that no perverted or impetuous affection shall ever claim it for its own.³²

However, in his properly theological work, Aquinas never speaks of the heart as a source of cognition.³³

In von Hildebrand's *The Sacred Heart*, we find a third account which differs from those of both Plato and Aquinas. He holds that, for the most part, it is "characteristic of the heart in its true and most specific sense that it is chosen as representative of man's inner life, and that the heart, rather than the intellect or will, is identified with the soul as such."³⁴ He goes on to identify the "heart" as the center of human affectivity. Thus, "just as the intellect is the root of all acts of knowledge, the heart is the organ of all affectivity: all wishing, all desiring, all 'being *affected*.'"³⁵ Von Hildebrand gradually explains his definition of the heart. More precisely,

---

29. Elders, "The Inner Life of Jesus," 79, referring the reader to St. Thomas Aquinas, *Q. d. de veritate*, 22.2; and *Super Io evang.*, c. 13, lectio 4, N. 1796.

30. Elders, "The Inner Life of Jesus," 79, referring the reader to St. Thomas Aquinas, *Super epist. I ad Thess.*, c. 5, lectio I, N. 120; and *Super Io evang.*, c. 14, lectio I, N. 1850: "*cor, id est spiritus.*"

31. Aquinas, *Summa Theologiae*, II-II.44.5.

32. "Prayer for a Priestly Heart."

33. Elders, "The Inner Life of Jesus," 79, referring the reader to Thomas Aquinas, *Summa Theologica*, III.90.3.ad.3.

34. Von Hildebrand, *The Sacred Heart*, 47. Von Hildebrand sees the intellect, will, and heart as the three fundamental "capacities" of the human person. It is to the heart that the "affective sphere" belongs (25–49).

35. Von Hildebrand, *The Sacred Heart*, 48.

the heart is the center of affectivity. It can be contrasted not just with the will and intellect, but with the less central strata of affectivity. These strata von Hildebrand characterizes as "non-spiritual," that is, the agreeable or disagreeable feelings which attend upon bodily pains and pleasures.[36] Distinguishing between bodily and psychic feelings, he holds that not all psychic feelings can be classified as "spiritual." There are psychic states such as "jolliness" and depression, and what he calls spiritual affective responses such as joy, sorrow, love or compassion. He distinguishes between them on the grounds that the psychic states are not "intentional," that is to say, they do not have "a meaningful conscious relation to an object."[37] Thus,

> [Psychic] states are "caused" either by bodily processes or by psychic ones, whereas affective responses are "motivated." Never can an authentic affective response come into existence by mere causation, but only by motivation. Real joy necessarily implies not only the consciousness of an object about which we are rejoicing, but also an awareness that it is this object which is the reason for this joy. In rejoicing over the recovery of a friend, we know that it is this event which engenders and motivates our joy. The recovery of our friend is thus connected with our joy by a meaningful and intelligible relation.[38]

Von Hildebrand further refines his definition of the "heart" by distinguishing between what he calls "energized" and "tender" affectivity. The former is "temperamental," for example, the pleasure experienced in sports or in displaying one's talents. According to him,

> [The latter] manifests itself in love in all its categories: filial and parental love, friendship, brotherly and sisterly love, conjugal love and love of neighbor. It displays itself in "being moved," in enthusiasm, in deep authentic sorrow, in gratitude, in tears of grateful joy, or in contrition. It is this type of affectivity which

---

36. Von Hildebrand, *The Sacred Heart*, 49–52. In this, is von Hildebrand following a "Thomistic" line of thought? Tóth sees Ricoeur as not taking the Thomistic line "of regulating vital affectivity to the animal nature of man, which is seen in this framework as showing an essential continuity with bodily materiality." See Tóth, *The Heart Has Its Reasons*, 47.

37. Von Hildebrand, *The Sacred Heart*, 54.

38. Von Hildebrand, *The Sacred Heart*, 54–55. Von Hildebrand goes on to contrast this with the conviviality caused by drinking alcohol.

includes the capacity for a noble surrender, affectivity in which the heart is involved.[39]

For von Hildebrand, this is the "affectivity" spoken of in the Song of Songs.

> The more the lover wants to dwell in his love; the more he aspires to experience the full depth of his love; the more he wants to recollect himself and to allow his love to unfold itself in a deep contemplative rhythm; the more he longs for the interpenetration of his soul with the soul of his beloved—a longing expressed in the words *cor ad cor loquitur*, "heart speaks to heart," and displaying itself in the eyes of the lover seeking the eyes of his beloved—the more he will possess true affectivity.[40]

For von Hildebrand, if one truly has a "tender affectivity," the more one's experience of the object of this affectivity will be "awakened," and the more one's affectivity is awakened, the greater the joy that one will experience. Thus, "[t]he more conscious a joy is, the more its object is seen and understood in its full meaning; the more awakened and outspoken the response, the more the joy is lived."[41] In other words, the deeper one's joy in the beloved, the deeper one's knowledge of the beloved, and the deeper that knowledge, the deeper the joy. Love, joy and knowledge mutually reinforce each other. Thus, "[i]t belongs to the very nature of affective experiences that a deep joy or a deep love, though each possesses a theme of its own, is penetrated by the awareness that our joy or our love is objectively justified and objectively valid."[42]

To sum up the analytical tradition, for Greek Fathers like Gregory Nazianzen, heart equals mind. For Aquinas, heart equals either the principle of animal life and movement, or the organ of the passions, or the *spiritus*, or the will. For von Hildebrand, heart equals a particular kind of affectivity.

The Synthetic Tradition

While not insisting that we need to choose definitively between these traditions, an attempt will be made to present a more balanced picture

39. Von Hildebrand, *The Sacred Heart*, 77.
40. Von Hildebrand, *The Sacred Heart*, 79.
41. Von Hildebrand, *The Sacred Heart*, 81.
42. Von Hildebrand, *The Sacred Heart*, 83.

by giving a brief outline and analysis of the synthetic tradition, which is based on how we experience being human. It will be maintained that having this picture is valuable, since a theological anthropology of the heart is more in accord with our immediate experience of being and acting humanly, and it may be of some help in countering a contemporary anthropological dualism.

The "Pedigree" of a Theological Anthropology of the Heart

Romano Guardini is one who identifies this focus upon the heart, which he calls the noblest tradition of the Christian Occident, a *philosophia* and *theologia cordis*. According to him, the pedigree of this tradition begins with Plato, and runs through Paul, Ignatius of Antioch, Augustine, Bernard of Clairvaux, Francis of Assisi, Gertrude the Great, Elizabeth of Thuringia, and Catherine of Siena. Its "system" is created by Bonaventure and its "poetry" by Dante. After a hiatus in the Renaissance, it continues through Teresa of Avila, Francis de Sales, Blaise Pascal, the Oratorians Charles de Condren, Pierre de Bérulle, and A. Gratry, Antonio Rosmini, and culminates in John Henry Newman. In the East it has been cultivated by Vladimir Soloviev, Aleksey Khomyakov and Pavel Florensky. Guardini also sees it, "in a strange Nordic modification," in Søren Kierkegaard, and, in an anti-Christian manifestation, in Friedrich Nietzsche.[43] To this pedigree, Tóth could add Paul Ricoeur, and Karol Wojtyła,[44] while Ratzinger could add the Old and New Testaments, the Stoics, and Origen.[45] To all of these could be added Jane de Chantal, Margaret Mary Alacoque, Claude de la Colombière, John Eudes, the Syrian Martyrius Sadhona, the Russian Theophane the Recluse, as well as Karl Rahner, Guardini, Tóth, and Ratzinger. Beginning with Sacred Scripture, an attempt will be made to trace this tradition through some of the most significant of these people, namely, Augustine, Pascal, Newman, Guardini, and Ratzinger.

---

43. Guardini, *Pascal for Our Time*, 128–29. For Augustine and Pascal, see also Peters, *The Logic of the Heart*. For Francis de Sales, see Wright, *Heart Speaks to Heart*.

44. Tóth, *The Heart Has Its Reasons*, 21–26, 29–60, 93–100, 214–30.

45. Ratzinger, *Behold the Pierced One*, 51–69.

The Heart in Sacred Scripture

While Scripture does, on occasion, distinguish between such faculties of the human person as "heart," "soul," and "mind" (cf. Matt 22:37), it generally uses the term "heart" across the whole spectrum of human faculties. It is the place of knowing, faith, willing, and conscience. It is drawn to what seems good and beautiful. It is the seat of the passions, imagination, and memory. It is the place of virtue and purity. It is the place of relationships with other persons. It is the place which God searches and knows, the place of revelation and the refusal of revelation, and the place of God's indwelling.[46]

Summing up the biblical understanding of the heart, the *Theological Dictionary of the New Testament* says that

---

46. In the Septuagint, for *kardia* as the locus of knowing, see Deut 29:3; Judg 16:17; 2 Sam 15:6; Job 12:3; Eccl 8:19; 21:6; Song 4:9; Isa 6:10; Hos 4:11; 7:11. For willing, see 2 Sam 7:3; 1 Kgs 11:2-4; Ps 111:7. For conscience, see 1 Sam 2:6; 2 Sam 24:10; 1 Kgs 8:38; Jer 17:1. As drawn to the good and beautiful, see Job 31:3, 9; Eccl 5:2. As the seat of the passions, see 2 Sam 17:10; Jer 4:9, 19; John 7:5. As being broken, see Pss 33:19; 50:19; Isa 57:15; 61:1; Jer 23:9; Ezek 6:9. In the New Testament, for *kardia* as the locus of the passions, see Matt 5:28; 6:21; John 14:1, 27; 16:6, 22; Acts 2:26; 7:54; 14:17; 21:13; Rom 1:24; 9:2; 10:1; 2 Cor 2:4; Jas 3:14; 2 Pet 2:14. For thought, see Matt 9:4; 24:48; Mark 7:21; 11:23; Luke 2:35; 9:47; Rom 10:6; Rev 18:7. For understanding, see Matt 13:15; 24:48; John 12:40; Acts 28:27; Rom 1:21; 1 Cor 2:9; Heb 4:12. For doubt and questioning, see Mark 11:23; Luke 24:38; Rom 10:6. For deception and belief, see Luke 24:25; Heb 3:12; Jas 1:26. For intention and decision, see Luke 6:45; 21:14; Acts 5:3-4; 7:39; 8:22; 11:23; 1 Cor 4:5; 7:37; 14:25; 2 Cor 9:7. For imagination and memory, see Luke 1:51, 66; 2:19, 51. For virtue, see Luke 8:15; Acts 2:46; 15:9; Rom 6:17; 10:9; 2 Thess 3:5. For conscience, see 1 John 3:20. For purity of heart, see Matt 5:8; Acts 15:9; Eph 6:5; Col 3:22; 1 Thess 3:13; 2 Tim 2:22; Heb 10:22. For relation with other human persons, see Matt 18:35; Acts 16:14; 2 Cor 6:11-13; 7:2-3; Phil 1:7. As that which God searches and knows, see Luke 16:15; Rom 8:27; 1 Thess 2:4. Of revelation, see Luke 24:32; Acts 2:37; Rom 2:15; 2 Cor 3:3; 4:6; Eph 1:18. Of the refusal of revelation, see Matt 13:19; Mark 3:5; 6:52; 8:17; John 12:40; Acts 8:21; Rom 2:5; Eph 4:18. Of God's indwelling, in Christ, see Gal 4:6; Eph 3:17; 2 Pet 1:19. On this question of the biblical language of the heart, see Becker, "The Heart in the Language of the Bible," 24-30. With regard to the heart as the place of pity and mercy, Becker makes the following point: "Biblical language prefers to assign to these feelings other terms, meaning approximately 'bowels'" (30). Hugo Rahner regards this term as equivalent to "heart." See Rahner, "On the Biblical Basis of the Devotion," 17-26. Rahner states that "[i]n the language of Revelation, the hallowed word 'heart' and its almost synonymous equivalents (Hebrew: *leb, lebab, beten, me(j)'im, kereb*; Greek: *kardia, koilia, splanchna*; Latin: *cor, venter, viscera*) have the same primal meaning as in all human language" (17). See also Bovenmars, *A Biblical Spirituality of the Heart*; Spidlik, *Prayer*, 250-51.

> [The] heart is the center of the inner life of man and the source or seat of all the forces and functions of the soul and spirit.... [In it] dwell feelings, desires and passions.... [It is] the seat of understanding, the source of through and reflection... the seat of the will, the source of resolves... supremely the one center in man to which God turns, in which the religious life is rooted, which determines moral conduct.[47]

Spidlik on the Heart in Eastern Christian Spirituality

We have already seen Spidlik point out how the Eastern Fathers tended to identify the heart with the mind. In the face of the difficulty of defining the heart, Spidlik proposes an insightful solution, one that turns the issue on its head.

> The psychological method to which people generally resort in discussions on this topic will never be able to clarify the question. There have been attempts above all to place the heart into a schematic presentation of man's psychological structure, and only then to ask which function such a "heart" can have in the spiritual life. This procedure really needs to be reversed. The biblical concept of the heart poses religious questions. Once these have been more or less clarified, we can ask how they are reflected in man's psychological structure.[48]

According to Spidlik the Eastern understanding of the heart developed over time. Eventually there was a reaction to the emphasis on the mind in favor of the "feelings." The classic definition of prayer changed from "an ascent of the mind to God" to "an ascent of the mind and heart to God."[49] For the Greeks, but especially for the Russians, the heart came to be seen as the principle of human integration.[50] For Theophane the Recluse (d. 1894), the heart is "the focus of all the human forces, those of the mind, of the soul, of the animal and corporeal forces."[51] As Spidlik explains, this principle has temporal significance.

---

47. Baumgärtel and Behm, "καρδια," 611–12. See also Tóth, *The Heart Has Its Reasons*, 11.

48. Spidlik, *The Spirituality of the Christian East*, 104.

49. Spidlik, *The Spirituality of the Christian East*, 104–5.

50. Spidlik, *The Spirituality of the Christian East*, 105.

51. Théophane the Recluse, *Načertanie christianskago nravoučenjia*, 306, quoted in Spidlik, *The Spirituality of the Christian East*, 105.

The heart, the principle of unity within a person, also gives stability to the multiplicity of successive moments of life. We cannot perform one act which continues forever. . . . For the Eastern Christian, however, the ideal has always been "the state of prayer" . . . an habitual disposition which somehow in itself deserves the name prayer, aside from the acts which it produces with greater of lesser frequency. This state of prayer is at the same time the state of the entire spiritual life, a steadfast disposition of the heart.[52]

Ratzinger on the Heart for the Fathers

When Ratzinger looks at the meaning of "heart" in the Fathers he gives a different though not necessarily contradictory perspective to that of Spidlik. Ratzinger maintains that much patristic writing reveals a failure to synthesize fully this biblical image of the heart with the Platonic world of ideas. However, according to him, the Fathers were often aware of these two contradictory anthropologies, the Platonic anthropology having its center in the intellect, and the Christian in the heart.[53] For example, according to Ratzinger, a reading of the *Confessions* reveals that "the stream of biblical theology and anthropology, has entered into his [Augustine's] thought and combined with an entirely different, Platonic conception of man, a conception unacquainted with the notion of 'heart.'"[54] Moreover, Ratzinger sees not just this opposition between Platonic and Christian views, but also an opposition between Platonic and Stoic anthropologies, an opposition that actually presented the Fathers with "the opportunity of drawing on the Bible to create a new anthropological synthesis."[55]

Ratzinger maintains that this Patristic synthesis draws upon Stoic anthropology. Whilst Platonic anthropology distinguishes the individual potencies of the soul—intellect, will, and sensibility—and relates them in a hierarchical order, Stoic thought is closer to the anthropology of the Bible, focusing, as it does, on the heart rather than the intellect. The Stoics conceived of the human person as a microcosm corresponding to

---

52. Spidlik, *The Spirituality of the Christian East*, 105.

53. Ratzinger, *Behold the Pierced One*, 65. Ratzinger refers the reader to Anton Maxsein's *Philosophia cordis*. Maxsein calls Augustine's anthropology a *philosophia cordis*.

54. Ratzinger, *Behold the Pierced One*, 65.

55. Ratzinger, *Behold the Pierced One*, 66. Ratzinger refers the reader to Ivánka, *Plato christianus*, 315–51.

the macrocosm. As this cosmos is fashioned by a formless primal fire which adopts the form of that which it creates, so the human body is fashioned and enlivened by this divine, primal fire, becoming hearing, sight, thought, and imagination. This primal fire in the cosmos is called "logos." In us, it is called "the logos in us." For the Stoics, as the sun is the "heart of the cosmos," the human heart is the body's sun, the seat of the logos in us.[56]

For Ratzinger, this displays a profound philosophical intuition, which offered the Fathers the opportunity of reaching a new synthesis of Platonic thought and biblical faith. For Ratzinger, it was Origen who made the most of this opportunity. Basing his thinking on John 1:26, "[a]mong you stands one whom you do not know," Origen went on to assert that, unbeknownst to us, the Logos is at the center of all human beings, since the Logos is present in the center of every human being, the heart. As Ratzinger states,

> It is [this] Logos which enables us to be logic-al, to correspond to the Logos; he is the image of God after which we were created. Here the word "heart" has expanded beyond reason and denotes "a deeper level of spiritual/intellectual existence, where direct contact takes place with the divine." It is here, in the heart, that the birth of the divine Logos in man takes place, that man is united with the personal incarnate Word of God.[57]

Both von Hildebrand and Ratzinger point out that "heart" is a key term in Augustine's *Confessions*.[58] For Augustine, the love of the heart is deeper than language, and can convey that which words cannot.[59] Indeed, he claims that we do not know our own hearts; they are an "abyss," a "great deep."[60] Augustine sometimes seems to speak of the heart as

---

56. Ratzinger, *Behold the Pierced One*, 66–67.

57. Ratzinger, *Behold the Pierced One*, 67–68. Here Ratzinger cites Ivánka, *Plato christianus*, 326.

58. See Hildebrand, *The Sacred Heart*, 28–29: "It is true that there is one great tradition in the stream of Christian philosophy in which full justice is done in a concrete way to the affective sphere and to the heart. St. Augustine's work from the *Confessions* onward is pervaded by deep and admirable insights concerning the heart and the affective attitudes of man." Hildebrand goes so far as to wonder why, when Augustine speaks of the reflection of the Trinity in the human soul, he "fails to give to the affective sphere and to the heart a standing analogous to that granted to the reason and will" (28). See also Ratzinger, *Behold the Pierced One*, 65.

59. Rist, *Augustine*, 33.

60. Rist, *Augustine*, 37.

RESOURCES FOR A THEOLOGICAL ANTHROPOLOGY OF THE HEART 243

equivalent to the "self." His famous "you have made *us* for yourself, and our *hearts* are restless until they rest in you" would seem to indicate as much.[61] At other times, he seems to equate the heart with the soul. For instance, in his account of the death of a friend, Augustine speaks of the heart as the place of the passions. It was black with grief. "I became a great enigma to myself and I was forever asking my soul why it was sad and why it disquieted me so sorely."[62] He also sees the heart as the place of encounter with God: "Let us return to the heart, that we may find Him."[63] Ratzinger maintains that Augustine

> is well aware that the organ by which God can be seen cannot be a non-historical "ratio naturalis" which just does not exist, but only the *ratio pura*, i.e. *purificata* [purified reason] or, as Augustine expresses it echoing the gospel, the *cor purum* ("Blessed are the pure in heart, for they shall see God"). Augustine also knows that the necessary purification of sight takes place through faith (Acts 15:9) and through love, at all events not as a result of reflection alone and not at all by man's own power.[64]

In other words, we do not think our way or work our way to salvation and deification. Beyond this, Augustine never precisely defines what he means by "heart." He simply describes it in action. For him, ultimately, it is an enigma, a mystery.

Pascal

After the Protestant Reformation, the rise of skepticism in religious matters led Pascal to pen his *Pensées*. There we find the famous, frequently quoted, and frequently misunderstood statement: "The heart has its reasons of which the reason knows nothing," a statement that can be understood as a reply to Michel de Montaigne's question: "Que sais-je?" (What do I know?)[65] In his answer, Pascal is being neither sentimental nor irra-

---

61. Augustine, *Confessions*, 1.1.1.

62. Augustine, *Confessions*, 4.4.9. Tóth finds the Ricoeurian heart to be akin, though not identical, to Augustine's "restless heart." See Tóth, *The Heart Has Its Reasons*, 40–41, 44.

63. Augustine, *Confessions*, 4.12.19, quoted in Ratzinger, *Behold the Pierced One*, 68.

64. Ratzinger, "The Church and Man's Calling," 155.

65. Pascal, *Pensées*, 423 (277). There are two common ways of numbering Pascal's "thoughts." Here the Krailsheimer number is given first, followed by the Brunschvicg number in brackets.

tional. By "reason" he means Cartesian "reasoning" by scientific analysis and calculation, what Aristotelian-Scholastic logic called the third act of the mind, the discursive reasoning by which one proves one truth, the conclusion, from another, the premise.[66] Pascal says that the heart has its reasons. These are first principles, self-evident truths. "Principles are felt, propositions proved, and both with certainty by different means."[67]

For Pascal, the first act of the mind, understanding the meaning of an essence, is carried out by the "heart." Furthermore, for him it is the heart that "feels" God (*sent Dieu*). This is Pascal's definition of faith: "It is the heart which perceives God and not the reason. That is what faith is: God perceived by the heart, not by the reason."[68] The heart "sees" God. It knows God. God gives faith to people by moving their hearts.[69] It is also the heart which chooses, which wills, to love God or self. "I say that it is natural for the heart to love the universal being or itself, according to its allegiance, and it hardens itself against either as it chooses."[70] Finally, for Pascal, the heart is "the unified center of inner life."[71]

Newman

Although, like Augustine, Newman frequently uses the term "heart," like Augustine, he does not give an explicit definition of what he means by it. We must infer the definition from the manner in which he uses the term. For Newman, "reason," in the sense of that faculty which is used in logic, mathematics, the scientific method and historical investigations, cannot establish faith in God. Even though Newman holds that conscience can establish the "reasonableness," though not the rationality, of faith, it too is not capable of establishing faith.[72] Reacting against an eighteenth century reduction of faith to nothing more than an acceptance of evidence,

---

66. Cf. Descartes, *Discourse on the Method*, 265–72. For Pascal's understanding of "reason" and "heart," see Kreeft, *Christianity for Modern Pagans*, 228–34.

67. Pascal, *Pensées*, 110 (282).

68. Pascal, *Pensées*, 424 (278).

69. Pascal, *Pensées*, 110 (282).

70. Pascal, *Pensées*, 423 (277).

71. Pascal, *Pensées*, 110 (282). For more on Pascal's understanding of the heart, see Tóth, *The Heart Has Its Reasons*, 5–12. Tóth finds the Ricoeurian heart to be akin, though not identical, to Pascal's sensitive *coeur*. See Tóth, *The Heart Has Its Reasons*, 41.

72. Shute, "Newman's Logic of the Heart," 233–35.

Newman argues from what might be called "existential" evidence that "[t]he Word of Life is offered to a man; and, on its being offered, he has Faith in it.... Faith is the reasoning of a religious mind, or of what Scripture calls a right or renewed heart."[73]

In a sermon entitled "Love the Safeguard of Faith against Superstition," Newman states,

> Right faith is the faith of a right mind. Faith is an intellectual act; right faith is an intellectual act, done in a certain moral disposition. Faith is an act of Reason, viz. a reasoning upon presumptions; right Faith is a reasoning upon holy, devout, and enlightened presumptions.[74]

Again, in the same sermon, he says,

> [This faith does not need] what is popularly called Reason for its protection—I mean processes of investigation, discrimination, discussion, argument, and inference. It itself is an intellectual act, and takes its character from the moral state of the agent. It is perfected, not by intellectual cultivation, but by obedience.[75]

Like Pascal, Newman held that there were two modes of reasoning, logical reasoning and a "logic of the heart." The latter is an insight or intuition.[76] Conversion comes, not by overcoming the reason, but by touching the heart.[77] Furthermore,

> The heart is commonly reached, not through the reason, but through the imagination, by means of direct impressions, by the testimony of facts and events, by history, by description. Persons influence us, voices melt us, looks subdue us, deeds inflame us.[78]

Rather than "reasoning," Newman sees that

> The safeguard of Faith is a right state of heart. This it is that gives it birth; it also disciplines it. This is what protects it from bigotry, credulity, and fanaticism. It is holiness, or dutifulness,

---

73. Newman, *Newman's University Sermons*, 202–3.

74. Newman, *Newman's University Sermons*, 239. See also Sands, *The Justification of Religious Faith*, 121.

75. Newman, *Newman's University Sermons*, 249–50.

76. Hughes, "*Une Source Cachée*," 29–44.

77. Newman, *An Essay in Aid of a Grammar of Assent*, 425.

78. Newman, *An Essay in Aid of a Grammar of Assent*, 92. See also Ferreira, "The Grammar of the Heart," 129.

or the new creation, or the spiritual mind, however we word it, which is the quickening and illuminating principle of true faith, giving it eyes, hands, and feet. It is Love which forms it out of the rude chaos into an image of Christ.[79]

Like Augustine and Pascal, Newman is convinced that it is only the "heart" which can "see" God. It is only the love-purified reason that can perceive him. Thus in a sermon entitled "Faith and Reason contrasted as Habits of Mind," he states,

> For is not this the error, the common and fatal error, of the world, to think itself a judge of Religious Truth without preparation of heart? "I am the good Shepherd, and know My sheep, and am known of Mine." "He goeth before them, and the sheep follow Him, for they know His voice." "The pure in heart shall see God": "to the meek mysteries are revealed"; "he that is spiritual judgeth all things." "The darkness comprehendeth it not." Gross eyes see not; heavy ears hear not. But in the schools of the world the ways towards Truth are considered high roads open to all men, however disposed, at all times. Truth is to be approached without homage.[80]

Guardini

The two main sources for Guardini's anthropology of the heart are his book on Pascal and another on the conversion of Augustine, both published in 1935. The more thorough-going exposition of Guardini's understanding of the human heart is to be found in that on Augustine. Guardini seeks to give a basis for understanding the whole of Augustine's development as described in *The Confessions*. As Guardini puts it,

> The long slow process of experience, of growth, unfolding, seizure and struggle, action and suffering by which the young man with his unfree sensuality on the one hand, his abstract, idealistic-aesthetic intellectuality on the other, pries open the realm of the heart; the manner in which that realm, strengthened, purified, and instructed, gains power and knowledge and

---

79. Newman, *Newman's University Sermons*, 234. See also Shute, "Newman's Logic of the Heart," 235.

80. Newman, *Newman's University Sermons*, 198.

certainty—all this forms the central skein of Augustine's rich and complicated development.[81]

In his reading of Pascal, Guardini identifies *le coeur* as the central reality of Pascal's anthropology. He also identifies what his understanding is not. It is not the emotional in opposition to the logical, feeling to intellect, or "soul" to "mind." Rather "heart" *is* mind, that is to say, the heart is a manifestation of the mind. For Guardini's Pascal, "[t]he act of the heart is an act productive of knowledge. Certain objects only become given in the act of the heart. But they do not remain there in a-rational intuition, but are accessible to intellectual and rational penetration."[82]

In summary, a close reading of his books on Augustine and Pascal reveals that, for Guardini, the heart is the place of reconciliation between the two halves of the human person, the sensual and the intellectual. It is the "heart" that makes us specifically human, since angels have spiritual intellects and animals have embodied senses. The heart is the place where spiritual mind becomes human soul, and animal corporeity becomes human body. The heart is also the place of reconciliation of the moral and the spiritual. The heart is evaluating mind, mind as eros-bearer. It is able to grasp not just truth, but also the transcendentals of goodness and beauty. It is the place of union of knowing and loving. The heart is the whole person participating in knowing, and the whole person participating in loving. Only when we love can we truly know. This is purity of heart. The heart is this organ of love. This love is both passive and active. Not only is it drawn to the good, true, and beautiful, but it actively seeks them out. Love is freedom. It is only through participation in the life of God that heart truly becomes heart, truly integrated, truly human, truly knowing, truly loving, truly pure, and truly free.

Ratzinger

Finally, turning to Ratzinger, in his analysis of the Beatitudes and the Lord's Prayer in his *Jesus of Nazareth: From the Baptism*, he constantly speaks of the human heart. Indeed, it is a theme that permeates the first two volumes of *Jesus of Nazareth*. As Ratzinger sees it, in the parable of the Prodigal Son, the conversion of the prodigal is a "change of heart."[83]

81. Guardini, *The Conversion of Augustine*, 45.
82. Guardini, *Pascal for Our Time*, 129.
83. Ratzinger, *From the Baptism*, 205.

In telling the parable, Jesus seeks to woo the hearts of the murmuring Pharisees and scribes through the words of the father to his prodigal.[84] Jesus also wishes to speak to the hearts of the poor and downtrodden, like Lazarus (cf. Luke 16:19–31). Rather than leave them with embittered hearts (cf. Ps 73:13–22), he wishes them to behold the form of God (cf. Ps 77:14–15), that their hearts may be "sated by the encounter with infinite love."[85] We are called to become like the "little ones" in the temple, who are able to praise Jesus with Hosannas because they see with pure and undivided hearts.[86] The alternative to faith in Jesus is a hardening of the heart. Whether it is in response to the parables, or to a miracle of Jesus (cf. John 11:45–53), putting God "to the test" leads to a "non-seeing" and "non-understanding," a "hardening of heart."[87] We are all in a position of "not knowing" what we do (cf. Luke 23:34; Acts 3:14–17; 1 Tim 1:13).[88] It is the failure to recognize one's ignorance that is fatal, because it blinds one to the need for repentance. It is a danger that especially threatens the learned.[89]

In *Jesus of Nazareth* Ratzinger explains what he means by "heart."

> "Blessed are the pure in heart, for they shall see God" (Mt 5:8). The organ for seeing God is the heart. The intellect alone is not enough. In order for man to become capable of perceiving God, the energies of his existence have to work in harmony. His will must be pure and so too must the underlying affective dimension of his soul, which gives intelligence and will their direction. Speaking of the *heart* in this way means precisely that man's perceptive powers play in concert, which also requires the proper interplay of body and soul, since this is essential for the totality of the creature we call "man." Man's fundamental affective disposition actually depends on just this unity of body and soul and on man's acceptance of being both body and spirit. This means he places the body under the discipline of the spirit, yet does not isolate intellect or will. Rather, he accepts himself as coming from God, and thereby also acknowledges and lives out the bodiliness of his existence as an enrichment for the spirit.

---

84. Ratzinger, *From the Baptism*, 209.
85. Ratzinger, *From the Baptism*, 214.
86. Ratzinger, *Holy Week*, 23.
87. Ratzinger, *From the Baptism*, 193, 216.
88. Ratzinger, *Holy Week*, 206–8.
89. Ratzinger, *Holy Week*, 208.

> The heart—the wholeness of man—must be pure, interiorly open and free, in order for man to be able to see God.[90]

For Ratzinger, the heart is not to be identified simply with the intellect, or the will, or the passions, or the senses, or the body, or the soul. Nor is it to be identified with the *ego*. Rather, it is the *locus* of the integration of the intellect, will, passions, and senses, of the body and the soul. One could say that, for Ratzinger, the human heart *is* the personal integration, the integration by the person, of these aspects of their human nature.

Ratzinger says that the heart is "the wholeness of man." In a sense, to call it the locus of anthropological integration is still inadequate. One is almost tempted to say that the human person is "all heart." However, what this phrase "the wholeness of man" leads us to is that, this side of the Beatific Vision, none of us are fully human. Rather, we all have wounded hearts, since none of us are fully whole. None of us are perfect as our heavenly Father is perfect. In this world, there have only been two who are and remain fully human, Jesus and Mary. In his *Mary: The Church at the Source*, Ratzinger goes so far as to make a comparison between the human heart and trinitarian perichoresis. Commenting on Mary's pondering "all these things" in her heart (cf. Luke 2:51), he writes,

> Mary sees the events as "words," as happenings full of meaning because they come from God's meaning-creating will. She translates the events into words and penetrates then, bringing them into her "heart"—into that interior dimension of understanding where sense and spirit, reason and feeling, interior and exterior perception interpenetrate circumincessively.[91]

What common ground is there between Augustine, Pascal, Newman, Guardini, and Ratzinger? They all acknowledge the heart as the place of encounter with God, and they all think of the heart as the place that "knows." For Augustine, Newman, Guardini, and Ratzinger, it is the "pure of heart" who see God. For Pascal, Guardini, and Ratzinger, the heart is the center of one's inner life.

---

90. Ratzinger, *From the Baptism*, 92–93.
91. Ratzinger, *Mary*, 70–71.

Do We Really Need a Theological Anthropology of the Heart?

We are suffering from a new dualism, one which has been called a disassociation of head and heart. However, expressing the disassociation simply in these terms could be misleading. We are actually suffering from a disassociation of the intellectual faculty from the sensual-emotional-volitional faculties. We could also call this disassociation a *de-kardia-zation* of reason. Furthermore, in our current separation of head and heart, more and more people are opting for the heart over the head. Our current age has been variously labelled post-modern, post-Enlightenment, and post-Christian. To these could be added post-rational. After the death of God, we are experiencing the death of human reason. We seem to be in the last stage of the fragmentation of the human person. That fragmentation has been occurring for some time. One could trace it back at least to Kant's focus on the will, turning Christianity into morality, Hegel's focus on the intellect, turning Christianity into philosophy, and Scheleiermacher's focus on the consciousness, turning Christianity into an experience. Or, one could go further back to the separation of faith from reason, either at the Protestant Reformation or at the rise of Nominalism. Or perhaps even further back to the separation of mystical theology from scholastic theology in the thirteenth century. However, at the moment, it would seem that experience's time has come. More and more, it appears that we are entering the Age of Emotion, or the Age of Affectivity, but this is an affectivity disassociated from rationality, an affectivity that dominates both the reason and the will. Whether it concerns identity politics, including the increasingly vexed question of transgenderism, or any of the other great moral issues of our time, the prevailing attitude of many people is: "I am what I feel," "I am what I desire." Developing a theological anthropology of the heart could have great therapeutic value and great evangelical potential for addressing this current malaise.

A Biographical Conclusion

I think that Guardini's anthropology of the heart deserves more consideration. At lot of attention has been given here, and rightly so, to Augustine, Pascal, Newman, and Ratzinger. Without the constraints of writing a chapter rather than a monograph, much more could have been said about the work of Ricoeur, Wojtyła, Tóth, and others. Yet I find myself being drawn in particular to the work of Guardini. This is the case although I have found it challenging to comprehend his understanding of the heart. His prose is so pithy, his thought so profound, and his terminology so idiosyncratic, that I have found it both difficult to understand it and to give a just account of it. I think that part of the challenge in understanding it is that, in order to do so fully, one must theologize in the same way that Guardini does. One cannot just think about it. One must live it. To do so is a challenge to the whole heart, not just to the mind. In order to develop a theological anthropology of the heart, one must learn how to theologize with the heart, something that I would say I still do very imperfectly. I would suggest it is the case that the more one's heart becomes integrated, the better one ought to be able to theologize according to the heart, and that the more one theologizes according to the heart, the more one's heart will become integrated. More and more I see my theological work, my theologizing, as therapeutic. Yet, I am also more and more aware that I myself am in need of some therapy for my heart.

Bibliography

Aquinas, Thomas. *Summa Theologiae*. Translated by the Fathers of the English Dominican Province. New York: Benzinger Brothers, 1947.

Augustine. *Confessions, Books I–IV*. Edited by Gillian Clark. Cambridge: Cambridge University Press, 1995.

Baier, Walter. "Key Issues in Medieval Sacred Heart Piety." In *Faith in Christ and the Worship of Christ: New Approaches to Devotion to Christ*, edited by Leo Scheffczyk, 81–99. San Francisco: Ignatius, 1986.

Baumgärtel, Friedrich, and Johannes Behm. "καρδια." In vol. 3 of *Theological Dictionary of the New Testament*, edited by Gerhard Kittel, translated by Geoffrey W. Bromiley, 605–14. Grand Rapids: Eerdmans, 1965.

Becker, Joachim. "The Heart in the Language of the Bible." In *Faith in Christ and the Worship of Christ: New Approaches to Devotion to Christ*, edited by Leo Scheffczyk, 24–30. San Francisco: Ignatius, 1986.

Bovenmars, Jan G. *A Biblical Spirituality of the Heart*. New York: Alba, 1991.

Descartes, René. *Discourse on the Method of Rightly Conducting the Reason and Seeking for Truth in the Sciences*. In vol. 28 of *Bacon, Descartes, Spinoza, Great Books of the Western World*, edited by Mortimer J. Adler et al., translated by Elizabeth S. Haldane and G. R. T. Ross, 265–91. 2nd ed. Chicago: Encyclopaedia Britannica, 1990.

Elders, Leo. "The Inner Life of Jesus in the Theology and Devotion of Saint Thomas Aquinas." In *Faith in Christ and the Worship of Christ*, edited by Leo Scheffczyk, 65–79. San Francisco: Ignatius, 1986.

Ferreira, M. Jamie. "The Grammar of the Heart: Newman on Faith and Imagination." In *Discourse and Context: An Interdisciplinary Study of John Henry Newman*, edited by Gerard Magill, 129–43. Carbondale: Southern Illinois University Press, 1993.

Guardini, Romano. *The Conversion of Augustine*. Translated by Elinor Briefs. London: Sands, 1960.

———. *Pascal for Our Time*. Translated by Brian Thompson. New York: Herder & Herder, 1966.

Hughes, Brian W. "*Une Source Cachée*: Blaise Pascal's Influence upon John Henry Newman." *Newman Studies Journal* 7.1 (2010) 29–44.

Ivánka, Endre von. *Plato christianus*. Einsiedeln: Johannes, 1964.

Kreeft, Peter. *Christianity for Modern Pagans; Pascal's Pensées Outlined, Edited, and Explained*. San Francisco: Ignatius, 1993.

Maxsein, Anton. *Philosophia cordis. Das Wesen der Persönlichkeit bei Augustinus*. Salzburg: Müller, 1966.

McGregor, Peter John. *Heart to Heart: The Spiritual Christology of Joseph Ratzinger*. Eugene, OR: Pickwick, 2016.

Newman, John Henry. *An Essay in Aid of a Grammar of Assent*. Westminster, MD: Christian Classics, 1973.

———. *Newman's University Sermons: Fifteen Sermons Preached before the University of Oxford, 1826–43*. London: SPCK, 1970.

Pascal, Blaise. *Pensées*. Edited by Léon Brunschvicg. Paris: Hachette, 1897.

———. *Pensées*. Translated by A. J. Krailsheimer. London: Penguin Classics, 1966.

Plato. *The Dialogues of Plato*. Vol. 3, *Timaeus & Other Dialogues*. Edited R. M. Hare and D. A. Russell. Translated by Benjamin Jowett. London: Sphere, 1970.

———. *The Dialogues of Plato*. Vol. 4, *The Republic*. Edited by R. M. Hare and D. A. Russell. Translated by Benjamin Jowett. London: Sphere, 1970.

Peters, James R. *The Logic of the Heart: Augustine, Pascal, and the Rationality of Faith*. Grand Rapids: Baker Academic, 2009.

"Prayer for a Priestly Heart." https://www.catholicity.com/prayer/prayer-for-a-priestly-heart.html.

Rahner, Hugo. "On the Biblical Basis of the Devotion." In *Heart of the Saviour*, edited by Joseph Stierli, translated by Paul Andrews, 15–35. New York: Herder & Herder, 1957.

Ratzinger, Joseph. *Behold the Pierced One: An Approach to a Spiritual Christology*. Translated by Graham Harrison. San Francisco: Ignatius, 1986.

———. "The Church and Man's Calling." In vol. 5 of *Commentary on the Documents of Vatican II*, edited by Herbert Vorgrimler, translated by J. W. O'Hara, 115–63. London: Burns & Oates, 1969.

———. *Jesus of Nazareth: From the Baptism in the Jordan to the Transfiguration*. Translated by Adrian J. Walker. New York: Doubleday, 2007.

———. *Jesus of Nazareth: Holy Week: From the Entrance into Jerusalem to the Resurrection*. Translated by Philip J. Whitmore. San Francisco: Ignatius, 2011.

———. *Mary: The Church at the Source*. Translated by Adrian Walker. San Francisco: Ignatius, 2005.

Ricoeur, Paul. *Fallible Man*. Translated by Charles Kelbley. Chicago: Regnery, 1965.

Rist, John M. *Augustine: Ancient Thought Baptized*. Cambridge: Cambridge University Press, 1994.

Rowland, Tracey. "The Role of Natural Law and Natural Right in the Search for a Universal Ethics." In *Searching for a Universal Ethic: Multidisciplinary, Ecumenical, and Interfaith Responses to the Catholic Natural Law Tradition*, edited by John Berkman and William C. Mattison III, 156–66. Grand Rapids: Eerdmans, 2014.

Sands, Paul Francis. *The Justification of Religious Faith in Søren Kierkegaard, John Henry Newman, and William James*. Piscatway, NJ: Gorgias, 2004.

Shute, Graham J. "Newman's Logic of the Heart." *Expository Times* 78 (1967) 232–35.

Spidlik, Tomas. *The Spirituality of the Christian East: A Systematic Handbook*. Translated by Anthony P. Gythiel. Kalamazoo, MI: Cistercian, 1986.

———. *Prayer*. Translated by Anthony P. Gythiel. The Spirituality of the Christian East 2. Kalamazoo, MI: Cistercian, 2005.

Théophane the Recluse. *Načertanie christianskago nravoučenjia* [*A Reading of Christian Ethical Teaching*]. Moscow, 1895.

Tóth, Beáta. *The Heart Has Its Reasons: Towards a Theological Anthropology of the Heart*. Eugene, OR: Cascade, 2015.

Von Hildebrand, Dietrich. *The Sacred Heart: An Analysis of Human and Divine Affectivity*. Baltimore, MD: Helicon, 1965.

Wright, Wendy M. *Heart Speaks to Heart: The Salesian Tradition*. Maryknoll, NY: Orbis, 2004.

13

Homo orans

The Human Person as Defined by Prayer

Paschal M. Corby, OFM Conv.

Introduction

This chapter proposes that the human person is not primarily defined by reason or ingenuity or the ability to make things, but according to the capacity to think about God and pray to him. He is *homo orans*, who through prayer exercises his relational nature as created in the divine image.

This proposal is not novel. The orthodox theologian, Fr. Alexander Schmemann, has previously written that "the only natural (and not 'supernatural') reaction of man, to whom God gave this blessed and sanctified world, is to bless God in return, to thank him, to see the world as God sees it and—in this act of gratitude and adoration—to know, name and possess the world."[1] From this essential attitude towards God, Schmemann identifies man in his basic and original form as priest, whose original vocation is to bless and adore the Creator, and offer back to him the fruits of the earth. In this basic orientation towards adoration,

---

1. Schmemann, *For the Life of the World*, 15.

Schmemann defines man: "'Homo sapiens', 'homo faber' . . . yes, but first of all, 'homo adorans.'"[2]

Assuming the proposition that worship/adoration is integral to human nature, this chapter nonetheless asks the question of whether adoration is itself the original stance of man before God—that which fundamentally characterizes human nature—or whether there is something even more basic that defines him? Drawing on the theology of Joseph Ratzinger, it is suggested that the human person emerges in the first place as one who *prays*: who thinks the thought of God and turns to him in prayer. Adoration presumes that we know the One to whom we offer our worship and that we are capable of addressing him. This faculty, I contend, is founded in prayer—the communion between God and man—that is made possible through our creation in the image of God.

The Cult of Worship

Schmemann's thesis regarding the indigenous nature of adoration is supported by the incidence of cults of worship that are proper to most established religions. In this, Christianity is no exception. Indeed, it would be proper to define the whole of the Judeo-Christian tradition as orientated towards worship of God. Joseph Ratzinger, in his seminal work *The Spirit of the Liturgy*, convincingly argues that the establishment of Israel as a nation, originating in the Exodus, is built on the refrain of Moses and Aaron to Pharaoh to "let my people go, that they may serve me in the wilderness" (Exod 7:16; cf. 8:1; 9:1, 13; 10:3). Ratzinger claims that the object of the Exodus was not primarily about freedom from slavery, but freedom to worship God. "The issue is not the Promised Land; the only goal of the Exodus is shown to be worship, which can only take place according to God's measure and therefore eludes the rules of the game of political compromise."[3] It this, Ratzinger deliberately negates a nationalistic reading of the Exodus. "The land is given to the people to be a place for the worship of the true God," he writes.[4] "Mere possession of the land, mere national autonomy, would reduce Israel to the level of all the other nations."[5] Possession of the promised land in itself is an "indeterminate

---

2. Schmemann, *For the Life of the World*, 15.
3. Ratzinger, *The Spirit of the Liturgy*, 16.
4. Ratzinger, *The Spirit of the Liturgy*, 17.
5. Ratzinger, *The Spirit of the Liturgy*, 17.

good." "It only becomes a true good, a real gift, a promise fulfilled, when it is the place where God reigns."[6]

It follows that worship, and right relationship with God, makes man free. Freedom is not liberation from servile structures, but an interior disposition that places things in right order. In the same mold, slavery is not primarily imposed from outside, but is a state of being in alienation from God. Accordingly, Ratzinger identifies that "whenever Israel falls away from the right worship of God, when she turns away from God to the false gods (the powers and values of this world), her freedom, too, collapses."[7] At those times, the land of promise means nothing. They might as well be back in Egypt, alienated from free worship of God.

What, then, does right worship of God look like in biblical tradition? It is not primarily a human initiative, but one ordained by God. This too is evident in the Exodus story. Moses says before Pharaoh: "We must go three days journey into the wilderness and sacrifice to the Lord our God as he will command us" (Exod 8:27).[8] But it is only when Moses reaches Sinai that the Lord's command becomes clear. God speaks to Moses on the mountain, and through him gives a law to his chosen people. He establishes a way of life. He forms a covenant with them that is sealed by an ordained and structured form of worship. "In this way," writes Ratzinger, "the purpose of the wandering in the wilderness, as explained to Pharaoh, is fulfilled. Israel learns how to worship God in the way he himself desires."[9] Thus, worship, as revealed by God, includes cult/liturgy. But it also embraces life, and law, and ethics. Right worship is covenantal. It is life lived in God.

As the renewal of the covenants of old (with Adam and Noah), the giving of the law on Sinai mimics the account of creation. As Ratzinger expounds,

> It is constructed in close parallel to the account of creation. Seven times it says, "Moses did as the Lord had commanded him," words that suggest that the seven-day work on the tabernacle replicates the seven-day work on creation. The account of the construction of the tabernacle ends with a kind of vision of the Sabbath. "So Moses finished the work. Then the cloud covered the tent of meeting, and the glory of the Lord filled the

---

6. Ratzinger, *The Spirit of the Liturgy*, 17.
7. Ratzinger, *The Spirit of the Liturgy*, 19–20.
8. All scriptural references will be from the RSV unless otherwise stated.
9. Ratzinger, *The Spirit of the Liturgy*, 17.

tabernacle" (Exod 40:33f.). The completion of the tent anticipates the completion of creation. God makes his dwelling in the world. Heaven and earth are united.[10]

This symmetry between creation and covenantal worship leads Ratzinger to suggest that "creation exists to be a place for the covenant that God wants to make with man. The goal of creation is covenant."[11] This realization harmonizes with a reading of the origins of man that places adoration in the first place and envisages the whole world as a temple ordered to the worship of God. The Garden in which man ministers is God's sanctuary. It is the place in which man is ordained to offer a sacrifice of praise to the Lord.

Man as Priest

In light of latter developments, exegetes therefore identify "sanctuary symbolisms" within the Garden narrative, drawing parallels between Eden and the Jerusalem Temple.[12] These symbolisms are many: (1) The Garden is entered from the East, as for later sanctuaries.[13] (2) The tree of life finds a parallel in the temple menorah. (3) The cherubim that guard the Garden are reminiscent of the cherubim that guarded the inner sanctuary of Solomon's temple (1 Kgs 6:23–28). There are also certain gestures or actions that hint at a connection between Eden and cultic worship: (4) In Genesis 3, the Lord is described as "walking in the garden in the cool of the day" (v. 8). In this instance, the verb "to walk to and fro" (*hithallek*), is the same form used in referring to the Lord's presence in the tent sanctuaries of Israel (see Lev 26:12; Deut 23:15; 2 Sam 7:6–7).[14] (5) Finally, Adam, the first man, is imaged as a priest, "ordained" to "till and keep" the Garden (Gen 2:15). The only other time these Hebrew verbs (*'abodah* and *shamar*) are used together are in reference to Levitical

10. Ratzinger, *The Spirit of the Liturgy*, 26–27.
11. Ratzinger, *The Spirit of the Liturgy*, 26.
12. See Wenham, "Sanctuary Symbolism in the Garden of Eden Story," 19–25. Or, for a more contemporary account, Davidson, "Earth's First Sanctuary," 65–89.
13. In another parallel between the Temple and the Garden, the East Gate in Ezekiel's Temple is closed shut (Ezek 44:1), just as the eastern entrance to the Garden was closed and guarded by the cherubim and flaming sword after the expulsion of Adam and Eve (Gen 3:24). I thank my colleague, Dr. Kevin Wagner, for alerting me to this parallel.
14. Wenham, "Sanctuary Symbolism in the Garden of Eden Story," 20.

duties in the tabernacle (see Num 3:7–8; 8:26; 18:5–6)[15]—further highlighting the sanctuary symbolism of the Garden and man's aboriginal priestly identity. Placed within the sanctuary of God's creation, man finds his purpose in blessing God for the goodness of what he has received. He is, as Schmemann rightly defines, a priest from the beginning.

Homo orans

In defining what is uniquely human, it is fitting that we should look back to our beginnings. However, such a backward glance cannot exhaust our particularity. Acknowledging this limitation, Ratzinger insists that man cannot be understood only by considering where he comes from. "We understand him only when we also ask where he can go. Only from his height is his essence really illuminated."[16] In other words, to discover the human distinctiveness, we must look forward to the fulfilment of our human nature. And while we who remain "on the way" have not yet reached that point, we have in Jesus Christ, true God and true man, the revelation of our true nature. It is, therefore, to the Incarnation that we must turn to discover what is most original in man.

Since the human form finds its fulfilment in the God-man, there must be something in human nature that tends towards this end. In response to the question of *whether human nature was more assumable by the Son of God than any other nature*, St. Thomas Aquinas answers that

> a thing is said to be assumable according to some fitness for such a union. Now this fitness in human nature may be taken from two things, viz. according to its dignity, and according to its need. According to its dignity, because human nature, as being rational and intellectual, was made for attaining to the Word to some extent by its operation, viz. by knowing and loving Him. According to its need—because it stood in need of restoration, having fallen under original sin.[17]

In other words, the *fittingness* of the Incarnation is not only determined by need (of redemption from sin), but it also conforms to the dignity of human nature. According to Aquinas, human nature, emerging as it does from the creative will of God, possesses an inherent capacity for the

15. Hahn, *A Father Who Keeps His Promises*, 54.
16. Ratzinger, *Images of Hope*, 58.
17. Aquinas, *Summa Theologiae*, III.4.1.

Word. This capacity defines the human person as a being in relation—as one to whom a word can be addressed, and who is capable of responding in turn. It defines the human person as communicable—not limited to the mastery of language in which one expresses oneself, but extended to the capacity to make oneself communicable as gift; of giving oneself and receiving the other in a communion of beings.

This capacity for the Word is premised on the creation of the human person in the image of God (Gen 1:27). God is Word. He is dialogical. He is inherently communicable as a relation of Persons that constitutes the Blessed Trinity. He does not speak into a void, but addresses another who is capable of receiving him. This dialogical God thus defines us also. The God who speaks gives form to the concept of "person" and thus identifies the human person as one to whom the Word is addressed.[18] In a particular way, the Word defines the Second Person of the Trinity: the Word that was from the beginning "with God" and "was God" (John 1:1); the Word that "became flesh and dwelt among us" (John 1:14). The Incarnation is the end to which the inherent capacity of human nature for the Word is directed. In God-made-man, the union of human nature and the Word is complete.

When constituted as an anthropology, this "fittingness" signifies that human beings are defined by their relation to the Word; by their capacity to know and love God, and by their ability to "hear" and respond to him. "Man was created to be a hearer of the word," as Balthasar writes. "His innermost constitution has been designed for dialogue."[19] In this realization, the human person cannot only be defined by reason, or ingenuity, or ability to make things; not simply *homo sapiens*, or *homo faber*, as Schmemann rightly insists. But neither is he primarily *homo adorans*, but, in the first place, one who can think the thought of God and pray to him. Adoration presumes that there is a prior relationship between the one who adores and the object of his adoration. It presumes a likeness: the capacity to speak and to be heard. Man is, therefore, primarily *homo orans*, who through prayer exercises his relational nature as created in the divine image and as existing with and for the Other.[20]

---

18. Ratzinger, "Concerning the Notion of Person in Theology," 443.
19. Balthasar, *Prayer*, 22.
20. "The image of God also means that human persons are beings of word and of love, beings moving toward Another, oriented to giving themselves to the Other and only truly receiving themselves back in real self-giving." Ratzinger, *In the Beginning*, 48.

Created in the divine image, the dialogical God is therefore the foundation of our capacity to pray. Ratzinger explains,

> The basic reason why man can speak with God arises from the fact that God himself is speech, word. His nature is to speak, to hear, to reply, as we see particularly in Johannine theology, where Son and Spirit are described in terms of pure "hearing"; they speak in response to what they have first heard. Only because there is already speech, "Logos," in God can there be speech, "Logos," to God. Philosophically we could put it like this: the Logos in God is the onto-logical foundation for prayer. ... Since there is relationship within God himself, there can also be a participation in this relationship. Thus we can relate to God in a way which does not contradict his nature.[21]

Prayer, therefore, does not exist as something peripheral to our human nature. It exists at its very core and origin. Human beings are those to whom God addresses himself in a particular way. They are those who are capable of making a response. To deny this capacity is to deny the human person.

The definition of the human person in terms of prayer has radical implications. It means, as Ratzinger writes, that human persons are "most profoundly human when they step out of themselves and become capable of addressing God on familiar terms."[22] This is the human distinction. This is what separates us from other creatures. We are "the beings that God made capable of thinking *and* praying."[23] As human beings we do not merely possess consciousness, or reason, but the capacity to "reflect on the wholly other, the concept of God."[24] We are creatures made to respond to the Word that has been addressed to us; a Word that is personal and calls us into communion with himself.

In the evolution of the human person, therefore, there must exist a defining moment; a moment characterized by the emergence of a being who is capable of personally relating to his or her Creator. Ratzinger proposes,

> The clay became man at that moment in which a being for the first time was capable of forming, however dimly, the thought

---

21. Ratzinger, *The Feast of Faith*, 25.
22. Ratzinger, *In the Beginning*, 47.
23. Ratzinger, *In the Beginning*, 48. Italics added.
24. Ratzinger, "Concerning the Notion of Person in Theology," 451.

"God." The first Thou that—however stammeringly—was said by human lips to God marks the moment in which spirit arose in the world. Here the Rubicon of anthropogenesis was crossed. For it is not the use of weapons or fire, not new methods of cruelty or of useful activity, that constitute man, but, rather, his ability to be immediately in relation to God.[25]

Alternatively, borrowing the language of Teilhard de Chardin, Ratzinger offers another image of the emergence of the human spirit: "Teilhard de Chardin once remarked that it is in the nature of evolution to produce ever better eyesight. If we take up this thought, we can describe man accordingly as that stage in the creation, (as) that creature ... for whom the vision of God is part and parcel of his very being."[26] The analogy is fitting, especially when we consider that the evolution of the human person finds its end in the Incarnate Son, who eternally exists in the sight of the Father, and who, by his own admission, "can do nothing of his own accord, but only what he sees the Father doing" (John 5:19). Like him, we are called to share in that divine gaze; to find our end in the beatific vision of contemplating or 'seeing' the glory of God.

In the presence of one's Creator, prayer might be defined as "an act of consent"; an affirmation of being. Before the God who wills our existence, who brings us into being, prayer is our "yes" to our existence. "Essentially it means this," writes Ratzinger, "I can affirm the world, being, myself, because I can affirm the ground of my being, for this ground is good. It is good to *be*."[27] Drawing on the *Yahwist* account of creation, this could correspond to John Paul II's concept of the original experience of *solitude* that is unique to the human person. This solitude, confirmed in the Lord's determination that "it is not good that man should be alone" (Gen 2:18), does not only refer to the absence of complementarity and difference of the sexes, but more fundamentally to the very being of man/person in the world. "Right from the first moment of his existence," suggests John Paul, "created man finds himself before God as if in search of his own entity."[28] In his solitude before his Creator, man is confronted with his uniqueness. He is not like the other animals who are brought to him to name.

---

25. Ratzinger, *Dogma and Preaching*, 142.
26. Ratzinger, *Eschatology*, 154.
27. Ratzinger, *The Feast of Faith*, 27.
28. John Paul II, "General Audience."

> With this knowledge which, in a certain way, brings him out of his own being, man at the same time reveals himself to himself in all the peculiarity of his being. He is not only essentially and subjectively alone. Solitude also signifies man's subjectivity, which is constituted through self-knowledge. Man is alone because he is "different" from the visible world, from the world of living beings.[29]

He is different because he alone amongst all of creation is capable of entering into personal communion with his Creator. Thus, with the first thought of God, the first prayer that forms on his lips, there is an affirmation of the goodness of his being, the realization of his uniqueness, and the knowledge that his being exists in intimate relationship to the Creator.

The experience of solitude also points to the necessity of prayer for human authenticity. Prayer is not something "that one can take or leave but, rather, [it is] the center of human self-realization."[30] Prayer is more than an individual moment. It is a decision, a determination, of life and reality. "In saying Yes or No to prayer, one in fact decides on a theory of life and does not merely perform or omit an incidental individual act."[31] In prayer we are confronted with the reality that, even if devoid of human companionship, we are never alone; that we are "watched and loved" and part of something greater than ourselves.

This attention to the subjective and spiritual nature of man, who finds his origin in freedom and love, stands in stark contrast to the narrow constraints of evolutionary theory. As Ratzinger contends, a world "conceived as pure 'chance and necessity'" has no reason for prayer.[32] Prayer in such a world would be either desperate or irrational—a wretched hope, an opiate against despair. True human prayer, on the other hand, is the expression of hope and love flowing from a relationship of persons. The definition of man as one who prays also stands in contrast to a crudely materialistic evolutionism that posits the spiritual nature of man as something incidental. The emergence of a being who is capable of the thought of God accords with a spiritually-defined world view which "regards spirit as the goal of the process and, conversely, matter as the

---

29. John Paul II, "General Audience."
30. Ratzinger, *Dogma and Preaching*, 106.
31. Ratzinger, *Dogma and Preaching*, 105.
32. Ratzinger, *The Feast of Faith*, 20.

prehistory of the spirit."³³ Such a spiritually defined world view recognizes that matter is teleologically orientated towards the spirit. The end to which the physical evolution of man moved ever so slowly was a being who would be "like" his Creator in a communion of spirit. The inbreathing of the spirit, personally created by God, does not appear "as something foreign, as second substance in addition to matter; the appearance of spirit . . . means rather that an advancing movement arrives at the goal that has been set for it."³⁴ Thus, with anthropogenesis determined by "the rise of the spirit," the moment of humanity's emergence cannot be defined exclusively by the human sciences. It cannot be "excavated with a shovel."³⁵ It is a profoundly personal and relational moment that escapes the limitations of evolutionary theory, that by itself cannot hope to explain the human complexity.

An Original Reason

Thus we recognize that the human capacity for receiving the Word is premised on two fundamental truths: (1) on the nature of God as Word; and (2) on our creation in that divine image. According to biblical theology, the Word is the *logos*, the reason, of God. It is that which, as the Evangelist teaches, existed since the beginning and through whom all things were made (John 1:1–2). Thus, at the origin of all things, and in a special way at the origin of our human nature, there stands the reason of God; an originating thought, a primordial reason, that gives meaning and intelligence and order to all things.

In contrast to certain evolutionary theories that are premised on chance and chaos—that presume that rationality proceeds as "a chance by-product of irrationality and floating in an ocean of irrationality"³⁶—belief in the Word points to our origins in thought, and premises an intellectual structure at the foundation of all that exists.³⁷ Living creation points to a rationality at the basis of all being, exhibiting the traces of reason in its intelligence and design, and with the discoveries of science,

---

33. Ratzinger, *Dogma and Preaching*, 141.
34. Ratzinger, *Dogma and Preaching*, 141.
35. Ratzinger, *Dogma and Preaching*, 142.
36. Ratzinger, *Truth and Tolerance*, 181.
37. Ratzinger, *Introduction to Christianity*, 152.

does so "more luminously and radiantly today than ever before."[38] This rationality exists even within matter itself. "One can read it," writes Ratzinger. "It has mathematical properties."[39]

Ratzinger insists that sensitivity to natural structures necessarily engages reason, because creation, as flowing from the mind of God, is inherently rational. Drawing on this reasoning, David Crawford writes,

> Because all of being is created, it bears the impress, the meaning, or logic, or reason, or language, of its Creator. Hence, in this important sense, there is no level of being that does not in some sense express divine reason. There is no level of being lacking an intrinsic intelligibility that is in deep accord with the intelligence of man.[40]

The world is not simply material, objectified by human reason. It is not pre-rational, in the sense of not yet participating in reason. Rather, "it is in itself an expression of divine reason."[41] Creation is intelligible, "saturated" with its own meaning through its participation in the divine *logos*. Creation "teaches us how we can be human in the right way," as Ratzinger suggests.[42] It offers us "signposts" that give direction to our lives.[43]

But in the economy of salvation, this *logos*, for which man has an inherent capacity, is revealed to us as something more than natural laws. As Ratzinger reflects, "the original thought, whose being-thought is represented by the world, is not an anonymous, neutral consciousness but rather freedom, creative love, a person."[44] Again, the God in whose image we are created is relational; He is a communion of persons.

A God Who Speaks

For the human person, therefore, the goal of creation is a special likeness to the God "who speaks" and "to whom man can speak" in return.[45] This likeness finds its end and perfection in Christ, the Word made flesh. He is

---

38. Ratzinger, *In the Beginning*, 56.
39. In Horn and Wiedenhofer, *Creation and Evolution*, 163.
40. Crawford, "Natural Law and the Body," 335.
41. Crawford, "Natural Law and the Body," 347.
42. Ratzinger, *A Turning Point for Europe?*, 44.
43. Ratzinger, *God and the World*, 164.
44. Ratzinger, *Introduction to Christianity*, 158.
45. Ratzinger, *The Feast of Faith*, 16.

the reconciliation of spirit and matter. He is the end to which our evolution looks forward. Through the Incarnation, Christ, the Son who is himself speech, Word, *logos*, now participates in human speech. By assuming human speech, the Son has also offered us the way of communicating with God. To this Ratzinger adds,

> The Christian God is characterized by revelation, that is, by the words and deeds in which he addresses man, and the goal of revelation is man's response in word and deed, which thus expands revelation into a dialogue between Creator and creature which guides man toward union with God. So prayer is not something on the periphery of the Christian concept of God; it is a fundamental trait.[46]

Christ has restored the lines of communication broken by sin. He has purified our language and opened our ears to God's voice. "As a result of the Incarnation, human speech has become a component in divine speech; it has been taken up, unconfusedly and inseparably, into that speech which is God's inner nature."[47]

But our participation in the prayer of Christ goes even beyond the Incarnation. Through his resurrection and ascension, our humanity is forever made a participant in the divine dialogue. Of this reality, and borrowing the language of evolutionary theory, Ratzinger envisages the risen humanity of Christ as "the greatest 'mutation', absolutely the most crucial leap into a totally new dimension that there has ever been in the long history of life and its development: a leap into a completely new order."[48] Reborn in grace, and enlivened by his Spirit, we enter into the Son's dialogue with the Father—the spirit that cries out within us *Abba, Father* (Gal 4:6). That which is most original in us—the capacity to pray—is thus elevated in Christ to a participation in God's eternal communication. We enter into the prayer of Christ, "which is the Son's act of being, as Son, and which thus is rooted in the ultimate ontological depths of reality."[49] This is nothing less than our filial adoption in Christ; the perfection of our nature which is created to be in communion with God. Therefore, as Ratzinger insists, in Christ, "in the man who is completely with God, human existence is not cancelled, but comes to its highest possibility, which

---

46. Ratzinger, *The Feast of Faith*, 16.
47. Ratzinger, *The Feast of Faith*, 26.
48. Benedict XVI, "Homily for Easter Vigil."
49. Ratzinger, *The Feast of Faith*, 27.

consists in transcending itself into the absolute and in the integration of its own relativity into the absoluteness of divine love."[50]

Obstacles to the Realization of Our Nature in Prayer

The characterization of the human person as one who prays—who enters into communion with God—does not mean, however, that prayer comes easily or (dare we say) "naturally." Indeed, it often seems that prayer is a struggle; that, more often than not, man feels animosity towards praying. In this context, Romano Guardini reflects, "It is a great mystery that man, whose life springs from God, should have such difficulty in communing with Him; that indeed he should experience disinclination to do so and should seize on any pretext to evade Him."[51]

This disinclination to prayer to the point of avoidance, may, to some ways of thinking, undermine the claim that man is *homo orans*. If man finds prayer onerous, and is content to exist without it, then it can hardly define his condition. But in labelling this disinclination a "mystery," Guardini insists that it does not correspond to man's proper condition. He acknowledges the disinclination to prayer as a reality, but he does not accept it as definitive. Like any other characteristic that defines the human person—reason, intelligence, creativity—prayer does not emerge unconsciously or without effort. Furthermore, communication with God is hindered by Original Sin, in which man's easy relationship with God is fractured, poetically illustrated in man hiding in fright from God after the Fall (Gen 3:10). Prayer must be cultivated and intended. The prayer that "springs from inner longing must, on the whole, be considered as the exception," writes Guardini. "Anyone who takes his relationship with God seriously soon sees that prayer is not merely an expression of the inner life which will prevail on its own, but is also a service to be performed in faith and obedience. Thus it must be willed and practiced."[52]

There is another potential obstacle to the determination of man as *homo orans*, and that concerns his stance before God. It appears that man is an unequal dialogical partner with God. When Ratzinger speaks of the "thought of God" arising in the mind of the emergent man, this thought of God must not be considered as a "thing" amongst other things; the

---

50. Ratzinger, "Concerning the Notion of Person in Theology," 452.
51. Guardini, *The Art of Praying*, 9.
52. Guardini, *The Art of Praying*, 4.

contemplation of a "being" alongside other beings.[53] No, the mere thought of God contains within itself a realization of his otherness; that "He is God; I am His creature. He made me; in Him I have my being."[54] As Guardini again writes,

> God *is*, as nobody and nothing is. He is from Himself and by reason of Himself. Thus He alone has substance; He alone verily *is*.... I, however, am not from myself and by reason of myself. I am through Him: not being, but existing by His grace; not absolute, but contingent. Between my way of being and His, the coordinating conjunction *and* has no place. The sentence "God and I are" is devoid of meaning. Were I to maintain it in all seriousness, I would be blaspheming.[55]

Prayer, therefore, presumes an attitude of humility. It acknowledges the gap that exists between Creator and creature—a distance that can only be crossed by God himself.

> My being stands in an entirely different relationship to God than does the being of a creature to that of his fellow. I am only *before* Him and *through* Him. In a state of true recollectedness, one experiences this truth. One will have learnt something very important when one knows that one *is* before God, and in reality *only* before Him. It is something very great; it can become frightening and at the same time joyous, and we shall see that on this realization rests one of the fundamental acts of prayer, that is, adoration.[56]

The natural capacity for prayer, therefore, necessarily includes adoration. Within an anthropology that recognizes "the only natural . . . reaction of man, to whom God gave this blessed and sanctified world, is to bless God in return," the prayer that defines the human person tends towards adoration and blessing.[57] It is eucharistic—an offering of thanksgiving for all that God has given. It is the prayer of the creature before its Creator. It is the prayer of the priest, who offers everything back to God.

Therefore, in contrast to the thesis of this chapter, Guardini would seem to claim that man is primarily, if not exclusively, *homo adorans*. In

---

53. Ratzinger, *Dogma and Preaching*, 142.
54. Guardini, *Faith and Modern Man*, 11.
55. Guardini, *The Art of Praying*, 20.
56. Guardini, *The Art of Praying*, 20.
57. Schmemann, *For the Life of the World*, 15.

highlighting the distance that exists between God and man, and insisting that man exists only *before* and *through* the Creator, the idea that prayer depends on a likeness between Creator and creature is brought into question. In response I would suggest that Guardini, in rightly stressing the Otherness of God, nonetheless creates an unnecessary separation between God and man—a separation that has been bridged by the Incarnation. The Word, to which (as Aquinas has noted) our human nature tends, is the origin of our speech. Our likeness to him from our creation is the foundation of our prayer. As already noted, "the Logos in God" in whose image we are created exists as "the onto-logical foundation for prayer," and the Logos made flesh is its expression.[58]

In Christ, therefore, man prays not only *before* God, but *in* him. Our prayer is joined to the prayer of the Son. From the beginning, therefore, prayer flows from an inherent likeness to God that is rooted in the Word. Thus, while adoration has its privileged place before God, it is dependent on man's capacity to pray. As noted at the beginning of the chapter, the cult of worship or adoration forms a part of nearly all religions. But in order to be an act of communion with God, such adoration depends on a fundamental likeness; a capacity to speak the same word, which is the capacity to pray.

Conclusion

Throughout this chapter, I have attempted to defend the thesis that the human person is intrinsically constituted as one who prays. He is *homo orans*, created in the divine image for the purpose of union with the Word. Man is essentially defined by this relation to the Word; by his capacity to "hear" the Word addressed to him, and to respond in kind. And this is precisely what we define as prayer: "a real exchange between God and man."[59]

As noted, this thesis exists in tension with a nuanced conception of man as *homo adorans*, who, in light of the difference that exists between Creator and creature, stands before God in an attitude of blessing and gratitude. This fundamental task of man to adore God is not denied by this chapter. The orientation of man as *homo adorans* is revealed from the beginning of man's existence in the Garden in his institution as priest and

---

58. Ratzinger, *Feast of Faith*, 25.
59. Ratzinger, *The Feast of Faith*, 26.

in the divine establishment of cult and worship. However, in emphasizing the dissimilarity between Creator and creature, the concept of *homo adorans* tends to diminish the likeness, union, and relation between God and man. And it is precisely here that the tension lies.

In response, I have argued that adoration presumes that we both know the One to whom we offer our worship, and that we are capable of addressing him. This faculty, I contend, is founded in a real likeness to God through our creation in his image, and our inherent capacity for the Word. It is realized in the Incarnation of that Word and is expressed in prayer as a real communion between God and man. And so man is rightly called *homo adorans*—a priest who blesses and worships his Creator. But he is *homo orans* first, who can think the thought of God and pray to him; who knows the object of his love and can enter into communion with him.

Bibliography

Aquinas, Thomas. *Summa Theologiae*. Translated by the Fathers of the English Dominican Province. New York: Benzinger Brothers, 1947.

Balthasar, Hans Urs von. *Prayer*. Translated by Graham Harrison. San Francisco: Ignatius, 1986.

Benedict XVI, Pope. "Homily for Easter Vigil." http://www.vatican.va/content/benedict-xvi/en/homilies/2006/documents/hf_ben-xvi_hom_20060415_veglia-pasquale.pdf.

Crawford, David S. "Natural Law and the Body: Between Deductivism and Parallelism." *Communio* 35 (2008) 327–53.

Davidson, Richard. "Earth's First Sanctuary: Genesis 1–3 and Parallel Creation Accounts." *Andrews University Seminary Studies* 53.1 (2015) 65–89.

Guardini, Romano. *The Art of Praying: The Principles and Methods of Christian Prayer*. Translated by Leopold of Loewenstein-Wertheim. Manchester, NH: Sophia Institute, 1985.

———. *Faith and Modern Man*. Translated by Charlotte E. Forsyth. New York: Pantheon, 1952.

Hahn, Scott. *A Father Who Keeps His Promises: God's Covenant Love in Scripture*. Cincinnati: Servant, 1998.

Horn, Stephan O., and Siegfried Wiedenhofer, eds. *Creation and Evolution: A Conference with Pope Benedict XVI in Castel Gandolfo*. Translated by Michael J. Miller. San Francisco: Ignatius, 2008.

John Paul II, Pope. "General Audience." https://www.vatican.va/content/john-paul-ii/en/audiences/1979/documents/hf_jp-ii_aud_19791010.pdf.

Ratzinger, Joseph. "Concerning the Notion of Person in Theology." Translated by Michael Waldstein. *Communio* 17 (1990) 439–54.

———. *Dogma and Preaching: Applying Christian Doctrine to Daily Life*. Edited by Michael J. Miller. San Francisco: Ignatius, 2011.

———. *Eschatology: Death and Eternal Life*. Translated by Michael Waldstein and Aidan Nichols. 2nd ed. Washington DC: Catholic University of America Press, 1988.

———. *The Feast of Faith: Approaches to a Theology of the Liturgy*. Translated by Graham Harrison. San Francisco: Ignatius, 1986.

———. *God and the World: Believing and Living in Our Time: A Conversation with Peter Seewald*. Translated by Henry Taylor. San Francisco: Ignatius, 2002.

———. *Images of Hope: Meditations on Major Feasts*. Translated by J. Rock and G. Harrison. San Francisco: Ignatius, 2006.

———. *In the Beginning: A Catholic Understanding of the Story of Creation and the Fall*. Translated by Boniface Ramsey. Grand Rapids: Eerdmans, 1995.

———. *Introduction to Christianity*. Translated by J. R. Foster and Michael J. Miller. San Francisco: Ignatius, 2004.

———. *The Spirit of the Liturgy*. Translated by John Saward. San Francisco: Ignatius, 2000.

———. *Truth and Tolerance: Christian Belief and World Religions*. Translated by Henry Taylor. San Francisco: Ignatius, 2004.

———. *A Turning Point for Europe? The Church in the Modern World: Assessment and Forecast*. Translated by Brian McNeil. 2nd ed. San Francisco: Ignatius, 2010.

Schmemann, Alexander. *For the Life of the World: Sacraments and Orthodoxy*. Crestwood, NY: St. Vladimir's Seminary Press, 1973.

Wenham, Gordan J. "Sanctuary Symbolism in the Garden of Eden Story." *Proceedings of the World Congress of Jewish Studies* (1985) 19–25.

14

Wisdom or Eloquence?

Insights from Josef Pieper's Anthropology for Secondary Religious Education

Paul G. Chigwidden

Wisdom or Eloquence?

It was Saint Augustine who argued that wisdom is of more importance than eloquence to the Christian teacher.[1] At present much of religious education is eloquent in the best traditions of that word—religion as a subject is clearly viewed by most students in generally positive terms.[2] Their time at Catholic schools is certainly influential.[3] As one study noted, "During teenage years Catholics who attended Catholic schools are more likely to attend services, pray frequently and report that religion is very important in their lives than their Catholic peers in non-Catholic schools."[4] However, despite the effort of countless teachers

---

1. Augustine, *On Christian Doctrine*, II.5.
2. Rymarz and Graham, "Australian Core Catholic Youth," 79–89.
3. See Rymarz and Cleary, "Examining Some Aspects," 327–36.
4. Smith et al., *Young Catholic America*, cited in Rymarz and Cleary, "Some Religious Beliefs," 69.

in countless religious education lessons, the same statistics generally indicate that "each of these differences has almost disappeared or even slightly reversed within five years when these Catholics reach emerging adulthood."[5] The increasingly fragmented and disenchanted views of young adults would indicate that eloquence is not enough; it informs but it struggles to transform. Wisdom is needed if schools are to reinvigorate their specific evangelical identity, enabling them to "build up the community of believers, evangelize the culture, and [thereby] serve the common good of society."[6]

The career of twentieth century German philosopher Josef Pieper, straddling both the modern and post-modern eras, was shaped by a relentless search for wisdom.[7] William J. Hoye summarized his career thus: "Pieper's attention was riveted first of all on the real and then on making the truth of reality transparent through language."[8] Across a career that spanned from 1931 until 1996, the year before his death, he developed three fundamental anthropological insights which form a unifying vision of the human person and, therefore, have much to say to those seeking the requisite wisdom to revitalize their work in secondary religious education.[9] Pieper begins with the receptivity inherent in our status as created beings. This receptivity points to our deep-seated need for contemplation and it is the blessedness of that contemplation that, in turn, points ahead to our heavenly destination. Pieper would argue that without these foundational anthropological ideas Catholic Schools cannot hope to form students in a "shared vision of the real."[10]

Using Charles Taylor's description of secularism, we will develop a theoretical overview of the phenomenon. Then, looking at the data, we will acquire a sense of the effects of this phenomenon in the world of Catholic religious education. Having established a sense of the contextual realities of religious education in a secular milieu, we will outline the three anthropological insights of Josef Pieper's *oeuvre*. The question then

---

5. Smith et al., *Young Catholic America*, cited in Rymarz and Cleary "Some Religious Beliefs," 69.

6. Miller, "Five Essential Marks of Catholic Schools," 63.

7. Hoye, "A Transparent Philosopher," 22.

8. Hoye, "A Transparent Philosopher," 17.

9. This connection between the philosophy of Josef Pieper and the revitalization of contemporary education owes much to the recent work of Nathaniel A. Warne. See Warne, "Learning to See the World Again," 289–303.

10. Dupré, *Metaphysics and Culture*, 42.

becomes—what do they suggest for contemporary religious education? We can then draw four warnings that Pieper would make to religious educators should they abandon these insights, and then develop three practical suggestions for how they might embed this wisdom in their work.

Diagnosing Secularism

Rejecting the traditional "subtraction theory" of secularism as simply "less religion," Charles Taylor's 2007 magnum opus *A Secular Age* focuses on the social imaginary characterizing the way in which "ordinary people 'imagine' their social surroundings."[11] In the classical world the social imaginary was such that atheism seemed an impossibility. In the twenty-first century it strikes many people as inescapable. Taylor defines this secular mindset as being primarily shaped by the gradual distancing of God; a process begun in the Middle Ages and accelerated by the Reformation, the Enlightenment, and industrialization. The cumulative effect being that, "we can [now] rationalise the world and expel the mystery from it,"[12] "we might say that we moved from living in a cosmos to being included in a universe."[13] Borrowing from Max Weber, Taylor refers to the world "charged with the grandeur of God" as enchanted. In contrast he refers to the secular world as disenchanted.

What is the result of this disenchantment? Our forebears were open, or porous, to the supernatural; it so characterized the world in which they lived that to accept the supernatural was simply to accept reality itself. To live was to be shaped and moved by the supernatural. In contrast, Taylor describes the modern person as buffered. In the enchanted world meaning exists outside of us, it is ours to receive.[14] In the disenchanted world, the self is buffered; suddenly we feel ourselves to be "master of the meanings of things,"[15] we give our "own autonomous order to life."[16] Thus, people might remain religious, but they are rarely creedal; the faith

---

11. Taylor, *A Secular Age*, 171–72.
12. Taylor, *A Secular Age*, 59.
13. Taylor, *A Secular Age*, 80.
14. Taylor, *A Secular Age*, 34.
15. Taylor, *A Secular Age*, 38–39.
16. Taylor, *A Secular Age*, 554–55.

is not so much received as constructed. In such a context students might be informed about the faith, but they are rarely transformed by the faith.

The result has been that, from the mid-twentieth century onwards, each individual has felt a compulsion to "discover their own fulfilment."[17] For Taylor the effect of this compulsion is a radical fragmentation of meaning, or hyperpluralism. Thus, he says that "We are now living in a spiritual super-nova, a kind of galloping pluralism on the spiritual plane."[18] A key product of this fragmentation is something Taylor terms mutual fragilization, this being when "the many forms of belief and unbelief jostle," and one's increasingly idiosyncratic beliefs are implicitly challenged and potentially re-shaped or strengthened by the contest with others. More likely however, the result is a form of self-imposed quietism in which beliefs remain private.[19] It is in this context of quietist subjectivism that our secondary religion teachers must pass on a creedal faith built on mystery and lived sacramentally. They may do so with great eloquence, but the call to respond to "our society's rampant individualism" by "open[ing] new prospects of evangelical hope"[20] demands a wisdom capable of enlarging and enriching students' fragmented and fragilized beliefs.

Secularism by the Numbers

Numerous sociological studies have produced findings underscoring the legitimacy of Taylor's diagnosis: our students remain buffered. Young people often remain attached to religion but in a fragmented and individualised manner. Perhaps the description of adolescent faith that has most resonated with reaserachers and teachers alike was that found in Christian Smith and Melina Lundquist Denton's 2005 *Soul Searching: The Religious and Spiritual Lives of American Teenagers*. Based on their study of over eight thousand American teens, the authors concluded that the religion of American teenagers was a product of the buffered social imaginary: "What legitimates the religion of most youth today is not that it is the life-transformative, transcendent truth, but that it instrumentally provides mental, psychological, emotional, and social benefits that teens

17. Taylor, *A Secular Age*, 299.
18. Taylor, *A Secular Age*, 300.
19. Taylor, *A Secular Age*, 531–32.
20. Congregation for Catholic Education, *Educating Today and Tomorrow*, no. 1.

find useful and valuable."[21] They termed this Moral Therapeutic Deism (MTD). Interestingly, they noted a direct link between MTD and, among other factors, education. "When the engagement and education of youth by their religious communities is weak, then the faith of teenagers in those traditions tends to degenerate into Moralistic Therapeutic Deism."[22]

More recently, the 2018 *Cardus Survey* interviewed 1,500 randomly selected American high school graduates aged twenty-four to thirty-nine and found the same evidence of MTD. These were not anti-religious graduates, but neither were they typically students for whom Christ is the source of all truth. Rather, they were young people who clearly recognized "the [utile] value of faith, and of belonging to a faith community, especially in light of troubling trends related to depression and loneliness."[23]

Despite such an outlook, the report showed that Catholic education still played a significant formative role. "[On balance] Catholic school graduates are more likely to remain or become Catholic" than to take up a different faith or to abandon all religion.[24] In fact, the Cardus Report noted that, compared with other faith schools, "the Catholic school sector seems [able] to work toward the spiritual formation of its students even when their family background would push their graduates in a less religious direction."[25] Whatever its challenges, Catholic education retains an enormous evangelizing potential even in the secular milieu.

Australian studies indicate broadly similar patterns. When the focus is on the elements of Catholicism linked with the objective truth claims of the church and its concomitant practices, they reveal a pattern of decline through the adolescent years. For instance, the 2018 Independent Schools Council of Australia published an analysis of 2016 census

21. Smith and Denton, *Soul Searching*, 154.
22. Smith and Denton, *Soul Searching*, 262.
23. When it focused in on Catholic graduates, it found significantly fragmented or individualized views which, in significant instances, were indistinguishable from attitudes found among students graduating from public schools. For instance, when it came to views of marriage, family, and sexuality, "Catholic school graduates are not distinctive . . . from public school graduates on views of divorce or gay marriage, but are slightly more likely than public school graduates to say that cohabitation and premarital sex is morally wrong." Additionally, their sense of being obliged to maintain spiritual practices actually trailed graduates of public and protestant schools. Cardus, "2018 US Cardus Education Survey."
24. Cardus, "2018 US Cardus Education Survey."
25. Cardus, "2018 US Cardus Education Survey."

data revealing that the number of students attending Catholic schools claiming "No Religion" had grown from 8 to 14 percent.[26] In the same year, the Australian Catholic Bishops' Youth Survey revealed that of the 12,170 respondents aged between sixteen and eighteen, only 16 percent identified with the statement: "I am Catholic and regularly attend Mass and other faith activities." This was the same percentage as those who ticked: "I don't identify with being Catholic or any other religion."[27] Studies released in 2007[28] and again in 2020[29] reveal a consistent data trend from 1991 to 2016: young people are least likely to attend Mass or even identify as a Catholic in their final years of secondary school, and the years immediately following graduation.[30] The only change has been the consistent percentage decline of young people aged fifteen to twenty-four who actually do attend Mass.[31] In short, students are interested in the faith and informed about the faith, yet its ability to transform the buffered self remains limited.

Indeed, when the questions are restricted to generalized attitudes or personal religious beliefs, they can often reveal very different trends.[32] A particularly illustrative finding came in a recent survey undertaken by the Sydney Archdiocese. There was the usual statistical decline in belief during the high school or adolescent years. There were also, predictably enough, a high number of students who remained neutral on religious questions. However, questions concerning such primary theological concepts as the incarnation revealed relatively traditional views. According to Rymarz and Cleary, "By Year 11, just over 67% agreed that Jesus is both truly God and truly man. . . . Given the influences on younger Catholics today . . . this figure can be seen as being somewhat higher than

---

26. Independent Schools Council of Australia, *The Changing Face of Australian Schooling*, 10.

27. Dantis and Reid, *Called to Fullness of Life and Love*, 4, 11.

28. Dixon, *Catholics Who Have Stopped Attending Mass*, 3–4, 14.

29. National Centre for Pastoral Research. *The Australian Catholic Mass Attendance Report 2016*.

30. Dixon predicted that "the steady fall in attendances will continue for some time to come, as the higher rates of attendance associated with older attenders are unlikely to be reached by younger Catholics as they get older." Dixon, *Catholics Who Have Stopped Attending Mass*, 3–4.

31. National Centre for Pastoral Research, *The Australian Catholic Mass Attendance Report 2016*, 20.

32. See Rymarz and Cleary, "Kids Today!," 12–18.

anticipated."[33] Belief in the incarnation is the doorway to the enchanted worldview. As the authors say "This is not a deistic sense of God but a strong affirmation of the personal Christian God."[34] Thus, they concluded from their study, "The figures for Catholic school students . . . still reflect a high level of support for a traditional Catholic teaching and religious educators should be aware of this."[35] The challenge is to work towards a model of religious education that can coherently and evocatively communicate the rich fullness of the Catholic faith to young people.

And yet what of the religious educators themselves? Unsurprisingly, teachers, much like students, are a group who are more and more shaped by the secular context in which they live. The 2014 Congregation for Catholic Education document, *Educating Today and Tomorrow*, argued that what is needed is "unity among the teachers, who together are willing to embrace and share a specific evangelical identity, as well as a consistent lifestyle."[36] But a 2015 study of teachers in Queensland's Catholic schools found that levels of faith commitment were lower among younger teachers in general and secondary teachers in particular.[37]

A subsequent study by the same authors looked into the beliefs and attitudes of student teachers. When asked to rank the goals of Catholic education, faith had the lowest overall mean score. Of the 134 students surveyed, only 22 percent of those identifying as Catholic rated their faith as being a very important/important factor in selecting a school for their practicum. This was actually lower than students from other Christian denominations doing practicums in Catholic schools.[38] A more recent work by Richard Rymarz revealed an increased difficulty among many young RE teachers in both eliciting questions from students and subsequently answering them when they arose.[39]

In short, it is fair to conclude that, "It is likely that many who enter teacher education programmes to work in Catholic schools may not have a strong cognitive grasp of Catholicism."[40] Teachers are often just as hun-

---

33. Rymarz and Cleary, "Examining Some Aspects," 330–31. Of the same Year Eleven cohort, 60 percent held that Jesus was truly present in the Eucharist.
34. Rymarz and Cleary, "Examining Some Aspects," 330.
35. Rymarz and Cleary, "Examining Some Aspects," 331.
36. Congregation for Catholic Education, *Educating Today and Tomorrow*, 1.J.
37. Gleeson and O'Neill, "Student-Teachers' Perspectives," 59.
38. Gleeson and O'Neill, "Student-Teachers' Perspectives," 62–63.
39. Rymarz and Belmonte, "The Questions Students Ask?," 120–28.
40. Franchi and Rymarz, "The Education and Formation of Teachers," 5.

gry for "new prospects of evangelical hope" as their students; prospects capable of enlivening their work, enabling it to cohere both for themselves and for their students. The alternative is that religious education risks acting as an accelerant to the process of fragmentation and fragilization among both students and teachers at Catholic schools.

Louis Dupré, the philosopher of religion, offered a warning when he wrote, "Once the human subject became solely responsible for the constitution of meaning and value, tradition lost its former authority. Each group, if not each individual, eventually felt free to advance a cultural synthesis of its own, ransacking the tradition for spare parts."[41] In contrast, the 2020 Directory for Catechesis argued that "the religious dimension is in fact intrinsic to culture. It contributes to the overall formation of the person and makes it possible to transform knowledge into wisdom of life."[42] Yet when the context in which religious education takes place is defined by fragmentation and fragilization—when its members no longer "share an overall vision of the real," such wisdom is in danger of being lost to mere eloquence. Modern religious education can only be fruitful with this unifying vision.[43] The only alternative to a shared vision is a growing subjectivism and, from an educational perspective, incoherence. Josef Pieper's anthropological vision of creaturely receptivity represents a much-needed "overall vision of the real" and, for that reason, has much to offer twenty-first century religious education.

Pieper's Thomistic Anthropology

Although widely regarded as an interpreter of St. Thomas, Pieper had a deep-seated suspicion of what he termed "movement Thomism."[44] For Pieper, Aquinas was "a witness of extraordinary rank"[45] for a tradition that "goes deeper than historical time."[46] In interpreting Aquinas, Pieper sought not a "closed system of propositions" but "language which is alive

---

41. Dupré, *Metaphysics and Culture*, 45.

42. Pontifical Council for Promoting New Evangelisation, *Directory for Catechesis*, 187–88.

43. Pontifical Council for Promoting New Evangelisation, *Directory for Catechesis*, 189.

44. Crim, "Josef Pieper's Critique of Western Civ."

45. Pieper, *Happiness and Contemplation*, 14.

46. Pieper, *Happiness and Contemplation*, 44.

and has a liquid clarity."[47] For Pieper, Aquinas simply gave the clearest evocation of "that great, integral, all-embracing tradition of wisdom fed by the Divine Logos which can be found in all ages."[48] Whilst Taylor considers the enchanted social imaginary impossible in the twentieth century, his intellectual history fails to fully appreciate the great stream of enchanted thinkers (including Pieper) who characterized so much of Catholic intellectual life throughout the disenchanted twentieth century; those men and women who subscribed to that "all-embracing tradition of wisdom fed by the Divine Logos."[49]

47. Crim, "Josef Pieper's Critique of Western Civ."
48. Pieper, *Happiness and Contemplation*, 44.
49. Taylor offers portraits of many twentieth century figures within this tradition: Chesterton, Knox, Dawson, and Eliot, but he focuses on feeling rather than wisdom. For this reason, he seems only capable of seeing nostalgia in their conversions. Such a summary is philosophically consistent with his argument, but it is not historically consistent. For instance, in part five of *A Secular Age*, Taylor considers intellectual converts such as Jacques Maritain, G. K. Chesterton, Christopher Dawson, Ronald Knox, Evelyn Waugh, and Walker Percy. He identifies conversion as a "paradigm shift" in which the individual breaks out of "the regnant versions of immanent order" (732). However, Taylor limits his discussion of motivation to notions of nostalgia for an overtly (and at times politically) Christian past. "The hold of the former Christendom on our imagination is immense . . . [but] of course the backward look here may deceive" (734–35). Here Taylor's work would benefit from closer study of the converts themselves; many of whom were very explicit about why it was they became a Catholic. G. K. Chesterton, for instance, wrote an essay not long after entering the Catholic Church in 1922. Entitled "Why I Am a Catholic," he began rather directly, "The difficulty of explaining "why I am a Catholic" is that there are ten thousand reasons all amounting to one reason: that Catholicism is true." Chesterton, *Why I Am a Catholic*, 125. Evelyn Waugh, in his turn, was equally explicit. In an article entitled "Come Inside," Waugh argued that culturally, liturgically, and even architecturally his preferences were Anglican rather than Catholic. So why did he convert to Catholicism? "On firm intellectual conviction but with little emotion" he was convinced that "Christian revelation was genuine." Waugh, "Come Inside," 149. In addition, where Taylor investigates what converts believed themselves to be finding in the Catholic Church, he points to an institution that, although threatened with "bureaucratic hardening" it is able to be a "network of agape" or a "network of living concern," prioritizing the "gut-driven response" of the person or even a "communion of different people and ages in mutual understanding and enrichment." Taylor, *A Secular Age*, 742, 743, 755. But here again, the converts have given their answers. As Waugh went on to explain, "If the Christian revelation was true, then the Church was the society founded by Christ and all other bodies were only as good so far as they had salvaged something from the wrecks of the Great Schism and the Reformation." Waugh, "Come Inside," 149. In his essay, Chesterton made a similar point, describing the Catholic Church as "not a movement but a meeting place; the trysting place of all the truths in the world." Chesterton, *Why I Am a Catholic*, 132. Taylor rightly criticizes the purely excarnational thinking of the twenty-first century,

Taylor argues that we cannot go back. But perhaps he is wrong to insist that so little of the past remains with us, that we only have our fragments. He describes "the tension, awkwardness and dilemma that exists for modern Christians between [what they draw] from the development of modern humanism, and [their] attachment to the central mysteries of Christian Faith";[50] between their "sense of God"[51] and the "official formulations of the faith."[52] It was precisely in response to such a tension that Pieper spent his career handing on the refreshing vitality of the all-embracing tradition of wisdom, transcending the passage of time. It is as the contemporary voice of that tradition that Pieper has much to say to contemporary religious educators.

Across his vast output, Pieper consistently stressed three interconnected elements of the human person. They are: (1) our receptivity as created beings, (2) our inherent need for contemplation, and (3) the blessedness of that contemplation betokening our eternal destiny. These three elements constitute the wisdom he offers to fragmented and fragilized religious education classrooms struggling to challenge, much less free the buffered self.

Pieper most clearly articulates this first insight in a somewhat neglected essay of his entitled "The Negative Element in the Philosophy of St. Thomas Aquinas." In this essay, Pieper argued that the philosophy of St. Thomas Aquinas always contained:

> A fundamental idea by which all the basic concepts of his vision of the world are determined: the idea of creation. The idea of creation, or more precisely, the notion that nothing exists which is not *creatura*, except the Creator Himself; and in addition, that this createdness determines entirely and all-pervasively the inner structure of the creature.[53]

This idea, so rarely expressed in commentaries on Aquinas,[54] becomes, for Pieper, the foundational idea in the anthropological vision emerging from his writing.

---

but perhaps he fails to appreciate the explicitly incarnational thinking evident in the motivations of the converts he discusses.

50. Taylor, *A Secular Age*, 654.
51. Taylor, *A Secular Age*, 654.
52. Taylor, *A Secular Age*, 656.
53. Pieper, "The Negative Element," 47.
54. Pieper, "The Negative Element," 48.

From Thomas's declaration that, "Because and in so far as God has creatively thought things into being, just so and to that extent have they a nature,"[55] Pieper concludes that our creaturely status therefore cannot be ignored in any discussion of education because it is what allows us to know anything. This gift of the "absolutely creative knowledge of God can then be known by the 'reality conforming mind' of man.... Things have their intelligibility, their inner clarity and lucidity, and the power to reveal themselves because God has creatively thought them."[56] At its best, then, our thinking is just a re-thinking; it is literally re-cognizing. Thus, it may be said that thinking can only be the act of a receptive creature. Like the reality to which our thinking seeks to conform, our thinking nature is created and received.[57] For Pieper, any model of Catholic education which loses sight of this understanding of our preternatural receptivity can only be impoverished.

Borrowing directly from the *Summa*, Pieper argues that, just as created things are knowable for the creature, they are also unfathomable because they are created.[58] Therefore, in the realm of "created natural reality" we might speak of truth in two senses. "When things are the norm and measure of the intellect, truth consists in the equation of the intellect to these things . . . but when the intellect is the norm and measure of things, then truth consists in the equation of things to the intellect."[59] Of these two senses of truth, the first rightly belongs to man the creature, the second to God, his creator. For this reason, then, it may be argued that

---

55. Aquinas, *Summa Theologiae*, I.93.6, cited in Pieper, "The Negative Element," 53.

56. Pieper, "The Negative Element," 54, 55–56.

57. Pieper also quotes Aquinas's use of Avicenna's definition: "the truth of every individual thing is the special character of its Being that has been given to it as its abiding possession." Aquinas, *Summa Theologiae*, I.16.1, cited in Pieper, "The Negative Element," 62.

58. Pieper describes St. Thomas's dictum that "knowledge is a certain effect of truth" as "a revolutionary sentence" (Aquinas, *Quaestiones Disputatae de Veritate*, 1.I). He then explains, "this relation on which the truth of things is fundamentally based—the relation between natural reality and the archetypal creative thought of God—*cannot, I insist, be known formally by us*. We can of course know things; we cannot formally know their *truth*." Pieper, "The Negative Element," 58–59.

59. Aquinas, *Summa Theologiae*, I.21.2 cited in Pieper, "The Negative Element," 57. He also cites, to the same effect, Augustine's distinction "that things exist because God sees them (whereas we see things because they exist)." Pieper, "The Negative Element," 61.

our status as created beings is completely at odds with the buffered social imaginary which posits itself as the author of meaning.

The second point can be summed up by his simple maxim, "the extent of a man's happiness is only as great as his capacity for contemplation."[60] Pieper consistently argues that since we are creatures rather than the creator, our good life is one "lived in contemplative assent to the world" which we have received.[61] Again, such a view is distinctly at odds with living as the "master of the meanings of things."[62]

Unsurprisingly, therefore, Pieper promotes the *vita contemplativa* as the good that alone can satisfy our radical desire for happiness:

> Man is, to the very roots of his being, a creature designed for and desiring vision; and this is true to such a degree that the extent of a man's happiness is only as great as his capacity for contemplation.... Only the vision of something we love makes us happy, and thus it is integral to the concept of contemplation that it represents a vision kindled by the act of turning towards something in love and affirmation.[63]

What are we to contemplate? All of reality. As Pieper poses the question, "What . . . is the drink known as happiness which can ultimately suffice this thirst of the whole human being?"[64] Thomas gives the reply "*bonum universale*" which Pieper translates as "the whole good" because it best expresses the radical boundlessness of humanity's desire for happiness.[65] And so Pieper concludes, "if anywhere in the world a given good exists which it has not yet received, the will desires that good also."[66] Yet the only way to possess such a good is cognitively. He does not mean the term in the narrow sense, which would limit itself to the physical brain. Rather, he means it in the classical sense which links mind and soul with the capacity for spiritual insights. For this reason he argues that it is only in the mind that "the totality of things has room."[67] In contrast, the secular mindset seeks satisfaction in fragments.

60. Pieper, *An Anthology*, 143.
61. Austenfeld, "Josef Pieper's Contemplative Assent to the World," 374.
62. Taylor, *A Secular Age*, 38.
63. Pieper, *An Anthology*, 143, 144.
64. Pieper, *Happiness and Contemplation*, 39.
65. Pieper, *Happiness and Contemplation*, 39.
66. Pieper, *Happiness and Contemplation*, 40.
67. Pieper, *Happiness and Contemplation*, 65–66.

Contemplation might seem an odd word to twenty-first century ears. Surely knowledge would be better in what many are calling a "knowledge society."[68] And yet, as Taylor himself argues, we are often dissatisfied with "the present immanent orders of psychological or moral self-understanding."[69] We are confronted by "an awareness of a larger order which can alone make sense of our lives."[70] We are in desperate need for a word more capacious than mere knowledge, a word which indicates, as "contemplation" does, that man's "means of ascertaining the nature of reality are not exclusively mental."[71]

In his three most famous essays, *Leisure the Basis of Culture*, *The Philosophical Act*, and *Happiness and Contemplation*, Pieper challenges our narrow materialist epistemology by distinguishing between *ratio* and *intellectus*. Whilst the faculty of mind is both of these things and "the process of knowing is the action of the two together,"[72] *intellectus* which is intuition should be regarded as being superior:

> Intuition is without doubt the perfect form of knowing. For intuition is knowledge of what is actually present; the parallel to seeing with the senses is exact. Thinking [*ratio*], on the other hand, is knowledge of what is absent, or may be merely the effort to achieve such knowledge; the subject matter of thinking is investigated by way of something else which is directly present to the mind, but the subject matter is not seen as it is in itself. . . . The validity of thinking, Thomas says, rests upon what we perceive by direct intuition; but the necessity for thinking is due to a failure of intuition.[73]

Pieper insists that contemplation is not passive but receptive. He defines "the contemplative vision of the *intellectus*" as being "truth offer[ing] itself like a landscape to the eye."[74] This receptivity ensures that the very process of knowing is "accompanied and impregnated by an effortless awareness, the contemplative vision of the *intellectus* . . . the activity of the soul in which it conceives that which it sees."[75] For Pieper, religious

---

68. Laurillard, "Rethinking Teaching for the Knowledge Society," 133.
69. Taylor, *A Secular Age*, 744.
70. Taylor, *A Secular Age*, 744.
71. Pieper, *An Anthology*, 144.
72. Pieper, *Leisure the Basis of Culture*, 28.
73. Pieper, *Happiness and Contemplation*, 74.
74. Pieper, *Leisure the Basis of Culture*, 28.
75. Pieper, *Leisure the Basis of Culture*, 28.

education which fails to engage the *intellectus* is, by definition, incapable of proving transformative in the life of students because it cannot give them insights into the very nature of reality.

The third point Pieper would introduce into this discussion is that the purpose of education is to prepare students for happiness. Such a goal might seem at odds with the growing focus on preparing students for "technology-rich globalised job markets."[76] Yet for Pieper, this contemplation, this seeing, gets right to the heart of the educational endeavor. He noted that the word "school" comes from the Latin word *scola*, meaning leisure. For Pieper leisure is, by definition, a receptive attitude of mind—a kind of silence.[77] At the heart of leisure is contemplation. "For leisure is a receptive attitude of mind, a contemplative attitude, and it is not only the occasion but also the capacity for steeping oneself in the whole of creation."[78] This potential for "steeping in," really a more specific verb than receiving, is for Pieper what constitutes "the greatness of man."[79] For Pieper it is at the heart of education. "Education concerns the whole man; an educated man is a man with a point of view from which he takes in the whole world. Education concerns . . . man *capax universi*, capable of grasping the totality of existing things."[80] This *capax universi*, in the Christian tradition, points ahead to the beatific vision—our heavenly destiny.[81]

In short, the *vita contemplativa* offers the only wisdom capable of providing an antidote to the unbounded and unsatisfying fragmentation of secularism. What is this wisdom? Pieper invokes a medieval maxim, "A

---

76. The Department of Education and Training. "A Student Focused National Career Education Strategy."

77. Pieper, *Leisure the Basis of Culture*, 46.

78. Pieper, *Leisure the Basis of Culture*, 46–47.

79. Pieper, *Leisure the Basis of Culture*, 92.

80. Pieper, *Leisure the Basis of Culture*, 39. One can see obvious links with Newman's insistence that education sought far more than mere knowledge, it sought "the perfection or virtue of the intellect" via what he termed "philosophical knowledge, enlargement of mind, or illumination." Newman, *The Idea of a University*, 125. In a similar vein, although writing over a century later, Luigi Guissani argued that the teacher must educate "the original element that is present in all of us . . . the human heart as God made it," in order to free the student from mental slavery. Guissani, *The Risk of Education*, xxvii, xxxi.

81. Pieper, *Leisure the Basis of Culture*, 92. In making this point Pieper cites Gregory the Great, "What do they not see, who see him who sees all things."

man is wise if all things taste to him as they really are."[82] However, he adds the warning that the opposite of this wisdom, this receptivity, is found in the man "who in all things tastes only himself."[83] These insights get right to the heart of Pieper's vision of evangelical hope. It is a vision in which the person is freed from the work of self-construction and is trained in the habit of receptivity—an orientation that allows us to stand in "gift relation" to the world and, ultimately, to God and his offer of salvation.[84]

The Alternative: The World of Total Work

Pieper understood that the alternative to this creaturely receptivity was "the world of total work."[85] This is the utilitarian reality in which the individual exists only to work. Leisure and contemplation may well exist in such a world, but they exist solely in order to refresh the worker and ensure that he or she remains productive. Thus, the modern worker (or student who is simply a worker in training) "is permitted spare time but no true repose."[86] Far from the *capax universi*, the world of total work is marked by a constant focus on the immediate needs of the individual and their economic context. Thus, Pieper warned, contemplation, which ought to break the individual out of their limited view and point to their eternal destiny, becomes, instead, a means "to screw down the dome more firmly than ever, to close every window" and imprison them in a world of work.[87]

In the world of total work contemplation and receptivity are not valued. What is valued, in contrast, is activity. In such a world, the "intellectual worker" limits knowledge to *ratio*. Instead of contemplating, a person observes. Instead of receiving, they produce knowledge via their own efforts. In this narrow world known by Kantian epistemology even philosophy becomes work.[88] In such a world of total work, Pieper warns, effort is suddenly mistaken as the assurance for "the material

---

82. Pieper, *The Christian Idea of Man*, 16.
83. Pieper, *The Christian Idea of Man*, 16.
84. Pieper, *Leisure the Basis of Culture*, 12, 16, 36.
85. Pieper, *Leisure the Basis of Culture*, 20, 25, 30.
86. Pieper, *Happiness and Contemplation*, 79.
87. Pieper, *Leisure the Basis of Culture*, 84.
88. Pieper, *Leisure the Basis of Culture*, 25–27.

truth of the knowledge acquired."[89] In such a context, the human person becomes suspicious of receiving anything as a gift. "To be passive is always senseless."[90] The creature prefers itself in the role of creator who thinks things into being.[91] In short, the buffered self is most at home in the world of total work.

The church has consistently warned against a "merely functional view of education, as if it were legitimized only if it served the market economy and the labour market."[92] And yet secondary education is certainly not immune to the world of total work.[93] The growing focus on determining the efficacy of all teaching and learning by results gained from standardized tests and the university placements thereby earned means that even Catholic secondary schools will remain haunted by what might be called a functional or utilitarian temptation. In recent years, in fact, numerous writers have become more explicit in their demands for education to be more overtly focused on preparing students for work.[94] There is great concern that students are ill-prepared for "the fourth industrial revolution, for the knowledge economy and the world of intellectual work."[95] Students are perceived as workers in training, the only real urgency is that they develop twenty-first century skills and become more employable.[96]

---

89. Pieper, *Leisure the Basis of Culture*, 31.

90. Pieper, *Leisure the Basis of Culture*, 31.

91. Pieper, *Leisure the Basis of Culture*, 35–36.

92. Congregation for Catholic Education, *Educating Today and Tomorrow*, 1.E.

93. Incidentally, nor are primary schools. As a recent article noted, "During the elementary years, students are at a crucial period when career beliefs and aspirations are being developed," consequently a greater focus on "career readiness interventions" for primary students are a growing concern. See Pulliama and Barteka, "College and Career Readiness," 355.

94. As Lyn Sharratt, the well-respected and influential Canadian educationalist put it, "We have an opportunity to shape education for our students' prosperity and our educators' professional success in the future. . . . [W]e know it is time for education policy and programming to be linked to economic development at every level in order to close the gap between perceived student needs by educators and what employers actually expect and want." Sharratt and Harild, *Good to Great to Innovate*, xv.

95. "At the core of the fourth industrial revolution and society are the cognitive skills of humans. This new order of economy can be called *cognitive capitalism* or *cognitive economy*. Consequently, cognitive work is ever-present in our lives. The work we do every day is technically with us everywhere, so we can colloquially call it anyplace working." Heikkinen, "Education, Work, and Life," 79.

96. It has been argued that often what are termed twenty-first century skills are

Preparation for the workplace is certainly a good. But if it becomes the predominant good of education, the anthropological vision thereby communicated to students is radically narrowed. It is in fact a false vision that students themselves are loathe to accept. There is even some evidence to suggest that students have a far more rounded and holistic understanding of their own education than many theorists, or indeed many of their own parents, might suspect.[97] Perhaps for this reason there has been a growing number of secular works written decrying the utilitarian tenor of modern education and calling for a rediscovery of wisdom and the pursuit of the good life.[98]

Catholic Schools have a particular reputation for providing a rounded education.[99] Thus, it is vital they continue to struggle against

---

simply those allowing people to flourish in that most unstable and utilitarian structure—the gig-economy. "What are called twenty-first century skills are just those skills and attitudes most desired by employers in the contingent workplace—skills for obtaining and performing 'gigs'. . . . Until recently, university students prepared for lifetime careers in professions, by digging deeply into real knowledge. Those days are mostly over." Waks, "Massive Open Online Courses," 193, 195. As many discovered during the recent covid lockdown, "any place work" is also total work—there is no place free from the call of work. Indeed, the lockdown ensured that many experienced the flexibility of the gig economy, only to discover that the worker is both slave and master—always working to ensure he or she always has work.

97. In a recent New Zealand study, students' views on the purpose of schools were much broader than those of parents and teachers. However, across all three groups, regardless of economic circumstance, "the more instrumental purpose of enabling future employment and economic well-being was less strongly supported as a purpose of school. Differentiation between the economic and learning purposes suggests that learning in a variety of forms was viewed as an end in itself, not simply as a means to economic ends." Widdowson et al., "Why Go to School?," 481.

98. Some of the more notable authors in this genre have been the philosopher Byung Chul Han who decried the utilitarianism of modern life and, in the chapter on "The Pedagogy of Seeing" wrote "of the need to revitalize the *vita contemplativa*." Although inspired by Nietzsche rather than Aquinas, the similarities between his conclusions and those of Pieper are striking. See Han, *The Burnout Society*, 21. Among the more noteworthy voices calling for an end to an increasingly utilitarian education are teachers like Robinson, *Trivium 21C*; Robinson, *Curriculum*; Hitz, *Lost in Thought*.

99. As a recent study revealed, many parents, although disconnected from any worshipping community, actively seek out Catholic schools citing, among other factors, the religious immersion being offered to their children. However, the utilitarian temptation always remains a factor. As that same study made clear, the religious elements of school life were "certainly not a decisive factor for parents," and in schools no longer perceived to be achieving good academic results, the provision of religious education made no difference in declining enrolments. Rymarz and Franchi, *Catholic Teacher Preparation*, 98.

this temptation. As Pieper makes clear, in a utilitarian context Catholic education in general and religious education in particular must always become "shallow, sterile and tautologous."[100] Pieper's anthropology would identify four reasons for such a stark warning.

> The first and most fundamental, as Pieper warned, is the troubling danger of *acedia*. Metaphysically and theologically the notion of *acedia* means that a man does not, in the last resort, give the consent of his will to his own being; that beneath the dynamic activity of his existence, he is still not at one with himself.[101]

In short, "despair and the incapacity for leisure are twins."[102] Without leisure, students cannot understand the greatness to which they instinctively feel called, nor can they find the courage or worse, the means, to respond to that call.[103] Students recognize the obvious limitations of a worldview which demands they work as hard as possible in order to earn the right to, well, work as hard as possible.[104] After all, once the practical demands of life have been met, what then are we to do with ourselves?[105] A Catholic school must be able to provide an answer to that question. It might well be argued that the growing fascination for mindfulness and the practice of gratitude in educational settings is a very reasonable, if anemic, response to the impoverished anthropology and accompanying sense of leisureless acedia it inspires.[106]

Second, at its core, religious education involves revelation. This crucial element means that religion cannot be the same as other subjects. As Pieper explained, revelation is a divine utterance. Because it is "given," it can only ever be communicated in a tradition,[107] however much that word may challenge what Taylor calls the super-nova of fragmentation

---

100. Pieper, "The Negative Element," 49.
101. Pieper, *Leisure the Basis of Culture*, 44.
102. Pieper, *Leisure the Basis of Culture*, 47.
103. Pieper, *Faith, Hope, Love*, 119.
104. Widdowson et al., "Why Go to School?"
105. Pieper, *Happiness and Contemplation*, 95.
106. Unsurprisingly, a recent educational article on acedia owes much to Pieper's work. See Aijian, "Acedia and Student Life," 186–96.
107. What is decisive in Pieper's account is the way in which the very nature of tradition requires something like a divine revelation at its origin. See Pieper, *Tradition*, 27–29.

defining the secular age. For Pieper, revelation is that holy core which one receives and then passes on, undisturbed.[108] As he says,

> there is in the last analysis only *one* traditional good that is absolutely necessary to preserve unchanged, namely the gift that is received and handed on in the *sacred* tradition. I say "necessary" because this tradition comes from a divine source; because each generation needs it for a truly human existence; because no people and no brilliant individual can replace it on their own or even add anything valid to it.[109]

According to Aquinas, the essence of the Christian faith, the holy core as it were, can be summed up in the words "Trinity and Incarnation."[110] As Pieper explains, while the "living process" of handing on this revelation should be dynamic, the holy core remains unchanging. The Trinity and the Incarnation cannot ever be the product of our intellectual efforts. Pieper even goes so far as to argue that they are not even, properly speaking, subject to discussion; they are something that we must receive.[111]

This may seem strange to modern ears for whom, as Taylor and Pieper both note, the buffered/non-receptive intellect is the source of meaning. Discussion is the bread and butter of education. And yet, this is true only of *ratio*. With revelation we are in the world of *intellectus*. Whilst an explanation for a historical event can be discussed, adjusted, or rejected in part or whole, the Trinity is not ours to adjust. We might note that the way in which the Trinity is revealed or the way in which we experience the world is, in a certain sense, trinitarian. Yet we could never argue that the Trinity is a theory of our own devising; its existence contingent on our words. Thus, Pieper notes the importance of a creaturely anthropology in making possible our assent to revelation. As he says, "belief in revelation, as a living act, can come about only if a man's self-understanding goes beyond mere conceptual thinking, if it shapes and governs the inner style of life if, in other words, the receptivity inherent in the created mind is 'realized' existentially."[112] In a world of total

---

108. Pieper, *Tradition*, 35.

109. Pieper, *Tradition*, 35.

110. Aquinas, *Summa Theologiae*, II-II.1.8; II-II.174.6, cited in Pieper, *Faith, Hope, Love*, 83.

111. Pieper, *Tradition*, 11.

112. Pieper, *Faith, Hope, Love*, 63.

work it is impossible for students to ever form such a realization. They are trained only to act, to produce, not formed to contemplate and receive.

This is not to say that God is absolute otherness who must simply be accepted or rejected. As Aquinas noted, "man could not believingly assent to any proposition if he did not in some way understand it."[113] This is why we have religion lessons and why those lessons must be coherent and convincing. However, Piper cautions, belief is not simply a conclusion from premises—coherence is not enough on its own. "It is the will, not cognition, that acknowledges the good."[114] Additionally, Pieper argues that those lessons should be obviously relevant to the lives of the students. "Before the human act of belief is possible, we must presuppose that the believer experiences the subject to be believed as something that really concerns him, as an object of hope, longing and love."[115] But crucially, this experience of relevance is not what engenders belief. As suggested in the title of this chapter, eloquence in the religious education classroom, though valuable, is not enough.

This leads us to the third challenge to the evangelizing mission of our Catholic secondary schools—belief relies on a witness—someone who is not a believer but who knows.[116] In theological terms, our belief rests on the witness of Christ and his perfect knowledge of the Father. As John writes, "No one has ever seen God. It is God the only Son, who is close to the Father's heart, who has made him known" (John 1:18; see also John 6:46; 14:9). Drawing heavily from Aquinas, Pieper argues that the will to believe, the volition, is a response to the witness of Christ.

> Toward what does the believer direct his will when he believes? Answer: Toward the warrantor and witness whom he affirms, loves, "wills"—insofar as he accepts the truthfulness of what that witness says, accepts it on his mere word. This wholly free, entirely uncoercible act of affirmation, which is enforced neither by the power of self-evident truth nor by the weight of argumentation; this confiding, acknowledging, communion-seeking submission of the believer to the witness whom he believes—this, precisely, is "the element of volition" in belief itself.[117]

---

113. Pieper, *Faith, Hope, Love*, 25.
114. Pieper, *Faith, Hope, Love*, 36.
115. Pieper, *Faith, Hope, Love*, 38.
116. Pieper, *Faith, Hope, Love*, 45.
117. Pieper, *Faith, Hope, Love*, 39.

In the world of total work the school is simply the place in which workers are prepared. *Ratio* is in the ascendant. Religious education in such a rationalistic context is in danger of seeming irrelevant or unconvincing or as an interesting arena for study and skill acquisition. In such a context, can the individual ever fully see Christ? Pieper advises, "whoever undertakes to defend belief against the arguments of rationalism should prepare himself by considering the question: How do we apprehend a person?"[118] It is through contemplation which seeks out their very being. "When we direct our gaze upon a human being, we engage in a rapid, penetrating and direct cognition of a unique kind."[119] Thus, Catholic schools must be places in which the gaze of the students is gently but consistently drawn to Christ. Such a gaze might seem useless, unproductive, perhaps even an attack on the time given to their pursuit of skills and ever improving results. Yet so, too, is the gaze of a baby into the eyes of its mother useless, and out of that gaze comes the unshakeable and life-long belief that one is loved.

The final cost of the utilitarian temptation is that virtue education or formation must fragment and therefore devolve into moralism. In his brief essay *The Christian Idea of Man*, Pieper continued to warn about the absolutizing of *doing* over and against the existence of the living person. Such a tendency can only produce moralism.[120] For this reason he begins with Meister Eckhart's dictum that virtue is not about "doing" but about "being."[121] No one can do good if they do not know how things really are; "for the good accords with reality."[122] In turn, Pieper advocates the "precedence of prudence," which is the training of oneself "to view objectively the reality surrounding our actions and making them have, depending on their kind and significance, a direct bearing on our actions."[123] Note the word *view*. Virtue, like belief, begins with contemplation, with a gaze trained upon created reality. It does not begin with action.

Gilbert Meilaender drew attention to creaturely receptivity at the heart of Pieper's philosophy of virtue when he wrote:

---

118. Pieper, *Faith, Hope, Love*, 48.
119. Pieper, *Faith, Hope, Love*, 47.
120. Pieper, *The Christian Idea of Man*, 10–11.
121. Pieper, *The Christian Idea of Man*, 5–6.
122. Pieper, *The Christian Idea of Man*, 13.
123. Pieper, *The Christian Idea of Man*, 15.

> For Pieper no such depiction [of virtue] can be adequate if it ignores our God-relation, if it lacks a vision of human beings as creatures. "To be a creature means to be continually receiving being and essence from the divine Source and Creator, and in this respect, therefore, never to be finally completed." Virtue is not finally or simply a possession; it is a quest for what can only be received.[124]

Far from being about our action, the quest is not even, strictly speaking, about virtue. "Creatures are made for God: that is Pieper's fundamental premise. And they can no more live by virtue alone than by bread alone."[125]

A recent article entitled, "What Catholic Schools can do about World Hunger," presents a reasonably accurate portrait of what moral education looks like in many Catholic secondary schools. The author rightly insists that teachers "have to help their students understand the problem and then motivate them to help as best they can as future citizens, scientists, statesmen, diplomats, and on-the-ground producers, consumers, and movers of food."[126] Yet the focus is generally on the problem, rather than the student, and they are motivated only for action; action which often has its fulfilment in the working or public life. "It proclaims a duty without perceiving and without showing that duty is rooted in what we are."[127] Aquinas argued, "the *whole* moral life of the person is related to the common good."[128] Thus, a wonderful goal such as the one sought in the article "is not achievable if the individual members of the community are not good, not only 'just' in the narrow sense, but 'good,' even in the sense of the most personal and hidden, and, so to speak, most private virtue."[129] The great limitation of moralism is that it is not transformative, inspiring conferences but not conversion.

Interestingly, this seems to be something that we already intuit. In a recent study, teachers generally argued that the most convincing moral teachers were personal role models, not simply those who were well-versed in the geo-political and economic causes of injustice. In other words, it was the goodness of the teacher, not their isolated virtues

---

124. Meilaender, "Josef Pieper," 116.
125. Meilaender, "Josef Pieper," 131.
126. Byron, "What Catholic Schools Can Do about World Hunger," 202.
127. Pieper, *The Christian Idea of Man*, 15–16.
128. Pieper, *The Christian Idea of Man*, 21.
129. Pieper, *The Christian Idea of Man*, 21–22.

and certainly not their arguments for action that proved convincing for students.[130]

Wisdom, the Antidote to Fragmentation

At its best, secondary religious education combines both *ratio* and *intellectus*, and is founded upon the receptivity of the student. In such a context the kerygma rings out,[131] enabling the student to encounter Christ and, crucially, preparing them to receive grace. As Paul wrote to the Ephesians, "For it is by grace you have been saved, through faith—and this is not from yourselves, it is the gift of God" (Eph 2:8).

If we lose sight of our createdness, our status of *creatura*, it becomes so easy to subsume the divine prerogatives. To borrow from Heraclitus, we cease to "listen to the essence of things."[132] Far from receiving, we construct. We cease to contemplate and begin to absolutize work. In such a context, religion can only ever attain the status of an epiphenomenon—providing therapeutic mechanisms, allowing us to work more effectively. In such a context, Pieper warns, "man can only enjoy with a good conscience, what he has acquired with toil and trouble; he refuses to have anything as a gift."[133]

How might Catholic secondary schools foreground our creaturely receptivity, train students in the *vita contemplativa*, and effectively prepare them for happiness? Pieper's anthropological vision provides a "shared vision of the real" but it also provides the means by which to inculcate such necessary and transformative wisdom in an educational setting.

The first is to ensure schools become places of leisure by fostering the ability to teach philosophically in all subjects.[134] Perhaps a place to

---

130. Interestingly, almost half the teachers aged fifty or more saw their role exclusively as that of a role model, compared with 19 percent of those under thirty. See Gleeson and O'Flaherty, "The Teacher as Moral Educator," 50.

131. Francis, *Evangelii gaudium*, no. 164: "On the lips of the catechist the first proclamation must ring out over and over: 'Jesus Christ loves you; he gave his life to save you; and now he is living at your side every day to enlighten, strengthen and free you.'"

132. Cited in Pieper, *Leisure the Basis of Culture*, 28.

133. Pieper, *Leisure the Basis of Culture*, 36.

134. At present subjects are divorced from each other and are often engaged in naked epistemological competition. See Warne, "Of All Things," 296: "Science [should be] embedded in a broader metaphysical and theological framework that has at its

start is to actively promote the experience of wonder in all subjects. This would emphasize the giftedness and interconnectedness of all reality. In his essay "The Philosophical Act," Pieper cites Plato's argument that contemplation "can only be realised in its pure state through the sense of wonder, in that purely receptive attitude to reality."[135] In the science classroom our students should study the universe primarily to marvel, to see that a single blade of grass is a miracle demanding gratitude. In the English classroom they should be moved by the artist's own experience of wonder; artists such as Gerald Manley Hopkins who wrote, "I do not think that I have ever seen anything more beautiful than the bluebell I have been looking at. I know the beauty of the Lord by it."[136] As Pieper continues, "the innermost sense of wonder is fulfilled in a deepened sense of mystery."[137] And so, paraphrasing Aquinas, he concluded that our capacity for wonder "sets our feet on the ladder that leads up to the beatific vision."[138] The promotion of wonder is not utile, it "does not make a man 'able.'"[139] Rather, it constantly shakes the boundary between heaven and earth; between God and man. It is the dawn of enchantment.

The second is, more specifically, to ensure that in every unit of religious education the student encounters Christ, our witness to the divine reality. The statistics cited earlier in this chapter tell us that many students are disengaged with the practice of their faith. Consequently, the religion classroom might be the only time in which they encounter Christ. While they must have their *ratio* engaged by coherent teaching,[140] this is not an end in itself. Students must also be given the space and time to gaze

---

heart mystery. All knowledge, whether scientific, theological, or philosophical, is partial and essentially only known by God, and any human claims at complete mastery are false. Human knowledge can only flourish when limits are respected."

135. Pieper, "The Philosophical Act," in Peiper, *Leisure the Basis of Culture*, 112.

136. Gerald Manley Hopkins's diary 18th May 1870, cited in Pieper, *Happiness and Contemplation*, 86–87.

137. Pieper, *Leisure the Basis of Culture*, 115.

138. Pieper, *Leisure the Basis of Culture*, 114.

139. Pieper, *Leisure the Basis of Culture*, 113.

140. I would suggest the three strategies of chronology, typology, and mystagogy. By keeping everything in historical order, chronology allows students are able to make connections between disparate fragments. By continually establishing the connection between Old and New Testament, typology allows students to develop a coherent overview of salvation history. Mystagogy allows students to see how and why the faith is lived liturgically. By cultivating the students' gaze it thereby deepens their prayerful participation in school masses.

attentively at Christ. Any acceptance of faith is the joyful, loving affirmation of Christ. This affirmation is impossible if religion lessons do not lead students to know Christ.

Thirdly, and most specifically of all, schools should do all they can to actively promote the Sunday Mass, which, according to Pieper, is the experience of "leisure" par excellence. This point alone is worthy of another chapter because in a world of total work it seems so counterintuitive. On this, we must content ourselves with a handful of points. Pieper argues that the celebration of God in worship must be done for its own sake. "Worship is either something 'given,' divine worship is fore-ordained—or it does not exist at all."[141] We have received an ordinance to "keep holy the Sabbath day" (Gen 2:3), and to "do this in memory of me" (Luke 22:19). Thus, Mass is not subject to feedback sheets. We are subject to the divine ordinance. It is something we receive.[142]

In the Sunday Mass we set aside the workaday world and we receive, contemplate, and experience our supernatural destiny. We live out all three of Pieper's anthropological insights within the Mass. When describing contemplation as man's happiness, Pieper gave several conditions for true contemplation: it must focus on something outside the soul,[143] it must be outside of time,[144] it must seek out the "whole good,"[145] or to put it another way, "the finite spirit by virtue of its essence is unquenchable and insatiable—unless it partakes of God."[146] It must pertain to the ultimate good, it must engage with the reality of suffering and death, and yet see them redeemed.[147] It must engage our actions or response, but the effect of our activity must reach inwards.[148] All of these conditions are perfectly and completely satisfied in the Holy Sacrifice of the Mass.

In summary, what makes us happy is the "infinite and uncreated richness of God."[149] Yet Pieper cautions,

---

141. Pieper, *Leisure the Basis of Culture*, 72–73.

142. A recent work drawing heavily on Pieper's anthropology and developing this point is Hughes, "The Ease of Beauty," 91–104.

143. Pieper, *Happiness and Contemplation*, 33.

144. Pieper, *Happiness and Contemplation*, 37.

145. Pieper, *Happiness and Contemplation*, 39–40.

146. Pieper, *Happiness and Contemplation*, 41.

147. Pieper, *Happiness and Contemplation*, 108.

148. Pieper, *Happiness and Contemplation*, 56–57.

149. Pieper, *Happiness and Contemplation*, 52.

> Participation in this, happiness itself, is entirely a "creatural" reality governed from within by our humanity; it is *not* something that descends overwhelmingly upon us from outside. That is, it is not only something that happens to us; we ourselves are intensely active participants in our own happiness.[150]

Indeed, Pieper cites a Spanish commentator on Aquinas who wrote, "the happy life does not mean loving what we possess, but possessing what we love."[151] This is what we do when we receive the Eucharist. As Pieper says, "We take possession of our real wealth."[152] To remove the Sunday Mass from any communication of our Catholic Faith is to mortally wound that faith's coherence. The statistics would suggest that this is precisely what has happened.[153]

Conclusion

Josef Pieper's anthropological vision can be captured in the psalm from which he quotes at the beginning of his essay on leisure, "Be still and know that I am God."[154] For Pieper, the fundamental reality of the human person is their creaturely receptivity. And yet, as he noted in another essay, in a statement that might well describe education in the secular era: "Man's ability to see is in decline. Those who nowadays concern themselves with culture and education will experience this fact again and again."[155] The obfuscation of our creaturely receptivity engendered by experiencing ourselves as buffered, proves antithetical to the *vita contemplativa* which, according to Pieper, impairs "the spiritual capacity to perceive the visible reality as it truly is."[156] Pieper's warnings have much to teach us in the twenty-first century. Any Catholic education seeking to educate the whole child can only do so if it is animated by an understanding of each student as being made *by* and *for* their creator God. It is only in such a context of creaturely receptivity that we can hope to coherently

---

150. Pieper, *Happiness and Contemplation*, 52.
151. Bartolome de Medina, cited in Pieper, *Happiness and Contemplation*, 63.
152. Pieper, *Happiness and Contemplation*, 67.
153. Dantis and Reid, *Called to Fullness of Life and Love*, 4, 11; Dixon, *Catholics Who Have Stopped Attending Mass*, 3–4, 14.
154. Pieper, *Leisure the Basis of Culture*, 17.
155. Pieper, "Learning How to See Again," 31.
156. Pieper, "Learning How to See Again," 31.

and convincingly prepare students for the only true happiness, which can be found on the *vita contemplativa*, pointing ahead towards the beatific vision for which we were all created.

Bibliography

Aijjian, J. L. "Acedia and Student Life: Ancient Christian Wisdom for Addressing Boredom, Distraction, and Over-Commitment in Undergraduates." *International Journal of Christianity & Education* 21.3 (2017) 186–96.

Augustine. *On Christian Doctrine*. https://ccel.org/ccel/augustine/doctrine/doctrine.

Austenfeld, Thomas. "Josef Pieper's Contemplative Assent to the World." *Modern Age* 42.4 (2000) 372–82.

Byron, William J. "What Catholic Schools Can Do about World Hunger?" *International Studies in Catholic Education* 7.2 (2015) 201–9.

Cardus. "2018 US Cardus Education Survey: Spiritual Strength, Faithful Formation." https://www.cardus.ca/research/education/reports/2018-us-cardus-education-survey-spiritual-strength-faithful-formation/.

Chesterton, G. K. *Why I Am a Catholic*. In vol. 3 of *The Collected Works of G. K. Chesterton*, 125–32. San Francisco: Ignatius, 1990.

Congregation for Catholic Education. *Educating Today and Tomorrow: A Renewing Passion*. http://www.vatican.va/roman_curia/congregations/ccatheduc/documents/rc_con_ccatheduc_doc_20140407_educare-oggi-e-domani_en.html.

Crim, Elias. "Josef Pieper's Critique of Western Civ." https://churchlifejournal.nd.edu/articles/josef-piepers-critique-of-western-civ/.

Dantis, Trudy, and Stephen Reid. *Called to Fullness of Life and Love: National Report on the Australian Catholic Bishops' Youth Survey 2017*. https://www.mn.catholic.org.au/media/3679/acbc-youth-survey-report-sm.pdf.

The Department of Education and Training. "A Student Focused National Career Education Strategy." https://web.archive.org/web/20201204150009/https://schooltowork.dese.gov.au/.

Dixon, Bob. *Catholics Who Have Stopped Attending Mass*. https://www.catholic.org.au/all-downloads/bishops-1/media-releases-1/219-bishops-welcome-new-research-1/file.

Dupré, Louis. *Metaphysics and Culture*. Milwaukee: Marquette University Press, 1994.

Franchi, Leonardo, and Richard Rymarz. "The Education and Formation of Teachers for Catholic Schools: Responding to Changed Cultural Contexts." *International Studies in Catholic Education* 9.1 (2017) 2–16.

Francis, Pope. *Evangelii gaudium*. https://www.vatican.va/content/francesco/en/apost_exhortations/documents/papa-francesco_esortazione-ap_20131124_evangelii-gaudium.html.

Gleeson, Jim, and Maureen Mary O'Neill. "Student-Teachers' Perspectives on the Purposes and Characteristics of Faith-Based Schools: An Australian View." *British Journal of Religious Education* 40.1 (2018) 55–69.

Gleeson, Jim, and Joanne O'Flaherty. "The Teacher as Moral Educator: Comparative Study of Secondary Teachers in Catholic Schools in Australia and Ireland." *Teaching and Teacher Education* 55 (2016) 45–56.

Guissani, Luigi. *The Risk of Education: Discovering Our Ultimate Destiny.* Montreal: McGill-Queen's University Press, 2019.

Han, Byung Chul. *The Burnout Society.* Translated by Erik Butler. Stanford: Stanford University Press, 2015.

Heikkinen, Hannu. "Education, Work, and Life." In *Education in an Era of Schooling: Critical Perspectives of Educational Practice and Action Research*, edited by Christine Edwards-Groves et al., 79–90. Singapore: Springer, 2018.

Hitz, Zena. *Lost in Thought: The Hidden Pleasures of an Intellectual Life.* Princeton: Princeton University Press, 2020.

Hoye, William J. "A Transparent Philosopher." *America*, November 8, 2004.

Hughes, Margaret I. "The Ease of Beauty: Liturgy, Evangelization, and Catechesis." In *Liturgy in the Twenty-First Century: Contemporary Issues and Perspectives*, edited by Alcuin Reid, 91–104. London: Bloomsbury T. & T. Clark, 2016.

The Independent Schools Council of Australia. *The Changing Face of Australian Schooling: An ISCA Analysis of the ABS 2016 Census of Population & Housing.* https://isa.edu.au/wp-content/uploads/2018/06/The-changing-face-of-Australian-schooling_FINAL_web.pdf.

Laurillard, Diana. "Rethinking Teaching for the Knowledge Society." *Educause Review* 37.1 (2002) 16–25.

Martínez-Ariño, Julia, and Sara Teinturie. "Faith-Based Schools in Contexts of Religious Diversity: An Introduction." *Religion and Education* 46.2 (2019) 147–58.

Meilaender, Gilbert. "Josef Pieper: Explorations in the Thought of a Philosopher of Virtue." *The Journal of Religious Ethics* 11.1 (1983) 114–34.

Miller, Michael J. "Five Essential Marks of Catholic Schools." In *The Holy See's Teaching on Catholic Schools*, 17–63. Atlanta: Sophia Institute Press, 2006.

National Centre for Pastoral Research. *The Australian Catholic Mass Attendance Report 2016: A Report Based on the National Count of Attendance, the National Church Life Survey and the National Catholic Census Project.* https://ncpr.catholic.org.au/wp-content/uploads/2020/12/Mass-attendance-in-Australia-2016-Final.pdf.

Newman, John Henry. *The Idea of a University Defined and Illustrated.* London: Basil Montagu Pickering, 1873.

Paletta, Angelo, and Italo Fiorin. "The Challenges of Catholic Education: Evidence from the Responses to the Instrumentum Laboris 'Educating Today and Tomorrow.'" *International Studies in Catholic Education* 8.2 (2016) 136–54.

Pieper, Josef. *An Anthology.* San Francisco: Ignatius, 1989.

———. *The Christian Idea of Man.* Translated by Dan Farrelly. South Bend, IN: St. Augustine's, 2011.

———. *Faith, Hope, Love.* Translated by Richard Watson et al. San Francisco: Ignatius, 2002.

———. *For the Love of Wisdom: Essays on the Nature of Philosophy.* Translated by Roger Wasserman. San Francisco: Ignatius, 2006.

———. *Happiness and Contemplation.* Translated by Richard Winston and Clara Winston. New York: Pantheon, 1958.

———. "Learning How to See Again." In *Only the Lover Sings: Art and Contemplation*, translated by Lothar Krauth, 29–36. San Francisco: Ignatius, 1990.

———. *Leisure: The Basis of Culture; The Philosophical Act.* Translated by Alexander Dru. San Francisco: Ignatius, 2009.

———. "The Negative Elements in the Philosophy of St. Thomas Aquinas." In *The Silence of St. Thomas: Three Essays*, translated by John Murray and Daniel O'Connor, 45–74. South Bend, IN: St. Augustine's, 1999.

———. *Only the Lover Sings*. Translated by Lothar Krauth. San Francisco: Ignatius, 1990.

———. *Tradition: Concept and Claim*. Translated by E. Christian Kopff. South Bend, IN: St. Augustine's, 2010.

Pontifical Council for Promoting New Evangelisation. *Directory for Catechesis*. Strathfield: St. Paul's, 2020.

Pulliama, Nicole, and Samantha Barteka. "College and Career Readiness in Elementary Schools." *International Electronic Journal of Elementary Education* 10.3 (2018) 355–60.

Robinson, Martin. *Curriculum: Athena versus the Machine*. Carmarthen: Crown, 2019.

———. *Trivium 21c: Preparing Young People for the Future with Lessons from the Past*. Carmarthen: Independent Thinking, 2013.

Rymarz, Richard, and Angelo Belmonte. "The Questions Students Ask? A Preliminary Examination of the Questions Raised in Religious Education Classes in Catholic Schools." *British Journal of Religious Education* 42.2 (2020) 120–28.

Rymarz, Richard, and Anthony Cleary. "Examining Some Aspects of the Worldview of Students in Australian Catholic Schools: Some Implications for Religious Education." *British Journal of Religious Education* 40.3 (2018) 327–36.

———. "Kids Today! A Perspective from Students in Australian Catholic Schools." *Compass* 50.1 (2016) 12–18.

———. "Some Religious Beliefs and Behaviours of Australian Catholic School Students." *Journal of Beliefs & Values* 37.1 (2016) 68–77.

Rymarz, Richard, and Leonardo Franchi. *Catholic Teacher Preparation: Historical and Contemporary Perspectives*. Bingley: Emerald, 2019.

Rymarz, Richard, and John Graham. "Australian Core Catholic Youth, Catholic Schools, and Religious Education." *British Journal of Religious Education* 28.1 (2006) 79–89.

Sharratt, Lyn, and Gale Harild. *Good to Great to Innovate: Recalculating the Route to Career Readiness, K–12+*. Thousand Oaks, CA: Corwin, 2014.

Smith, Christian, and Melinda Lundquist Denton. *Soul Searching: The Religious and Spiritual Lives of American Teenagers*. Oxford: Oxford University Press, 2005.

Taylor, Charles. *A Secular Age*. Cambridge: Belknap, 2007.

Waks, Leonard J. "Massive Open Online Courses and the Future of Higher Education." In *Contemporary Technologies in Education: Maximizing Student Engagement, Motivation, and Learning*, edited by Olusola Adesope and A. G. Rud, 183–214. Cham: Palgrave Macmillan, 2019.

Warne, Nathaniel. "Learning to See the World Again: Josef Pieper on Philosophy, Prudence, and the University." *Journal of Moral Education* 47.3 (2018) 289–303.

———. "Of All Things, Seen and Unseen: Josef Pieper's Negative Philosophy, Science, and Hope." *Theological Studies* 79.2 (2018) 294–313.

Waugh, Evelyn. "Come Inside." In *A Little Order: Selected Journalism*, edited by Donat Gallagher, 147–49. London: Penguin, 2010.

Widdowson, Deborah A., et al. "Why Go to school? Student, Parent, and Teacher." *Asia Pacific Journal of Education* 35.4 (2015) 471–84.

www.ingramcontent.com/pod-product-compliance
Lightning Source LLC
Chambersburg PA
CBHW050622300426
44112CB00012B/1609